frontiers, read Chinese novels and Persian poetry and knew a dozen languages. The breathtaking scope and infectious enthusiasm of this book are a tribute to that ideal."

—*The Sunday Times* (U.K.)

"For those whose refuge is the word—on-screen, on paper, or chiseled in ancient stone—and for those who appreciate a tale well told, *The Written World* is a book you will want to read from cover to cover."

—*Santa Barbara Independent*

"An episodic history of human civilization as shaped by and told through its literature . . . Mr. Puchner, a professor at Harvard University, places the written word at the very heart of things, bringing scribes and scribblers out from the shadows and giving them their moment in the sun. . . . Puchner is a clear-eyed and helpful guide."

—*The Economist*

"In a globetrotting, epoch-spanning history, Puchner argues that written works—and the ever-changing technologies used to sustain them—have defined societies since the beginning of recorded time."

—*The Atlantic*

"[Puchner] emphasizes the ubiquity of storytelling across human history, elevating it in the manner of the historian Yuval Noah Harari's *Sapiens: A Brief History of Humankind* into perhaps the defining human trait, necessary to instill the trust on which so much else is built. . . . The book builds a convincing case that writing technologies are more foundational in major historical moments than we may have otherwise thought."

—*Financial Times*

"Martin Puchner's vivid new history of writing . . . eschews a straight survey in favor of a series of vignettes which capture what is gained and what lost from writing things down. . . . Puchner is brilliant on the role paper has played in shaping literature. . . . Never short of engaging, Puchner leaves you full of admiration."

—*Times Literary Supplement*

"Puchner, an English professor at Harvard, makes the case for literature's pervasive importance as a force that has shaped the societies we have built and our very sensibilities as human beings. His fieldwork takes him to every continent, digging inexhaustibly into cultures for their foundational and sacred stories."

—*The New York Times Book Review*,
Editor's Choice

"In *The Written World*, Puchner traces the history of literature in the rise and fall of empires and nations." —*Forbes*

"Our brains appear to be hard-wired to respond to stories, and reading appears to be a uniquely powerful way to experience narrative. Martin Puchner's recently released [*The Written World*] makes a case that stories are the building blocks of civilization itself, that literature has "shaped the lives of most humans on planet Earth."

—*Chicago Tribune*

"[Puchner] shares the stories behind the stories and the change they created with verve and affection."

—*Zócalo Public Square*, ten best nonfiction books of 2017

"Fascinating . . . The book excels at showing the global nature of the written word." —*The Scotsman*

"*The Written World* is an informative, relentlessly entertaining account of the development of literature."   —*The National*

"A hugely engaging exploration of how writing changed civilizations, cultures, and the history of the world . . . *The Written World* tells the riveting story of the development of literature. . . . Through vivid storytelling and across a huge sweep of time, *The Written World* offers a new and enticing perspective on human history."
                    —*DCB News*, Editors' Picks

"Spellbinding and expansive, *The Written World* will be enjoyed by academic scholars and literature buffs."   —Bookriot

"Taking in its sweep the invention of paper, the alphabet, movable type, etc., [*The Written World*] examines certain foundational texts. But this is more than a textual analysis—and as he travels across continents, Puchner manages to give his inquiry feisty shape. . . . The most riveting portion on the power of storytelling is on Derek Walcott, the West Indian poet who won the Nobel Prize in 1992 and passed away a year ago."   —*The Hindu*

"[Puchner] makes a breathtaking leap from Homer to Derek Walcott, illustrating why it is impossible to imagine a world without literature."   —*Harvard Magazine*

"Enthralling . . . [an] entertaining saga of how literature shaped civilization . . . Puchner has penned a fascinating celebration of literature. . . . [He] is a generous, natural teacher who brings these works and their origins to vivid life. . . . Erudition and enthusiasm combine seamlessly in Puchner's sweeping narrative, which comprises history, biography, technology and ideas. And while it is a cliché to say that he brings literature to life, he does exactly that, connecting the dots of civilization in new and interesting ways. *The Written World* is perfect reading for a long, chilly night, and it will leave you thinking in new ways about the wondrous thing called literature that, perhaps, we sometimes take for granted."

—*BookPage*

"What is better than a book? A book about books! In this ground-breaking book, Martin Puchner leads us on a remarkable journey through time and around the globe. . . . A book that history buffs, techno-geeks, and book lovers alike will savor."

—*Free-for-All* (Peabody Institute Library)

"[A] thoughtful treatise . . . The book provides a nice collection of oddments of the bibliophilic nature, fitting neatly alongside works by Nicholas Basbanes and Alberto Manguel. . . . In mounting a learned and, yes, literate defense for literature as an instrument of mind and memory, Puchner also argues against literary fundamentalism, allowing texts to be seen as living things and allowing 'readers of each generation to make these texts their own.' A lucid entertainment for the humanists in the audience."

—*Kirkus Reviews*

"Puchner doesn't just tell us about the important works of literature that have shaped civilization over 4,000 years, from *The Epic of Gilgamesh* to *Don Quixote* to J. K. Rowling's Harry Potter series. He tells us about the people whose personal persuasions led them to create those works. It's literature not as mirror, then, but as potent force."

—*Library Journal*

"In this timely chronicle, Puchner, a professor of English and comparative literature at Harvard University, tells the story both of the ideas that shaped civilization and the equally crucial technology that transmitted and preserved those ideas. . . . By providing snapshots of key moments in the written word's evolution, Puchner creates a gripping intellectual odyssey." —*Publishers Weekly*

"Well worth a read, to find out how come we read."
—Margaret Atwood, via Twitter

"*The Written World* is not only an expansive, exuberant survey of the central importance of literature in human culture but also a great adventure story—a story of letters and paper and rocket ships, of ruthless conquerors and elegant court ladies and middle-class entrepreneurs, of the will to power and the dream of freedom. Leading the reader across a vast landscape of space and time, Martin Puchner is the perfect companion and guide. Restless, witty, learned, and endowed with seemingly infinite curiosity, he brings home to us how much we have been formed over the millennia by the tales we have invented and recorded."
—Stephen Greenblatt, author of
The Swerve: How the World Became Modern

"A unique and spellbinding book . . . Martin Puchner's dramatic storytelling leads us through the mazes and underworlds of civilization at key moments when it is being built or unbuilt. *The Written World* shows the way 'great books'—and the alphabets, clay tablets, and printing presses by which they were spread—provided both the rudder and the sails for humanity's voyage across vast oceans of time."
—Elaine Scarry, author of *Naming Thy Name:*
Cross Talk in Shakespeare's Sonnets

"From Mesopotamia to the moon, *The Written World* is an imaginative, informative, and ingenious history of civilization in the form of a narrative of what people have written and read over the last four thousand years. It's an exhilarating feat of intellectual athleticism. The big picture doesn't get much bigger."

—Louis Menand, author of
The Metaphysical Club: A Story of Ideas in America

THE
WRITTEN WORLD

The

WRITTEN WORLD

THE
POWER OF STORIES
TO SHAPE PEOPLE,
HISTORY, AND
CIVILIZATION

Martin Puchner

RANDOM HOUSE

NEW YORK

2018 Random House Trade Paperback Edition

Copyright © 2017 by Martin Puchner
Map copyright © 2017 by David Lindroth Inc.

All rights reserved.

Published in the United States by Random House,
an imprint and division of Penguin Random House LLC, New York.

RANDOM HOUSE and the HOUSE colophon are
registered trademarks of Penguin Random House LLC.

Originally published in hardcover in the United States by Random House,
an imprint and division of Penguin Random House LLC, in 2017.

Illustration acknowledgments can be found beginning on page 389.

LIBRARY OF CONGRESS CATALOGING-IN-PUBLICATION DATA
NAMES: Puchner, Martin, author.
TITLE: The written world : the power of stories to shape people,
history, and civilization / Martin Puchner.
DESCRIPTION: New York : Random House, 2017. | Includes index.
IDENTIFIERS: LCCN 2017002438| ISBN 9780812988277 |
ISBN 9780812998948 (ebook)
SUBJECTS: LCSH: Literature and society. | Literature—History and criticism. |
Books and reading. | BISAC: HISTORY / Civilization. | BIOGRAPHY &
AUTOBIOGRAPHY / Historical. | LITERARY CRITICISM / Books & Reading.
CLASSIFICATION: LCC PN51 .P79 2017 | DDC 809/.93358—dc23
LC record available at lccn.loc.gov/2017002438

Printed in the United States of America on acid-free paper

randomhousebooks.com

246897531

Title-page art map © by iStock

Book design by Barbara M. Bachman

For
Amanda Claybaugh

CONTENTS

—

Chapt 7 & 24
only ones
need to
read

EARTHRISE

SOMETIMES I TRY TO IMAGINE A WORLD WITHOUT LITERATURE. I would miss books on airplanes. Bookstores and libraries would have a lot of extra shelf space (and my own bookshelves would no longer be overflowing). The publishing industry wouldn't exist as we know it, nor would Amazon, and there'd be nothing on my bedside table when I can't sleep at night.

All this would be unfortunate, but it barely scratches the surface of what would be lost if literature had never existed, if stories were told only orally and had never been written down. Such a world is almost impossible for us to imagine. Our sense of history, of the rise and fall of empires and nations, would be completely different. Most philosophical and political ideas would never have come into existence, because the literature that gave rise to them wouldn't have been written. Almost all religious beliefs would disappear along with the scriptures in which they were expressed.

Literature isn't just for book lovers. Ever since it emerged four thousand years ago, it has shaped the lives of most humans on planet Earth.

As the three astronauts aboard Apollo 8 were to find.

———

"ALRIGHT, APOLLO 8. YOU are go for TLI. Over."

"Roger. We understand we are go for TLI."

By late 1968, circling the earth was no longer a novelty. Apollo 8, the latest American mission, had just spent two hours and twenty-seven minutes in terrestrial orbit. There had been no major incidents. But Frank Frederick Borman II, James Arthur Lovell, Jr., and William Alison Anders were on edge. Their ship was about to attempt a new maneuver, translunar injection, TLI. They were pointing away from Earth, ready to shoot straight into space. Their destination was the moon. At any moment, they would speed up to 24,207 mph, faster than anyone had ever traveled before.

The mission of Apollo 8 was relatively simple. They wouldn't land on the moon; they didn't even have a landing vehicle on board. They were to see what the moon was like, identify an appropriate landing site for a future Apollo mission, and bring back photos and film material that experts could study.

TLI, the translunar injection that would power their flight to the moon, proceeded as planned. Apollo 8 sped up and took the plunge into space. The farther they went, the better they could see what no one had ever seen before: the earth.

Borman interrupted procedures to call out the landmasses that were rotating below him: Florida; the Cape; Africa. He could see them all at once. He was the first human ever to see the earth as a single globe. Anders took the picture that would capture this new sight, Earth rising above the surface of the moon.

As the earth was getting smaller and smaller and the moon bigger and bigger, the astronauts had trouble capturing everything on camera. Ground control realized that the astronauts needed to rely on a simpler technology: the spoken word. "We would like you, if possible, to go into as much of a detailed description as you poets can."

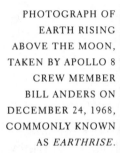

PHOTOGRAPH OF
EARTH RISING
ABOVE THE MOON,
TAKEN BY APOLLO 8
CREW MEMBER
BILL ANDERS ON
DECEMBER 24, 1968,
COMMONLY KNOWN
AS *EARTHRISE*.

Becoming poets was a task for which the astronauts' training hadn't prepared them and to which they brought no particular skills. They had made it through the ruthless selection process of NASA because they were the best fighter pilots and knew something about rocket science. Anders had attended the Naval Academy and then joined the Air Force, where he had served as an all-weather interceptor at Air Defense Command in California and Iceland. But now he needed to come up with words—the right words.

He singled out the "lunar sunrises and sunsets." "These in particular bring out the stark nature of the terrain," he said, "and the long shadows really bring out the relief that is here and hard to see at this very bright surface that we're going over right now." Anders was painting a stark picture of bright light hitting the hard surface of the moon and making precise shadows—perhaps his job as all-weather interceptor helped. He was becoming a poet in the great American tradition of imagism, perfectly suited to a stark and brilliant thing like the moon.

Lovell had also trained at the Naval Academy, after which he had joined the Navy; like the others, he had spent most of his life on air bases. In space, he showed a predilection for another school of poetry: the sublime. "The vast loneliness up here of the moon is awe-inspiring," he ventured. Philosophers had reflected on the awe that nature could inspire; waterfalls, storms, anything grand, too grand to be neatly captured and framed, would serve. But they could not have imagined what it would be like to be out there, in space. It was the ultimate sublime, the awe-inspiring experience of vastness that was certain to dwarf them, crush them, make them feel small. Just as these philosophers had predicted, this experience made Lovell relish the safety of home. "It makes you realize just what you have back there on earth. The earth from here is a grand oasis in the big vastness of space." Dr. Wernher von Braun, who had built the rocket for Apollo 8, must have understood; he liked to say that "a space scientist is an engineer who loves poetry."

Finally, there was Borman, their commanding officer. Borman had graduated from the United States Military Academy at West Point, entered the Air Force, and become a fighter pilot. On board Apollo 8, he waxed eloquent: "It's a vast, lonely, forbidding-type existence, or expanse of nothing." Lonely, forbidding, existence, nothing: It sounded as if Borman had been hanging out on the Left Bank reading Jean-Paul Sartre.

Having become space poets, the three astronauts had arrived at their final destination: They were circling the moon. With every rotation, Apollo 8 disappeared behind the moon, where no one had ever been before, and each time, they lost radio contact with Earth. There was much nail-biting in Houston, the Texas headquarters of ground control, during their first fifty-minute absence. "Apollo 8, Houston. Over." "Apollo 8, Houston. Over." Ground control kept calling, sending radio waves into space, but with no response. One, two, three, four, five, six times. The seconds, the minutes passed. Then, on the seventh try, they got an answer: "Go ahead, Houston. This is Apollo 8. Burn complete." Ground control was audibly relieved and exclaimed: "Good to hear your voice!"

Over the next fifteen hours, the astronauts kept disappearing and reappearing, changing their position, maneuvering the capsule, trying to get some sleep, and preparing for their return to Earth. It would require them to fire up the rocket on the dark side of the moon, without radio contact, in order to escape the pull of the moon and gain enough momentum to make it back home. They had only one shot at it; if they failed, they would be orbiting the moon for the rest of their lives.

Before that maneuver, they wanted to send a special message to Earth. Borman had written it down on a fireproof piece of paper beforehand and had even made them rehearse. Not everyone seemed equally enthusiastic about the idea. Before the broadcast, Anders said: "May I see that blurb—that . . . thing?" "The what, Bill?" Borman asked, somewhat passive-aggressively. This was not how he wanted them to be talking about their upcoming performance. "The thing we're supposed to read?" Anders replied, more carefully. Borman let it go. All that mattered now was the reading itself.

They returned from the dark side of the moon and announced to Houston, "For all the people back on earth, the crew of Apollo 8 has a message that we would like to send to you." And then they read that message, even though they had fallen behind schedule and still faced the perilous final burn and return voyage to Earth, where people were celebrating Christmas Eve. Anders, the space imagist, began:

In the beginning, God created the heaven and the earth; and
the earth was without form and void, and darkness was upon

the face of the deep; and the spirit of God moved upon the face of the waters. And God said: "Let there be light" and there was light. And God saw the light, and that it was good. And God divided the light from the darkness.

Then Lovell read:

And God called the light Day, and the darkness He called Night. And the evening and the morning were the first day. And God said, "Let there be a firmament in the midst of the waters. And let it divide the waters from the waters." And God made the firmament and divided the waters which were under the firmament and the waters which were above the firmament, and it was so. And God called the firmament Heaven. And the evening and the morning were the second day.

Now it was Borman's turn, but he had his hands full. "Can you hold this camera?" he asked Lovell. Borman, his hands now free, grabbed the piece of paper:

And God said, "let the waters under the heaven be gathered together into one place and let the dry land appear," and it was so. And God called the dry land Earth, and the waters that were gathered together he called Seas. And God saw that it was good.

Back on Earth, an audience of 500 million people was spellbound. It was the most popular live transmission in the history of the world.

There had been doubts about the necessity of sending men to the moon. For many purposes, an unmanned probe equipped with cameras and other scientific instruments would have been enough. Or NASA could have used a chimp, as it had done on previous missions. The first American in space had been Ham, a chimp from Cameroon, captured and sold to the United States Air Force. Between the Russians and the Americans, a whole zoo had been sent up there, as if on some doomed Noah's Ark: chimps, dogs, turtles.

But while the human Apollo crew might not have contributed much to science, it did contribute to literature. Ham the chimp would not have shared his impressions about space. He would not have tried his hand at poetry. He would not have thought of reading those passages from the Bible, which unexpectedly expressed what it was like to have left the orbit of the earth and shot straight out into space. Seeing earthrise from afar was the perfect position for reading the most influential creation myth devised by humans.

WHAT IS MOST MOVING about the Apollo 8 reading is that it was done by people without literary training who found themselves in an unusual situation and who used their own words, as well as the words of an ancient text, to express that experience. The three astronauts remind me that the most important protagonists in the story of literature aren't necessarily professional authors. Instead I encounter an unexpected cast of characters, from Mesopotamian accountants and illiterate Spanish soldiers to a lawyer in medieval Baghdad, a Maya rebel in southern Mexico, and the pirates of the bayou in the Gulf of Mexico.

But the most important lesson from Apollo 8 was the influence of foundational texts such as the Bible, texts that accrued power and significance over time until they became source codes for entire cultures, telling people where they came from and how they should live their lives. Foundational texts were often presided over by priests, who enshrined them at the center of empires and nations. Kings promoted these texts because they realized that a story could justify conquests and provide cultural cohesion. Foundational texts first arose in very few places, but as their influence spread and new texts emerged, the globe increasingly resembled a map organized by literature—by the foundational texts dominating a given region.

The increasing power of foundational texts put literature at the center of many conflicts, including most religious wars. Even in the modern era, when Frank Borman, James Lovell, and William Anders returned to Earth, they were greeted by a lawsuit brought by Madalyn Murray O'Hair, an outspoken atheist, asking the courts to keep NASA from any future "reading of the sectarian Christian religion Bible . . . in space and in relation to all future space flight activity." O'Hair was aware of the shaping force of this foundational text, and she didn't like it.

O'Hair was not the only one to challenge the reading of the Bible. While Borman was circling the moon, he received periodic news updates from ground control in Houston, the Interstellar Times, as they called it. He heard about soldiers being released from Cambodia and updates on the fate of the U.S.S. *Pueblo*, a U.S. Navy ship captured earlier that year by North Korea.

The *Pueblo* was front-page news on the Interstellar Times every single day, ensuring that Borman would never forget that he was up there so that the free world would win the race to the moon against the Soviet Union and Communism. The Apollo 8 mission was part of the Cold War, and the Cold War was very much a war between foundational texts.

The Soviet Union had been founded on the ideas articulated in a much more recent text than the Bible. *The Communist Manifesto*, written by Marx and Engels, and avidly read by Lenin, Mao, Ho, and Castro, was a mere 120 years old, but it sought to compete with older foundational texts such as the Bible. When Borman was planning the Bible reading, he must have remembered the Soviet astronaut Yuri Gagarin, the first man in space. Gagarin hadn't thought to bring *The Communist Manifesto* into space, but he had been inspired by its ideas to declare, upon his triumphant return to

Earth: "I looked and looked but I didn't see God." Out in space, a battle of ideas and of books was raging. Gagarin had beaten Borman to space, but Borman had prevailed there with a powerful foundational text.

The Apollo 8 reading from Genesis also spoke to the importance of the creative technologies behind literature, invented in different parts of the world and brought together only gradually. Borman had written out the lines of Genesis using an alphabet, the most efficient written code, that had been created in Greece. He had written the lines on paper, a convenient material that originated in China and came to Europe and America via the Arabic world. He had copied the words from a Bible that had been bound as a book, a useful Roman invention. The pages were printed, a Chinese invention that had been further developed in northern Europe.

It was only when storytelling intersected with writing that literature was born. Previously, storytelling had existed in oral cultures, with different rules and purposes. But once storytelling was connected to writing, literature emerged as a new force. Everything that followed, the entire history of literature, began with this moment of intersection, which meant that in order to tell the story of literature, I had to focus on both storytelling and the evolution of creative technologies, such as the alphabet, paper, the book, and print.

Storytelling and writing technologies didn't follow a straight path. Writing itself was invented at least twice, first in Mesopotamia and then in the Americas. Indian priests refused to write down sacred stories for fear of losing control over them, a feeling shared by West African bards who lived two thousand years later and halfway around the world. Egyptian scribes embraced writing but tried to keep it secret, hoping to reserve the power of literature to themselves. Charismatic teachers such as Socrates refused to write, rebelling against the idea of foundational texts having authority and against the writing technologies that had made them possible. Some later inventions were only selectively adopted, as when Arab scholars used Chinese paper but showed no interest in another Chinese invention, print.

Writing inventions often came with unexpected side effects. Preserving old texts meant that their languages were kept alive artificially. Students have been studying dead languages ever since. Some texts ended up being declared sacred, causing bitter rivalries and wars among readers of different scriptures. New technologies sometimes led to format wars, such as the battle between the traditional scroll and the newer book in the first centuries C.E., when Christians pitted their holy books against Hebrew scrolls, or when Spanish adventurers later used their printed Bibles against hand-crafted Maya scripture.

As the larger story of literature slowly took shape in my mind, I saw it as unfolding in four stages. The first stage was dominated by small groups of scribes, who alone had mastered the early, difficult writing systems and therefore controlled the texts they assembled from storytellers, texts such as the *Epic of Gilgamesh,* the Hebrew Bible, and Homer's *Iliad* and *Odyssey.* As the influence of these foundational texts grew, they were challenged, in a second stage, by charismatic teachers such as the Buddha, Socrates, and Jesus, who denounced the influence of priests and scribes and whose followers developed new styles of writing. I began to think of these vivid texts as teachers' literature.

In a third stage of literature, individual authors started to emerge, supported by innovations that made access to writing easier. While these authors first imitated older texts, more daring ones such as Lady Murasaki in Japan and Cervantes in Spain soon created new types of literature, above all, novels. Finally, in a fourth stage, the widespread use of paper and print ushered in the era of mass production and mass literacy, with newspapers and broadsides, as well as new texts such as *The Autobiography of Benjamin Franklin* or *The Communist Manifesto*.

Together, these four stages, and the stories and inventions that made them possible, created a world shaped by literature. It is a world in which we expect religions to be based on books and nations to be founded on texts, a world in which we routinely converse with voices from the past and imagine that we might address readers of the future.

BORMAN AND HIS CREW were fighting their literary Cold War with an old text, and they were also using old technologies: book, paper, and print. But in the cone of their spaceship were new tools, computers that had been reduced in size to fit into their Apollo 8 capsule. Soon these computers would usher in a writing revolution whose effects we are living with today.

The history of literature in this book is written very much in light of this, our latest revolution in writing technologies. Revolutions of such magnitude don't happen often. The alphabet revolution, begun in the Middle East and Greece, made writing easier to master and helped increase literacy rates. The paper revolution, begun in China and continued in the Middle East, lowered the cost of literature and thereby changed its nature. It also set the stage for the print revolution, which first occurred in East Asia and then, hundreds of years later, in northern Europe. There were smaller revolutions, such as the invention of parchment in Asia Minor and of the codex in Rome. In the last four thousand years, there have been a handful of moments when new technologies radically transformed literature.

Until now. Clearly, our current technological revolution is throwing at us every year new forms of writing, from email and e-readers to blogs and Twitter, changing not only how literature is

GREEK SCRIBE WRITING ON A TABLET, AS DEPICTED ON A CUP FROM THE
FOURTH TO THE SIXTH CENTURY B.C.E. GREEK SCRIBES USED
WAX TABLETS, WHICH COULD BE ERASED AND REUSED.

distributed and read but also how it is written, as authors adjust to
these new realities. At the same time, some of the terms we have
recently begun using sound like earlier moments in the deep history of literature: Like ancient scribes, we are once again scrolling
down texts and sitting hunched over tablets. How to make sense of
this combination of old and new?

As I was exploring the story of literature, I became restless. It felt
strange to think about the way literature had shaped our history and
the history of our planet solely while sitting at my desk. I needed to
go to places where great texts and inventions had originated.

And so I went from Beirut to Beijing and from Jaipur to the Arc-
tic Circle. I searched literary ruins in Troy and Chiapas and spoke
to archaeologists, translators, and authors, seeking out Derek Walcott in the Caribbean and Orhan Pamuk in Istanbul. I went to
places where literature had been buried or burned, where it had
been rediscovered and brought to life again. Wandering the ruins
of the great library of Pergamum, in Turkey, I pondered how parchment had been invented there; I marveled at the stone libraries of
China, where emperors endeavored to make their canon of litera-

ture permanent. I followed in the footsteps of travel writers, retracing Goethe's steps in Sicily, where he had gone to discover world literature, and went looking for the leader of the Zapatista uprising in southern Mexico because he had used the old Maya epic *Popol Vuh* as a weapon of resistance and insurrection.

On those travels, it was hardly possible to take a single step without coming across some form of written story. In what follows, I have tried to convey my experience by telling the story of literature and how it turned our planet into a written world.

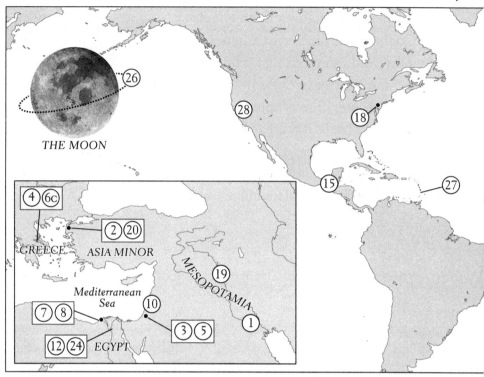

THE MOON

GREECE ASIA MINOR

Mediterranean Sea

MESOPOTAMIA

EGYPT

TIMELINE *of the* WRITTEN WORLD

① ①
C. 2100 B.C.E.

First tales of Gilgamesh, in cuneiform writing

TODAY'S IRAQ

②
C. 1200 B.C.E.

Troy destroyed by Greeks

ASIA MINOR, TODAY'S TURKEY

③
C. 1000 B.C.E.

Oldest sources of Hebrew Bible

JERUSALEM

④
C. 800 B.C.E.

Homeric tales of Trojan War, in Greek alphabet

GREECE

⑤
C. 458 B.C.E.

Ezra declares Hebr writings sacred

JERUSALEM

⑪
868

Diamond Sutra, *earliest surviving printed work*

DUNHUANG, WESTERN CHINA

⑫
879

Earliest paper fragment of One Thousand and One Nights

EGYPT

⑬
C. 1000

Lady Murasaki writes The Tale of Genji, *the first novel*

KYOTO, JAPAN

⑭
C. 1440S

Gutenberg reinvents the printing press, probably drawing on East Asian models

MAINZ, GERMANY

⑮
C. 1550S

Popol Vuh *written Roman alphabet*

CHIAPAS, SOUTHWE MEXICO

㉑
1827

Johann Goethe announces "era of world literature"

WEIMAR, GERMANY

㉒
1848

The Communist Manifesto is published

LONDON

㉓
1930S

Akhmatova writes, then burns, secret poetry

ST. PETERSBURG, RUSSIA

㉔
1947

A scrap from One Thousand and One Nights *is discovered*

EGYPT

㉕
1960

Epic of Sunjata written down

GUINEA, WEST AFRICA

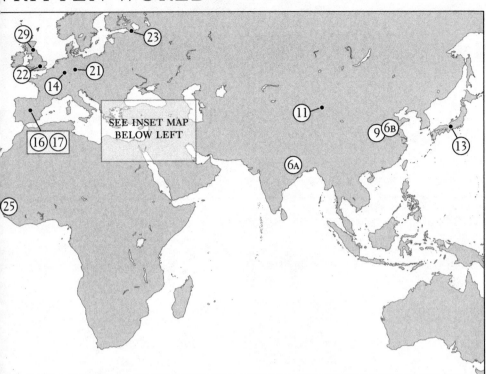

SEE INSET MAP
BELOW LEFT

THE
WRITTEN WORLD

CHAPTER 1

ALEXANDER'S PILLOW BOOK

336 B.C.E., MACEDONIA

ALEXANDER OF MACEDONIA IS CALLED THE GREAT BECAUSE HE managed to unify the proud Greek city-states, conquer every kingdom between Greece and Egypt, defeat the mighty Persian army, and create an empire that stretched all the way to India—in less than thirteen years. People have wondered ever since how a ruler from a minor Greek kingdom could accomplish such a feat. But there was always a second question, more intriguing to me, which was why Alexander wanted to conquer Asia in the first place.

In contemplating this question, I found myself focusing on three objects that Alexander carried with him throughout his military campaign and that he put under his pillow every night, three objects that summed up the way he saw his campaign. The first was a dagger. Next to his dagger, Alexander kept a box. And inside the box, he placed the most precious of the three objects: a copy of his favorite text, the *Iliad*.

How did Alexander come by these three objects, and what did they mean to him?

Alexander slept on a dagger because he wanted to escape his

father's fate of being assassinated. The box he had seized from Darius, his Persian opponent. And the *Iliad* he had brought to Asia because it was the story through which he saw his campaign and life, a foundational text that captured the mind of a prince who would go on to conquer the world.

Homer's epic had been a foundational text for the Greeks for generations. For Alexander, it acquired the status of an almost sacred text, which is why he carried it with him on his campaign. It is what texts, especially foundational ones, do: They change the way we see the world and also the way we act upon it. This was certainly the case with Alexander. He was induced not only to read and study this text, but also to reenact it. Alexander, the reader, put himself into the story, viewing his own life and trajectory in the light of Homer's Achilles. Alexander the Great is well-known as a larger-than-life king. It turns out that he was also a larger-than-life reader.

A Young Achilles

Alexander learned the lesson of the dagger while still a prince, at a turning point in his life. His father, King Philip II of Macedonia, was marrying off a daughter, and no one could afford to decline his invitation. Emissaries from the Greek city-states would have been sent, along with visitors from recently conquered lands in Thrace, where the Danube met the Black Sea. Perhaps even some Persians were in the crowd, attracted by King Philip's military successes. Alexander's father stood on the eve of a major assault on Asia Minor, striking fear in the heart of Darius III, king of Persia. The mood in the old Macedonian capital, Aegae, was exuberant, because King Philip was famous for throwing lavish parties. Everyone had assembled in the great theater, eager for the proceedings to begin.

Alexander must have watched the preparations with ambivalence. He had been groomed to be his father's successor from an early age, with forced marches and training in the martial arts. He had become a famous horseman, astonishing his father by breaking an unmanageable horse when he was in his early teens. King Philip had also seen to Alexander's education in public speaking and had made sure that his son would learn proper Greek in addition to the mountain dialect spoken in Macedonia. (Throughout his life, Alexander would revert back to the Macedonian dialect when enraged.) But now it seemed that Philip, who had invested so much in Alexander, might alter his plans for succession. He was marrying his daughter to his brother-in-law, who might well become Alexander's rival. If the marriage produced a son, Alexander could be replaced altogether. Philip was a master at knitting new alliances, preferably through marriage. Alexander knew that his father would not hesitate to break a promise if it served his purpose.

There was no more time for musing: Philip was entering the theater. He came alone, without his usual guards, to demonstrate confidence and control. Never had Macedonia been more powerful and more respected. If the campaign into Asia Minor succeeded, Philip would become known as the Greek leader who had attacked and defeated the Persian Empire on its own shores.

Suddenly, an armed man rushed toward Philip. A dagger was drawn, and the king fell to the ground. People ran toward him. Where was the attacker? He had managed to escape. A few bodyguards spotted him outside and gave chase. He was running toward a horse. But his foot became entangled in vines; he stumbled and fell. His pursuers caught up with him, and, after a short fight, he was put to the sword. Back in the theater, the king was lying in his blood, dead. Macedonia, the Greek alliance, and the army assembled to take on Persia were without a head.

For the rest of his life Alexander would protect himself with a dagger, even at night, to avoid his father's fate.

Had Darius of Persia sent the assassin to prevent Philip's assault on Asia Minor? If Darius was behind the murder, he had miscalculated. Alexander used the murder as a pretext to get rid of his potential rivals, seize the throne, and launch an expedition to secure the Macedonian borders to the north and the loyalty of the Greek city-states to the south. Then he was ready to take on Darius. He crossed the Hellespont with a large force, retracing the path the Persian army had taken when it invaded Greece generations ago. Alexander's conquest of Persia had begun.

Before he confronted the Persian army, Alexander made a detour to Troy. He didn't do so for military reasons. Even though Troy was well situated near the narrow waterway between Asia and Europe, it had lost the importance it once had. Nor did he go there to capture Darius. In making Troy his first stop in Asia, Alexander revealed a different motivation for his conquest of Asia, one that could be found in the text he carried around with him everywhere: Homer's *Iliad*.

Homer was the avenue by which many people had approached Troy ever since the stories of the Trojan War had become a foundational text. It's certainly the reason I went to Troy. I had read a children's version of the *Iliad* while growing up before graduating to more faithful translations. When I studied Greek in college, I even read parts in the original, with the help of a dictionary. The famous scenes and characters from this text have been in my mind ever since, including the opening, which finds the Greek army having laid siege to Troy for nine years and Achilles withdrawing from battle because Agamemnon had taken Achilles' female captive, Briseis, for himself. Without their best fighter, the Greeks are hard-pressed by the Trojans. But then Achilles returns to battle and kills the most important Trojan, Hector, and drags his body around the city walls. (According to other sources, Paris manages to retaliate and kill Achilles by aiming his arrow at Achilles' heel.) I also remembered the war among the gods, Athena fighting on the side of the Greeks and Aphrodite on the side of the Trojans. And the strange backstory of Paris crowning Aphrodite the most beautiful goddess and receiving Menelaus' wife, Helen, as a reward, which sets off the war. The most striking image of them all was of course the Trojan horse with Greek soldiers hidden inside its belly, although I realized, to my surprise, once I read more accurate translations, that the last part of the war was actually not recounted in the *Iliad* and only briefly in the *Odyssey*.

When I think of the story of Troy in the *Iliad,* there is one scene that has stayed in my mind above all others. Hector has returned from the battle that is raging down below the city and is looking for his wife, Andromache. He can't find her at home because she has rushed out into the city in search of news of him. Hector finally finds her near the city gate. She pleads with him not to risk his life, but he explains that he must fight to keep her safe. In the midst of this high-stakes exchange, a nurse brings their son:

> With these words, resplendent Hector
> Reached for his child, who shrank back screaming
> Into his nurse's bosom, terrified of his father's
> Bronze-encased face and the horsehair plume
> He saw nodding down from the helmet's crest.
> This forced a laugh from his father and mother,
> And Hector removed the helmet from his head
> And set it on the ground all shimmering with light.
> Then he kissed his dear son and swung him up gently
> And said a prayer to Zeus and the other immortals.

In the middle of a brutal war that is raging right outside the gate, and of a heated exchange between husband and wife about the meaning of the war, suddenly the mood changes as the father laughingly removes the helmet that is frightening the child. It is a moment of domestic reconciliation, the helmet giving way to Hector's laughing face before he kisses his son. But the helmet is still there, sitting on the ground shimmering with light, and perhaps the child is still sobbing, a reminder that this is but a brief reprieve from the war that will end with the death of Hector and the destruction of the great city of Troy.

All of this was in my mind when I first approached the ruins of Troy, situated high upon a hill. The citadel was once located close to the sea, but since the fall of Troy around the year 1200 B.C.E., the sea has receded due to the sediments brought by the river Scamander. Whereas in ancient times Troy had commanded the waterway between Asia and Europe, it now simply rose from a wide plane, cut off from the sea, which I could barely see on the horizon.

What was even more disappointing than the city's position in the landscape was its size. Troy was tiny. I was able to cross within five minutes what I had imagined as a gigantic, towering fortress and city. How this minifortress had withstood the mighty Greek army for so long was difficult to fathom. Was this what epic literature did, taking a small fortress and blowing it out of proportion?

As I was mulling over my disappointment, it struck me that Alexander reacted in exactly the opposite way: He loved Troy. Like me, Alexander had dreamed of the epic since childhood, when he had first been introduced to the Homeric world. He had learned to read and write by studying Homer. Pleased with Alexander's success, King Philip had found the most famous living philosopher, Aristotle, and persuaded him to come north to Macedonia. Aristotle happened to be the greatest commentator on Homer and regarded Homer as the fount of Greek culture and thought. Under his tutelage, Alexander came to regard Homer's *Iliad* not just as the most important story of Greek culture, but also as an ideal to which he aspired, a motivation for crossing into Asia. The copy of the *Iliad* that Alexander put under his pillow every night was annotated by his teacher, Aristotle.

The first thing Alexander did upon his arrival in Asia was to pay homage at the grave of Protesilaus, praised in the *Iliad* as the first to leap ashore when the Greek ships landed. This act proved to be only the beginning of Alexander's Homeric reenactment. Once they had made their way to Troy, Alexander and his friend Hephaestion laid wreaths at the graves of Achilles and Patroclus, showing the world that they were following in the footsteps of that famous pair of Greek warriors and lovers. They and their companions raced naked around the city walls, in Homeric fashion. When Alexander was given what was allegedly Paris's lyre, he complained that he would have preferred that of Achilles; and he took armor preserved from the Trojan War. He would conquer Asia in Homeric armor.

While Troy had no direct strategic significance, it revealed the secret springs of Alexander's campaign: Alexander had come to Asia to relive the stories of the Trojan War. Homer had shaped the way Alexander viewed the world, and now Alexander carried out that view through his campaign. When Alexander arrived in Troy, he took it upon himself to carry on the epic story—beyond that which Homer could have imagined. Alexander made Homer bigger by reenacting the conquest of Asia on a grander scale. (He also seemed to have preferred different parts of the *Iliad* than I did: Whereas I gravitated to the domestic scene of Hector, Andromache, and their son, Alexander identified with Achilles and his prowess in battle.)

While Alexander was at Troy, Darius of Persia sent an army that included Persian commanders and Greek mercenaries. The first clash between Alexander and the Persians, on the Granicus River, left the Persian army defeated, and Darius learned that this young Macedonian was a bigger threat than he had thought. Seeing that he needed to take things into his own hands, Darius began to assemble a large army to put an end to this troublemaker.

Alexander's Macedonian and Greek army was smaller than the Persian force but better trained, and the Greeks had developed formidable battle tactics. Alexander's father had inherited the Greek phalanx, rows of interlocking foot soldiers who wielded a shield in one hand and a spear in the other, protecting and supporting each other. By tightening the discipline of his soldiers through training,

Philip had been able to increase the length of their spears, turning the rows of soldiers into an impenetrable movable wall. Upon resuming the throne, Alexander had combined the improved phalanx with a swift cavalry that could encircle an army and attack from the rear. His own fighting style was uniquely calculated to inspire his soldiers. While his adversary Darius usually hung back when his armies fought, Alexander would lead the attack, throwing himself into the fray whenever he could. Once, when laying siege to a city, he scaled the walls before any of his men and jumped down without them, finding himself with only two guards by his side facing a swarm of the city's defenders. When his men finally caught up with him, they found him pressed hard on all sides and wounded, but still defending himself vigorously.

The two armies finally met late in the year 333 B.C.E. at Issus, near the border separating today's Turkey from Syria. The coast here quickly gave way to mountains, leaving relatively little room for Darius's large army. Confident in his superior numbers, Darius attacked the Greek phalanx, which was guarding the left wing, with a massive assault. But ultimately better training prevailed. The phalanx did not break, and the Greeks even gained on the Persians. When Alexander, in charge of the right wing, spotted an opening in the guard around the Persian king, he aimed directly at him; Darius panicked and fled rather than engage his adversary directly, with Alexander in hot pursuit.

The Battle of Issus had loomed large in my mind ever since as a young child I came across a painting of it by the Renaissance painter Albrecht Altdorfer. In the painting, the sun is setting, illuminating a dramatic sky of clouds and light, which is mirrored by the thicket of lances and armor and horses on the battlefield below. In the middle of the chaos is Darius, standing on a chariot drawn by three horses, with Alexander, riding alone on a horse, chasing after him. What I have always loved was the detail and the texture of this painting. I would examine the painting, which I had chanced upon in a picture book, inspecting the battle scenes or the encampment or the ruins of a castle in the distance. (When I finally saw the painting in the original, it, too, was much smaller than I had imagined, merely 60 by 47 inches.)

Even though in the painting it looks as though Alexander will get Darius at any moment, Darius in fact got away again. In every other respect, however, it was a decisive victory. Alexander captured a large quantity of treasure, as well as Darius's mother, daughters, and wife. Was he imagining Darius's wife as Andromache, wife of the Trojan warrior Hector?

It was at this battle that Alexander captured Darius's box, in which he would place his copy of the *Iliad*, a reminder that he had not yet defeated this foe in a properly Homeric fashion.

Alexander wasn't done playing Achilles. For the time being, he ignored Darius, who was threatening him with letters and demanded the return of his family. Instead he marched down the coast, making sure that the powerful Persian navy would not be able to attack from the sea. He went all the way to the Levant, forcing cities to surrender and sacking them when they refused. When he conquered Gaza, he killed its recalcitrant leader, Batis, who had resisted his offer of peaceful surrender, and dragged his body around the city as Achilles had dragged Hector's. It was as if Alexander had decided that faithful reenactment of scenes from Homer was the path to victory.

But to Alexander's Homeric mind, the true Hector was not this minor Gazan commander but Darius. As soon as Alexander secured his possession of Egypt, he entered Mesopotamia, where he found Darius waiting for him. Darius no longer underestimated Alexander. This time, he had assembled the entire might of the Persian Empire. The armies met in the heartland of Mesopotamia, near today's Mosul, in Iraq. Alexander first marched his phalanx toward the Persian forces, but then cleverly combined this assault with a daring maneuver. His cavalry drew the Persians far to the right side, then turned unexpectedly and struck a decisive blow to the center. Alexander had achieved his goal: The Persian Empire was his.

The only thing that spoiled the triumph was that Darius had gotten away once again. Even though the Persian king no longer represented a threat, Alexander went after him. Was Alexander hoping to avenge his father's murder? He didn't behave vengefully to Darius's mother, wife, and daughters, treating them with the utmost respect. No, Alexander was still reenacting his epic. He wanted to meet Darius in a traditional battle and defeat him in single combat, the way Achilles had met and defeated Hector. Alas, that desire was never fulfilled. Darius was killed by one of his own commanders, his body left behind for Alexander. Alexander grieved over this worthy opponent and angrily hunted down the murderer who had deprived him of his Homeric victory.

The Sounds of Homer

—

800 B.C.E., Greece

The *Iliad* originated not as literature but as a tradition of oral storytelling. The story was set in the Bronze Age, around 1200 B.C.E., in a world before the modern warfare used by Alexander—and before writing. True, the Minoan civilization on the Greek island of Crete had developed an early writing system similar to Egyptian hieroglyphics that has not been deciphered. In Mycenae, on the Greek mainland, a related writing system, called Linear B, had emerged, but it was mostly used for economic transactions. No one thought to write down the stories of the Trojan War. Those stories were sung by specialized bards to audiences large and small.

Around 800 B.C.E., travelers from Phoenicia, today's Lebanon, brought news of a writing system that was fundamentally different from all the others, so different that it was at first difficult to under-

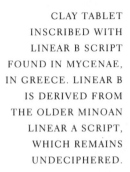

CLAY TABLET
INSCRIBED WITH
LINEAR B SCRIPT
FOUND IN MYCENAE,
IN GREECE. LINEAR B
IS DERIVED FROM
THE OLDER MINOAN
LINEAR A SCRIPT,
WHICH REMAINS
UNDECIPHERED.

stand how it would actually work. Older writing systems such as the one used in Mycenae had emerged from signs that stood for objects, such as cows, houses, grain. Over time, these signs also came to stand for the syllables that made up those objects' names, or even individual sounds, but all signs were originally meaningful, connected in shape to an object or idea, which also made them easier to remember.

Drawing on earlier experiments from Egypt, the Phoenicians recognized that the strength of these writing systems was also their weakness. As long as signs were based on meaning, there would be no end of them. In response, they came up with a radical solution: Writing needed to cut its ties with the world of objects and meaning. Instead it would simply represent language, and more specifically sound. Each sign would represent a sound, and the signs could then be combined to make meaningful words. Giving up on objects, giving up on meaning, was a difficult thing to do, but it had one enormous advantage: The number of signs would be reduced from hundreds or thousands to a few dozen, making reading and writing infinitely simpler. Writing would be attached much more directly to speech. (The Phoenician idea spread in the region: Hebrew is based on the same concept.)

The Phoenicians had applied this idea systematically to their language, but they had not followed it to its logical conclusion. Only consonants were represented. It was as if, in English, *rg* could mean *rug* or *rig* or *rage*. Readers needed to guess from context which word was meant, supplying the vowels themselves. This is where the Greeks saw room for improvement, completing the Phoenician system by adding vowels. Now it was no longer necessary to guess which word was meant by *rg*. The entire word, its complete sound sequence, would be written out: *r-a-g-e*.

The new system was particularly well suited to the meter used to sing stories of the Trojan War: the hexameter, composed of six feet (each consisting of one long and two shorter syllables or of two long syllables). This sound pattern couldn't easily be captured by the Phoenician system; the most important part, the long, stressed sound at the core of syllables—the *a* in *rage*—would have been missing. The Greek modification supplied the long, stressed vowels. The new phonetic alphabet was perfect for the stories of the Trojan War—and pretty much the first thing scribes did with the new alphabet was to write those stories down. It's even possible that the Greek alphabet was first invented expressly to capture the hexameter of these bards. In any case, the new system ensured that readers weren't thinking of the *rig* of Achilles' sailboat, nor of the *rug* he slept on at night, but of the *rage* he felt when Agamemnon deprived him of his well-deserved prize after a hard-fought battle, as rendered in the famous first line of the epic: "*Rage: Sing, Goddess, Achilles' rage, / Black and murderous, that cost the Greeks / Incalculable pain.*"

The name of one singer, Homer, has become famous (though

we can't even be sure that there ever was a singer by that name), but the name of the ingenious scribe who wrote down the story of the Trojan War is unknown. And yet it was their collaboration that made Homer's version unique. Because the anonymous scribe probably wrote down one singer's version, because the *Iliad* wasn't cobbled together by different scribes and different singers over many generations, the result was much more coherent than other scriptures such as the Hebrew Bible. Significantly, there is no description of writing in the world of the *Iliad* (with a single exception); the epic presents itself as being sung rather than written. The *Iliad* and the Greek alphabet, an alphabet based on pure sound, were a powerful combination, and together they were going to have far-reaching consequences. Within a few hundred years, Greece became the most literate society the world had known, witnessing an extraordinary explosion of literature, drama, and philosophy.

Making Asia Greek

The Greek alphabet and Homer had preceded Alexander to Asia Minor, but once Alexander arrived, they went much farther than they could have gone without him. The power of the new alphabet, and the culture of literacy that came with it, in turn helped Alexander's mission. Having conquered Asia Minor and defeated Darius in Mesopotamia and Persia, Alexander pressed onward, across the Hindu Kush into Afghanistan in the spring and across the Indus River during the monsoon, fighting formidable battle elephants as he went. Neither armed opponent nor nature could stop him. With each new battle won, with each new territory subjected, it became clear that the world was much larger than previously known to Greeks.

As Alexander's realm kept expanding, he started to believe that he was a half god like Achilles, the son of a goddess. He demanded that the Greek city-states officially accord him this divine status,

said no

and many complied. Only Sparta, which had always kept him at arm's length, sent back a characteristically laconic answer. "Since Alexander wishes to be a god, let him be a god," they replied, suggesting that divinity was all in Alexander's head.

The more territories Alexander conquered, the more trouble he had holding them. The western and southern periphery of the Persian sphere of influence, regions like Anatolia and Egypt, were happy enough to accept Alexander, since he usually left the local rulers and governing structures in place. But the task of holding the occupied lands became increasingly difficult the farther east Alexander got from Greece, once he found himself in control of the Persian heartland, and still more difficult once he entered remote Afghanistan and India.

To retain possession of these territories, Alexander made a decision that ran counter to what he had been taught, namely that non-Greeks were inferior. Alexander started to wear foreign clothes. He admitted foreigners into the Greek army. He married a princess from Afghanistan in an elaborate Bactrian ceremony. He paid homage to foreign gods. And he let his Eastern vassals worship him by falling to the floor, facedown.

Alexander's Greek and Macedonian comrades, who had followed him loyally, were shocked. They felt displaced by foreign rivals, and they no longer recognized their king. Their resentments were forced into the open when Alexander invited his old comrades to a private dinner. Each of them was expected to follow Eastern protocol and prostrate himself before the king. As a reward, Alexander would kiss them and let them rise again. The battle-worn warriors didn't need to be Athenian democrats to be repulsed by this custom. And yet, under pressure, they did it, one by one, grudgingly. Only one would not submit: Callisthenes, Aristotle's great-nephew, whom Alexander had hired to be his chronicler. "I shall be poorer for the kiss," he declared, drawing Alexander's wrath, with far-reaching consequences, as we shall see. Alexander no lon-

ger thought of himself as the king of Macedonia. In possession of
Babylon, he began styling himself "king of Asia."

So focused were his commanders on Alexander's foreign clothes
and customs that they failed to see how under his rule the four
quarters of Alexander's world were actually becoming Greek. Alexander had left a trail of Greek and Macedonian garrisons to keep
local rulers in check. Soon a whole network of Greek settlements,
some named after him, dotted his empire. The empire comprised
dozens of languages and cultures, and Greeks were famously reluctant to learn foreign languages, let alone foreign writing systems.
Their disdain for most non-Greek peoples was closely tied with language and writing; they called foreigners barbarians precisely because their speech was incomprehensible to them, sounding to
Greek ears like *barbarbar*. For this reason, there was never any
question about what language the Greek and Macedonian settlers
would speak: Of course they would speak Greek. Even Alexander
with his new foreign friends and new foreign clothes never bothered to learn any other language.

Homer played a central role in this linguistic conquest, and not
only because Alexander favored him. The *Iliad* was the text through
which everyone learned how to read and write, the chief vehicle for
spreading the Greek language and alphabet. It became a foundational text par excellence. This also meant that it gave rise to professional interpreters, not only philosophers like Aristotle but also
critics who wrote extensive commentary on this text.

Alexander's Greek soldiers and settlers spoke a special kind of
Greek. It wasn't the cultured Greek of Athens, nor Alexander's
Macedonian dialect. Instead, it was a somewhat simplified form of
spoken Greek called Common (*koiné*) Greek. This was the language that had originated in the Greek trading empire in previous
centuries, and it now became the common language of Alexander's
realm, the language in which its different parts could speak to each
other. Local rulers often continued to use native languages and

writing systems, but Common Greek and its phonetic system were a means of communicating across the borders that Alexander's conquest had obliterated. He also circulated a common currency, the

THE TETRADRACHM COIN BROUGHT THE IMAGE OF ALEXANDER THE GREAT AND GREEK WRITING TO THE OUTER REACHES OF HIS EMPIRE.

Attic coin (tetradrachm), which bore his face and Greek writing. Alexander wasn't just a faithful reader of a text; he created the infrastructure necessary for its survival.

As Greek became a world language, the people who spoke it felt like world citizens. Alexander turned out to be not so much a betrayer of Macedonian and Greek culture as the embodiment of a new identity that stretched across cultures and territories, from Greece to Egypt and from Mesopotamia to India. A new word was gaining traction that described this new identity, no longer firmly tied to one particular tribe or nation. Needless to say, it, too, was Greek: *cosmopolitan*, or "citizen of the world." Alexander's export of the *Iliad* proved that a foundational text could be carried far outside its place of origin and yet retain its power, becoming a truly cosmopolitan text.

Greek was profiting from Alexander's conquests, but also from the power of the alphabet. The alphabet revolution was unfolding, and it soon would wipe out nonalphabetic writing systems like Egyptian hieroglyphics (and later still, Maya glyphs). It is a revolution that is still going on. Today, only East Asia is holding out against the alphabet, and even there phonetic writing systems and syllabaries have been advancing.

In Asia Minor, other cultures and languages were also in retreat. Lydian ultimately died out in Anatolia, while Parthia (now northeastern Iran) and Bactria (now Afghanistan), home to Alexander's wife, became more familiar with Greek. Even in Phoenicia, where the idea of the alphabet had originated, Greek was making headway. The effects of this unprecedented language export could be felt as far away as India, where the Greek phonetic alphabet influenced several writing systems. When a new Indian king, Ashoka, emerged, he ordered inscriptions to be made in Greek.

A HOMER OF HIS OWN

Alexander kept going, taking his *Iliad* and his coins, his language and his alphabet, farther and farther east. He would have gone all the way to China if he had been able. But discontent was brewing within his ranks. Divided between increasingly resentful Greek and Macedonian commanders and an assortment of foreign legions, his soldiers wanted to return home. His own army finally accomplished what no foreign army had been able to do: It made Alexander turn back. He punished his soldiers with a forced march through the desert that left many dead before grudgingly leading them back to Babylon, which had become the center of his realm. But Babylon was only supposed to be a temporary stop. Alexander started to hatch plans for an invasion of Arabia, even of the entire African continent. Would these cultures have adopted the Greek phonetic system and Greek culture? We will never know, because after a night of drinking, Alexander became ill and died a few days later, of unknown causes. Perhaps he was assassinated like his father. He was thirty-two years old.

Alexander died with one regret: His life's story was still unwritten. Even though he did more for Homer than anyone before or after, there was something tragic about his dedication to this poet, because what he really wanted was not so much to follow Homer's heroes as to have a Homer follow him. This idea had been on his mind ever since he first set foot in Asia, near Troy. Anticipating that his own deeds would outshine those of Homer's half gods, he publicly complained that he didn't have his own Homer to celebrate them.

It was not in Alexander's nature to complain about the absence of a Homer and do nothing about it. He hired Callisthenes to chronicle his exploits, but the arrangement didn't work out as planned. Callisthenes refused to bow to Alexander, was later implicated in a revolt against him, and died in prison.

Picking a fight with his chronicler was not the wisest thing Alexander did. Before his death, Callisthenes wrote an account of Alexander's exploits. The narrative itself has been lost, but it included harsh words about Alexander's new Persian manners that found their way into most subsequent biographies. Callisthenes, in any case, was not really what Alexander had in mind when he called for a new Homer. He wanted a proper poet; sadly, he did not live to see the day.

Callisthenes was only the beginning. Alexander's life was simply too amazing, too unprecedented, to be left in the hands of a single writer. Several contemporaries wrote their own accounts, which in turn inspired others to try their hand at Alexander's life, with each writer further embellishing this fantastic tale, hoping to become the Homer to this new Achilles. In one version, Alexander searches for eternal life; in another, he travels to the land of the Blessed. Alexander's life, conceived by him in light of literature, was being transformed into a literary story.

These accounts coalesced into the *Alexander Romance*, as this story came to be known. It is not associated with a single famous author, let alone a new Homer, but it became the most-read text in late antiquity and the early Middle Ages, apart from religious texts. Some authors boldly adapted the story to local circumstances. The Greek version claimed that Alexander was the son not of Philip but of the last Egyptian pharaoh. In the Persian *Book of Kings*, he is identified as the son of the Persian king Darab, who had taken a Greek princess as his wife. Literature turned Alexander into the cosmopolitan king of the East he had always wanted to be.

ALEXANDER'S LITERARY MONUMENTS

When I traveled in Alexander's wake, visiting cities such as Pergamum, Ephesus, and Perge in what is now Turkey, I found that most buildings from the era had disappeared. But invariably the ruins of two types of buildings were left standing, at least partially, dominating the sites: theaters and libraries. These were the buildings to which the greatest resources were devoted, a testament to their significance. Both were connected to literature. The libraries were the place where literature was preserved, and where librarians copied important texts and wrote commentaries. The theaters were devoted to bringing the world of Homer to contemporary audiences. Hellenistic theaters held audiences of up to 25,000, who gathered to see the old Homeric stories updated by tragedians. Alexander was so devoted to theater that he sent for plays and actors during his eastern campaign to entertain him and his troops.

Alexander's most important service to literature took place in Egypt. After conquering the country early in his campaign, Alexan-

der had paid reverence to Egyptian gods and accepted the title Pharaoh. Greeks generally admired Egypt's culture and complicated
writing system, which they did not understand, as a source of ancient wisdom. But even in Egypt, Alexander's tolerance for local
culture had limits. His most important act in making Egypt Greek
was prompted, as so often, by Homer. Alexander was planning to
found a new city when he dreamed of a passage in Homer that suggested the most suitable location.

In contrast to the old Egyptian cities, which were inland, Alexandria was situated by the sea and designed for seafaring and trade.
It contained a large natural harbor on one side and a lake and canals, fed by the Nile, on the other, with plenty of sites for docks. At
its center stood the imposing buildings that expressed the ideals of
Greek culture. There was a school, where pupils would learn Greek
by studying Homer. Next to the school was a gymnasium, with a
colonnade allegedly measuring over six hundred feet, for exercise
and conversation. And, of course, there was a large theater.

Alexandria boasted all of these institutions, but another was
more consequential in making Egypt Greek: the library. The strategic location of the city, which quickly became a major port, was
crucial for the library's success. When ships arrived to do business
in Alexandria, they were told that they must first share with the library whatever literature they had on board. The library employed
an army of copyists to preserve it all, creating the largest collection
of scrolls anywhere in the world, aiming to include all existing
tools, an ambition recently rekindled by Google's plan to organize
the world's information and make it universally accessible. The library also boasted intellectuals and philosophers who pioneered
the study of literary texts. At the center of the library were the epics
of Homer, which were copied, edited, and annotated with a painstaking intensity otherwise reserved for scripture. Not only did Alexander export the Homeric epics to his entire realm, his successors
also built the institutions that would transmit them to the future.

Under Alexander's successors, Alexandria became the largest Greek city in the world, changing the Egyptian writing culture. Egypt had developed one of the earliest writing systems, hieroglyphics, with an enormous history and cultural significance attached to it. But even though hieroglyphics had been simplified over the centuries, with some phonetic signs in increasing circulation, they remained difficult to use, and most Egyptians had to hire scribes for even the simplest transactions. The ease of the Greek phonetic alphabet was too great a temptation, and Egyptians eventually adopted letters inspired by the Greek alphabet to capture the sounds of their own language. The new system, known as Coptic writing, soon displaced hieroglyphics.

There was one writing culture that was even older than Egyptian hieroglyphics: Sumerian cuneiform. This writing system, too, was displaced by Alexander's alphabetic writing and forgotten entirely. It was rediscovered only by chance in the nineteenth century. The story of that discovery takes us to the very origin of writing and to the first great foundational text in human history.

CHAPTER 2

KING OF THE UNIVERSE:
OF GILGAMESH AND ASHURBANIPAL

MY FATHER ONCE TOLD ME THAT AS A STUDENT ON AN archaeological dig, he was taught to detect subtle changes in chemical composition by tasting the soil. I did not like the idea of eating dirt that was probably crawling with insects and had touched dead bones. Was my father just trying to gross me out? The idea has stayed with me ever since, and it popped into my mind many years later when I was contemplating Austen Henry Layard and the trench he had dug into a mound near Mosul, in present-day Iraq. What Layard found there, without quite realizing it, was the first masterpiece of world literature, going back before Homer.

An Englishman who had grown up in Italy and Switzerland, Layard had traveled across the Middle East in 1839, on his way to Ceylon, where he was supposed to take up a position with the colonial civil service. A born traveler, he liked to blend in, adopting local foods and customs and seeking out encounters and adventures whenever he could. He made his way to Constantinople and from there explored the Levant and points east as far as Persia, but he never got to India. Instead he found work with the British ambassador in Constantinople and stayed in the Middle East, whose history he found particularly intriguing. His interest intensified in 1842 when a French archaeologist, Paul-Émile Botta, unearthed the ruins of an ancient palace near Mosul, on the banks of the river Tigris. Layard knew that this was the approximate location of the ancient city of Nineveh, whose destruction was mentioned in the Bible.

Layard wasn't an archaeologist, and if he ever tasted soil, he didn't report on it. But he might well have done something like it. He was endlessly curious, unafraid of physical hardship, and didn't give up easily. In 1845, he cut a trench into a mound in Mosul and hit something. When he dug deeper, he found walls, rooms, and foundations, and he realized that he was in the process of unearthing an entire city.

It was a city made of clay. The spades of his hired workmen uncovered walls built of clay bricks mixed with straw that had been dried in the sun or baked in a kiln. Vessels of various kinds for storing food, even water pipes, were made of clay, which was plentiful in the "land between the rivers" ("Mesopotamia" in Greek), referring to the rivers Tigris and Euphrates. During subsequent digs Layard found more marvels, breathtaking bas-reliefs offering him glimpses onto an unknown civilization, images of cities besieged, of armies clashing, of captives in shackles, and of winged lions and bulls with human heads. Clearly, great kings had ruled a great empire.

The walls, bas-reliefs, and statues were covered with inscriptions in cuneiform, a writing system designed for making wedge-shaped indentations or incisions into clay or stone. Individual bricks could be inscribed that way, as could bas-reliefs and statues—anything, really, made of clay.

Layard soon found small clay seals that contained signatures to be impressed onto moistened clay. He even uncovered an inscription hidden behind a wall that would have been inaccessible to the

A DRAWING BY THE BRITISH ARTIST FREDERICK CHARLES COOPER,
WHO ACCOMPANIED LAYARD'S EXCAVATION AT NINEVEH,
OF A CARVED RELIEF DEPICTING A WINGED BULL.

inhabitants of this palace and became visible only when the wall crumbled. Apparently, the rulers of this writing-obsessed city had anticipated that their empire would eventually fall and had left a message for someone like Layard who would excavate their palace in the future.

The clay city and its inscriptions held the promise of telling Layard their story—"Their meaning was written upon them," he observed. The problem was that he could not decipher anything other than a few names that were known from other sources. No one could. Knowledge of the cuneiform script had died out almost two thousand years ago in the wake of Alexander's conquest and no one knew how to read it anymore.

The more inscriptions that surfaced, the more tantalizing was the question: What was this ancient civilization saying? Then, by chance, a new system of rooms was discovered that contained piles of broken tablets.

A RELIEF WITH CUNEIFORM INSCRIPTIONS FOUND AT NIMRUD.

That find changed Layard's view of this world yet again. Not only had the rulers written on every available clay surface, they had also amassed an entire collection of tablets and constructed a building to house their precious texts. Layard was ecstatic. This extraordinary discovery made it all the more urgent that he decipher the cuneiform script. It would create the possibility, as Layard wrote breathlessly in an account of his excavation, of "restoring the language and history of Assyria, and for inquiring into the customs, sciences, and, we may perhaps even add, literature, of its people." It turned out Layard was right. Given how much writing he saw had existed in this world, it was now likely that these people had created an entire literature, allowing the world to learn not only their names and histories but also their imaginative lives and beliefs.

Some of the clay was delicate, and Layard soon realized that digging up these tablets and exposing them to the sun caused some to crumble. He needed to capture this writing fast; otherwise his dig would destroy a lost civilization at the same time that he discovered it. Layard used moistened brown paper to make imprints of the most endangered inscriptions, and he packed the sturdier tablets off to London, along with some of the bas-reliefs.

THIS ENGRAVING, MADE BY LAYARD HIMSELF, SHOWS LAYARD DIRECTING
THE EXCAVATION OF A LARGE BAS-RELIEF AT NINEVEH.

In London, the inscriptions didn't give up their secret easily. Many years went by before they were deciphered by a succession of Assyriologists. Beginning with names known from other sources, they slowly worked out the meaning of these cuneiform signs. Nineveh—for this was the city Layard had discovered—could finally make itself heard. It revealed an unknown masterpiece: the *Epic of Gilgamesh*.

A Foundational Text and
the Invention of Writing
—

Humans had been telling stories orally ever since they had learned how to communicate with symbolic sounds and use those sounds to tell tales of the past and of the future, of gods and demons, tales that gave communities a shared past and a common destiny. Stories also preserved human experience, telling listeners how to act in difficult situations and how to avoid common pitfalls. Important stories, of the creation of the world or the founding of cities, were sometimes sung by specially appointed bards who had learned these stories by heart and performed them on special occasions. But no one wrote them down, even long after the invention of writing. Bards remembered stories with precision, and before they grew old, they would pass the stories on to their students and successors.

Writing had been invented in Mesopotamia, five thousand years ago, for other purposes, such as economic and political transactions. One story about the origin of writing tells of a king of Uruk who came up with the idea of sending a threatening message, pressed onto clay, to a rival king. When presented with the incomprehensible signs that stored the words spoken by the king of Uruk, the rival king declared his allegiance, so impressed was he by this miraculous way of making clay talk. Writing was used by scribes to centralize power in cities and to control the hinterland.

And yet at some point, hundreds of years after the invention of writing, one of these highly trained scribes had used his skills in practical applications and started to turn stories into a sequence of written marks. He may have been especially intrigued by a story told by one of the bards and wanted to preserve it. Perhaps he had known a bard who had taken a story to his grave, having failed to pass it on. Or, looking up from bookkeeping tablets, this accountant might have tried to remember a story he had heard a long time ago and found that his memory was failing him. Or it was for another reason entirely that a scribe realized that with enough patience and enough clay the cumbersome code he used every day to record sales or send messages could also be used to write down an entire story.

No matter how it happened, the first writing down of a story was a momentous event. For the first time, storytelling, the oral province of bards, intersected with writing, the province of diplomats and accountants. It was not exactly a natural combination, but the result of this unlikely alliance proved fertile beyond imagination: It produced the first great written narrative.

The *Epic of Gilgamesh* received its standard form around 1200 B.C.E., but its origins were hundreds of years older. The epic took its readers even further back in time to the reign of Gilgamesh, king of Uruk. The story boasted of Uruk's clay walls, clay stairways, and clay foundations, all made from "kiln-fired brick," enclosing lush gardens as well as a square mile of clay pits. Uruk, where writing may have been invented, was one of the first cities in the world, giving readers a window into the origin of urban settlement.

But in the story of Gilgamesh, not all was well. The ruler, King Gilgamesh, was headstrong and unjust and needed to be reined in. To check him, the gods created a troublemaker roaming the countryside. Here the epic took its readers to a place that was both fascinating and horrifying to city dwellers: the wild. The troublemaker, Enkidu, was a strange creature, a human unwilling to associate with other humans, preferring instead the company of animals. Enkidu needed to be made fully human, and this meant he needed to be brought from the wild into the city. King Gilgamesh, the city builder, took charge of the matter himself and sent an alluring woman, Shamhat, to offer herself to the wildling. The strategy worked. After having enjoyed her company for seven days, the wild man was changed, with the result that he was rejected by his animal companions. Enticed by Shamhat to come with her, he had to cast his lot with humans. Enkidu became a friend of Gilgamesh. The city had won.

Enkidu's loyalties to his new life and friend were put to the test when they ventured forth to the wildest place of them all, a remote mountain forest in what is now Lebanon. Forests were alien to Mesopotamia, which had been deforested ever since the first cities started to rise. While small huts could be built entirely from clay, larger structures such as palaces, temples, and libraries needed good timber, and timber was difficult to come by. City builders had to go farther and farther afield to get wood, ultimately as far as Lebanon. This was the underlying reality of the greatest adventure of the epic.

When the two friends arrived at the forest, they encountered the monstrous Humbaba, guardian of this wilderness. Slaying this forest monster allowed them to get their hands on all the high-quality trees they wanted, which they promptly did, completing a mission that was dangerous but indispensable for city builders. Literature was taking the side of the city against the hinterland, perhaps because writing was so closely connected to urban civilization.

In the story, Gilgamesh and Enkidu returned home to Uruk in triumph, but not all was well. The monster Humbaba, it turned out, had been under the protection of a god, and together the gods decided to punish Gilgamesh with the death of his friend Enkidu. When the punishment was carried out, Gilgamesh was so stricken at the loss of Enkidu that he did not believe Enkidu was really dead until he saw a worm crawling out of his nose—a lesson for all kings who build cities too greedily.

Inconsolable over the death of Enkidu, Gilgamesh left the city and roamed in the wild, becoming almost as wild as his friend had once been. Ultimately he found his way to a netherworld on a distant island. It was here that Gilgamesh encountered Utanapishtim. Impossibly old, Utanapishtim and his wife were the only survivors of the great flood. The only ones to be warned, they had given up their worldly possessions and built a ship to house pairs of animals. The flood came, the rains subsided, and the ship came to rest on a mountain. Utanapishtim let out a dove, which returned. Another bird, a swallow, was sent out, and it, too, returned. Only when a raven returned with a twig in its beak were they certain that land must have surfaced somewhere. But even as a survivor of the flood, Utanapishtim could not give Gilgamesh eternal life. Painfully, Gilgamesh had to face his own mortality, like an ordinary human.

When Assyriologists deciphered the clay tablet that contained the story of the flood, it caused a sensation: Victorian England had to acknowledge that the biblical story of the flood had been borrowed from the older *Epic of Gilgamesh*, or that both derived from an even older text.

For Mesopotamians, imagining the remote past as a time before the flood was not unusual. Floods were common, and mostly welcome. When contained through canals, they allowed for the intensive agriculture necessary to maintain urban spaces. But when the two rivers, the Tigris and Euphrates, flooded at the same time, the canals could not contain the rising waters, and everything would be destroyed, with clay particularly vulnerable. Unbaked clay was great for building and writing, but only as long as it was kept dry. A

TABLET FOUND
AT NINEVEH
CONTAINING THE
STORY OF THE
FLOOD, WHICH
WAS ALSO
INCORPORATED
INTO THE
HEBREW BIBLE.

great flood would wipe out everything this clay-based civilization was built on, would crush everything "like a clay pot," the epic warned. Even humans were believed to have been molded from clay.

The *Epic of Gilgamesh* not only asked its readers to admire urban civilization and shudder at its destruction, it also boasted of the tablets on which the story was written. Unlike many other epics, such as the Homeric epics that imagine themselves sung live, *Gilgamesh* incorporated writing. The fact that it was written down made Gilgamesh, the hero, the author of his own tale:

> Gilgamesh, who saw the wellspring, the foundations
>   of the land,
> Who knew the ways, was wise in all things, . . .
> He saw what was secret and revealed what was hidden,
> He brought back tidings from before the flood,
> From a distant journey came home, weary, at peace,
> Engraved all his hardships on a monument of stone.

Gilgamesh was a writer-king, and his epic boasted of a written story as its culture's most significant achievement.

ASHURBANIPAL'S SCRIBAL EDUCATION

CIRCA 670 B.C.E., MESOPOTAMIA

Layard had stumbled upon the first significant literary text, a text much older than the palace in Nineveh where he had unearthed it. What kind of city was Nineveh, and why had the *Epic of Gilgamesh* been preserved there? As more inscriptions and clay fragments were deciphered, the answer emerged: It had to do with a king by the name of Ashurbanipal.

Living hundreds of years after the *Epic of Gilgamesh* had been written down, Ashurbanipal was an admirer of the ancient text. He had it brought to Nineveh, copied, and preserved in his great library. On a single dig, Layard had discovered both the first masterpiece of world literature and its most important reader.

Ashurbanipal had grown up in a royal family amid the magnificent palaces and temples of Nineveh. Between the imposing buildings were gardens, green oases giving shade and shelter from the relentless sun. Wandering through the streets and gardens, young Ashurbanipal would see inscriptions telling of the kings who had built them. For those capable of reading, the entire city of Nineveh was one big clay tablet waiting to be deciphered. Exposed to writing everywhere, Ashurbanipal would go on to learn the craft of pressing words onto clay, so much so that he would claim in a hymn that he was an orphan, and in another that his true father was the god of writing, Nabu.

In truth, Ashurbanipal's father was powerful and very much alive. His father was Esarhaddon, one of the younger sons of the king who had founded the dynasty. Things became complicated when Esarhaddon was made crown prince, which aroused the jealousy of his demoted brothers, who forced the crown prince into exile. When news came to Esarhaddon that his angry brothers had assassinated their father, the king, Esarhaddon fought his way back to Nineveh, defeating his brothers in a civil war that lasted six weeks. In that same year, 681 B.C.E., Esarhaddon became king.

Not only did Ashurbanipal have human parents, his father was the most powerful man in the world.

Taking possession of Nineveh, Ashurbanipal's father built a new palace for himself. The city was the center of a large territory, the largest empire yet known in human history, stretching from the Mediterranean coast all the way to Babylon. This control of territory, the concentration of power in a single place, was made possible by the facts that decrees could be delivered by messengers (written on clay tablets and placed in clay envelopes), and that records could be kept in archives.

A younger son, Ashurbanipal was not in the line of succession. To prepare him for the priesthood, he was sent to scribal school. The foundation for his later admiration for the *Epic of Gilgamesh* was laid there.

Originally, scribes had passed their craft down within families, from father to son. But as writing gained in importance, demand for these highly prized professionals increased, and scribal schools were set up. Students needed to learn how to flatten moist clay into a tablet, draw lines across it, and make wedge-shaped impressions using a pointed reed (giving cuneiform writing its name; the Latin word for "wedge" is *cuneus*). Surviving two-sided tablets with the teacher's neat handwriting on one side and students' awkward attempts on the other show how difficult it was for students to attain the required dexterity.

When visiting the British Museum, where Layard brought his treasure of bas-reliefs and clay tablets, I am always struck by the skill and symmetry of the teacher's writing, especially given the size of the tablets. Many tablets were quite small, often only two by three inches, each bearing many lines of minuscule wedge-shaped incisions. In one surviving fragment, a Babylonian apprentice scribe, writing in Sumerian, complained of the difficulties of writing: "My teacher said, 'Your handwriting is not good!' and he beat me." Teachers complained as well: "Like you, I was once a youth and had a mentor. The teacher assigned a task to me—it was man's work. Like a springing reed, I leapt up and put myself to work." These universal complaints about cruel teachers and lazy students were recorded here perhaps for the first time in human history.

Looking at these tiny pieces of clay, I can also imagine the pride felt by those who had mastered this craft, pride that something this small could have such power. A teacher writing in faraway Egypt praised the exalted status of being a scribe: "Do you not remember the condition of the field hand [. . .]? The mice are numerous in the field, the locust descends, and the cattle eat. [. . .] But a scribe, he is the taskmaster of everyone." Scribes were the first bureaucrats, sitting comfortably indoors counting grain, fixing contracts, and keeping records while their brothers labored in the fields.

EGYPTIAN SCRIBAL SCHOOL. STUDENTS COMPLAINED ABOUT CRUEL TEACHERS, AND TEACHERS ABOUT LAZY STUDENTS.

The scribes left images of themselves. We see them sitting, tablet in hand, or cross-legged, writing on their laps. Next to them might be a jar of clay, which needed to be moist, otherwise it would harden and become unusable. The scribes look confident, proud of their own god, the god of writing. There was nothing literary about them. They were the original accountants and functionaries, administering a growing empire and conveying religious teachings.

Kings and princes usually didn't submit to the tortures of scribal school. They simply hired trained scribes to do the hard work for them. Ashurbanipal himself would never have to earn a living as a scribe; one of his brothers would be king. But Ashurbanipal's father, Esarhaddon, was an unusual king in that he himself knew how to read and write, well enough to appreciate the power and mystery of the technology. (Ashurbanipal's sister also knew how to write, and she later wrote a letter to Ashurbanipal's wife admonishing her not to neglect her own writing practice.)

THE SWORD AND THE REED

Everything changed when Ashurbanipal's older brother died and Ashurbanipal suddenly found himself named crown prince. Given his father's constant health problems, Ashurbanipal now needed to be trained in the skills that a king would require. A rigorous regime of horseback riding, physical exercise, and shooting with a bow and arrow was set up. Still a teenager, Ashurbanipal was being turned into someone who could lead men into battle.

For all the emphasis on a martial education, Ashurbanipal did not abandon his earlier education in literature. Instead, he intensified it. The best scribal teacher, Balasî, was hired to initiate the new crown prince into the higher arts of writing. While his father had only mastered the basics of reading and writing, Ashurbanipal knew that more advanced training would gain him access to a whole new world of literacy, one far more difficult and sophisticated than merely sending messages to vassals or reading inscriptions on buildings. Ashurbanipal had seen these higher literary skills on display every day. The most influential scribes had access to the inner sanctum of power, and the source of their power was the ability to read omens and signs that portended the future. They could tell his father when to go to war, when to lay the foundation of a building, and when to stay at home.

Divination practices required interpreting special calendars and reading commentaries, but they also included skills beyond written words. To the trained eyes of scribes, not just the buildings of

Nineveh but the whole world was full of traces that could be read. One could find written messages in the entrails of rams and in the sky—the secret writing of the gods. Writing was so powerful that humans now imagined this technology to be everywhere, legible to those trained in reading its signs. Writing, begun as an accounting technique, had changed the way humans viewed the world around them.

To Ashurbanipal's father, the scribes recommended cures for his frequent illnesses and controlled his movements and decisions. If something happened to the king, they were to blame, so they usually counseled extra caution. In Nineveh, scribes could be more powerful than a king, even a king with rudimentary knowledge of reading and writing.

For Ashurbanipal, rising to the highest rungs of scribal art meant that he would be the first king not at the mercy of his interpreters, because he would be capable of disputing the findings of his divinatory scribes. He would be able to converse with the priests as an equal and to counter their interpretation of the stars. He would have access to the source code of power. As a high scribe, he would be in control of his own destiny.

Combining the sword and the reed, Ashurbanipal made full use of both his military and scribal training while his father was on military campaigns. When his father died en route to Egypt, Ashurbanipal was ready to take his place. Aided by his grandmother, who secured the loyalty of relatives, Ashurbanipal found himself crowned the next year, 668 B.C.E. His long title included the epithet "King of the Universe."

After seizing power, Ashurbanipal built upon the imperial successes of his father and extended the empire, finally securing Egypt (Layard found Egyptian-looking artifacts among the ruins of Nineveh). Unlike his father, Ashurbanipal did not lead his army into battle; he controlled it remotely. Thanks to writing and the bureaucratic apparatus made possible by it, power could now be centralized as it had never been before, allowing a king to stay at home while extending his reach. For Ashurbanipal, remote warfare did not mean a lack of dedication. Ashurbanipal conducted his campaign with brutality and force. If a city refused to submit, he would decapitate the rebels and put their heads on stakes.

Ashurbanipal didn't just expand his territory. Conscious of the power of writing, he also expanded his father's collection of tablets, paying scribes to copy old texts. Most of those texts were found not in Nineveh but farther to the south, at older centers of learning such as Uruk and Babylon. In transferring these treasures north, Ashurbanipal was doing more than indulging a personal interest. He understood that writing meant power, that power could be displayed not only through the heads of enemies on stakes but also through writing skills and a large collection of cuneiform tablets. Writing played a larger role in Ashurbanipal's life than it had for any king before him, perhaps because he was, unusually, a second-generation scribal king.

While transferring written knowledge from Babylon to Nineveh, Ashurbanipal had to be careful with his brother. To avoid succession wars and rivalries, Ashurbanipal's brother had been appointed crown prince of Babylon. Technically his brother would be subject to Ashurbanipal, but for the most part the brother would be in control of his own city, the grand city of Babylon. Relations with Babylon had always been difficult. Their grandfather had razed it to the ground and removed the statue of its most important god, Marduk, from the temple and transferred it to Nineveh. But since that time, Babylon had reluctantly become a part of the Assyrian Empire controlled by Nineveh, and the city would receive additional prestige by being ruled almost independently by Ashurbanipal's brother.

The scheme worked for a while. When Ashurbanipal had secured the throne, his brother, whose mother had come from Babylon, was sent off to take possession of that city. He brought the large statue of Marduk back with him to Babylon in triumph. It was not an easy journey, but thanks to irrigation and canal systems that had been built over centuries, an engineering wonder without rivals, the journey could be made by boat. The statue of Marduk was shipped down the Tigris and then through the Sirtu canal to the Euphrates and on to Babylon via the Arahtu canal (Layard transported some of his loot in a similar fashion). Ashurbanipal's brother was invested as ruler, and the two kings maintained cordial relations, at least on the surface. Even when his brother refused to address Ashurbanipal as "king," Ashurbanipal did not force the issue. He maintained informers in Babylon and used his influence to have scribes copy ancient tablets from Babylon and nearby Uruk.

The arrangement did not last. His brother, whom he had praised on every occasion, whom he had called his twin even though they were born of different mothers, conspired with enemies of the state and rebelled against Nineveh. The history of bloody succession that their father had hoped to end had only been postponed, and it now erupted with unprecedented force. Whereas their father had been able to finish off his brothers in six weeks, the great civil war of the next generation took four years. The rebellious brother, whom Ashurbanipal now called his "non-brother," was well guarded in Babylon, with its famous, ancient city walls, and Ashurbanipal had to use all his might and determination to seize the town; he succeeded only after systematically starving the city for many months.

Despite his brother's treachery, Ashurbanipal did not punish Babylon by putting the rebels' heads on stakes. Instead he used his conquest to enlarge his holdings in old clay tablets. He raided his brother's own collection and took what he could find with him to Nineveh. He also took scribes, sometimes by force, to increase his copying power. Ashurbanipal had realized that writing was not just useful for long-distance warfare and administration, or for economic transactions. Because cuneiform tablets were artificial extensions of human minds, they would allow him to accumulate more knowledge than anyone before him. The entire library would be like an artificial memory, making him the most knowledgeable human in the history of the world.

A LIBRARY FOR THE FUTURE

To make room for his library, Ashurbanipal razed his own palace in Nineveh and built a new one in its place. One reason was technical: Clay did not endure for long, especially when subject to prolonged rain or floods. Clay bricks were often just dried in the sun, not baked in a kiln, and tended to degrade after a few decades, requiring constant rebuilding and restoration. The other reason was prestige. With his brother vanquished, Ashurbanipal was at the height of his power; his Assyrian Empire was as strong as it had ever been. This new power would be reflected in new and more magnificent palaces, and at the center of those palaces was his ever-growing collection of cuneiform tablets, which Layard would find in the middle of the nineteenth century.

The collection was much more than a hoard of scribal loot. It was the result of the unprecedented resources Ashurbanipal spent on writing. Perhaps owing to his early training as an accountant—computation had been among the skills he had learned—Ashurbanipal also organized his tablets in a new way. Each tablet was carefully classified, and each room had an inventory: Historical documents and transactions were in one place, omens and divination texts in another, calendars of auspicious days and commentaries on astrology in a third. Having accumulated more information than anyone had before, Ashurbanipal realized that his store of knowledge was useful only if it was organized. Confronted with this challenge, he created the first significant system of information management.

Of all his texts, his favorite was not an account tablet, nor a calendar or omen text, but the *Epic of Gilgamesh*. It was written on a dozen clay tablets, larger than the small letters sent to vassals and military commanders but still no larger than a hardcover book today.

The first poems about Gilgamesh had come from Sumerian scribes using the language of Uruk. The Sumerian Empire didn't last. Despite the city walls and the power of writing praised in the *Epic of Gilgamesh*, Uruk and Babylon and the other Sumerian cities were taken over by Akkadians, nomadic speakers of a Semitic language. But once Akkadians were in possession of a territorial empire, they found themselves in need of a writing system to maintain the city's bureaucracy. They ended up adopting Sumerian cuneiform writing to record their own language. Sumerian scribes couldn't save their civilization, but they could pass it on to their captors by teaching Akkadians how to write.

It was in Akkadian that the *Epic of Gilgamesh* received its final form, which Ashurbanipal came across several empires later. Ashurbanipal was fascinated by how old the *Epic of Gilgamesh* was and how long it had endured—something Layard and his colleagues slowly understood as more and more cuneiform texts were deciphered. In an unusual autobiographical inscription, Ashurbanipal bragged: "I was brave, I was exceedingly industrious [. . .] I have read the artistic script of Sumer and the obscure Akkadian, which is hard to master, taking pleasure in the reading of the stones coming from before the flood." Ashurbanipal had to master an archaic version of his language, Old Babylonian Akkadian, and an even older writing system, cuneiform, to decipher writing so old that he imagined it as hailing "from before the flood."

As long as languages were only spoken, they died when all their speakers disappeared. But once stories were fixed by marks on clay, the old languages persisted. Inadvertently, writing had kept alive a language that no one spoke anymore (and since Ashurbanipal, the number of preserved dead languages has been steadily growing).

Thanks to Ashurbanipal, the *Epic of Gilgamesh* was copied

many times and carried far afield, as far as Lebanon and Judea, Persia and Egypt, as a way to secure territory and to assimilate foreign cultures. Writing, it turned out, was a tool for building an empire, not only because of its effects on governance and the economy but also because of literature. Writing, centralized urban living, territorial empires, and written stories were closely aligned and would remain so for the next several thousand years. Ashurbanipal realized the strategic importance of having a foundational text. He even modeled his conquests on those of Gilgamesh by adopting Gilgamesh's title: Mighty King, Without Rivals.

Cherishing the *Epic of Gilgamesh*, Ashurbanipal did his best to preserve it for the future. Did he sense that his own empire would crumble? Was he building a library and making copies of the epic because he wanted to increase the chances that his favorite text would survive whatever catastrophes the future had in store? The story of the flood itself was a reminder of how quickly destruction might come, an apocalyptic vision of the annihilation of almost all life on earth. Some of the texts copied by scribes in Ashurbanipal's library contained a prayer that dealt with the future: "I, Ashurbanipal, king of the universe . . . wrote down on tablets Nabu's wisdom . . . I placed them . . . for the future in the library." Writing not only allowed readers access to the past but also allowed them to imagine how literature might endure into the future and inspire readers not yet alive.

Soon after Ashurbanipal's death, his empire did crumble. Nineveh was taken and destroyed, and slowly the *Epic of Gilgamesh*, which had survived several empires and languages, started to lose readers. No new Ashurbanipal stepped forward to rescue the epic, and no powerful ally versed in dead languages took it up. Newer and simpler writing systems were devised, but the epic was never transcribed into them; its fate was bound to that of cuneiform script. The future that Ashurbanipal had envisioned for his library was all but dead. The world was changing, thanks to Alexander's

alphabetic conquest, and this suggests a painful lesson about literature: The only thing that can assure survival is continual use. Don't
place your trust in clay or stone. Literature must be used by every
generation. Overly impressed by the endurance of writing, the
world forgot that everything was subject to forgetting, even writing.

The world almost lost the *Epic of Gilgamesh*. When destruction
came to the library of Nineveh, it came not as flood, but as fire.
Ashurbanipal's library was burned, and everything in it as well: the
wooden shelves, the wood-backed wax tablets, and the woven bas-
kets containing the tablets. Everything but clay. While clay can be
destroyed by flood, it cannot be destroyed by fire, except with the
greatest heat. Some tablets bubbled and melted like hot glass or
magma, but others hardened, as if fired in a kiln. Buried beneath
the library built to protect them, the clay tablets lay for two thousand years, waiting to be discovered.

They waited until the nineteenth century, when Austen Henry
Layard and Paul-Émile Botta, his French rival, started to dig up
Nineveh and its environs and the cuneiform script was painstakingly deciphered over the ensuing decades. For the first time, a
piece of literature was unearthed after having disappeared from all
memory for thousands of years.

Giving readers access to the past was a most profound consequence of writing. As long as stories were told orally, they were
adapted to new audiences and listeners, coming alive in the present. Once captured by writing, the past endured. For those versed
in this difficult technology, for people like Ashurbanipal, it brought
back the voices from centuries, even millennia ago, voices so old
they might very well come from before the flood. Writing created
history.

While old objects and buildings can give us access to the external habits of our ancestors, their stories, fixed and preserved by writing, give us access to their inner lives. This was why Layard had

been so frustrated by not understanding the cuneiform script. He could admire reliefs and statues, but he could not hear their voices, their language, their thoughts, their literature. The invention of writing divides human evolution into a time that is all but inaccessible to us and one in which we have access to the minds of others.

CHAPTER 3

EZRA AND THE CREATION
OF HOLY SCRIPTURE

SIXTH CENTURY B.C.E., BABYLON

FOUNDATIONAL TEXTS SUCH AS THE *EPIC OF GILGAMESH* OR THE HO-
meric epics survived by inspiring powerful kings to create institutions that increased their longevity. But some of these foundational
texts developed into something new: sacred scriptures. These scriptures shared all the features of foundational texts, but they did
something more: They bound people to them, demanding service
and obedience. In doing so, they established a survival mechanism
that was independent from the sponsorship of great kings like
Ashurbanipal and Alexander.

The search for the origins of sacred scripture led me back to
Babylon and a group of exiled Judeans who had settled there after
587 B.C.E., when the Babylonian ruler Nebuchadnezzar II (a successor of Ashurbanipal's) had razed Jerusalem to the ground and
driven its ruling class, about four thousand of them, into exile. After
a period of hardship following the forced migration, Judeans had
been allowed to settle in Nippur, south of Babylon, forming a community in which they were able to preserve their language, their
way of life, and the memory of the old kingdom of Israel and Judea.

Among them was a scribe by the name of Ezra. Born in exile

and living in the heartland of literacy, with its scribal kings and libraries, Ezra had gone to scribal school, mastered different writing
systems, and enjoyed a successful career as a scribe. Had he learned
the cuneiform script, he would have been able to read the *Epic of
Gilgamesh*, but instead he specialized in Aramaic and worked as an
imperial accountant, part of the bureaucracy that held this vast territory together.

But Ezra and the Judean scribes who had come before him
didn't just work for their victors. They had brought with them some
of their own stories, written during the time when Jerusalem had
served as the capital of the kingdom, ruled by the House of David.
Inspired by Babylonian literacy, these exile scribes not only preserved their texts by copying them but also wove them into a more
coherent narrative, beginning with the very creation of the world.
This they followed with a story of their first ancestors, Adam and
Eve, and their fall from grace, and with a story of a flood that almost
wiped out humanity, strikingly similar to the flood included in the
Epic of Gilgamesh. They continued with the story of the generations coming after the flood, from Abraham, originally a Mesopotamian, to the exodus from Egypt under Moses and the claiming of a
homeland in Judea.

These writings exhibited many of the features that had charac-
terized the *Epic of Gilgamesh* and other foundational texts. They
told a story of origin; they set their readers apart from their neighbors; and they claimed the territory and the towering city of Jerusalem as belonging to the readers of this text, allowing them to
imagine the land as their own, even though they had been driven
from this land into Babylonian exile.

By the time Ezra was born, these texts had become central for
the exile community, the cherished guarantors of their faith. The
scrolls preserved rituals and practices from the past, assembling wisdom and detailing rules covering everything from worship to the
preparation of food. They also kept alive the exile's language, He-

brew, even though more of the exiled Judeans began speaking Aramaic, increasingly the common language of the region.

The Hebrew writings were different from the *Epic of Gilgamesh* or the Homeric epics in important ways. Far from being a single, coherent text, they formed a text bundle, assembled from a large variety of sources. The greatest difference between the Hebrew writings and other epics was that the Hebrew collection was shaped by a people enduring long periods of exile. If foundational texts were important for kings, they were even more important, it turned out, for a people without kings and without an empire.

In weaving together different stories, exiled scribes recast them in light of their own position and values, the values of scribes. Moses was important to them because he was traditionally seen as the person who had written down the book of laws, Deuteronomy, making him a fellow scribe (just as the *Epic of Gilgamesh* celebrated its protagonist as a writer-king). In the same manner, the scribes populated the later parts of the scriptures with scribes such as Baruch, who writes down Jeremiah's words, in each case giving an account of how the stories they were preserving and arranging had been turned into writing.

In one of the most dramatic episodes of the Bible, the exiled scribes even imagined their god as a scribe. God first summons Moses to dictate the rules by which he wants the chosen people to live. Moses writes everything down faithfully and delivers the message to the people. This is a familiar scribal situation: someone in authority dictating to a scribe. Then, without much explanation, God changes his mind and decides to continue without a scribe. Instead of dictating to Moses, he hands Moses stone tablets that already contain words engraved upon them—engraved by none other than God himself. A god willing to go to the trouble of writing with his own hand was not unusual. Among their many gods, the Mesopotamians worshipped Nabu as the god of the scribes. What was unusual here was that the Judeans had concentrated all divine power in a single god, and they still wanted to think of this god as a writer.

But the drama is not over yet. In the famous scene, Moses goes down the mountain with his tablets and sees the sons of Israel dancing around a golden calf. He is overcome with such anger that he takes the stone tablets, engraved by the finger of God, and breaks them. Now everything has to be done over again. God summons Moses again and tells him to prepare two tablets, similar to the ones he had broken in his anger; he, God, would write everything down again. It sounds as if we are to expect a replay of the earlier scene. But this isn't what happens. God repeats the commandments, but he doesn't write them. This time, Moses has to do it himself. He stays with God for forty days and works without eating or drinking, chiseling God's words into stone. "And the Lord said unto Moses, Write thou these words: for after the tenor of these words I have made a covenant with thee and with Israel." It is a return to the scribal arrangement—an overpowering master dictating to his scribe—with which the episode had begun.

The scene reads like a scribe's worst nightmare. First the scribe is supposed to take dictation from God, then he is handed the finished tablets, then the replacement tablets, and finally he finds himself taking dictation again. Along the way, precision is crucial; any mistake would be fatal, surely angering this god who is himself an expert scribe. The exiled scribes who preserved and embellished this scene had used all their imagination to create a drama out of writing, detailing just how complicated and fraught writing could be, especially when it was used to communicate with God.

Scribes also generated the greatest and best-known part of the Bible: its creation myth. Most such myths, including the Mesopotamian ones, imagine a god molding the world and its inhabitants laboriously from clay. The older Hebrew creation stories, which were retained in the Hebrew Bible, do the same and have God engage in an act of divine craft, laboring with his hands. These creation stories were imagined by humans who were used to manual labor. Not so the opening of Genesis. God does not get his hands dirty. He does not work with them; indeed, he does not touch his creation at all. From nowhere in particular, he simply brings the world into being through the sheer power of words. This is creation as imagined by scribes who sit at a remove from manual labor and whose work takes place entirely in (spoken) language acting across great distances.

458 B.C.E., JERUSALEM

The scribes didn't just preside over increasingly important texts; these texts exerted a peculiar force over the exile community, making it long to return to the land of its ancestors so powerfully evoked in these stories.

Ezra took the lead. In the year 458 B.C.E., he issued a call to his fellow exiles to leave behind the life they knew and migrate to their ancestral land. Descendants from the different tribes and from different professions followed Ezra's call, flocking to his camp north of Babylon, on the river Ahava. There was no question that the journey would be dangerous. There would not even be soldiers to protect them. Ezra had boasted that the Judeans would be safeguarded by their singular god, Yahweh, so asking the Persian king for soldiers would have shown a sacrilegious lack of faith.

Ezra was carrying something that might give them protection along the way: a letter from Artaxerxes I, the king of Persia. It stated that the traveling Judeans were to be given protection and that local rulers were to support their activities. Bandits might not be able to read the king's letter, but the imperial stamp might impress them. In fact, Ezra was coming to Jerusalem in an official capacity: He had been charged by Artaxerxes to investigate the situation beyond the river Jordan. He was an official emissary.

Judeans rarely enjoyed the protection of a large empire. Usually it was best for the Jews when their larger neighbors didn't pay attention to them, as the example of Nebuchadnezzar, the Babylonian destroyer of Jerusalem, had taught them. But their old enemy had since fallen to the Persians, who had captured Babylon and were now extending their realm into Egypt. Judea was suddenly of strategic interest, a crucial link between Egypt and Babylon. In sending Ezra and his party back to their ancestral homeland, the Persian king wasn't acting out of charity. He was sending Ezra to secure an imperial outpost.

Ezra and his companions traveled unmolested and after more than eight hundred miles finally crossed the river Jordan. For the first time in their lives, they were setting foot in the fabled lands of their ancestors.

But as they made their way from the river valley up into the mountains, they found that things weren't as they had expected. Hardly anyone seemed to be living here anymore, and there were signs of abandonment and depopulation everywhere. No fortified towns and settlements could be seen, only downtrodden farmers, the descendants of those insignificant enough to have escaped deportation seventy years ago. Those remaining few were barely able to live from the land and bore little resemblance to the Judean court of the stories, let alone of the high civilization the returning exiles knew from Babylon. These rude farmers spoke in a rough dialect, and their way of life was different as well. True, some claimed to be adherents of the god Yahweh, but they lived side by side with other tribes, and their manner of worship was lax. The exiles had developed strict rules about keeping the Sabbath as well as other purity rituals and laws, none of which seemed to play much of a role here.

These sights were nothing compared with what greeted them when they reached their destination: Jerusalem. The city had been famous for its walls and imposing gates, but both the walls and the gates were in ruins. The city was open to anyone intent on taking it.

But who would want it? Entire quarters were abandoned, others barely inhabitable. Jerusalem, the city of stories and dreams that Ezra and his followers had heard so much about, was a heap of rubble.

There was one consolation: While the walls and gates were in ruins, at least the temple was standing, restored by an earlier group of returnees. The loss of the temple had been especially hard for the Judeans because it was the dwelling place of their god. Other places of sacrifice had been given up long ago, often against the protests of locals, in order to concentrate the power of this one god in a single place. This concentration was what set them apart from their neighbors. When they had lost Jerusalem, they had lost not only the seat of their king, but also the seat of their god.

Some decades earlier, a group had returned and rebuilt the temple. Ezra and his group knew about the earlier mission and were looking forward to the new temple; they would not have to do the heavy lifting themselves. Like the earlier group of exiles, Ezra and his followers would now be able to worship their god in his own land once again. Three days they rested, and on the fourth they collected the gold and precious possessions each had brought, weighing each sum precisely and recording it. And then they did what they had been waiting to do throughout their exile, sacrificing bulls and rams, lambs and goats, in the traditional manner.

It wasn't just the walls and buildings that were in disrepair. The irregular religious practices Ezra had observed along the way had made it all the way into the city. All kinds of people had taken up residence here, and Judeans were openly marrying into these other groups. People started to come to Ezra reporting the violations the Judeans were guilty of, violations of the careful purification rules and rituals that had kept the exile community together. It was hard enough to bear the physical ruin of the city, but it was the city's spiritual ruin that made Ezra despair. He withdrew, contemplating the fallen state of the city and its inhabitants for half a day.

When the time for the evening sacrifice came, Ezra forced himself to go to the temple, but he could not go through with the ritual. Despairing, he rent his garments and his coat, threw himself onto the ground, and cried out in agony. Finally, he uttered a prayer that was also an accusation against the people of the land, as he had come to call them, those who had stayed behind and whose habits were so horrifying to the returning exiles.

More and more people gathered to watch the spectacle of the latest returnee, the highly placed emissary of King Artaxerxes, who had come with astonishing riches and who now lay before them on the ground accusing them of having mortally offended their god. They felt the rightness of what he said, and wept. He proposed that they should swear to a new covenant, and only when they agreed did Ezra rise and take their oaths. Then he withdrew, still stricken by the experience, and fasted.

A proclamation was issued to all who had returned from Babylon. The sons and daughters of exile came and waited for Ezra. They were shivering in a terrible rain, as if their god was weeping. Finally, Ezra appeared and uttered his strict proclamation: They had to cast away their foreign wives and children. They, the returnees, had to separate themselves from the people of the land. They who had brought with them from exile their purer and more elaborate form of worship vowed to stick together and undertake the spiritual renewal of Jerusalem.

But how to bind the exiles to their new oaths? Ezra realized he needed something else to secure their faith in God. To this end he had brought the scriptures of his people. But what role would those scriptures play in Jerusalem? Ezra the scribe had a plan he was now carefully putting into action. He constructed a raised platform of wood. He placed it strategically at the rebuilt Water Gate and arranged for twelve representatives, symbolizing the twelve tribes, to join him. They were arranged symmetrically, six on each side. Everyone had been told that Ezra was going to do something important.

When Ezra climbed the platform, he looked out on a large crowd of people. He revealed scrolls and presented them to the people. They immediately bowed their heads to the ground, as they would bow in the presence of their god, or their god's representative, in the temple. But they were not in the temple, and Ezra was not appearing before them as a priest. He was merely holding a scroll. For the first time, people worshipped their god in the form of a text.

Ezra began to read, but a problem emerged: Not everyone could understand him. Bringing the scrolls from the scribal chamber into the street and to the people was difficult. The words of the scripture weren't meant for continuous reading to a general audience because they had been cobbled together from many sources. Biblical Hebrew was arcane and some in the audience knew only Aramaic, the common language of the region. Noticing the difficulties his listeners were having, Ezra realized that he needed to translate and explain the stories and the laws he was reading to his audience. For hours Ezra read and explained and translated in this manner, transmitting the text even to those who were illiterate. After he was finished, he ended with a prayer that replicated the story he had been telling them, from the creation of the world to Abraham and the exodus, summing up the grand narrative that one day would make it to the moon.

It was in this scene, in which the people bowed before a text, that Ezra revealed the true significance of his return to Jerusalem. He wanted to do more than take possession of an imperial outpost for a Persian king or rebuild the physical city. Ezra was drawn to Jerusalem and the temple because he wanted to change the manner in which the Judeans worshipped their god. In exile, scriptures had remained, technically, a substitute. Only in Jerusalem could they become a sacred object rivaling the temple.

The Hebrew writings had long ago become a foundational text, a text bundle that set one group apart from its neighbors, that captured its collective experience, that told a powerful story of origin, that endured over time, and that commanded significant resources for its maintenance, including schools and scribes. But now, in Ezra's hands, an additional feature emerged: A foundational text was declared sacred, itself an object of worship.

A People of the Scroll

Ezra's reading triggered a battle between scribes and priests—the priests who had traditionally been granted exclusive rights of ritual. Ezra himself was a priest, but he had transformed his religion because in order to be a scribe, it wasn't necessary to be a priest. Ezra's reading was a coup that threatened to dethrone the most powerful class of Judeans.

The struggle between priests and scribes played itself out over the next two centuries, during which Judeans were able to live in Jerusalem with an increasing degree of autonomy, especially during periods when the Persian Empire was engaged elsewhere. The stronger Jerusalem became, the better for the priests and their holy shrine, the temple, the most carefully guarded place in the city. The temple still mattered, but with his text made sacred, Ezra had introduced a competing force.

The writings dealing with Ezra had been transmitted separately, and like so many parts of the Hebrew Bible, they contained different layers of text written at different times. Scribes living during the period of relative calm following Ezra's lifetime edited these stories, which captured the physical and spiritual rebuilding of Jerusalem, into an integrated narrative, producing the distinct but connected books of Ezra and Nehemiah we have today (my reconstruction of Ezra's return is largely based on those books, as well as historical scholarship).

As long as Judeans were allowed to live in Jerusalem, power in the city remained divided among the governor, priests, and scribes, all of whom presided over a population that increasingly regarded themselves as an ethnic group called the Jews. But this period of relative peace did not last long, and Jerusalem found itself overrun by Alexander the Great and at the mercy of his quarreling successors.

Then Jerusalem attracted the attention of the rising Roman Empire. In 70 C.E. Rome attacked, Jerusalem was taken, and the temple, so laboriously rebuilt, was destroyed again. Since no more temple service was possible, the hereditary rules regulating the holiest of holies, on which the privilege of the Levites rested, were moot.

In this situation, Ezra's decision to establish portable scripture as the means to worship their god proved crucial. An idea born from the experience of Babylonian exile, it suited the new exile equally well. With the temple gone again, Jews would worship in synagogues, and their services would be administered not by priests but by rabbis, scribes who could read and interpret the scripture.

Nothing is more familiar to us than a rabbi holding a scroll, reading from a sacred text to an assembled congregation. But like all things, this familiar practice had to be invented, and it was invented by the scribe Ezra upon his return to Jerusalem. Ezra's reading created Judaism as we know it. At the moment when Jews were forming an ethnic identity by setting themselves apart from the people of the land, they were also becoming a people of the book—or rather, given the form in which Ezra's scripture was presented, a people of the scroll.

The transition of the Hebrew Bible from a foundational text to scripture, and from a text rooted in territory to one that could function in exile, is also what made it survive, whereas the *Epic of Gilgamesh* got buried. The Hebrew Bible survived because it was not dependent on land, on kings and empires; it could do without them and create its own worshippers who would carry it wherever they might be.

This new survival mechanism meant that when Austen Henry Layard was excavating Nineveh, he was looking at it through the eyes of the Bible and its view of the city, not through the eyes of the *Epic of Gilgamesh*. Nineveh gets a bad press in the Hebrew Bible, as does Ashurbanipal, who is sometimes identified by Roman sources with the legendary Sardanapalus, and described as an ineffective, decadent king. In the struggle between two foundational texts, the Hebrew Bible was, for the time being, winning. It was only when the cuneiform script was deciphered that a different story of Nineveh and of the heroism of Ashurbanipal emerged.

So crucial did Ezra's reading look in retrospect that he was credited not only with having preserved, edited, and explained the Hebrew scriptures, but even with having written them. The spirit of those stories was certainly true: It was Ezra, along with other exiled scribes working on the scriptures, who had established the idea of a sacred text. Other commentators, scribes all, were more interested in the technical aspects of Ezra's work. They credited him with having introduced a new, modernized writing system, replacing the old Hebrew letters with the simpler, square letters, gleaned from Aramaic, that are still used today. Ezra was even seen as having translated the Hebrew scripture, increasingly incomprehensible to ordinary Judeans, into Aramaic, the common language of the Near East.

As Ezra's fame grew, so grew also a small but vocal group of detractors. Some Jewish writers accused Ezra of having introduced errors and alterations into the sacred text. Later Christian and Muslim writers continued this theme and blamed Ezra for any fault they saw in the Hebrew Bible. Why were Jesus or Muhammad not prophesied more explicitly? Somehow, Ezra must have made mistakes in his Hebrew Bible, or even deliberately falsified the text to suit his own purposes. These accusations contained a grain of truth. Ezra, and the later commentators editing this portion of the Bible, created the scriptures with a particular purpose in mind: to knit the community of returning exiles closer together. It was an act calcu-

ONE OF THE OLDEST MANUSCRIPTS OF THE TORAH, FROM BETWEEN
1155 AND 1225, WRITTEN IN THE SQUARE SCRIPT INSPIRED BY
BABYLONIAN SCRIBAL TRADITIONS. THE MANUSCRIPT WAS
MISCATALOGED AND REDISCOVERED ONLY IN 2013.

lated to establish a text at the center of a culture. And it worked: Thanks to its continuous use, the Hebrew Bible was able to bind the exile communities together, ensuring its own survival.

The idea of sacred writing became central not only for Judaism but also for Christianity and Islam, what we now call the religions of the book. Reading aloud and interpreting written words became important religious activities, making religion a matter of literature. Since there was always something hidden and unknowable about God, sacred words could not be taken at face value. It became necessary to read between the lines and come up with ingenious interpretations that might reveal hidden truths. Soon, rival schools of interpretation would set religions based on literature on divergent paths. Ashurbanipal had learned the art of divination and bragged about knowing obscure texts from before the flood. In the wake of Ezra, poring over obscure passages, connecting distant parts of a text, and bringing ingenuity to the interpretation of scripture became tantamount to religious service.

JERUSALEM — CITY OF SCRIPTURES

As I was contemplating Ezra and the creation of sacred scripture, I decided to visit the city where this creation had taken place. Jerusalem is a vertical city, and not only because it is built on hills. Everything is on top of everything else: people, religions, memories, histories. But in contrast to Nineveh and other ruined ancient cities, here all the layers were alive. As I approached the Old City, the first thing I saw was the imposing walls that circle the city. To enter, I had to make my way through one of the large fortified gates. Once inside, I found myself in a labyrinth of narrow streets. On the rare occasion when I got a wider view, I would see different flags flown from the higher buildings, different groups asserting their presence, marking territory. I walked by a number of churches of strange old Christian sects that had established their presence here. The Via Dolorosa, Jesus' path through the city and up the hangman's hill, was marked, as were other stations of his passion. Roman ruins abounded. But the focal point of different religions invested in a single place is the Temple Mount, whose upper part is claimed by Islam and lower part, the Wailing Wall, by Judaism.

The city is built not only upward but also deep into the ground. There are layers upon layers of basements, subbasements, and tunnels. I visited in July, and the air outside was hot and dry, but the deeper I went the colder it was, and the air became ever damper until, upon descending yet another staircase and tunnel, I heard dripping and found myself staring into a pool of water.

The presence of water was certainly one reason why Jerusalem was so contested throughout its history. In this arid land, water was a precious commodity. The story of the flood, a common experience for Mesopotamians living between two enormous rivers that were prone to overflow, must have seemed very different when it made its way to arid Jerusalem, strange and almost unthinkable.

The need for water alone did not explain the sheer concentration of religions and peoples, all intensely invested in this one place. Contemplating the history of Jerusalem, I realized that this city was not just the place where the idea of sacred scripture had been born, but also where it continued to exert its influence most fully. What had brought all of these people to this one place, what had endowed these hills with so much significance, was the concentration of sacred scriptures, beginning with the Hebrew Bible, followed by the New Testament, and finally the Qur'an, in a single location.

Jerusalem may be the best place to study the effects of sacred texts, but it is far from the only one touched by them. Since Ezra, we have been living in a world dominated by sacred scriptures. Sacred scriptures are a subset of foundational texts, all of which create cultural cohesion, tell stories of origin and destiny, and connect cultures to the remote past. In addition to these features of foundational texts more generally, sacred scriptures inspire worship and obedience. This is true not only of the so-called religions of the book—Judaism, Christianity, and Islam—but also of those of other cultures, for example the Sikhs, who worship their scripture in temples, and Buddhists, who placed short sacred sutras in statues.

Sometimes these worshipped texts hold cultures hostage to ancient ideas, binding them strictly to the past, to the letters of a text. One might call this effect *textual fundamentalism*. The religions of the book, Judaism, Christianity, and Islam, are perhaps most prone to textual fundamentalism, but all religions based on sacred scripture have experienced waves of textual fundamentalism at some point in their history. Nor is textual fundamentalism limited to religious texts. The Constitution of the United States, a modern foundational text with sacred overtones, has its share of fundamentalist interpreters (hoping to read it according to its literal meaning and the original intention of its authors), and another modern foundational text, *The Communist Manifesto,* does as well. A good indicator that we are in the presence of a sacred text is the existence of an exclusive group of readers charged with interpreting it, from religious authorities to the United States Supreme Court. (I sometimes think about my own profession, the study of literature, as an offshoot of these official interpreters, although our authority is much weakened.)

Textual fundamentalism rests on two contradictory assumptions. The first is that texts are unchanging and fixed. The second acknowledges that texts need to be interpreted but restricts the authority to interpret them to an exclusive group. Seeing the extent to which textual fundamentalism has emerged in almost every literate culture, I have come to think of it as an inevitable side effect of literature, its dark side. How can we guard against it?

Through a robust culture of interpretation, readers will invariably bring their own ideas and values and culture to a text and understand in new ways the same words that have existed for a hundred, or a thousand, or three thousand years. We should not seek to curtail this process or limit it. We can worship texts, their stories, wisdom, and sheer age. Foundational and sacred texts are awesome monuments of culture, our shared human inheritance. But for precisely this reason, we should allow readers of each generation to make these texts their own.

Today, a vast majority of humans claims adherence to some form of sacred scripture. How we choose to interpret these texts has become one of the crucial questions of our time.

CHAPTER 4

LEARNING FROM THE BUDDHA, CONFUCIUS, SOCRATES, AND JESUS

I WAS NEVER A TEACHER'S PET, BUT THE TEACHERS I ADMIRED HAVE remained important figures throughout my life, protagonists in my mental narrative. For the most part they were remote, or perhaps I kept them at arm's length, preferring to admire them from a distance. But I was nevertheless fascinated by everything they said and did, how they dressed, and what little I knew about their lives. Now that I have become a teacher myself, I am wary of creating, consciously or unconsciously, a cult of personality, of playing up the role of the teacher.

These are the thoughts that go through my mind every time I pick up one of the philosophical or religious texts associated with the great teachers of the classical world: the sutras showing the Buddha in conversation with his followers, the texts describing how Confucius lived and taught, the dialogues between Socrates and his students, the gospels of Jesus. I like teaching these texts because they turn me into a student again, allowing me to admire these charismatic teachers alongside my own students.

Reading and teaching these texts is a much more personal experience than teaching *Gilgamesh*, Homer, or the Hebrew Bible, which depict the lives of kings and emperors utterly different from us. The texts revolving around teacher and students, by contrast, tap into an experience almost everyone can share: We all were students once and carry that memory with us for the rest of our lives.

It was only in the course of trying to understand the story of literature that I noticed a striking pattern in the teachings of the Buddha, Confucius, Socrates, and Jesus. Living within a span of a few hundred years but without knowing of one another, these teachers revolutionized the world of ideas. Many of today's philosophical and religious schools—Indian philosophy, Chinese philosophy, Western philosophy, and Christianity—were shaped by these charismatic teachers. It was almost as if in the five centuries before the Common Era, the world was waiting to be instructed, eager to learn new ways of thinking and being. But why? And what explains the emergence of these teachers?

These teachers emerged in the literate cultures of China, the Middle East, and Greece (India may have had little or no writing, but it had significant storytelling traditions)—and so I found one answer in the history of writing. In these literate centers, scribes, kings, and priests had created bureaucracies, libraries, and schools, collected stories, and entrenched these stories as foundational texts and even as holy scripture. Yet what these new teachers had in common was that they did not write. Instead, they insisted on gathering students around them and teaching them through dialogue, talking face-to-face.

The decision not to use writing—to avoid producing literature—is a fascinating development in the history of literature. It arose at the precise moment when writing was becoming more widely available, as if these cultures were suddenly worried about the effects of a technology that was gaining ground and decided to question its use.

But then something else happened, something even more interesting: This avoidance of writing, this insistence on personal, live teaching, was channeled back into literature. The teachers' words became texts, texts that we can now read and that draw us into the circle of students that formed around these teachers. They seem to be addressing us, too, and very personally, across time and space. This was the birth of a new form of literature: *teachers' literature.*

Who were these teachers, and how did their words become the basis of a new class of texts in the story of literature, so different from earlier foundational texts and scriptures?

The Buddha

FIFTH CENTURY B.C.E., NORTHEAST INDIA

One of the earliest teachers was a prince living in the northeast of India. His dates are disputed, but his life became a legend, and as a legend it became the source of a powerful movement.

His awakening began when he heard lovely things about the forest near his father's palace. Trees as far as the eye could see, giving shelter from the sun, and ponds adorned with the prettiest lotus flowers, surrounded by a carpet of tender grass. He himself could barely imagine such wonders. His chambers, exquisitely decorated, were hidden away in the interior of the sprawling palace. Everything he needed was brought to him by an army of servants or by his beloved wife. Except that now the prince didn't want anything brought to him; he wasn't asking that someone go to the forest and fetch him a lotus flower from one of the ponds. He wanted to go and see for himself.

The king, who had kept the prince protected from the world, was worried and prepared the outing with the utmost care. Nothing must disturb his son's refined sensibilities; cripples, beggars, anyone sick or unseemly was strictly banished from sight. By the time the prince and his charioteer emerged from the palace gates, the roads were decorated with garlands and banners, and flowers were strewn everywhere.

The prince loved the outing and took it all in, the people, the flowers, the city, the adoring crowds. But then his eyes caught a strange sight. Out of nowhere, a creature was creeping toward him with uncertain movements, barely able to walk, its face disfigured by heavy folds. Was this a cruel jest? The prince turned toward his charioteer and demanded an answer. The charioteer had been instructed by the king to protect the prince from everything that might disturb him, but something compelled him to come out with the terrible truth: "Old age has done it." What was this "old age," the prince wanted to know. And could it afflict him as well? Yes, it could, the charioteer replied, unable to deceive. In fact, it would do so, with certainty. The prince returned home bewildered, desperately trying to make sense of this experience.

After two similar encounters that confronted him with illness and death, the prince decided to break with what he felt was a false life and everything associated with it. He became a wandering mendicant, living on what people were willing to give him. People were surprised to see a young man of great fortune choose a life of poverty, but ascetics were not unknown in India (Alexander encountered some of these naked philosophers, as he called them, during his campaign). The prince followed an established path and joined five other mendicants, who together submitted to the harsh life of poverty. He gave up his few remaining possessions and needs, subsisting on less and less, until a woman found the emaciated mendicant, his mind feverish, and offered him milk. He accepted it thankfully. After his body had regained some strength and his mind calmed, he took refuge under an old fig tree and meditated on his experience. Was extreme deprivation a solution, or only a reaction to his shock and rage, his fall from innocence? The mortification of the flesh had not freed him from his body but only drawn more attention to it. It had not calmed his mind but only led to delirium. There must be another solution to his disappointment with the world.

As the prince sat under the fig tree, he felt the effects of his encounters with old age, illness, and death drift away. Dimly at first, he became aware that his life, which had brought him from the seclusion of the palace to the harsh world outside and then to extreme suffering and deprivation, was not his only life. He had lived many times before, and those earlier lives now came floating back to him, strange lives of animals and of humans, thousands, tens of thousands, even hundreds of thousands of them. And his lives were not the only things to multiply. The world that had so shocked him was not the only world, but one of many worlds he was now able to behold. Contemplating the wonders of these lives and worlds, he knew that he had attained what he was never able to attain during his six long years of mortification: enlightenment. He had become enlightened, a Buddha.

Freed now from worldly attachments, the Buddha attracted followers. First were his fellow ascetics, who had been disappointed at his departure from the strictures of their lives. When they encountered the prince, however, they realized that it was they who had chosen the wrong path. More and more came, ascetics and non-ascetics, Brahmins (members of the priestly class) and non-Brahmins, wanting to be in his presence, hoping to be taught by him, seeking enlightenment through him.

The Buddha continued to live his life, moving from place to place, going on his daily rounds of begging, eating his simple meal, washing his feet, arranging his seat, and finally sitting down to teach. He didn't deliver lectures. Instead he invited his followers to ask questions and then answered them patiently, sometimes in short sentences or images, sometimes in riddles or parables that needed explaining. It wasn't teaching so much as unteaching, undoing their former habits of mind and life. He urged them to abandon their worldly attachments to persons and things, even to their own selves. This teaching of the benefits of detachment from this world was difficult, sometimes even paradoxical. In withdrawing from the world, where should his students withdraw to if not to their own selves? Some teachings became famous, as when, after teaching in Shravasti, the Buddha was asked what this particular teaching should be called, and he answered that it should be called the *Diamond of Perfect Wisdom* because, like a diamond, it cut through false ideas.

Why were the Buddha's teachings so compelling despite being shrouded in paradoxes and riddles? One reason was their universal appeal. Here was the former prince turning even to the humblest of them, speaking to them, addressing them, offering them the promise of something completely different. This was not a message addressed to the privileged group but to each of them. They could all follow him and seek enlightenment if only they dared to do it. They could engage him in debate. This was very different from the exclusive teachings of the Brahmins, which the Buddha critiqued. While these teachings were controlled by Brahmins and princes, the Buddha addressed each person individually, powerfully, exhorting them to change their lives.

As the Buddha became old, he did not think it wise to elevate one of his students above the others and therefore refused to appoint a successor. Since so many of them had progressed in their search for enlightenment, they could all teach, as they had been doing, by supporting one another. Despite this encouragement, his followers found themselves deeply saddened and disoriented when their master died. How could they be sure that they weren't making errors of doctrine, errors in the conduct of their lives? Hitherto, they had been able to turn to the Buddha for correction, which he had freely given, admonishing, even shaming, those who clung to false beliefs. To whom should they turn now?

Honoring their dead master's wish that there not be a single leader, they turned to one another and called a large gathering of former disciples. Together they would remember and fix rules of conduct and belief, together they would agree what henceforth it would mean to be a follower of the Buddha. The collective memory of his students would preserve the precious words spoken by the Enlightened One, would prevent errors from being introduced into precious teachings such as the *Diamond of Perfect Wisdom*, would ensure that the right words would be passed down through the generations. If disagreements arose, another convocation of followers would have to be called to eliminate error and doubt.

If it was so important to remember the Buddha's words correctly, why had no one thought to write them down? Some form of writing may have existed in India during the Buddha's time (the so-called Indus Valley script may not have been a full writing system and remains undeciphered). What mattered above all were the age-old hymns and stories of the Vedas, which were transmitted orally by specially appointed Brahmins for whom remembering the Vedas was an obligation and a privilege. This priestly class had created an elaborate division of labor to preserve this large body of chants and stories. Doctrines and verses were divided into smaller pieces and distributed to different groups. While no single person could remember the entire doctrine, collectively the Brahmins preserved it with precision and ensured a seamless transition from generation to generation.

So well did the system work, so deeply was it woven into the social fabric of society, that religious leaders did not need to write down these holy chants, which originated before the introduction of writing into India. But even after the introduction of writing, these priests avoided it, fearing that once the sacred words were given over to writing, everything would change. Writing wasn't just an alternative to the old ways of memorizing words. It was something entirely new, a technology that would bring with it profound changes that were difficult to predict.

One thing the priests could predict right away: If they allowed sacred words to be written down, these words would be in the hands of those controlling the new technology. Those hands were not the

THE DISPUTED INDUS VALLEY SCRIPT,
DATING TO THE THIRD MILLENNIUM B.C.E.

hands of Brahmins and priests, but of unworthy merchants and accountants. Who knew what kind of corruption they would introduce? Better to stick to oral transmission by the privileged few and
the carefully initiated. The oldest Indian epic, the *Ramayana*, was
also orally composed and only later written down, much like Homeric epics.

The followers of Buddha disagreed with the Brahmins about
many things, but they nonetheless shared with them the practice of
oral transmission. Only centuries later did they turn to writing, but
still sooner than the Brahmins, because unlike the Brahmins they

were not invested in keeping their teaching in the hands of a privileged few. Writing would help the Buddhists to spread the teaching farther afield.

Finally wielding the technology, Buddhist scribes produced texts that captured as vividly as possible the life of the Buddha. Often they showed the Buddha in dialogue with students or adversaries, explaining rules for conduct and observations about the world. All the accounts of the Buddha we have today are based on texts written hundreds of years after his death, texts that would ultimately acquire the status of sacred scripture. (And once Buddhist scripture had been established, poets imagined the life of the Buddha; the biography of the Buddha I sketched is based on an early such account by the poet Ashvaghosha, who lived in the early second century C.E.) The Buddha's charisma, his effect on his listeners, his every word and deed were the product of a new type of literature, teachers' literature, which captured the appeal of a charismatic master who was long dead but whose life and teachings had finally intersected with writing technologies.

CONFUCIUS

FIFTH CENTURY B.C.E., NORTHERN CHINA

Around the year 500 B.C.E., news of an unusual teacher was spreading in the East, in the region where Mount Tai rises boldly from the northern plains of China. Forests had been cut down to create large fields, and over these fields the north wind raged. Below the imposing peak, leaders of rival states and clans made sacrifices to ensure victory in their constant internal wars. Even though the state was supposed to be run by a duke, it was controlled by three powerful families, each struggling to undermine the others.

Master Kong had worked for one of the families and become embroiled in the wrangling. He had advised younger functionaries how to navigate this tricky terrain until he felt that he could no longer reconcile his service with his conscience, whereupon he withdrew from government service and went into exile. There his teachings took on a more universal character and attracted more students, until he became a famous teacher, who would be known in the West by the Latin name Confucius.

His students were usually found crowding around him, sitting on their heels, transfixed by his words. He wasn't difficult to understand—he didn't like complicated phrases—but it often took a while for his simple words to sink in. One student, Yu, once asked him straight out what knowledge was. Kong replied calmly: "Yu, shall I teach you what knowledge is? When you know a thing, to hold that you know it; and when you do not know a thing, to allow that you do not know it; this is knowledge." It sounded simple, but the concept required thought and meditation. Kong wasn't angry about forward questions because he had such affection for his students. When he traveled, he was eager to return to them. He loved some of his former students even more, students like Yan Hui. He was the best, Kong had said. But Yan Hui was dead, and it was touching to know how much the teacher missed him.

When famous people came to talk to Kong, the students were usually allowed to listen in. Many dukes came, the governor of a province, a master musician. Kong talked to simpler people as well. Once a border warden wanted to speak to him, and the teacher acquiesced. And then there was the time when he took an interest in a messenger boy, taking him as seriously as his regular students.

The students didn't just listen to Kong's words. His every deed, the way he lived, was fascinating to them. He ate in moderation, they observed, but particularly enjoyed ginger. He always made sure that his bamboo mat was exactly straight. He loved order in all things. Even though he himself had withdrawn from government service, he considered stability and good governance central and impressed these values on his students.

What Kong cared about most was the past. This wasn't surprising, since the world around them was in violent chaos. He made his students read the old poetry collection *Classic of Songs*, because it improved their command of language and expression. But when some of them quoted from it all the time, Kong warned them that quoting from the *Classic* was not enough. Their entire lives needed to change. The point remained, though, that things had been better in the past, when political power was more centralized, the state more ordered. Confucius said, "I am not one who was born in the possession of knowledge; I am one who is fond of antiquity, and earnest in seeking it there."

In Kong's view, the chaos of the present had infected even the meaning of words:

> When names are not correct, what is said will not sound reasonable; when what is said does not sound reasonable, affairs will not culminate in success; when affairs do not culminate in success, rites and music will not flourish; when rites and music do not flourish, punishments will not fit the crimes; when punishments do not fit the crimes, the common people will not know where to put hand and foot.

Finding the right names and words was important because China was one of the great early writing cultures, and one of the few that has endured until our own time. The earliest Chinese writing, dating at least to 1200 B.C.E., was done on turtle shells and animal bones, so-called oracle bones, which were used for divination (much like the divination practices Ashurbanipal learned in Mesopotamia). It is possible, although ultimately unproven, that China invented writing independently from Mesopotamia and Egypt, though the very idea of devising a code to capture language may have been borrowed from Mesopotamia. The Chinese writing

THE EARLIEST CHINESE SCRIPT WAS WRITTEN ON
FRAGMENTS OF OX BONES OR THE FLAT UNDERSIDE OF
TURTLE SHELLS, DATING FROM 1600 TO 1050 B.C.E.

system itself was certainly unique. Words were not divided into single sounds, as in alphabetic writing; rather, concepts and things received their own signs, which grew in complexity and number. Today's Chinese writing is directly derived from this ancient origin, resisting the spread of alphabetic writing to this day.

By the time of Confucius, writing had touched many aspects of life, from religious divination to state bureaucracies and the creation of a literary canon, including the poetry collection *Classic of Songs*. Living in one of the great literary cultures of the world, Confucius might well have resorted to writing (much more easily than the Buddha), but he didn't. He died without having written down any of his teachings.

But soon after his death, students began to write down his words, capturing dialogues and scenes of teaching, questions and answers, from which emerged what we now call Confucianism. One volume of the sayings that came to be known as the *Analects* contained no account of his speeches at all, only descriptions of how he had conducted himself in different situations, what ceremonies he had observed, and which protocols he had obeyed. The *Analects* sketched the master in his most memorable moments and became a guide on how to live your life.

As in the case of the Buddha, these texts became influential. They also spawned imitators. Over the ensuing generations, some students rose to prominence, inspiring followers of their own to commit new ideas to writing. The sayings of the various teachers became so popular that a name was needed for this new genre: *masters' literature*. In a way, this term is a misnomer, for these master teachers did not write the texts themselves; their students did. One might also call these texts *students' literature*, written by students to commemorate their dead teachers.

Because so much of the teaching of Confucius revolved around the past and because he had recommended the study of the oldest songs and rituals, Confucius became associated with the most important foundational texts of China. Unusually, these texts were not long narrative tales of gods and heroes like Gilgamesh, Achilles, or Moses, but collections of poetry, deceptively simple songs, often quite short and only loosely connected. While the world had fallen into chaos, these ancient texts had survived, thanks to writing. Now they were able to bring readers in tune with a better past that would otherwise have been lost. Not only lyrical songs had been collected, but also anthologies of rituals, historical chronicles, and other ancient texts, and since they, too, were survivors of a distant past, they were all attributed to Master Kong.

Thus, without having written down his own teachings, Master Kong became the authority of the entire canon of Chinese literature, now known as the Confucian classics.

Socrates
—
399 B.C.E., ATHENS

The deaths of the Buddha and Confucius had been traumatic for their students. In the case of Socrates and Jesus, the deaths of these teachers turned them into martyrs.

Socrates' most intense teaching moment occurred just before his death, in 399 B.C.E., in prison, when he told his students that philosophy was nothing other than a preparation for dying. In retrospect, it was perhaps not surprising that he would come to a violent end. He had made his name by going against received wisdom and styling himself the gadfly of the city, questioning its most popular institutions, from democratic votes and appointments by lottery to theater festivals. His irritating questions had won him a small group of dedicated followers, but also many enemies. Sooner or later, someone was bound to drag him before the law. When the time came, Socrates played into the hands of his enemies, cheerfully declaring that he simply couldn't stop doing what he was doing, that there was a voice inside his head compelling him to do it. Everyone understood this to be his last, his most public provocation, and it led to the inevitable result: a death sentence.

But his students weren't going to let their teacher die just like that. Pooling their resources, they had bribed the prison guard and arranged to take Socrates to safety. There were plenty of Greek-speaking colonies and cities where he could hide, even thrive. When they revealed their plan, perhaps with a touch of pride, Socrates surprised them by refusing to go along with it. He, the provocateur, the misfit, the irritant, was determined to obey the law. Even though the trial had been a sham, he would submit to its verdict.

It wasn't just recalcitrance. Socrates had reasons—he always had reasons—and he walked his students step by step from the premises to a conclusion they hadn't expected but couldn't argue with. He called this process philosophizing, and this was what he was doing now, in prison, in the face of certain death. The students were still stunned by his refusal to flee and tried not to think of their master's inevitable death, but Socrates just kept talking. Before long, he was philosophizing about his own impending death, trying to convince them that it was the best thing that could happen to him. Since philosophy, according to him, was all about freeing yourself from the shackles of the body, wasn't death the ultimate liberation? And since he had taught them that the world was nothing but a shadow play, wasn't liberation from this shadow what any truth-seeking philosopher should hope for? Argument after argument came rolling at them, forcing them to think about death, about his death.

But he wanted more, their teacher: He wanted them to *admit* that his death was actually the best possible thing that could happen to him. Some tried to argue with him, but they didn't get very far. Even when their minds were fully engaged, they usually lost their arguments with Socrates. With Socrates in prison, their hearts full of grief, they didn't have a chance. He kept coming at them from different directions. You know about swan songs, he would ask them, when swans sing most beautifully just before dying? Swans sing that way because they are looking forward to dying, celebrating their death. The students may well have thought that the swans didn't sound so celebratory—they may even have realized that they were hearing their teacher's own swan song—but they tried to hide their tears because they knew that he wanted them to be happy about his death, and they wanted him to be proud of them and regard them as fellow philosophers.

Sensing distress among his students, Socrates switched modes. In an almost bantering tone, he said:

"You have the childish fear that when the soul goes out from the body the wind will really blow it away and scatter it, especially if a man happens to die in a high wind and not in calm weather." And Cebes [one of the students] laughed and said: "Assume that we have that fear, Socrates, and try to convince us; or rather, do not assume that we are afraid, but perhaps there is a child within us, who has such fears. Let us try to persuade him not to fear death as if it were a hobgoblin." "Ah," said Socrates, "you must sing charms to him every day until you charm away his fear."

Then abruptly, before it was time, Socrates called in the prison guard and asked for the poison to be brought. The guard returned with a cup and handed it to Socrates. He took it, calmly, and emptied it in one gulp. He kept talking to his students, who were no longer able to say anything, providing them with an account of how the poison was making its way through his body. First his legs went numb, and he had to lie down. Then the poison crept upward; he became increasingly paralyzed, but he was still talking to them. Finally, the poison reached his head, and Socrates became quiet at last. Another moment passed, and he was still. Socrates, their beloved teacher, was dead.

What would his legacy be? The problem was that Socrates, too, had refused to write anything down. It wasn't because he was illiterate. As the son of a sculptor and a midwife, he didn't belong to the highest class of citizens, and almost anywhere else, writing would have been reserved for a small class of privileged specialists far above his station. But not in the Athens of the late fifth century, which was one of the most literate places on earth. Thanks to the alphabet, Greek writing was much easier to learn than many other writing systems, twenty-four letters neatly matched to sounds, which meant that written Greek was close to spoken Greek. No need to learn some ancient literary language like Hebrew or Old Akkadian. And the political system made sure that a citizen, even a lowly one, perhaps even a slave, a migrant, or a woman, could learn to read and write. Only the expense of papyrus, which had to be imported, was a drag on literacy.

There was much to read. The stories of the Trojan War had been written down hundreds of years before in the *Iliad* and the *Odyssey*. Most people continued to experience these epics live by listening to specially trained bards who recited them to large audiences. But the epics were also taught in schools, which meant that those who knew literature prided themselves on being able to recite Homer from memory. More recently there had been an explosion of writing, above all by playwrights, who adapted stories from Homer's mythological world to be performed during festivals in large open-air theaters, and the trade in papyrus scrolls was brisk.

Socrates himself had studied Homer, but he didn't use writing in his teaching method. Instead he found potential students at the gymnasium or in the marketplace by drawing them into conversation. He wasn't always successful, because he was so odd. He was ugly, with a broad face and snub nose, and not well groomed. He rarely went to the public bath, didn't oil his skin and hair, and didn't usually use perfume. Sometimes he forgot to wear sandals. But despite his frequently disheveled appearance, he had developed a following among the aristocratic youths of the city. What Socrates offered them was a new way of thinking in which everything was open to questioning, even Homer.

In fact, Socrates raised many questions about Homer and about the playwrights adapting Homer's stories. What did Homer know about warfare or chariot racing? Socrates himself had fought as a foot soldier in the famous Greek phalanx. Did Homer ever fight in a war? Or build a chariot? Or plow a field? Everyone quoted Homeric maxims on these topics as if he were the universal expert, but Socrates was not so sure. Some lines didn't make sense; others seemed downright wrong.

Socrates' argument against writing went deeper than just a complaint about Homer's authority and expertise. One day he was sitting with Phaedrus, one of his companions, under a sycamore tree outside Athens, where the wind god, Borealis, had once abducted a young woman. Phaedrus had brought a speech by Lysias, one of the most famous intellectuals of Athens, and, prompted by Socrates, he read it aloud, with Socrates interrupting and questioning him in the shade of midday. Gently, Socrates had steered the conversation to the topic of writing. Writing was all the rage in Athens, Socrates observed, especially among the most ambitious citizens and politicians. So, should he adopt this powerful technology?

Socrates' answer was no, and he explained his position by going back to the origins of writing. For the Greeks, this inevitably meant Egypt, a culture more ancient than Greece and endowed with a beautiful and impossible-to-learn writing system. We know this system, in fact, by its Greek name: *hieroglyphics*. The term meant "sacred writing," which was also to say enigmatic, religious, mysterious writing, writing that was difficult to decipher but that might reveal secret meanings to the initiates. It was therefore not surprising that Socrates would tell Phaedrus an Egyptian legend about the origin of writing. A god brought writing to an Egyptian king, praising the advantages of the new technology, which would miraculously make fleeting words permanent. Writing would improve memory and lead to knowledge and wisdom. But the Egyptian king rejected the offer because he realized that the opposite would be true. People would no longer bother to remember things, relying instead on the new technology, and their ability to think would deteriorate.

Characteristically, Socrates didn't stop there. He used the anecdote to argue that the effect of writing was even worse than in the Egyptian story. Writing was just a mute shadow of speech, a technique that captured words but without their sound, their breath, their soul. It was just a mechanical contraption, a technology, with enormous disadvantages. You couldn't ask a piece of writing follow-up questions; words would be taken out of the context in which they were spoken, which would make them bound to be misunderstood, beyond the control of their author; words would survive the speaker's death, so that he would be unable to refute false interpretations that might arise later.

Among all the great teachers who refused to write, Socrates was the one to reject writing most explicitly. This rejection showed the extent to which writing had become a cultural force. Socrates was in the best position to recognize this precisely because he lived in one of the most literate societies of the time. As a technology keyed to language, writing had extended and altered how humans communicated and even how they thought. This triumphal rise of writing was causing a backlash spearheaded by charismatic teachers like Socrates.

In prison, Socrates' indictment of writing left his students incapable of preserving the words of their teacher, who had just died before their very eyes. Only one student had a plan: Plato. He had not been with Socrates during the teacher's final hours. Was he unable to bear the thought of Socrates in prison, dying? Did he know that Socrates would refuse to go along with the illegal escape plot? All he tells us is that he was ill at the time.

Plato, in any case, had developed a plot of his own. Despite his teacher's arguments against writing, Plato was in the process of securing his master's legacy through written words. He wasn't writing down Socrates' words as speeches. That would have been too much of a betrayal. He honored his teacher's method of question and answer by writing everything as dialogues. Since Socrates had accused writing of not answering back, Plato tried his best to make it responsive to the give-and-take of actual conversation. And since Socrates had accused writing of uprooting words from their original context, Plato took care to note the setting of each conversation and the changing interactions of the speakers, as if enabling readers to reenact these conversations on a stage. Plato was creating a drama of ideas.

As the living memory of Socrates faded, these written dialogues preserved him with all of his foibles, strange manners, and charisma. In fact, everything we know about Socrates—his ability to drink his companions under the table, his disheveled appearance, the love he inspired in his students—comes to us through Plato's dialogues. One other writer, Xenophon, authored Socratic dialogues, but his are less significant. The Socrates we know is Plato's Socrates, a Socrates transmitted by the written word.

Jesus

First decades c.e., Sea of Galilee (Israel)

Four hundred years after Socrates, another teacher emerged, this time in the Middle East. It was fortunate that he knew the Hebrew Bible so well. After he had fasted in the wilderness for forty days, an evil spirit came to tempt him. "Command that these stones be made bread," it said. "If thou be the Son of God, cast thyself down: for it is written, He shall give his angels charge concerning thee."

Jesus was hungry, his body and mind weakened, but in this hour of need he could turn to the scripture and recite verses that defended him from the cunning temptation the Evil One had put in his ear. He would remember reading the precept "Man does not live by bread alone." And "Do not tempt your God." Whatever the Evil One tried, he ran up against Jesus' knowledge of the scripture. A very good thing it was that God, with the help of the scribe Ezra, had produced a holy text, a weapon against which the Evil One was powerless, at least for now; a very good thing, too, that Jesus had learned to read this text.

After the fasting and the temptations, Jesus emerged a changed man, and he began to preach. First he gathered only a few students around him, persuading them to leave their families and homes, to abandon everything they knew and cherished, and to follow him.

And follow him they did, first a few, then more as word spread of a teacher wandering around the Sea of Galilee. In synagogues and courtyards he preached, asking questions, giving answers, sometimes straightforward ones but more often enigmatic parables and riddles.

Soon the crowds he attracted were too large for the synagogues and courtyards, and Jesus led them up a mountain overlooking the Sea of Galilee. It was there that he delivered his most famous sermon, a sermon that spoke to people directly in words they could understand, a speech about poverty, powerlessness, and persecution, but also about a new way of life. He told them that the world as they knew it was ending, and that their lives as they knew them would end as well. He told them to prepare themselves, to change, to follow him. Everyone he addressed, even the lowliest.

There was only one group he did not like, whom he attacked directly: the guardians of the Bible. These scribes were charged with interpreting the foundational text of their culture, the text Ezra had instituted as scripture upon his return from exile. But Jesus did not accept the authority of these scribes. Like other rebels against foundational literature, like Confucius and Socrates (and perhaps the Buddha) before him, Jesus could have written words down. Like these other teachers, he chose not to. He had been raised in a scribal culture built on a sacred text, as he showed when battling the demon in the desert. But he refused to create a writing of his own.

Only once did Jesus actually write. He was sitting in the courtyard of the temple, teaching those who had gathered around him, when a group of priests and scribes dragged in a woman who had committed adultery. According to the law, written in the Hebrew Bible, she should be stoned to death, and the scribes were hoping that he would come out publicly against the sentence, and therefore against the law, so they could attack him. But Jesus did not rise to the bait. He knew the law encoded in the scripture and did not call it false. Instead he shamed them by saying that those who were without sin should cast the first stone. Then he waited for them to slink away one by one until he was alone with the woman and could talk to her. But while he waited, he wrote with his finger in the sand. The Gospels don't record what he wrote. Perhaps it is enough to know that he did write, and at just the moment when the priests were confronting him with scripture. He wrote not on papyrus, but in sand, which the wind would blow away. Jesus' writing, if that is what it was, was not meant to be permanent.

He had a different plan when it came to scripture. Producing new scripture would have been an unheard-of act of blasphemy. He would accept the existing scripture, declaring, "Do not think that I have come to abolish the law or the prophets; I have come not to abolish but to fulfill." What did this mean, to fulfill the scriptures? It meant putting himself into these scriptures. It was John the Baptist who had first spelled it out: "For this is he that was spoken of by the prophet Esaias, saying, 'The voice of one crying out in the wilderness: "Prepare ye the way of the Lord, make his paths straight."'" Jesus presented himself as the one prophesied in the scriptures. He didn't say to the crowds that he had written new scripture; he said, "This that is written must yet be accomplished in me." He *was* the scripture, its living manifestation: "The Word was made flesh."

The authorities in Jerusalem hated the idea of their text being made flesh—literature had long since become a matter of power and authority. The Roman overlords didn't like it, either. They didn't care about the scripture, but they sensed the rebellion in what he said. The result was yet another sham trial and death sentence. Socrates had been lucky, having been allowed to die a painless death in the company of his students. Jesus was publicly mocked, a crown of thorns was pressed onto his head, and he was made to drag his heavy wooden cross through the streets and up the executioner's hill. He was nailed to the cross, the cross was set up with its heavy human load, and Jesus was left hanging there until he died of asphyxiation. The flesh was dead.

What would be his legacy? The same dilemma that had confronted the students of other teachers confronted his followers now. In their first desperation, Jesus came to their aid: His corpse vanished and then appeared to his followers, encouraging them to spread his teachings by word of mouth. To aid them in this endeavor, he sent a second miracle, the miracle of words, Pentecost. Tongues of fire appeared, and his students could understand all human languages, a perfect condition for proselytizing.

These miracles only postponed the problem of his legacy, and ultimately the solution was writing. Written accounts of Jesus emerged less than a century after his death, based on oral traditions among his students. Later called the Gospels, they preserved the story of Jesus' words and deeds as if reported by eyewitnesses. The Gospels were powerful, and not only because Jesus' words had been powerful. By focusing on their master's humiliation and death, the authors of the Gospels created an unusual type of hero, a rebel who was also a victim. This was not how a hero was supposed to be represented, but the writers realized that part of Jesus' strange appeal was that he had come as a common man. They described their master's humiliation because they, and their readers, could identify with it.

The Gospels were not the only texts about Jesus in circulation. Some of the most fervent writers lived far from the circle of disciples that had survived their teacher's death and didn't even pretend to write eyewitness accounts.

A Jew and Roman citizen, Paul had been involved in persecuting the followers of Jesus, but he had a conversion experience on the road to Damascus, when he believed the resurrected Jesus had appeared to him. After his conversion, he began to work as a preacher, traveling far and wide to visit Christian communities in Asia Minor. He interpreted Jesus' words and deeds and turned them into a system of belief called Christianity (much as Plato had done with Socrates, creating a system called Platonism, and as Lenin would do with Marx, creating a system called Marxism).

In this effort, Paul appreciated the power of writing. He also excelled at public speaking, most famously in the great Hellenistic theater of Ephesus, where his attack on local deities created a riot. But his most influential mode was writing open letters, which suited his itinerant life. These letters, addressed to Christian communities among the Romans, Corinthians, Galatians, Ephesians, Philippians, Colossians, and Thessalonians, helped to turn the scattered followers of Jesus into an organized network of groups.

Over the first centuries after Jesus' death, Christian scribes selected from among the many gospels the four that were deemed most accurate; they added the letters of Paul and others, now known as the Epistles, as well as accounts of the deeds of Paul and other apostles, and finally an apocalyptic story of the end of time. Once again a charismatic teacher who had not produced a single line of writing (except once in sand) had become the protagonist and anchor of a new type of literary collection. Having presented himself as the living fulfillment of the Hebrew Bible, Jesus had at last acquired his own scripture.

TRANSLATION AND FORMAT WARS

Students turned the words of these four teachers, the Buddha, Confucius, Socrates, and Jesus, into texts that address each reader individually, channeling back into literature their teachers' desire to speak to their students directly. Once these teachings had become writings, they were promoted by technological innovations such as parchment, the book, paper, and print. To gauge the effects of these technologies, I traveled again, this time to Pergamum, in what is now Turkey.

The library of Pergamum was one of the great literary institu-

tions of the ancient world, and like the library of Alexandria it had
been founded by one of Alexander's heirs. According to a classical
source, the origin of the library was a collection of scrolls by Aristotle, the first Greek to collect texts systematically.

Unlike the library of Alexandria, which was burned down by
repeated waves of conquests and has vanished, parts of the library of
Pergamum are still visible today. When I visited, I could see the
ruins of this city from afar. As I made my way up the serpentine
road, I passed a theater before I entered the fortified section of the
town. Pergamum has a commanding view of the sea and the hinterland, a strategic position that contributed to its prominence. The
foundations and some walls of the library occupied a prominent
place at the center of the citadel. It was here that librarians amassed
a treasure of scrolls, but also attracted some of the best scholars, giving rise to influential schools of thought. Libraries like those at Pergamum and Alexandria housed the writings of Plato, as well as
Homer, and were part of the export of Greek culture across Alexander's realm.

Even though Pergamum looks like a typical Hellenistic town,
with Greek statues, a theater, and the ruins of the famous library, it
was also one of the places where Greek-based literary culture intersected with the followers of Jesus. Though conversant with the Hebrew Bible, Jesus had spoken Aramaic, the common language of
the Middle East. But when his students turned his words into writing, they did so in the most prestigious language of the region,
brought by Alexander: Common Greek.

The choice of Greek was not just one of convenience. Along
with the language, early Christians (and Jews sticking to their traditional scriptures) absorbed Greek thought and letters, including
Plato's dialogues. This influence of Greek literature culminated in
the Gospel of Saint John, which used the Greek word *logos*,
"reason"—a word so dear to Socrates—to characterize the Chris-

tian God. Born out of Judaism, early Christianity was absorbing the lessons of Socrates, Greece's most important teacher.

Now that Jesus' teachings had been written down, a new problem arose. How would these texts relate to the Hebrew scriptures? Jesus had presented himself as their fulfillment. At first, the followers of Jesus considered the texts that had sprung up around their master to be independent of the Hebrew Bible. Because these writings of Jesus were so much more recent and born of a lived experience, and since they were promoted so aggressively by Paul as a repudiation of Judaism in its orthodox form, these new texts developed a dynamic of their own. Ultimately, they demoted the Hebrew Bible to the status of an older text, a preamble to what really mattered, namely its fulfillment in the texts of Jesus.

And so it came to pass that the Hebrew Bible was dubbed the Old Testament, followed and brought to completion by the New Testament. This way, the teachers' literature centered on Jesus became its own sacred scripture, with all the luster that went along with that status. Tending to these texts became a religious duty, the guiding principle for monks to produce beautiful editions as a form of religious service.

As with other sacred texts, the New Testament would also develop its own tradition of textual fundamentalism, with devout followers seeking in these texts unchanging guidelines for life in a changing world.

Assimilating the Hebrew Bible to the new canon of Jesus literature was made easier by the fact that the Hebrew Bible had already been translated into Greek. This translation took place in Alexandria, the center for the dissemination of Greek culture to the rest of Egypt. A sizable Jewish community had formed there, the result of repeated waves of exile and upheaval, held together by the Hebrew Bible as established by Ezra. Most of the community had lost Hebrew, the language of its scriptures, as well as Aramaic, the common language of the Near East, adopting instead Alexander's Common Greek. This threatened the people's access to their sacred scripture. There was only one solution: The Hebrew Bible needed to be translated into Greek.

The translation, which was undertaken in Alexandria's famous library, was a tricky process because the Bible was sacred scripture and closely linked to Hebrew. Could Yahweh create the world in the language of Greek pagans? Could he carve the Ten Commandments using a script devised for capturing the hexameters of Homer? Perhaps to soften this blow, a legend emerged that the librarians of Alexandria had called upon seventy-two Alexandrian Jews to translate the Hebrew Bible, and that all of them had come up with the same translation separately. The resulting Greek Bible was called the Septuagint after the number of translators. At first, only Greek-speaking Jews used it, but soon it was adopted by others as well.

The Greek Bible could now serve the Greek-speaking Christians as the prequel for the accounts of Jesus given to them by the Evangelists. Not everyone was happy with this new use of the translated Hebrew Bible, especially the various Jewish communities, for whom their Bible, no matter whether in Hebrew or in Greek, was not old but ageless and not in need of additions or completion.

The ensuing struggle between Christians and Jews over the Hebrew Bible became a struggle over different writing formats. Jews stuck with the traditional papyrus scroll, such as the one Ezra in Jerusalem had held up to be worshipped. Christians, by contrast, availed themselves of two complementary inventions. One was born of the rivalry between the libraries of Pergamum and Alexandria. Even though Pergamum was gaining ground, Alexandria still had one great advantage: ready availability of the plant from which most scrolls were made and which undergirded the writing culture of the Hellenistic world. The scrolls were made from pressed leaves of the papyrus plant native to the Nile Delta, right next to Alexandria—but hundreds of miles from Pergamum. Importing papyrus was expensive and uncertain. If the librarians at Pergamum wanted to become independent from Egypt, they needed to come up with another writing material.

There existed as an alternative to papyrus a technique of using sheepskin. Raising animals was expensive and the preparation labor-intensive, but over time librarians at Pergamum perfected the process, producing an important technological invention that is still named after them: *pergamentum*, or parchment. The skin of sheep was first soaked in water for cleansing and then dried while stretched on a wooden frame. The resulting thin and durable surface was refined by adding powders to make it smooth and to allow it to absorb ink better. The librarians became so successful in perfecting this writing surface that they began to export it, in particular to Rome, their ally and master.

Christians used parchment, and they combined it with a Roman invention that favored this new writing surface, a new system of stacking sheets, binding them on one side, and placing them between covers. The Romans called it the *codex*, and we know it as the book. It had a number of advantages. It took up less room, and the covers provided protection. It could be opened and searched more easily. The codex worked better with parchment because parchment was tougher than papyrus (originally wax-coated wooden tablets were used). A new format was born: the parchment codex.

Initially, the parchment codex didn't have as much prestige as the papyrus scroll and was primarily used to jot down notes in the moment. In this it was perfect for the followers of Jesus, who wanted to avoid the permanence and reverence of scripture associated with the Hebrew Bible, preferring to preserve the spontaneous, oral flavor of their master's teachings. Soon a format war was raging among Jews and Christians in which Jews faithful to the Hebrew scripture stuck to the papyrus scroll, used in Jewish services to this day, while Christians adopted the parchment codex. Paul was an early adopter of this new form.

In the long run, the codex became the dominant format. Compact, easy to handle and transport, it also enabled readers to flip through pages and browse. The two formats had been drawn into a battle between an older type of scripture, based on a foundational text, and a newer type of scripture, based on the recent lessons of a charismatic teacher.

TWO CHINESE INVENTIONS: PAPER AND PRINT

While Christians adopted the parchment codex, followers of the two Eastern teachers, the Buddha and Confucius, enjoyed even more exciting developments in writing technology. To inspect the main exhibit of these innovations, I directed my steps once more to the British Library, which houses the *Diamond Sutra*, one of the teachings of the Buddha that had been committed to writing, transported from India to China, and translated into Chinese. It took the form of a scroll, like the Hebrew Bible, and looks extremely brittle. One part is covered in regular writing, faded black on a light gray surface, and much discolored by use and mold. The other part is covered with a black-and-white image showing the Buddha in conversation with students.

The journey of this scroll to the British Library began in the late nineteenth century, when a wandering preacher, Wang Yuanlu, stumbled upon a system of caves containing old Buddhist sculptures and wall paintings. Even though he was not a Buddhist himself, he was so struck by these objects from the distant past that he decided to devote the rest of his life to recovering them.

While working in one of the caves, Wang discovered a crack in the wall, which revealed a hidden storeroom full of bronze statues, paintings, and more than fifty thousand literary documents. They were miraculously preserved thanks to the dry desert climate and the fact that the cave had been sealed at some point in the fourteenth century, shielding it from intruders, daylight, and moisture, creating the perfect conservation conditions for what remains one of the world's most remarkable literary treasures. The cave contained fragments from more than five hundred copies of the *Diamond Sutra,* many of them worn to tatters, almost illegible. The heavily used sutras had been put in the cave because they were considered sacred scripture and therefore could not be thrown away or destroyed.

The *Diamond Sutra* was also explicit about its status as writing. Even though the Buddha had not cared for writing, later students had put into the Buddha's mouth an uncharacteristic emphasis on the written word. When the Buddha was asked how much spiritual benefit one could obtain by filling the river Ganges with jewels, he had replied that it would be better still to teach one of his sutras. The *Diamond Sutra* even encouraged its worshippers to transcribe and copy it. This emphasis on writing culminated in the declaration "Wherever this sutra is present, it is as if the Buddha and the Buddha's reverent disciples were also present." The Buddha and the written text had become one. Like an organism seeking to replicate itself, the *Diamond Sutra* was spawning versions of itself, becoming something similar to what Ezra had created: sacred scripture.

The cave contained Buddhist sutras written in Sanskrit and brought to China from the centers of Buddhism in India, but most of the scrolls and folding books were written in Chinese. This was unsurprising, since the caves were located in predominantly Chinese Dunhuang, between the Taklamakan Desert and the Gobi, a stopping point on the Silk Road that connected China to northern India and Persia. Buddhism had been able to exert influence in China because its sutras were not addressed to a particular culture, nor tied to a particular territory, as many older texts such as the *Epic of Gilgamesh,* the Homeric epics, or the Hebrew Bible had been. The universal appeal of these texts, and the missionary zeal of many Buddhists, allowed these texts to find adherents in all classes and far outside India.

In China, Buddhist sutras encountered two crucial innovations. While the Sanskrit texts in the Caves of the Thousand Buddhas were written on palm leaves, most of the Chinese texts were inscribed on a new writing surface, one that would transform the world of literature: paper.

Paper was made of plant fibers, mostly from the abundant mulberry tree, that had been broken down through repeated beating and were then soaked in water, which first separated the fibers and then bonded them again without the need for glue or any other bonding agent. It was a process I observed firsthand during a papermaking workshop in Taiwan. The pulp, made of broken-down plant fibers, was drained, flattened, dried, and pressed. The result was a writing surface that was smooth and light and could be folded or rolled. The alleged inventor of paper, Cai Lun, who lived during the Han Dynasty (206 B.C.E.–220 C.E.), is still greatly revered today.

Paper made a difference. Previously, texts in China were written on bones, strips of bamboo, or silk, all either cumbersome or expensive. Paper, by contrast, was cheap yet durable, so that written matter could be efficiently stored and preserved. Its smooth surface and thinness allowed much more information to be condensed into a small space, making it feasible to keep extensive records, which laid the foundation for sophisticated bureaucracies. It was also easy to transport; indeed, some of the Chinese texts in the Caves of the Thousand Buddhas had come from more than a thousand miles away.

One copy of the *Diamond Sutra* was different. It, too, was a paper version, in the form of a scroll, containing a note: "Reverently made for universal free distribution by Wang Jie on behalf of his two parents on the 13th of the 4th moon of the 9th year of Xiantong [May 11, 868]." It was common for wealthy Buddhists to sponsor the replication of sutras, either for their own benefit or for the benefit of loved ones. This, apparently, was what Wang Jie had done on behalf of his parents.

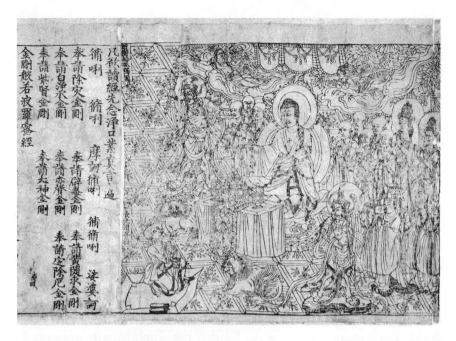

THIS COPY OF THE
DIAMOND SUTRA,
PRINTED WITH
WOODBLOCKS ON PAPER,
IS THE EARLIEST
SURVIVING PRINTED
BOOK IN THE WORLD,
DATING FROM
868 C.E. THE ENGRAVING,
ALSO PRINTED,
SHOWS THE BUDDHA
SURROUNDED BY
HIS DISCIPLES.

PAUL PELLIOT, AUREL
STEIN'S FRENCH RIVAL,
EXAMINING MANUSCRIPTS
IN THE HIDDEN
STOREROOM OF THE
CAVES OF THE
THOUSAND BUDDHAS.

To be sure, Wang Jie had not written the lines himself; wealthy Buddhists would usually hire scribes to copy sutras for them. But this copy of the *Diamond Sutra* was not written by human hand. It was printed—the first dated printed text to survive.

The printing method relied on blocks of hardwood. A scribe would write out the text, which would then be carved in relief on wooden blocks, which would be inked and pressed on paper. Printing was first used for administrative records, but Buddhists, driven by the desire to accrue merit, were quick to adapt the new technology. Printing made sense only for special texts, given the labor required to carve each page into wood. But once the carving was done, a printer could produce thousands of copies in a single day, which was perfect for the followers of Buddha, who wanted to spread the words of their teacher as rapidly as possible and obtain merit in the process. Thus Buddhism became an early adopter of print in China and soon also in Korea, where printing would ultimately be performed with movable letters made of ceramic or metal.

Four world-changing inventions are attributed to China: the compass, gunpowder, paper, and print. Two of four were inventions in writing technology. Small wonder that they helped propel literature in China to an unheard-of prominence, including the flowering of literature during the Tang Dynasty (618–907), the golden age of Chinese poetry. Later, woodblock printing would also set the stage for the rise of the Chinese novel.

There was one more journey in store for the printed version of the *Diamond Sutra* and many other texts in the caves. As Wang's discovery began to attract attention, several Western adventurers organized expeditions. A Hungarian-British explorer, Aurel Stein, was the first to reach the caves. An admirer of Alexander the Great, he shared his hero's interest in literature and managed to pilfer a large number of the manuscripts, paying only a pittance for them. He secretly stowed them away in a wooden crate, put them on the backs of camels, and took to the road, moving westward along the Silk Road. He survived the Taklamakan Desert, made his way across the Hindu Kush, then proceeded to Iran and, via Baghdad, reached Antioch, in what is now Syria, on the Mediterranean Sea. From Antioch, he sailed via Gibraltar to London, where I was able to see the scrolls more than a hundred years later.

Others, both Westerners and Chinese, raided the caves as well, and one of the most important collections of texts ever to be discovered was scattered. Only recently have these scrolls been brought back together, thanks to yet another revolution in writing technology: An early beneficiary of paper and print, the *Diamond Sutra* has been reunited with a number of its companion texts in digital form.

FIRE AND STONE

Chinese Buddhists were quick to use paper and print, but how did the followers of Confucius use these technologies? The written accounts of Confucius, as well as of the classics attributed to him as an editor, had emerged well before the age of paper and print. These texts almost did not survive long enough to avail themselves of these new technologies.

In 213 B.C.E., Chancellor Li Si had remarked to Qin Shi Huang, the first emperor of China, that the different accounts of the classics had contributed to the chaos associated with a previous period. Since the emperor was trying to unify China, it was seen as expedient to exert control over the canon of these writings. The result was a book burning. The emperor retained copies only for his own library as a way to centralize literary power.

It is unclear how much literary knowledge and culture was lost in the book burning, but one thing is certain: The sayings of Confucius and the classics associated with him had circulated too widely and inspired too many readers to be suppressed that easily.

Even though followers of Confucius did not expect the same kind of religious benefit that accrued to Buddhists replicating sutras, the book burning taught later Confucians the advantages of paper and print for ensuring the wide circulation and hence the survival of their texts.

Because Confucius had been a servant of the state and had taught the importance of maintaining public order, his teachings became of particular interest to rulers and bureaucrats. Less than a hundred years after the book burning, the Confucian classics were elevated to the rank of official state-sanctioned texts. An Imperial Academy was created, which laid the foundations for the earliest form of the imperial examination, an institution that would last, in one form or another, until 1905.

The exam became the chief vehicle for recruiting servants of the state, the bureaucratic class that was charged with running the vast Chinese Empire. It required students to know the Confucian classics, among other texts, and tested that knowledge in a three-day ordeal. On a trip to Nanjing, which had been the southern capital of the Chinese realm, I visited the site of the exam system. The candidates would sit in stone cells, perhaps four feet by five feet, subsisting on whatever provisions their families had prepared. It was December and cold, just above freezing. The stone cells, arranged in rows that formed a large quadrant, were open to the air, so candidates would be exposed to the weather. One wooden board served as desk, another as bench, and if the candidates chose to waste time sleeping, they would have to curl up on the bench as best they could. If they did well, they would advance to the next round of tests and then to the next until they arrived at the final and most prestigious exam, held in the capital. The reward was a lucrative government job. This exam system, unique in the world, put the study of literature at the heart of the Chinese political system (indirectly it inspired the creation of the SAT exam system in the United States). Designed to exclude military aristocrats from the highest levels of government, it gave unprecedented power to literary education. For two thousand years, China was ruled by an elite schooled primarily in literature.

The vast exam system required candidates to have access to the classics, which was made easier by paper and print. Beginning in the tenth century, the state responded to rising demand by having the Confucian classics replicated by woodblock printing on paper.

The same desire to create a canon of Confucian literature led to another, more unusual phenomenon, one seemingly at odds with the new world of paper and woodblock print. In the second century C.E., the classics were ordered to be carved in stone, what became the stone classics of Xiping, the first of many such endeavors. (Buddhist sutras were carved in stone as well.) Were these stone libraries a throwback to earlier times, before the invention of paper and print? More likely, these libraries were a reaction to the early effects of paper, which had led to a proliferation of unreliable versions of these important texts.

I visited one such stone library, in the Imperial Academy in Beijing. The texts were carved on stone steles that were eight or nine feet tall and carefully arranged in columns and rows. Wandering through them was like walking through a labyrinth of words. The writing was small, almost delicate, yet one never doubted its permanence. There was no room for alterations or corrections, or for commentary, and rearranging their order would be difficult. No wonder that the statue of Confucius looked serene, proud of the stone library carved in its name.

CHAPTER 5

MURASAKI AND
THE TALE OF GENJI:
THE FIRST GREAT NOVEL
IN WORLD HISTORY

1000 C.E., KYOTO

———

I STILL REMEMBER MY SURPRISE WHEN I LEARNED THAT THE FIRST great novel in world literature was written by a lady-in-waiting at the Japanese court around the year 1000 C.E. We don't even know the real name of the author, who came to be known by the name of her unforgettable female protagonist—Murasaki. This anonymous court lady created a literary world of screens, fans, and poems that was unlike anything written before. It revolved around the romance between a prince who found himself demoted to the status of a commoner and an aristocratic woman hidden away in the countryside. In developing this story, Murasaki Shikibu gave her readers unparalleled access to the thoughts and desires of her characters, whose lives were confined by strict court etiquette and gender roles. But despite the limits imposed on them, these characters kept growing in complexity chapter after chapter, to the delight of her courtly readers. By the time *The Tale of Genji* was complete, it had become an intricately woven narrative of great depth and elegance.

The writer knew firsthand about the restricted lives of women at the Japanese court. As the daughter of a provincial governor, she was one rung below the sphere of the protagonists of the book, but still part of the world she described. In order to be able to operate in that world, Murasaki Shikibu had been taught to compose short poems in Japanese. But Murasaki Shikibu was not content with the poetry and calligraphy deemed appropriate for a woman of her station. Above all, she wanted to learn the mysterious and challenging Chinese writing system, which alone promised access to the ancient literary traditions of China, so highly revered in Japan. But Chinese literature was traditionally reserved for men.

Determined to achieve her goal, she learned Chinese writing secretly by eavesdropping when her brother took Chinese lessons and by practicing in private when no one was watching. Soon she was outdoing her brother in Chinese letters. When her father became aware of her accomplishments, he lamented: "Just my luck. What a pity she was not born a man." When she reached marriageable age, Murasaki Shikibu was given to an older man in a typical arranged match. She was fortunate in that her husband possessed a library of literary texts, which allowed her to continue her studies, thus profiting from her arranged marriage much as her young protagonist would.

Murasaki Shikibu's secret study of Chinese literature came on top of a thorough education in Japanese literature. For this, she had been born into the right family. Her great-grandfather had his poetry included in one of the first major poetry anthologies written in Japanese. Like so much in Japan, this anthology was indebted to Chinese models. While most cultures revere long epic narratives such as the *Epic of Gilgamesh* or the *Odyssey* as the foundation of their culture, in China it had been the so-called *Classic of Songs*, a carefully arranged poetry collection, that served as the most studied text (and was later attributed to the editorial hand of Confucius as part of the Confucian classics). The very idea of establishing Japanese literature through a poetry anthology thus followed a Chinese tradition. At the same time, Japanese writers had begun to keep historical records, a sign of increasing cultural independence, and Murasaki Shikibu studied these texts with great interest as well.

Learning Chinese and the historical records of Japan was a risky undertaking. Even though Murasaki Shikibu tried to hide her knowledge, sometimes she let it slip inadvertently. The emperor himself once remarked, half admiringly, how deeply Murasaki Shikibu must have studied Japanese history, giving rise to rumors that Murasaki was flaunting her knowledge. She knew that she had to be more careful in the future. For a woman, learning Chinese letters and Japanese history just wasn't done. In a world where gossip and politics were indistinguishable, attracting the wrong kind of attention, or seeming not womanly enough, could have dire consequences. To protect herself, she began to pretend that she couldn't read even the most common Chinese inscriptions on paper screens.

When her husband died, Murasaki Shikibu suddenly found herself with enough freedom to put her hard-won literary education to use, and she began to write individual chapters of what ultimately would become *The Tale of Genji*. Even though the work was called a "tale," it soon expanded beyond the scope of a simple story into a minute account of life at the Heian court. Murasaki Shikibu's secret knowledge of Chinese literature shone through in many allusions to Chinese poetry, but the final work bore little resemblance to Chinese literature. A new literary form, it signaled Japan's growing sense of cultural independence.

This type of literature was not something that a male scholar immersed in the Chinese literary tradition would ever have dreamed of writing. Paradoxically, the discrimination against women had put them in a better position to innovate than their privileged male colleagues, who remained fixated on tradition and Chinese writing.

A World of Paper and Screens

In portraying the inner workings of the Japanese court, Murasaki Shikibu knew she was doing something daring. She carefully set the story a hundred years in the past in order to spare the feelings of the powerful Fujiwara clan, to which she belonged. The Fujiwara clan controlled the emperor through careful marriage politics, a topic to which *The Tale of Genji* pays minute attention. The head of the clan—Murasaki Shikibu's patron—would not appreciate a candid account of the levers of power (a history of the Fujiwara clan, written anonymously, is sometimes attributed to Murasaki).

The court was located in today's Kyoto, a rectangle of three and a half by two and a half miles, surrounded by a stone wall and modeled on the Chinese city grid and building style. The city's population numbered about a hundred thousand, and Japan's overall about five million, but the novel was not written for or about these multitudes. It was written for the few thousand who lived close to the court and who had at least an inkling of the restricted world of high society. Proximity to the emperor was everything.

Courtiers might venture outside the city in search of Buddhist temples or hidden-away beauties, or both, but they quickly returned to the urban grid that was their natural habitat. Outside the city, the houses were drab, the dialects strange, the poems flat, and the calligraphy hopelessly crude.

In *The Tale of Genji*, such a trip sets off the main plot. On a foray to an out-of-the-way temple, Genji catches a glimpse of a girl through the blinds of her dwelling, but she quickly retreats deep into the women's quarters, protected by a small army of attendants. Highborn women were difficult to see, and almost impossible to approach. The barriers separating women from men came in layers: stone walls, wooden fences, bamboo blinds, fabric curtains, and paper screens. Light, six-panel folding screens were made of rice paper; other screens came in heavier, richly ornamented and lacquered frames, but they, too, would be made of paper. If a man got too close, a fan, also made of paper, would protect a woman's face from his sight. Even sons, male siblings, and uncles might never meet their female relatives face-to-face. A woman of marriageable age could go about her life unseen by any man other than her father.

Women were strictly protected, but the protection was often literally paper-thin; it blocked sight, not sound. Lurking outside the compound, Genji, the Shining Prince, had overheard someone inside compose an impromptu poem referring to the girl as a shoot of spring grass. He now composed a short response poem picking up on that theme and recited it to an attendant. He hoped the girl would overhear him and respond. Everyone in court society was able to compose short poems—elegant sentences, really—written on special paper. Of all the things made of paper, poems were the most important. A good poem was supposed to take something from the natural world—a plant, a flower, an animal—and relate it to the occasion being written about. Every poem demanded a response. Even everyday business was sometimes conducted through these short poetic exchanges, which allowed people to hint at their true intentions without having to spell them out.

In a society in which much depended on hints and allusions, poems were a crucial means of communication. During a normal day at court, hundreds of such poems would be exchanged. The more delicately indirect, and the more a poem resonated with other poems, the better. But if someone could not think of a good poem on the spot, a mediocre one would do, as long as it fulfilled its purpose of communicating through allusions what should not be said directly.

When the girl did not respond and her warden rejected his advances, the Shining Prince returned to the capital. But he didn't give up. He composed another poem, alluding to the fact that he had caught a glimpse of her through screens, and he took care with his handwriting. He folded the poem into a knot and wrapped it casually to make it look as if he was not making much of an effort. Knowing how to handle paper was everything in this paper-made world, in which even hats, clothing, all kinds of household implements, and weapons were manufactured from this miraculous material. Every paper surface was an invitation for a poem. There were poems composed on the paper-paneled folding screens that dominated the interior of aristocratic quarters. In the story, the Shining Prince might compose a poem on a lady's fan or exchange fans with poems already written on them with her. In Genji's present situation, however, it was best to stick to the usual method of crafting a poem on special paper, wrapping it in another layer of paper, and sending it through a messenger.

This time there was a response, but it was not what he had hoped for. The girl's attendant, a nun, told him that her charge was too young for an amorous dalliance. The Shining Prince knew that the object of his affection was only ten years old. This was admittedly young, but not unheard-of. He himself had been married off at the age of twelve, and some women were married earlier than that. Arranged marriages of this kind were part of the elaborate social system at court, with rival clans striving to place daughters close to the center of power, ideally as principal wife of the emperor. Children of the emperor's lesser wives had more uncertain prospects, as the Shining Prince knew only too well. His own father was the emperor, but his mother was only a lesser wife and was therefore looked down upon by wives with more influential backers.

When faced with the most powerful clans, even the emperor was powerless. Forced to recognize the weak position of his favorite son, the emperor had decided to take the Shining Prince out of the power game by demoting him to the status of a commoner. This was how the Shining Prince had acquired the name of Genji, which signaled his new status, even though people still referred to him as the Shining Prince out of deference.

What should Genji do about the girl and her recalcitrant attendants? Even though marriages happened at an early age, this ten-year-old girl was immature for her age, her attendants had insisted. They had given her Genji's poem, as demanded, but to no avail. The problem was that the girl hadn't learned to compose poems yet. This, Genji had to admit, was indeed a sign that she was young for her age. A girl incapable of writing poems was too young for love.

When, shortly thereafter, Genji heard that the girl's father, who had long neglected her, was planning to remove her from Genji's reach, Genji knew he needed to act swiftly. Under a pretext, he drove to the girl's residence. This time, he cast aside all convention and decorum and barged through the blinds, curtains, and paper screens, ignoring the shrieks of protest from her startled attendants. The girl was sleeping, but the prince simply wrapped her in his arms, soothed her when she stirred, lifted her into his carriage, and drove off. It was all for her own good, as he saw it. At his compound, he could take her under his wing and make sure that she would have proper attendants and prospects. He could personally take charge of her education, which had clearly been neglected, and turn her into a proper young woman.

For many readers (myself included), this opening is deeply disturbing: Kidnapping a ten-year-old girl, against the wishes of her father, doesn't sound like a great recipe for a healthy relationship. Murasaki Shikibu's early readers reacted differently. They might be mildly scandalized by a male lover's abducting a ten-year-old girl, but they would not pass censure on the larger marriage system that made such acts possible. And they admired the Shining Prince despite his flaws, applauding the process by which he matured.

Above all, they would admire how Genji taught the girl to write poetry, watching *The Tale of Genji* become a story of literary education. There was more to poetry than natural images and allusions. What mattered above all was how the words were written. The ability to manufacture high-quality paper had ushered in a golden age of calligraphy, an art required of women and men who hoped to succeed at court. Since poems were such a central form of communication, much could be revealed about temperament and breeding through one's style of writing, which was done with various kinds of brushes. Anyone unlucky enough to be living outside the capital and its court society might practice outmoded styles (or, unthinkably, not know how to write calligraphy at all). Genji wanted to make sure this would not happen to his young ward. He himself would take care to compose model characters that the girl could use for her practice.

Once the girl had been established at his home and meddling relatives dealt with, Genji wrote another poem. There were many kinds of paper to choose from, of different colors, types, and qualities. He chose a paper of deep purple, a color achieved through a dye using the roots of a special plant, the gromwell. This poem, and the plant to which it alludes, would give the girl her name: Murasaki. Through this poem, Genji names his great love: "I've yet to see the purple roots of the gromwell—how I long for the wisteria's little kin."

The novel continues:

"Why don't you try writing something?" Genji encouraged her. . . . "But I can't write well," she protested, looking up at him. She was so lovely he couldn't help but smile. "Even if you can't write well, you must at least try. You won't get better if you don't write anything. Let me show you." He found it charming the way she held her brush and how she turned away from him when she wrote. . . . Her writing was quite immature, but he could see at once that she had the talent to be accomplished in composition. The lines of her brushstrokes were rich and gentle, and they resembled the hand of her late grandmother. If she practiced more modern models, he knew that she would be able to write very well.

Encouraged by this show of promise, Genji continued to teach the girl the art of writing beautifully. He improved on her brushstrokes. He showed her how to choose the right paper and how to wrap a poem. He was making a proper court lady of her.

CHINESE WRITING, BRUSH TALK, AND JAPANESE LITERATURE

The paper culture of the Heian court originated in China. For hundreds of years, Japan had adopted Chinese civilization and science, an extreme case of one culture accepting most of the products of another. While usually such wholesale cultural transfer was the result of military occupation, Japan adopted Chinese culture of its own free will (Rome had similarly assimilated Greek culture).

In order to stay in touch with Chinese culture, Japan had periodically sent official missions across the narrow Korea Strait separating Japan from the mainland. The languages the Japanese emissaries and their Chinese hosts spoke were mutually incomprehensible, but they could communicate by writing in Chinese signs. Because Chinese signs were not phonetic, the Japanese had been able to adapt them to their own language, pronouncing the Chinese signs in Japanese. It was much as speakers of different languages might negotiate over the price of a purchase by writing down numbers on a piece of paper. Even though they might pronounce the numerical signs differently in their respective languages, they could all understand the meaning of the written numbers. In the same way, Chinese and Japanese emissaries could thus communicate by writing shared signs. This form of writing-based communication across languages, the great advantage of nonphonetic writing systems, was called *brush talk*.

Among the cultural products imported to Japan were the literary works written in Chinese characters, including the Confucian classics. They didn't need to be translated because the educated elite was taught to read the Chinese signs directly, simply pronouncing them in Japanese. The poems exchanged at Genji's Heian court often subtly alluded to the Chinese classics as well as to more recent literature, and a Chinese academy had been created in the capital as a center of learning and education, based on the Confucian classics.

In China, the Confucian classics had led to the imperial exam system, which guaranteed successful candidates lucrative government jobs and sinecures. This exam system had never taken hold in Japan because Japan's powerful clans and families wanted to control access to power through marriage politics, not through an exam system over whose outcome they might not have much control.

Thus, in Murasaki's story, when Genji decided to send his son to the Chinese academy, the son was not thrilled. He would have preferred to receive a high-level government appointment based on his family connections, as was the custom, without having to labor at the university alongside students of much lower rank.

But there was no question of Genji's ever sending young Murasaki to the university or teaching her Chinese characters. Chinese literacy was officially the preserve of men and was focused on serving the state (in addition to praising the past). Perhaps the complicated Chinese writing system, with its thousands of signs, was considered beyond the grasp of women, or else keeping women away from this cultural source code was simply a way of preserving male privilege, as the author, Murasaki, knew only too well. Women were supposed to use a different writing system known as the *kana script*—the script in which *The Tale of Genji* was written as well.

The kana script was originally invented to serve another Chinese import: Buddhism. Buddhism emphasized detachment from the world and an appreciation for fleeting moments of beauty. Many poems exchanged at the Heian court were written to capture this sense of an ephemeral world. Buddhism had also profited from the paper and print revolution, perhaps even more so than Confucianism. The earliest surviving examples of print in China, Korea, and Japan were all of Buddhist sutras. The *Diamond Sutra*, the earliest surviving printed work in the world, and the *Lotus Sutra* were particularly influential in Japan, where both were reproduced and recited frequently. It was while practicing Buddhist devotions at a temple outside the city that Genji had first discovered the young Murasaki, who, later in the novel, would sponsor mass reproductions and readings of sutras, including the *Diamond Sutra*.

Buddhism brought along an entire writing system. Japanese monks had traveled all the way back to India in search of original texts. There they had encountered Sanskrit and the Sanskrit alphabet in which a number of the original Buddhist sutras had been composed. Because Japanese monks were keen to proselytize their Buddhist faith, they recognized the advantages of the phonetic Sanskrit writing system over the thousands of signs in Chinese writing. They decided to attempt something similar for the Japanese language and created the kana script.

The new system identified forty-seven distinct sounds used in spoken Japanese, and expressed them with forty-seven signs. Some signs captured syllables instead of individual sounds, a phonetic system known as a *syllabary*.

The kana syllabary was somewhat more complicated than a phonetic alphabet because spoken languages contain more syllables than individual sounds. But it was still infinitely simpler than the nonphonetic Chinese system. Another advantage of the new Japanese writing system was that it represented the specific sounds of Japanese rather than bending Chinese signs to a language they were not intended for. In keeping with the Buddhist origin of the new writing system, young students memorized the forty-seven signs by reciting a Buddhist poem that used each of the forty-seven sounds exactly once.

Initially, the kana script was less prestigious in Japan than the traditional Chinese characters, but it was deemed good enough for women, such as the writer Murasaki. In *The Tale of Genji*, the prince trained the young character Murasaki to write in the kana script, and it was in this script that all courtiers had to write when they communicated with women through short poems. The kana script had found a foothold in court society. It made possible the everyday poems on which this society depended for its most important communications.

In *The Tale of Genji*, when Genji had succeeded in teaching the girl calligraphy, poetry, and the kana script, he took her as his wife. She was then twelve years old, the same age at which he himself had first been married. Despite the care Genji had lavished on her, she was taken by surprise. The morning after their wedding, Genji left a poem for her, as custom required. Overwhelmed by the sudden change in their relationship, she did not respond. Genji looked in the box in which she was supposed to leave her response to his morning-after poem, and it was empty. But the marriage was accomplished anyway. It was confirmed when Genji ordered that rice cakes be served, the conventional signal that a marriage had been consummated. Before long, his young wife got used to the new relationship and put her training to better use, writing poems when Genji initiated an exchange. One of the great love stories of world literature had begun.

A GUIDE TO COURTLY LIFE

In the world that the writer Murasaki portrays, life is so intensely focused on the capital and the court that exile constitutes an unbearable hardship, a punishment just short of death. In *The Tale of Genji*, the Shining Prince experiences this form of hardship when he is exiled from court for a particularly outrageous affair with one of the emperor's lesser wives. An affair like that, if handled discreetly, might be fine, but in this case Genji made the mistake of focusing his attention on the sister of his enemy at court, the member of a rival clan. When the affair became public, banishment was the only answer.

He decided that he could not take his wife, Murasaki, with him. When the time came for parting, the lovers looked at their reflection in the mirror and then took leave of each other, naturally enough, in the form of poetry:

> Though my body must wander in exile
> My image will never be far away
> Reflected in this mirror by your side.

Murasaki replied:

> Though we are apart, I may find solace
> If perhaps by gazing in this mirror
> I should glimpse your image lingering there.

And thus the afterimage lingered in the minds of the two famous lovers until their reunion.

For Genji, living away from court was a hardship that required much Buddhist meditation on the vanities of a fleeting world. Ultimately he was allowed to return from exile two years later. He picked up his old life, enjoyed new promotions, and won new glories, but the experience of exile lingered. He had returned a changed man. The feeling that only life in the capital was a life worth living ran deep. Even becoming a provincial governor was seen as banishment. And as for commoners, they clearly were beyond the pale, in the countryside even more than in the city.

Only someone who had once lived at court could appreciate how much the minute details and rules Murasaki Shikibu captured in her novel really mattered: how women should hold their fans; what kinds of scents were most attractive in men (Genji spent hours mixing the most unusual perfumes and was widely admired for it);

under what circumstances a man could move closer to the screen concealing a woman; when he might actually reach through the screen and take hold of a woman's sleeve; and when he could push aside the screen and force his way onto a reluctant lady without getting into trouble. It is difficult to imagine a more restricted world, especially for courtly women, who were confined to interior rooms and banned from speaking to anyone but their attendants. Courtly men at least could venture outside the city and occasionally visit a relative or friend, but they, too, were everywhere hemmed in by rules and conventions.

All the attention the writer pays to protocol and decorum has the effect, on her readers, of inducting them into this society. After reading the thousand pages that comprise *The Tale of Genji*, I almost felt as if I could begin to operate in this strange world, that I had passed a crash course in its most basic rules and rituals. As Genji was educating Murasaki, so the author was educating me, and her other readers.

While Murasaki Shikibu did not attack the court system that allowed men to abduct young women and then confine them to their rooms, she showed her readers how little that system of rules could do to control the desires, fears, and fantasies of those living under them. These rules drove characters into illicit affairs or destructive jealousy, an emotion from which the character Murasaki suffered late in life. And everywhere, characters struggled with the restrictions imposed on expressing their emotions. When the new emperor learned that Genji was his real father (the result of Genji's affair with one of his father's lesser wives, his most indiscreet act), the emperor was so confined by court protocol that he could rarely speak to Genji or visit him for fear of arousing suspicions. He felt he could not reveal what he knew directly. Instead, the emperor communicated with his father on the occasion of his fortieth birthday by sending sketches and calligraphy.

Poems were the place where etiquette and raw emotion met.

Murasaki Shikibu composed, for the novel, almost eight hundred poems. In the book, they are sent back and forth between friends and courtiers, between fathers and sons, and above all between lovers. Not all her poems were perfect—and they weren't meant to be. Forced to compose in the moment, some characters, like Genji, excelled at the art of poetry from the beginning, while others, like young Murasaki, needed to learn before they could write poetry at a high level. But in aggregate, the poems formed the center of the novel; they were the chief manner in which characters communicated. For Murasaki Shikibu the poems were also a way to establish her tale as serious literature. In a culture based on poetry collections—Chinese collections and Japanese kana collections such as the ones associated with her great-grandfather—the long prose tale she was writing could gain legitimacy and authority only by including as many poems as possible.

I was not surprised to learn that in Murasaki Shikibu's time, *The Tale of Genji* taught readers how to behave so effectively that it was used as a manual of court etiquette. Both women and men would read it in order to write better poems, strike more effective poses, and learn when to withdraw from a suitor's unwanted advances (and when to give in to them). No doubt, it also allowed its readers to enjoy more elegant and radiant characters than real life had to offer. From *The Tale of Genji*, they would learn that if a courtier visited a woman three nights in a row, this constituted a marriage (and would be made public by serving rice cakes to the beloved). A reader might learn how to appreciate the moon, and with whom (only with a carefully chosen companion). At the same time, readers living in the confined world of the Heian court could also recognize the emotions beneath these conventions, the struggle between rules and desires that was expressed so poignantly in the novel's pages.

It is possible that *The Tale of Genji* was originally written for an audience of one. With her early chapters, Murasaki Shikibu had attracted the attention of the empress Shoshi and had been offered a position as attendant to her daughter. This position had many advantages, giving Murasaki Shikibu access to the inner sanctum of power, including the emperor himself. It allowed her to expand on the earlier versions of her tale, perhaps conforming them more fully to the needs and preferences of her new patron. The empress requested more installments, and Murasaki Shikibu kept producing them, until *The Tale of Genji* grew beyond the lifetime of its heroine, who died after having become a Buddhist nun halfway through the novel. Murasaki Shikibu continued the tale into the next generation and then into the one after that, creating a true multigenerational novel. None of the younger characters could approach the radiance and grace of Genji and his Murasaki, even as they found themselves compelled to repeat many of their patterns. Just as Genji had fallen in love with a woman living in obscurity outside the capital, so his grandson would do the same. While Genji had been driven to his great love for the young Murasaki because she reminded him of his stepmother, with whom he had been in love throughout his life, so his grandson fell in love with a hidden-away woman because she reminded him of someone he had loved in vain (both resemblances were the result of family relations). In this way, Murasaki Shikibu used the ever-expanding scope of her work to weave an intricate pattern of repetition and variation that gave her novel its distinctive shape. Ultimately *The Tale of Genji* grew twice as long as *Don Quixote*, the first important novel in the European tradition, written half a millennium later.

The size of the work and its tiny audience meant that there was never a question of using the technology of print, which had made its way long before from China to Japan. Woodblock printing made sense only for short works that would be reproduced by the thousands, such as Buddhist sutras, not a large work written for an extremely small readership. *The Tale of Genji* circulated in copies that had been written by hand on paper, still a precious commodity, and remained expensive even for this privileged readership. A complete set was a highly prized possession. Around 1051, a young court woman recorded the best present she had ever received: "the fifty-odd volumes of the *Genji,* all in their own box." She went on: "When I lay down alone behind my screens and took it out to read, I would not have changed places even with the empress. All day and as far into the night as I could keep my eyes open I read with the lamp close by me." Those eager to show off their wealth, or their dedication to *The Tale of Genji,* could purchase deluxe editions on special paper or with illustrations (many precious and illustrated editions survive). Those who could not afford their own private copy might get their hands on individual chapters, which circulated separately, or listen when a chapter was read aloud in company.

Only hundreds of years later, beginning in the sixteenth century, did printed copies emerge to satisfy a new market driven by a growing merchant class and rising literacy rates. By that time, Japanese court life had changed so much that the novel was read no longer as a manual but much as we read it today (and as Ashurbanipal had used the *Epic of Gilgamesh*), namely as a window into the remote past. Because the novel had been written for a small audience familiar with the rules governing behavior at court, it now had to be explained to later readers, leading to extensive commentaries on the text. Even today, we know much more about life at the Heian court during the Middle Ages than about almost any other place on earth during that time because of the incomparable *Tale of Genji.*

The most magical capacity of literature has always been that it gives readers access to the minds of others, including those long dead. In Murasaki's hands, that capacity increased significantly over earlier works. Like no one before her, she allowed her readers to observe the thought processes of her characters and to view their distinctive world through their eyes.

The success of the novel, first through handwritten copies and then through print, caused jealousy. Even though *The Tale of Genji* paid homage to the two literary sources of Japanese culture, Buddhist sutras and the Confucian classics, the novel itself was very different from either, and Confucians and Buddhists sensed that a new and powerful type of literature had emerged on the scene. Before long, Confucians warned against the novel, and Buddhists described its author as suffering for her sins in hell. Despite such powerful detractors, *The Tale of Genji* proved unstoppable. This expansive novel with its hundreds of poems became a cultural reference point, a common stock for quotations and pieces of wisdom rivaling earlier literature, solidifying Japan's cultural identity and independence from China.

For hundreds of years, *The Tale of Genji* enjoyed its reign over Japan, first as a manual, then as a historical picture, and finally as a classic, but it remained confined to the island nation. Only after 1853, when Japan was forced to open trade relations with the West, did the rest of the world get a first inkling of this text—appropriately enough, in the form of *Genji* screens. This novel had become so significant to Japan that scenes from it were commonly depicted on screens, and some of those screens had made it to Europe at a time when new trade opportunities had created a fashion for all things Japanese. Fans, too, arrived, beautifully adorned with Murasaki's writing. The paper culture that Murasaki had described was now sending her work to Europe and from there to other parts of the world.

Western collectors began to wonder where those scenes, so stunningly painted on paper screens and fans, came from, and they got a first glimpse of the text through a partial translation in the late nineteenth century. But the entire *Tale of Genji* erupted into Western consciousness only with the translation by Arthur Waley in the early twentieth century, almost a thousand years after this text was first composed. The Western world found, to its great surprise, that novel writing, which many considered among the distinct Euro-

A SIX-PANEL FOLDING SCREEN BY KANŌ TSUNENOBU (1636–1713),
DEPICTING SCENES FROM *THE TALE OF GENJI*.

pean contributions to literature, had been invented a thousand years earlier by a Japanese woman whose name we don't know.

AN AUTHOR LOOKS BACK

One day, when the woman we know as Murasaki Shikibu was no longer working on *The Tale of Genji*, she looked out onto a lake, where the waterbirds were increasing in number day by day. Her rooms at home had been much simpler than the splendor of the palace, to which she had grown accustomed. She was reminded of how she used to take note of the flowers, the birdsongs, the way the skies changed from season to season, the moon, the frost, and the snow. But she had since withdrawn, watching the seasons listlessly, painfully aware of the loneliness she had felt ever since her husband had died. Much had changed since then; she had become an attendant at court, and an author. In the course of this new life, she had lost touch with some of the old companions with whom she used to exchange poems. What could she do now to chase away her loneliness, her bitter mood?

Sometimes when this mood struck, she would turn to her library, which was now neglected, the paper crawling with silverfish, and take up an old Japanese tale or even one of her Chinese scrolls. She would remember how Her Majesty, the lady she had served, had asked her to read Chinese poetry to her, and how she had regretted it because word had gotten out and gossip started about her unusual learning. But today she took up her own book, *The Tale of Genji*. Earlier, the head of her clan, the most powerful person in Japan, had taken her fair copy of the text and given it to his second daughter. But rather than enjoy this success, Murasaki Shikibu worried that certain passages in *The Tale of Genji* would hurt her reputation at court. Perhaps reading her tale, which had grown to such large proportions, would dispel her loneliness. It didn't work. *The Tale of Genji* didn't give her the pleasure it used to, and Murasaki Shikibu was deeply disappointed. Finally, she took a brush and wrote a poem to a fellow attendant, realizing that those who served with her at court were now her only intimates. When her friend wrote back, Murasaki Shikibu admired the calligraphy and began to feel a little better.

How do we know, a thousand years later, what this enigmatic author thought on that particular day? Murasaki Shikibu had given us access to the intimate thoughts and musings of her characters with the hope that readers and listeners would care about the ambitions and disappointments of her fictional creations. But she had done something else as well, something equally modern: She had recorded her own thoughts and musings in the form of a diary.

Her diary is the source of what we know about Murasaki Shikibu, from her clandestine education in Chinese literature to her role at court. It spans only two years, but it is enough to give us a snapshot of her life at court, supplementing the fictional picture that emerges from her novel. In the diary, she showed an eye for etiquette, for screens and fans, for poems and printed curtains. She described how she had concealed her knowledge of Chinese letters when it had become a matter of gossip. Even more than the novel, the diary was written for a small, intimate audience. It, too, might have been written for a single reader; it is addressed to an unnamed young woman who might be Murasaki Shikibu's own daughter. Was Murasaki Shikibu trying to teach her daughter what Genji had taught her fictional namesake?

Murasaki Shikibu was not the only court lady to keep a diary. After the introduction of the kana script, diaries had flourished among court ladies, who reported in them about love affairs, poems exchanged, and many other daily matters with elegance and wit. Sometimes these diaries were seen as verging on gossip, but through the sharp pens of their more ambitious practitioners, they became an art form. Murasaki Shikibu's contemporary and rival, the quick-witted Sei Shonagon, enjoyed success with her frank and licentious diary called *The Pillow Book*. Similarly, the diary of the young girl who had been given *The Tale of Genji* as a present became a late Heian classic. Like Murasaki Shikibu, most of these women were daughters of provincial governors, close enough to court society to know it well but not in actual positions of political influence, which would have precluded them from becoming authors. So clearly was this new form of literature associated with women that when a male author published his own diary, the *Tosa Diaries*, he presented it as the writings of a fictional female writer.

An author who writes a confessional diary—nothing could be more familiar to us today. We live in an age of the diary, of the memoir, of the blog. A first rule of creative writing programs is "Write what you know." But the history of literature shows just how unusual autobiographical writing really was. Like all things, it had to be invented. There is a widespread belief that autobiographical writing was invented by Saint Augustine, writing in late antiquity in order to give an account of his conversion to Christianity. But self-writing was independently practiced at the Heian court by highly literate women. Their very seclusion within the restricted world of the court must have played a role in helping them come up with this form. Sequestered by walls and blinds and screens and fans, these women were thrown back onto themselves, observers of life around them but also observers of themselves. For Murasaki Shikibu, the two literary forms, the novel and the diary, were driven by a similar impulse to give us a glimpse into the inner lives of human beings real or imagined. Indeed, she gave us a second diary, this one entirely poetic and therefore highly allusive, a diary composed of personal poems that were arranged chronologically, providing us with indirect hints of their elusive author, as if spied through a screen.

Toward the end of her prose diary, Murasaki Shikibu fell back into a melancholy mood. She no longer worked on *The Tale of Genji* or corresponded with intimates through poems. All she cared about now was her diary. The diary was not written on special paper or even on new paper. Murasaki Shikibu, who described a world of splendid paper fans and paper screens, of paper lamps and paper poems, of calligraphy and paper dyes, found herself writing her diary on old, used paper. In her diary, she wrote:

> Recently I tore up and burned most of my old letters and papers. I used the rest to make dolls' houses this last spring and since then I have had no correspondence to speak of. I feel I should not use new paper so I'm afraid this will look very shabby, but I am not trying to be rude; I have my reasons.
>
> Please return this as soon as you have read it. There may be parts that are difficult to read and places where I have left out a word or two, but just disregard them and read it through. So you see—I still fret over what others think of me, and if I had to sum up my position now I would have to admit I still retain a strong sense of attachment for this world. But what can I do about it?

Even though Murasaki Shikibu was despondent and had lost faith in *The Tale of Genji,* she still cared about her writing. After having been made a wife to an older man and an attendant to a princess, the identity she chose to retain was the one she had acquired by her own initiative: that of an author.

CHAPTER 6

One Thousand and One Nights with Scheherazade

The First Millennium c.e., Baghdad

When did you first encounter *One Thousand and One Nights*? I don't remember when I did; it feels as if I have always known some of the stories. Perhaps it was Popeye meeting Ali Baba? Sinbad the Sailor in a children's book? Or someone saying "Open sesame"? *One Thousand and One Nights* is everywhere. Like a Jinni, the stories in this collection change their shape and assume any number of guises, thriving on the page and in the theater, in comic books and in animated films. As soon as a new form of entertainment is invented, *One Thousand and One Nights* presents itself, ready to inspire wonder and suspense, delight and horror, in new audiences yet again.

Realizing that I had been exposed to stories from *One Thousand and One Nights* my entire life without always knowing it, I wanted to know where these stories came from.

The earliest source is a small fragment from the ninth century c.e. One side of the fragment contains the draft of a legal agreement, written by a lawyer for a client, but the flip side, badly worn, bears the title page of *One Thousand and One Nights*. What clues about their provenance can we extract from this small piece of evidence?

The first is that the lawyer didn't seem to like this story collection very much, or else he wouldn't have used it as scrap paper. Perhaps the licentious nature of these tales, populated as they are by flamboyant thieves and passionate lovers, didn't appeal to his legal mind. But why did this lawyer have a fragment from this story collection lying around in his office in the first place? Had he indulged in guilty reading and was now trying to eliminate the evidence by recycling it? No matter what the lawyer was doing with these tales, there can be no doubt that they were already popular enough to have been written, sold, bought, and finally reused, in a surprisingly negligent manner, in the ninth century. In order to find the origin of *One Thousand and One Nights,* I needed to go further back.

My search brought me to a Baghdad bookseller, Ibn Ishaq al-Nadim. He lived a hundred years after the lawyer, but fortunately he had studied the history of this story collection as part of a catalog of Arabic literature. In the course of this enormous project, Al-Nadim had posed the same question I had, namely where these stories had come from. He surmised that they originally came from a Persian collection called *A Thousand Stories*—in Persian, *Hazar Afsan.* Probably the Arabic collection had begun as a translation of *A Thousand Stories* into Arabic as *Alf Layla,* which means "a thousand nights." Once the collection was available in Arabic, it must have acquired more tales, because many of the tales have Arabic themes and characters, with some of the best set in Baghdad during the reign of the great Islamic caliph Harun al-Rashid, who often wanders through these stories in disguise in order to get to know the commoners.

My favorite invocation of Baghdad, in the collection of tales that make up *One Thousand and One Nights,* is the opening of the story "The Porter and the Three Ladies of Baghdad":

Once upon a time there was a Porter in Baghdad, who was a bachelor and who would remain unmarried. It came to pass on a certain day, as he stood about the street leaning idly upon his crate, behold, there stood before him an honourable woman in a mantilla of Mosul silk, broidered with gold and bordered with brocade; her walking shoes were also purfled with gold and her hair floated in long plaits. She raised her face veil and, showing two black eyes fringed with jetty lashes, whose glances were soft and languishing and whose perfect beauty was ever blandishing, she accosted the Porter and said in the suavest tones and choicest language, "Take up thy crate and follow me."

The Porter was so dazzled he could hardly believe that he heard her aright, but he shouldered his basket in hot haste saying in himself, "O day of good luck! O day of Allah's grace!" and walked after her till she stopped at the door of a house. There she rapped, and presently came out to her an old man, a Nazarene, to whom she gave a gold piece, receiving from him in return what she required of strained wine clear as olive oil; and she set it safely in the hamper, saying "Lift and follow." Quoth the Porter, "This, by Allah, is indeed an auspicious day, a day propitious for the granting of all a man wisheth." He again hoisted up the crate and followed her; till she stopped at a fruiterer's shop and bought from him Shami apples and Osmani quinces and Omani peaches, and cucumbers of Nile growth, and Egyptian limes and Sultani oranges and citrons; besides Aleppine jasmine, scented myrtle berries, Damascene nenuphars, flower of privet and camomile, blood red anemones, violets, and pomegranate bloom, eglantine and narcissus, and set the whole in the Porter's crate, saying, "Up with it."

So he lifted and followed her till she stopped at a butcher's booth and said, "Cut me off ten pounds of mutton." She paid him his price and he wrapped it in a banana leaf, whereupon she laid it in the crate and said "Hoist, O Porter." He hoisted accordingly, and followed her as she walked on till she stopped at a grocer's, where she bought dry fruits and pistachio kernels, Tihamah raisins, shelled almonds and all wanted for dessert, and said to the Porter, "Lift and follow me." So he up with his hamper and after her till she stayed at the confectioner's, and she bought an earthen platter, and piled it with all kinds of sweetmeats in his shop, open worked tarts and fritters scented with musk and "soap cakes," and lemon loaves and melon preserves, and "Zaynab's combs," and "ladies' fingers," and "Kazi's tit-bits" and goodies of every description; and placed the platter in the Porter's crate. Thereupon quoth he (being a merry man), "Thou shouldest have told me, and I would have brought with me a pony or a she camel to carry all this market stuff." She smiled and gave him a little cuff on the nape saying, "Step out and exceed not in words for (Allah willing!) thy wage will not be wanting."

They are not even done shopping yet.

This story celebrates the markets of Baghdad, situated at the center of a trade empire that brought goods from as far away as Tibet, the Balkans, and Egypt. We see these goods through the eyes of the overawed yet quick-witted porter, whose adventure has just begun. *One Thousand and One Nights* delights in the market because the market was the environment in which this story collection came into its own. Intended for a broader audience than court literature, it was born and for sale in the market, a favorite among merchants.

If the story collection came to Arabia from Persia on the same trade network that brought all these delicious foodstuffs to the markets of Baghdad, the next question was: Who had assembled it? Ibn Ishaq al-Nadim, the bookseller, came up with a surprising answer:

A MARKET IN CAIRO, FROM A NINETEENTH-CENTURY EDITION
OF *ONE THOUSAND AND ONE NIGHTS*.

Alexander the Great. Alexander the Great, Al-Nadim reported, was
eager to hear such stories at night, in his camp, in the company of
his friends and associates.

But wait—didn't Alexander have plenty of bedside reading already? After all, he had brought Aristotle's copy of the *Iliad* on his
world-spanning campaign and put it under his pillow every night.
Apparently, the great Macedonian king didn't always find Homer
quite suitable when he lay awake at night. For this purpose, Alexander preferred different fare, stories such as the ones told by
Scheherazade. Being Alexander, he didn't just enjoy these stories;
he also collected them and had them written down to preserve

them for posterity. To be sure, these tales weren't going to displace Homer from his central position; perhaps they didn't even make it into the library of Alexandria. But Alexander nevertheless wanted them to endure and did what was necessary to make sure that they did.

It was a wild theory, identifying Alexander as the collector of *One Thousand and One Nights*, but Al-Nadim was onto something. After all, Alexander's own life was fantastic enough to gain him admission to this collection.

On night 464 of *One Thousand and One Nights*, we hear the story of Alexander's encounter with a people that possessed nothing (much like the wise Indian philosophers Alexander encountered, according to other sources). Alexander summoned their king, who refused to present himself. Alexander, with his usual determination, sought him out, posed questions, and finally received a word of wisdom: "Everyone is your enemy because you are rich, while everyone is my friend because I possess nothing."

But just because Alexander appeared in *One Thousand and One Nights* didn't mean that he assembled the collection. In fact, many of the tales came from sources that were considerably older than the Macedonian king. Take the story of the two thieves who each planned to kill the other after a successful robbery. When they sat down to dinner after the deed was done, one killed the other with his sword. Satisfied with his handiwork, he ate his food, started to choke, and realized that his dead companion had plotted to kill him by poisoning the food. The story comes from the *Jataka Tales*, one of the earliest existing story collections, put together by Buddhist priests in India. (Later, John Huston would use this story for his film *The Treasure of the Sierra Madre*.) Another story, of the ebony horse that could fly through the air, also comes from India, while others hail from the Mediterranean world or Persia.

When I contemplated these sources, I wondered whether Al-Nadim was thinking of Alexander because the great conqueror was in a perfect position to collect these tales. Not only was he a confirmed promoter of literature, as his dedication to Homer showed; his empire also brought into constant contact some of the regions, from Greece to India, that were most closely associated with story collections. All across Alexander's empire, people were borrowing and exchanging stories and making them their own. Alexander might not be the actual collector, but his short-lived realm covered much of the Eurasian landmass that supported the network of tales behind *One Thousand and One Nights*.

Still without an answer to my question about the origin of these tales, I returned once more to the earliest piece of evidence, the flip side of the legal contract. As I was scrutinizing it, my eyes fell on something I hadn't thought much about before: Scheherazade. The fragment contained not only the title page but also the opening, and that meant the famous frame tale of Scheherazade, her sister, and the king. The key to *One Thousand and One Nights* was not the origin of this or that story but what held them all together, namely their unforgettable narrator. I began to read the framing story with new interest.

WHY SCHEHERAZADE KNEW SO MANY STORIES

It was a provocative and strange tale that began with Scheherazade's father, the most important minister of the realm, who couldn't believe his ears when his daughter announced that she would offer herself as the next wife to the king. Scheherazade knew all too well that the king had gone mad after catching his wife in the arms of another man, a dark-skinned slave. In his pain and shame, the king had not known what to do except to flee, seeking solace in the company of his brother, who would soon be in a similar state of mind, discovering his own wife with a lover and killing them both. With this brother, the king had roamed the countryside and returned, declaring that he would take revenge on women. He ordered that a

new bride be brought to him every night. After having had his pleasure with her, she would be killed. Scheherazade's father was in
charge of procuring the women and killing them afterward. And
now his own daughter was volunteering to become the next victim.

Scheherazade's father tried everything to dissuade his daughter.

THIS NINETEENTH-
CENTURY LITHO-
GRAPH BY THE
PERSIAN ARTIST 'ALI-
KHÂN DEPICTS THE
SCENE OF INFIDEL-
ITY MENTIONED IN
THE FRAME TALE OF
*ONE THOUSAND AND
ONE NIGHTS.*

He pleaded with her and he threatened her, but nothing worked.
In his desperation, he told her stories of stubborn folly as a warning
of what would happen to her, but she stuck to her plan. In the end,
he ran out of stories and was forced to announce to his astonished
master that Scheherazade would be joining him that night.

Scheherazade was stubborn, but not suicidal. She had a plan,
which required the presence of an assistant, for which role she
chose her own sister. The sister would join them in the king's bed-
chamber, discreetly waiting for the lovemaking to end, and then
ask Scheherazade for a story. The plan worked, the king agreed to
the sister's request, and Scheherazade started to tell stories, stories
of great kings and clever commoners, of wisecracking animals and
frightening demons, of dark passages and fantastic adventures, sto-

ries of magic, morality, and wisdom. Scheherazade made sure that as dawn approached each night, the story was unfinished. This way she had to be allowed to live another day, so the king could hear the end of the story.

The king listened and was hooked. He wanted to hear the end of each story and the beginning of a new one, living from cliff-hanger to cliff-hanger. More and more nights were spent in this manner, lovemaking followed by a story, with no end in sight. Scheherazade was safe, provided she kept on telling stories that had to be continued the next night. From now on her fate, and the fate of all remaining women of the realm, would reside in a woman's powers of storytelling.

But how had Scheherazade come up with all these stories? Surely she could not have invented them on the spot. Rather, she was tapping into the great ocean of stories humans had been telling one another, stories of adventure, love, and crime; fairy tales; stories of famous kings; and stories of wisdom and instruction such as the ones with which Scheherazade's father had tried, unsuccessfully, to change his daughter's mind.

The impulse to tell stories, to put events into a sequence, to form plots and bring them to a conclusion, is so fundamental that it is as if this impulse is biologically rooted in our species. We are driven to make connections, from A to B and from B to C. In the process, we develop ideas of how to get from one point to the next, what drives a story forward, whether the answer is cosmic fate, chance, social forces, or the will of a protagonist. Often characters harbor a secret they must not reveal, and yet we long to pry into it, and by the law of storytelling, their secret is forced out of them, if only to satisfy the king's and our curiosity. No matter what forces drive these protagonists, we watch them make their way through hostile or friendly circumstances, and before we know it, a story-teller has created an entire world.

The worlds of our stories often obey different rules, some fantastic, some sober, some set in the remote past or remote parts of the world, others more familiar and closer to home. This is what imagination and language allow us to do, to create scenes that are different from what we see right in front of our eyes, to make up worlds with words. Scheherazade excelled at this task, taking the king and her sister from plot to plot, protagonist to protagonist, world to world. In this storytelling universe, anyone you meet on the street harbors a story, often full of marvels and coincidences; a beggar might have been born a king, and even a simple porter may have something to tell: Everyone is a story.

For the longest time, storytelling had existed prior to and then below the radar of literature. Stories were told orally by professional storytellers or amateurs, and only on rare occasions did stories insinuate themselves into the exclusive world of literature. But ultimately, more and more popular stories found scribes willing to preserve them and assemble them into larger collections. Less prestigious than sacred scripture, and not as rarefied as Murasaki's *Tale of Genji*, these tales were for sale in the marketplace. While they sometimes were collected in libraries, their primary audience consisted of merchants (who could relate to the inventory of the market of Baghdad given in the story "The Porter and the Three Ladies of Baghdad").

Once I reread the framing story of Scheherazade and the king, I realized that what had looked like an account of an ingenious oral storyteller was in fact an account of an avid reader. Unwittingly, her own father had prepared her for this task when he had given her the run of his library. Throughout her childhood and adolescence, Scheherazade had spent her days devouring everything within the library, from literature to history and philosophy; even medical tracts didn't escape her attention. She had acquired the reputation of a reader and scholar, a bookish heroine, whose natural home was the library, not the king's bed, until she combined the two by turning the king's bed into a place of storytelling.

In order to find the origin of *One Thousand and One Nights*, I needed to find out who had invented Scheherazade. The answer was hidden in her function, in what she did for the collection of stories. Scheherazade not only told the stories but also selected, arranged, and adapted them to the situation in which she found herself, faced with a king who had gone mad. In this she resembled the scribes who selected, arranged, and adapted the stories they had heard from all over the world, wrote them down, and put them into this and other story collections. I began to think of Scheherazade as the personification of these scribes, and the way in which they wrote themselves into the story. Scheherazade was the one in control of the stories, the queen of the scribes.

By inventing Scheherazade as a more appealing version of themselves, the scribes who left us *One Thousand and One Nights* had stumbled upon a powerful tool, what we now call a *frame-tale narrative*, a tale such as the one in which Scheherazade was forced to come up with stories in order to save her life. Frames provided drama and increased the stakes for each story. They created suspense by making it necessary to gain time. They also gave the stories a new purpose. Many a night, Scheherazade told of marital betrayals and infidelities, by men and women alike, as if to tell the king that infidelity is part of life; other stories showed examples of constancy, as if to remind him that fidelity was possible. A good number of stories revolved around good kings, above all Harun al-Rashid, the famous caliph of Baghdad, as if to implore the king to become a good ruler again.

Eventually, Scheherazade succeeded. Her stories turned the king from his murderous hatred of all women, teaching him how to be a good husband and a good king once again. This is the happy ending of the unforgettable frame of some versions of *One Thousand and One Nights:* The king was cured; he gave up on his revenge and married Scheherazade, who moved in with her entire library. Her sister, who had patiently asked for more and more stories, was given in marriage to the king's brother.

HOW TO FRAME TALES

Over time, frame tales became magnets that drew certain tales toward them while filtering out others. With Scheherazade as their primary storyteller, *One Thousand and One Nights* attracted those tales that spoke of love and kingship, tales that might have a chance of transforming the king. Tales unsuitable to this task were more likely to be neglected. Frames didn't always control all the tales within them, but over time they acted as sorting mechanisms, giving shape and identity to an entire collection.

   One Thousand and One Nights was not the only, nor the earliest, story collection with a frame tale. One famous frame tale comes from the Indian *Jataka Tales* (from which *One Thousand and One Nights* borrowed several stories), which consists of animal fables, but the frame adds a completely different twist to them: They are told by the Buddha. The Buddha used them to instruct his students, to teach them lessons, and to help them remember important points of doctrine by putting himself in them. After telling the tale of the duck who bore golden feathers only to be plucked clean, for example, the Buddha revealed that it was he, the Buddha, in a previous incarnation, who was the generous duck so greedily abused. The scribes putting together this collection had used animal fables as a vehicle to spread the words of the Buddha. The *Jataka Tales* is one of the written records of the Buddha (along with the Buddhist sutras), showing just how much a particular frame could add direction and purpose to what otherwise would have been just another collection of animal fables.

   If the Buddha seemed a far cry from Scheherazade, she did have a relative in India, where another scribe created a collection told by a parrot. Like Scheherazade, the parrot needed to distract his owner night after night with his storytelling prowess, although for a different purpose: His mistress had begun to cast eyes on other men while her husband was away, and the faithful parrot wanted to keep her from committing adultery.

The most frightening frame tale comes from India as well. It began when a king was induced by a visiting hermit to enter a fearsome cemetery to fetch a corpse that was hanging on a nearby tree. When the king touched the dead body, harrowing laughter erupted from within, and he realized that a vampire inhabited this corpse. Brave king that he was, he plucked the body, including its resident vampire, off the tree, slung it across his shoulder, and started to leave. The vampire seemed happy enough to go along, and to pass the time it told a story and then asked the king about its moral. When the king failed to come up with a satisfactory answer, the vampire flew back to the tree and the whole thing started over again.

This framed collection was included in the *Katha Sarit Sagara,* the *Ocean of Streams of Stories,* collected by a Brahmin scribe from Kashmir named Somadeva in the eleventh century. Faced with so many story collections, Somadeva had drawn the only sensible conclusion: He had created a supercollection, which housed within its eighteen volumes different discrete collections, many with frames of their own, and he combined them all within a frame tale.

The number of tales is unfathomable, like drops in the streams that form the ocean of all existing stories. Scribes have created frames with which to catch these stories, fishing them out of the ocean of stories and arranging them in different ways. Scribes preserve them, putting them in the mouths of speakers who tell them for their own purposes, to convince their listeners, or amuse them, or distract them, or educate them, or simply to pass the time. Clever frames, whether they featured wise men, brave women, forward parrots, or condescending vampires, became a way to assemble as many stories as possible and yet give them structure and purpose and meaning and to create resonances among them. This framing device was so powerful that later authors borrowed it freely, so much so that they wrote up their own story collections and their own frames. Literary history is full of these modern story collections, from Chaucer to Boccaccio, making framed collections one of the great forms of world literature, stretching from the classical age all the way to the present.

This was all very interesting, but I still didn't have an answer to my question about the origin of *One Thousand and One Nights*. As I was pondering this question, I had a dream. In my dream, I overheard Scheherazade tell the following story: *During the reign of Harun al-Rashid*, Scheherazade said to the king, *there lived a scribe in the city of Baghdad. He was a copier of documents and contracts. He had no wife or children, and he spent his time in the company of books and ledgers. One night, he heard a knock. He did not expect visitors, but the knock sounded friendly and he opened the door. In the dancing light of his candle, he saw a strange creature, clad in foreign clothes. At first the scribe thought it might be the caliph of Baghdad, who was known to wander the streets in disguise. Uncertain, he asked the creature's name, but it only answered with some words that sounded like "Hazar Afsan," the Persian phrase for "a thousand stories." Seeing that it had no home, the scribe let it into his house. The creature proved to be such a delightful companion that the scribe decided to let it stay. He taught it Arabic words and manners and gave it a proper Arabic name: Alf Layla. Alf's easy ways soon made it a favorite among the merchants, who let it linger among their stalls in the marketplace, where it often slept during the day. When the sun went down, Alf came alive, diverting and amusing merchants and townspeople, anyone who wanted to come, until they forgot their fears and worries.*

News of Alf reached the ears of a jealous Jinni. The Jinni hid behind a sack of almonds in a remote corner of the market, and when Alf passed by, weary from a night of entertainment, the Jinni sud-

denly stepped forward and made itself as large as a house. Alf looked up at the imposing figure and said: "My dear Jinni, I am so glad you have come. I have always wanted to meet you. Only my neck hurts from looking up so high. Could you please make yourself smaller so we can converse more easily?" No one had ever spoken to the Jinni in this way, as if they had been friends all along. In its astonishment, the Jinni forgot its evil design and the two became friends.

When the time came for parting, the Jinni gave Alf a flying machine made out of the best paper. "It is better than a flying carpet because it is very light. Just be careful and don't tear it," the Jinni warned. Carefully Alf stepped onto the paper carpet and flew with it wherever it wanted to go, as far as Cairo and Damascus, winning admirers everywhere. Untouched by age, it lived in this fashion for centuries, until it became restless again and used the paper carpet to fly across the sea to Europe. First Alf was taken up by an enthusiastic Frenchman, who taught it the French language. In England, it kept company with a British traveler of uncertain sexual proclivities. Despite this questionable company, Alf was soon feted across Europe.

The more famous it became, the more people kept asking: Who are you? Where are you from? Looking for Alf's parentage became an obsession. Scholars arrived from far away to examine it, often taking hold of the creature in the most impolite manner. Some declared it had Arabic origins; others noted its Persian name; a third group suspected Indian blood. Their inopportune approaches threatened to tear the delicate paper machine to bits. Exasperated, Alf finally exclaimed: "Enough! Don't you understand that I am an orphan? Those who go looking for my parents will only find themselves. I am the offspring of your own dreams and longings. Accept me as part of yourself, or be rid of me." Then it patched up its paper carpet and flew away.

As I woke up, I understood the dream as a warning against the futile search for the origin of *One Thousand and One Nights*. Clearly, I had been asking the wrong question. As my thoughts returned over and over again to the dream, I imagined that Scheherazade was telling me something else. I went back to the earliest fragment of the tales, the one used by the lawyer as scrap paper, and realized that I had overlooked the most important clue, which was not Scheherazade's frame story.

The most important clue was the fact that the lawyer's fragment of *One Thousand and One Nights* was the earliest evidence of a paper book in the Arabic world. Instead of origins, I needed to look for the technology—in this case, paper—that gave these stories wings to fly from India to Persia and from Baghdad to Cairo as if driven by the magical powers of a Jinni.

THE ARABIC PAPER TRAIL

Invented in China, the art of making paper was kept secret for hundreds of years, during which time it transformed society—for example, by changing how quickly Buddhist sutras could be multiplied. Because paper was unusually smooth and yet could absorb ink cleanly, it allowed for unheard-of precision in writing, which resulted in a flowering of calligraphy.

Korea and Japan eagerly learned the art of papermaking as a result of their close cultural ties to China (as reflected in *The Tale of Genji*). China's neighbors to the west could see and purchase this miraculously thin and light writing material, but they didn't know how to produce it. Papermakers were sworn to secrecy. For hundreds of years, the secret of papermaking remained in the Chinese cultural sphere.

The story of how this secret was finally disclosed is probably unreliable, but it shows how highly the knowledge of papermaking was regarded, as well as the route by which papermaking reached Arabia. The transfer of knowledge occurred when the expanding Chinese cultural sphere encountered the ancestors of Harun al-Rashid, residing in Baghdad, who were trying to expand eastward.

The two powers collided in July 751 at the Battle of Talas, in today's Kazakhstan.

The city of Talas was crucial because it was located on the Silk Road connecting China and Persia. In the battle, the Arabs prevailed thanks to defections on the Chinese side, and many of the ten thousand Chinese warriors were killed. Some were taken prisoner, among them professional papermakers. It is not recorded whether the Arabs extracted the papermaking secret by force, and if so how they managed to do it. But extract it they did, and the most powerful writing technology was in the hands of the rising Arab world. (The Battle of Talas also diminished the influence of Buddhism in the region, ultimately leading to the closing of the Caves of the Thousand Buddhas, where the earliest surviving printed work was found in the late nineteenth century.)

The Arabs improved on the newly acquired technology. Chinese paper was usually made from fibers of the mulberry tree, important to Chinese culture because it also hosted silkworms. Mulberry trees did not grow well in most of the Arabic world, and a substitute had to be found. The Arabs came up with a perfect solution: old rags. Through beating and other physical treatment, the fiber contained in rags could be decomposed to form the basis for paper. This substitution proved crucial for the history of paper, allowing it to leave its ancestral homeland in East Asia. From then on, rag collectors would be roaming the world wherever the secret of papermaking was known.

At first, papermaking was centered in Samarkand, today's Uzbekistan, but before long it spread along the Silk Road via Persia to the Arabic heartland and the capital, Baghdad, governed by its most famous caliph, Harun al-Rashid. A large territory such as this needed a large bureaucracy, and the advantages of paper over its alternatives, papyrus and parchment, soon became clear. Following the recommendation of his wise vizier, Harun al-Rashid turned Baghdad into the center of papermaking in the Arabic world, boasting its own stationer's market. The stories in *One Thousand and One Nights* follow the same route, from Samarkand to Persia and then to the Baghdad of Harun al-Rashid.

Paper powered an explosion of writing and intellectual activity, ushering in a golden age of Arab letters. Harun al-Rashid established the first public library in the Arabic world, an institution that his son would turn into Houses of Wisdom, centers of learning, scholarship, science, and mathematics (the reason we use Arabic, rather than Roman, numerals in the West). The Houses of Wisdom soon propelled the Arabic world to the forefront of knowledge at a time when the fall of Rome ushered in an era of decline in Europe. Because of the importance of Baghdad to writing culture, large sheets of fine paper became known as Baghdadi.

The biggest question was whether paper should be used for holy scripture. Like other charismatic teachers, the prophet Muhammad did not write. He received the Qur'an by divine inspiration, beginning in 610 C.E., and recited what he received to his followers. But some of his followers began to write down what they heard (or to recite it to scribes), either during his life or after his death in 632 C.E. Originally, this writing was done on palm branches, palm leaves, papyrus, or other materials. When a more complete text was created, these fragments were written on parchment sheets and bound into codices, the preferred format used by Christians in the Roman Empire. In this way, yet another teacher who had not written a single word ended up as the figure behind a new sacred scripture, which, like all other sacred scripture, inspired traditions of textual fundamentalism that have reached all the way into our own era.

When paper arrived in the Arabic world, scribes accustomed to parchment soon recognized the advantages of the new material. At first they continued to use parchment for the holy Qur'an, in light of that material's greater traditional status. But ultimately they ended up using paper for copying the Qur'an as well, the final sign that paper had conquered the Arabic world. Paper was perfect for the art of calligraphy (a quality equally appreciated in East Asia) giving rise to elaborate writing styles now closely associated with Arabic culture and productions of the Qur'an.

Because paper was cheaper to make, because it lowered the cost of producing literature, it was also perfect for popular tales such as the ones found in *One Thousand and One Nights*, which managed to thrive in its environment better than any other piece of literature. This is why the earliest paper fragment is not from the Qur'an but from this popular story collection. The collection acquired more and more stories, flourishing in the paper environment. Perhaps this is why this story collection turned the biggest promoter of paper in the Arab world, Harun al-Rashid, into the ruler of so many of its tales.

In Japan, the greatest impact of paper had been on the sophisticated creator of *The Tale of Genji*, Murasaki Shikibu. In the Arab world, it ushered in an early form of popular fiction. An Indian story collection, the *Panchatantra*, designed to educate princes, was translated into Persian as *Kalila and Dimna* and then into Arabic just around the time when paper was taking off. Changes in writing technology tended to have this double effect. On the one hand, they allowed older, foundational texts to thrive (though sacred texts sometimes adopt new technologies more hesitantly, as was the case with the Qur'an). This is not surprising, since foundational texts are often at the center of a writing culture and are therefore in the best position to profit from new technologies. At the same time, new technologies tended to make writing cheaper, thus lowering the bar for entry into the written world. The result was invariably a flowering of popular literature. *One Thousand and One Nights* profited from this effect: Having existed below the radar screen of scribes, the tales now asserted themselves as a new and compelling form of literature. And thanks to paper, literature became more compact and lighter than ever before, letting *One Thousand and One Nights* circulate among Damascus, Cairo, and Istanbul with ease.

The expansion of the Arabic empire finally brought both paper
and *One Thousand and One Nights* to Europe when Muslim in-
vaders captured a large part of Spain. We still count paper in reams,
a word that was adopted into Spanish from the Arabic *rizma*. From
there, paper slowly filtered into Christian Europe, where it first encountered resistance from scribes accustomed to parchment (just
as it had first encountered resistance from Arabic scribes charged
with duplicating the Qur'an). But such resistance did not last long,
and ultimately Christian Europe recognized the advantages of
paper. First came Sicily, long the home of a sizable Arab population, then northern Italy. One of the earliest papermaking facilities
north of the Alps was set up in 1390 in Nuremberg. Astonishingly,
it had taken more than six hundred years for paper to travel from
Samarkand to Europe. *One Thousand and One Nights* soon traveled in its wake, fueling the imagination of European writers such
as Boccaccio and Chaucer, who were so intrigued by story collections that they created their own versions, freely plagiarizing, or
rather adapting, what they could find.

When *One Thousand and One Nights* was translated into
French, it caused such a sensation that the translator, Antoine Galland, couldn't translate fast enough. People mobbed him in the
streets, asking for the next installment. With their fantastic plot
turns, the tales were not beloved by all, but their popularity made
them unstoppable. Then the unthinkable happened: Galland ran
out of stories. In his hour of need, in 1709, he thought of his heroine Scheherazade and realized that he needed to find more stories.
Instead of a Persian lady, he found a young Syrian man, an accomplished storyteller, Hanna Diyab, who produced more and more
tales by combining different stories in inventive ways. Some of the
most famous stories, such as Aladdin and Ali Baba, were produced
in this manner; no Arabic or Ottoman original has ever been found
for them.

All early versions of *One Thousand and One Nights*, including the longest, Syrian manuscript, are written on paper, but they were not printed; they were all written by hand. In retrospect, it is surprising that the Arabic world was an enthusiastic adopter of paper, possibly extracting the secret by force, but showed little interest in print, which in China was so closely associated with paper. One reason was that Arabic script was cursive, which made it more difficult to capture letters in discrete typefaces. Arabic scribes also created an efficient technique for reducing copying mistakes. A reader would recite a text to a whole battery of scribes, who in turn would recite it to a group of their own, thereby limiting the number of generations of copies. Reproduced by hand (and mouth), *One Thousand and One Nights* was popular, but it remained precious. Storytellers would borrow the text to learn stories by heart, like Scheherazade herself, and then pass them on. The first printed version of *One Thousand and One Nights* in Arabic was not produced until the nineteenth century, a sign of the ambivalence many felt about this collection of tales (the first printed version of the Qur'an was made in 1537, in Venice).

This makes the Arabic world a great test case for the transformative effects of paper without print, resulting not just in beautiful versions of the Qur'an, adorned by calligraphy, but also popular literature such as the tantalizing tales told by Scheherazade. Paper here reveals its two sides, leading to a high culture based on its calligraphic qualities and a popular culture based on its widespread availability. It was thanks to these two features that paper, a technology worthy of a Jinni, helped *One Thousand and One Nights* to travel the world.

Orhan Pamuk's Istanbul

If it was impossible, and pointless, to trace *One Thousand and One Nights* to a single origin, then I wanted to gauge its influence on contemporary writers. I decided to go to Istanbul to meet Orhan

Pamuk, a recent Nobel Prize laureate, whose novels include themes and characters from the famous story collection.

With the kind help of friends, I was able to meet Pamuk at his apartment, near the Taksim neighborhood of Istanbul, recently gentrified to boast a charming mix of trendy cafés, secondhand stores, antiques dealers, and old bathhouses. A guard was posted at the door, a reminder that Pamuk had had a difficult time of late. While at first many Turks had been pleased to have a Turkish writer break into the international market, more recently Pamuk had become an object of controversy when he used the term "Armenian genocide" in an interview with a foreign newspaper, referring to the killing of millions of Turkish Armenians at the end of World War I. He was promptly sued by the Turkish government for "defaming Turkishness" and received death threats from right-wing thugs. He moved to New York until the lawsuit was dropped as a result of pressure from the international community. Back in Istanbul, he still had to be careful. His apartment—he referred to it as his office, though he had been mostly based here for sixteen years—overlooked the Bosporus and—ironically, given his contentious relation to Islam— a beautiful mosque.

Pamuk's work often dwells on the Ottoman Empire and its long history, so I expected him to embrace *One Thousand and One Nights* as well. With his singsong Turkish intonation, Pamuk explained to me that for the longest time he had instead avoided these stories, because they suggested an exotic and unrepresentative view of the Islamic world—more Galland than authentic Islamic literature. Pamuk didn't say so, but I also suspect that the stories were too popular. After all, Pamuk was writing in the tradition of the European novel, especially the Russian novel, as he later explained during a lecture series at Harvard. I could see the point: Baghdad storytellers don't usually get the Nobel Prize in Literature.

And yet even Orhan Pamuk couldn't avoid the story collection entirely. When I pointed out that figures and motives from the story collection show up in his work with frequency, he admitted that somehow these stories had found their way into his writing.

Pamuk's reaction makes sense in light of the surprising journey of *One Thousand and One Nights* from East to West. They are as much a product of Europe as of India and Arabia, a strange hybrid between East and West, properly belonging to neither. Truly, what matters is not the origin of the stories but the ingenuity of those who collect them, write them down, distribute them, and use them. So what if they inspired a Syrian storyteller of the eighteenth century to add to their store, following the demands of the market?

Encouraged by this conversation, I wandered the streets of Istanbul, headed for the upscale neighborhood of Nişantaşı, where Pamuk had grown up in an apartment building named after the family that owns it: Pamuk Apartments (in an autobiographical book, *Istanbul*, he describes the move of Western-oriented families from traditional compounds to "modern" apartment buildings). What I was looking for was not Pamuk's youth, however, but Aladdin, the name of an all-purpose store that features prominently in his novel *The Black Book*.

A kind of murder mystery, Pamuk's *The Black Book* revolves around strange disappearances and two murders that take place in and around Alâaddin's shop. When I located the store, it looked more like a kiosk, overstuffed with everything you could desire and didn't need, from toys to books. As I tried to make sense of this strange place, I realized that Alâaddin's kiosk was a brilliant choice: Truly, *One Thousand and One Nights* is the toy store of literature, to which every reader and writer can go for amusement and enlightenment.

I was here with Pelin Kivrak, one of Pamuk's assistants, and Paulo Horta, an expert on *One Thousand and One Nights*. We were strolling around the neighborhood and Pelin was pointing out different sites that were part of Pamuk's novel. At one point, she took us to a perfectly ordinary house and identified it as the residence of the protagonist of *The Black Book*. Pelin, Paulo, and I were standing there, craning our necks, looking at the apartment. I wasn't sure what to think. Suddenly a window opened and someone looked back down at us, wondering suspiciously why three people were looking and pointing at his apartment. The two worlds, normal Istanbul and Pamuk's Istanbul, were beginning to overlap, or even clash.

That was when it struck me how absurd travel can be, the desire to go looking for traces of fiction in the real world. At the same time, the scene also spoke to the power of literature. Somehow, Pamuk had managed to transform this perfectly ordinary apartment house into something special, suffusing it with a fiction that was drawing us into its orbit. Perhaps at some point the residents will realize that they are no longer ordinary inhabitants of this part of Istanbul but have been miraculously transported into a novel, a marvel worthy of *One Thousand and One Nights*.

CHAPTER 7

GUTENBERG, LUTHER, AND THE NEW PUBLIC OF PRINT

CIRCA 1440, MAINZ

JOHANNES GENSFLEISCH WAS LOOKING FORWARD TO THE FAIR OF 1439. Every seven years, the cathedral of Aix-la-Chapelle (Aachen), on the border between Germany and France, would display its precious relics to pilgrims. On the appointed day, the clergy and the city council would enter the cathedral from different sides and converge on the wooden case housing the relics. A silversmith would remove each item, read the tag attached to it, and carefully place the precious object in a wooden carrying case. When full, the case would be marched ceremonially to the altar. A band of musicians would go first, followed by the clergy and councilmen, all bearing candles. The church bells would be rung, a trumpet would be sounded, and when the relics arrived at the altar, a gun would be discharged.

These were just the preliminaries before the main show began. The bells would chime nonstop for half an hour and then suddenly fall silent. Then each relic would be held up high for all to see and carefully placed on a black velvet cloth, accompanied by the deafening sounds of hundreds of horns that pilgrims had brought, called

Aix-la-Chapelle horns, to mark the occasion. The yellow-white gar-
ment of the Mother of the Savior would be shown in this way, as
well as the swaddling clothes of the Savior. The cathedral also
boasted the cloth that was laid on the body of Saint John the Baptist
after his decapitation and the cloth that the Savior wore around his
loins in the dreadful hour of his death. In addition to these major
relics, the cathedral possessed part of the rope with which the Savior was tied in his passion and a small fragment of the sponge that
had served to refresh him upon the cross; a fragment of that cross;
and two teeth of the apostle Saint Thomas. In addition, of Saint
Mary Magdalene, the cathedral claimed both a shoulder bone and
a leg bone.

The crowd gathering to witness these treasures would be immense. Tens of thousands, perhaps even a hundred thousand, pilgrims would descend upon this medieval town, eager to set eyes
upon the sacred objects. There was no way the cathedral could
hold them all, so guards would be posted around the building.
Those barred from entering would occupy every open space around
the cathedral and climb onto nearby roofs in order to catch a
glimpse of these mysterious objects, which promised to transport
their beholders all the way to the Near East, to Jerusalem and the
religious passion that had taken place there fourteen hundred years
earlier. The greatest miracle of all was that merely by being in the
presence of these relics, pilgrims were promised remission of all
sins. Small wonder that they were eager to be near them.

Gensfleisch was not thinking about the relics themselves or
about the remission of his sins. Instead, he was pondering a technical problem: Many pilgrims would be too far away to see, feel, and
experience the relics. Aix-la-Chapelle had come up with a solution
to this problem. Pilgrims could buy a small ornament, about four
inches high, showing holy figures cast in tin. When the relics were
displayed, pilgrims could lift these ornaments and catch the light

rays emanating from the relics. Some ornaments had a small mirror attached to them to heighten this effect, which is why they were called *pilgrims' mirrors*. The mirrors worked across distance and allowed each pilgrim, no matter how far from the shrine, to take home some of the luster of the relics themselves.

Demand for these mirrors had been so great that the smiths of Aix-la-Chapelle, whose guild enjoyed the monopoly of making them, couldn't keep up with it. In anticipation of the upcoming fair, the city council had therefore decided to suspend the guild's monopoly for the duration of the fair. Anyone would be allowed to come and sell pilgrims' mirrors. This was what Gensfleisch was thinking about: He sensed a business opportunity.

Gensfleisch was contemplating this prospect 170 miles to the south, in Strasbourg, where he had recently moved from his native city of Mainz. Gensfleisch came from a family of rich Mainz merchants and had received a decent education, acquiring proficiency in Latin, which had given him access to the religious and philosophical literature available in that language. In addition to this scholarly education, he had learned practical skills such as casting metals. But he was not a member of the goldsmiths' guild, nor a certified master of that trade. His family drew its income from lands in and around Mainz and from long-distance trade along the river Main. Members of this class were known by the name of their principal residence in town. In the case of Gensfleisch, it was the Hof zum Gutenberg, which is why he was sometimes called Johannes Gutenberg.

It was his skill in metalwork that Gutenberg was now seeking to bring to the making of pilgrims' mirrors. Through trial and error and his experience with casting coins, he had come up with a better way of manufacturing these trinkets than the usual technique, cumbersome and imprecise, of casting them using sand. He had invented a new casting instrument, and he knew that he could produce the mirrors in greater quantities and with greater precision. Given the large market, this technical advantage could translate into a handsome profit.

In order to set up shop, he needed manpower and materials, which meant he needed capital. Where to get it? His time in Strasbourg had not been without its difficulties. First, there was the breach-of-promise suit brought by a prominent burgher's daughter. Gutenberg didn't want to ponder the details of this unfortunate affair, nor of the trial, during which he had cursed a witness and promptly been charged with a fine by the city. Since he wasn't even a citizen of Strasbourg, he needed to be more careful in the future. Then there had been all kinds of financial worries. His family had settled a pension on him, to be paid by the city of Mainz. Suffering from financial difficulties, Mainz had simply stopped the payments. But Gutenberg didn't let them get away with that. When an official Mainz city scribe showed up in Strasbourg on unrelated business, Gutenberg took the law into his own hands and seized him. This episode showed traits crucial for invention: ruthlessness, even recklessness, in the face of opposition.

After much negotiation between Mainz and Strasbourg, Mainz relented and agreed to pay the pension. But even with the Mainz money flowing again, Gutenberg needed more funds. Rather than borrow the money outright, he set up a company to which he would bring his invention while the others in the company would bring additional technical skills and capital. With the suspension of the guild's monopoly on producing mirrors, Gutenberg and his company could make and sell mirrors at will. But the flip side of this freedom was that they were entirely on their own, without the protection that a guild normally provided to its members. If others got wind of the matter, nothing would prevent them from simply copying his new method. The only solution was absolute secrecy, which Gutenberg sought to ensure with elaborate contracts.

Then, surprisingly, Aix-la-Chapelle postponed the festival for a year, probably on account of the plague, which had made an appearance again in this part of Europe. Gutenberg and his partners would have to wait another year to realize the profits they anticipated. But the gamble paid off. The fair of 1440 was so popular that an entire roof collapsed under the weight of pilgrims who had crowded onto it to catch a glimpse of the relics.

Gutenberg had not risked everything on his mirrors. There was a second, even more secret venture. This second enterprise had begun when the fair at Aix-la-Chapelle was postponed and had required a second infusion of capital from Gutenberg's partners, in return for which Gutenberg had promised to reveal an even more promising scheme. From the way Gutenberg had set up the partnership, it was clear that he was working on something big. It had to do with applying his technique of casting pilgrims' mirrors to the making of books.

Whatever it was, Strasbourg increasingly became a difficult place to do business, and Gutenberg decided to move back to his hometown. The first thing he did in Mainz was to raise funds again. At first he turned to relatives, but it became clear that he needed more money than they could provide. He needed to form another partnership, one much larger than the one he had formed in Strasbourg, with a major investor who would understand his new project and commit significant funds. In Johann Fust, a rich patrician, he found a financier willing to bet what would eventually be large sums on a risky venture. Thanks to those funds, Gutenberg assembled a small workforce consisting of various trades and talents, including a trained scribe, Peter Schöffer, and various metalworkers. After swearing them to secrecy, Gutenberg revealed to them the invention that would change the world.

How Inventions Are Made

There is a temptation to think of an invention as the work of a genius who single-handedly changes the world. But this is rarely how inventions are made. In order to get a better sense of how the invention so often attributed to Gutenberg actually occurred, I traveled to the city of Mainz.

Today, Mainz feels small and provincial, dwarfed by nearby Frankfurt, but it was once well connected by the river Main to long-distance trade routes. Proudly, Mainz has dedicated a museum to its most famous accomplishment. The museum is in the center of town, near its large cathedral. Both the cathedral and long-distance trade turned out to be important for the invention of print in this part of the world.

Gutenberg was not the first to think of using movable letters and combining them to form pages that could be printed. Just as with the pilgrims' mirror, others had done so before him. He had long known about the relatively simple technique of carving images into wood and using them like stamps to make copies, as was routinely done in making playing cards. As long as one didn't care too much about quality, the same could be done with words. Small booklets had been made this way, with awkward wooden letters allowing readers to decipher the printed words with some difficulty.

This woodblock technique had come from the Far East via the Silk Road, which connected China to the Mongols and Uighurs, who in turn maintained trade with faraway Constantinople and thus indirectly with the rest of Europe. In Mainz, known for long-distance trade, Gutenberg was also in a good position to hear rumors that the Chinese were now producing printed books not just by carving text page by page onto whole blocks, but also by making individual letters and then assembling them to form sentences. Such letters were sometimes made of harder, more precise materials, including ceramic and metal alloys.

Whatever Gutenberg had heard, he was embarking on his own project along similar lines. His invention, if we still want to call it that, was based on an idea transfer, at the very least. The Gutenberg

Museum, which used to celebrate Gutenberg as the inventor of print with movable letters, has adjusted its narrative accordingly. It has added an annex devoted to East Asian printing, to acknowledge that what took place in Mainz was a reinvention, an adaptation of techniques already developed elsewhere.

But ideas are one thing; putting them into practice is another. The printing techniques that had been developed in Europe following East Asian models hadn't amounted to all that much. Gutenberg was the first to see the advantage of scaling up production—and the first to figure out how to do so. If books could be produced in large numbers, just as his pilgrims' mirrors had been, the advantage of a retooled printing process would be immense.

In order to mass-produce books, every step of the process needed to be rethought. The first and perhaps most crucial step was not how to print, but how to make individual letters. In order to achieve the quality produced by the best scribes, each letter needed to be designed with sharp edges. Wood was much too soft for this degree of precision and would wear out too easily. The letters needed to be cast in an alloy that would be hard enough to withstand frequent usage. And they all had to be exactly the same size and length so that they could be assembled to form a uniform line.

Unlike Chinese printers, who had to deal with thousands of different signs, Gutenberg had to deal only with an alphabet of two dozen letters, a great advantage for making print with movable type efficient. That was the theory, anyway. Once Gutenberg examined handwritten books, he realized that scribes used capital letters, punctuation, abbreviations, and ligatures, combinations of letters that were partially merged. He would need almost three hundred distinct letters and signs, all of which had to be carefully cast. In order to form a single page, thousands of these letters would need to be combined. Once a page was printed, the letters could be disassembled, but it was much more efficient to leave some pages intact so that errors could be easily corrected and the corrected page printed again. This meant that there needed to be enough letters to form several pages simultaneously, amounting to tens of thousands or perhaps as many as a hundred thousand individual letters. Here, Gutenberg's experience with mass-producing pilgrims' mirrors turned out to be crucial, and he invented a hand-casting device that allowed a single person to cast more than a thousand letters per day. Mass-producing letters made it possible to mass-produce books.

Once a page was set, it needed to be inked. Normal inks were too liquid and needed to be thickened through a process of trial and error. The thickened ink was more difficult for the pages to absorb, so the pages needed to be carefully moistened beforehand. These interlocking improvements led to Gutenberg's second great contribution. Because European paper (made from rags, as the Arabs had taught them) and parchment were thick, much thicker than what was used in East Asia, simply placing the page onto the letters was not enough; more pressure was needed. Here Gutenberg used something that was in ample supply in the region around Mainz: a wine press. The composed page of metal letters was placed faceup beneath a wine press, and the paper or parchment was pressed with great force onto the letters. A separate frame made sure that the paper was in the right place and could be turned for printing on the reverse side (something that wasn't done in East Asia). This series of improvements together amounted to a completely new prospect, namely the mass production of books of high quality.

With the basic production process worked out, the big question was what Gutenberg should print. This first printed book should be in high demand and relatively small. To come up with a promising candidate, Gutenberg consulted his own reading habits. Along with all educated Europeans, Gutenberg had learned Latin, the common language of the educated classes, and the rise of new universities, all based on instruction in Latin, had further increased the

WOODCUT OF AN EARLY PRINTING PRESS, CIRCA 1520.

demand for this language. The most common Latin grammar book, which had dominated the market for hundreds of years, was named after its author, Donatus, and was most likely used by Gutenberg himself. Donatus was so popular that publishers had gone to the considerable trouble of carving the entire text, page by page, into wooden blocks in order to produce cheap woodblock-printed versions. If it was worth doing that, then Gutenberg's superior process stood an excellent chance of succeeding. The book he produced was small, only twenty-eight pages, with twenty-six lines per page, using the more expensive but durable parchment since he knew how much wear and tear each copy would have to endure. The result was a great success: The Donatus would remain one of the most often reprinted books in the coming decades, going through 260 editions by 1500.

While Gutenberg was working on the Donatus, in 1453, news reached Mainz, so shocking that at first it was hard to believe: The Turks had taken Constantinople, the eastern bastion of Christianity. To many Christians, it felt as if they had been cut off from a vital source of their history and faith. For Mainz's merchants who dealt with long-distance goods, such as Gutenberg's financier, Fust, it also meant that the trade network that brought spices and ideas such as paper and print from the East was suddenly disrupted. With Constantinople fallen, it was only a question of what was next. Greece? The Balkans? Cyprus?

The Church called on all Christian kings and emperors to take back Constantinople, or at least to stop the advance of the Turks. An army had to be organized, and soldiers were promised remission of their sins in return for the defense of Christendom. Such an army was expensive, but fortunately, the Church had developed a useful vehicle for raising funds. Those who could not themselves fight could pay the Church instead and still get remission of their sins. A donor would receive a sheet of parchment that detailed his name, the date, and the order of sins remitted; those rich enough were able to wipe out their sins entirely. All that was necessary was to take this sheet of parchment to their confessor, who would go through the ceremony of remission, after which they could emerge relieved of their burden. This was the birth of indulgences, and to anyone with foresight it was clear that the Church was going to sell a great many indulgences very soon.

It didn't take Gutenberg long to figure out this new business opportunity. Indulgences always used the same Latin formula. He could set a single page, with the name, date, and type of remission left blank to be filled in by hand. He lobbied for the commission and succeeded. The first indulgence he printed, on behalf of Pope Nicholas V, was for the defense of Cyprus. Others followed. Gutenberg knew that the Church would need hundreds, even thousands of indulgences, and he could print them with ease, as many as were needed and the market could absorb. In East Asia, print and paper had been combined to form paper money. Marco Polo had marveled at this almost magical invention whereby valueless paper

AN INDULGENCE PRINTED BY JOHANNES GUTENBERG IN 1454,
SEEKING CONTRIBUTIONS TO THE WAR AGAINST THE TURKS.

could be made to stand in for gold. Europe didn't have paper money yet, but the mass-produced indulgences Gutenberg was printing were nearly as good.

War indulgences were not the only business opportunity provided by the fall of Constantinople. In order to sell indulgences, the Church needed to whip up hatred of the Turks, and Gutenberg was happy to put his invention in the service of this further goal as well. He printed an anti-Turkish tract, written in the somewhat unusual form of a lunar calendar in which each month a different ruler, emperor, or the Pope himself was urged, in rhymed couplets, to join the fight. Indeed, most of Gutenberg's texts were printed for the Church. As a patrician of Mainz, a city that was under the control of an archbishop, Gutenberg was in a perfect position to offer the products of his workshop to the Church.

THE WORDS OF GOD,
WRITTEN BY INHUMAN HANDS

While Gutenberg was printing his Latin grammar, his indulgences, and his propaganda tracts, he was also pursuing another project. In contracts with his associates, he called it, enigmatically, "the work of books." With this project, Gutenberg was hoping to apply his method to the most important book of all time, and the one with the largest market share: the Bible. Without realizing it, Gutenberg was repeating the pattern that had been established in East Asia, where print had been used primarily for religious texts such as the *Diamond Sutra*. Once again a foundational and sacred text proved an early adopter of new writing technologies.

For Gutenberg, printing the Bible was an ambition on a whole new scale. So far, he had printed only single-page indulgences and small booklets such as the anti-Turkish calendar and the short Latin grammar. The Old and New Testaments together would be thousands of pages. Based on the methods Gutenberg had used so far, it would take decades to produce this book. He needed to scale up the process by using several presses at once, which meant more letters needed to be cast, which in turn meant that the whole process needed to be made more efficient. Every step would have to be calibrated precisely so that as little time as possible was wasted. Gutenberg was turning his workshop into an early industrial production process, anticipating the assembly-belt production system of Henry Ford in the early twentieth century.

Ordinary citizens, even relatively well-off ones, wouldn't be able to afford such a large and expensive book; the market would be churches and monasteries. This meant that the Bible would need to be printed in a large format, folio-sized, as it was called when a large sheet of paper or parchment was folded once to produce two large leaves, rather than folded twice, forming four leaves (quarto), or three times, forming eight small leaves (octavo). Only a folio volume would be large enough for a monk or priest to read on a lectern in a dimly lit church. And many more lines and columns could be crammed onto such a large page. Even with these savings, Gutenberg would have to print about thirteen hundred pages.

The challenge wasn't just scale. With the Bible, Gutenberg was touching the most revered and sacred text of them all. He would have to demonstrate that his machines could produce something as neat, as precise, as accurate and elegant, as those Bibles produced by the best-trained scribes, who were often monks who had dedicated their lives to this purpose. His scribe, Peter Schöffer, had created the model for new, more elegant letters. And Gutenberg planned to print in two colors, adding a ruby red, the way many calligraphers did when they copied the Bible in two different colors, to make the mechanical Bible look like a handwritten one.

The printing proved even more difficult and laborious than Gutenberg had anticipated. His workshop managed to cram two columns of forty lines each onto each page, printing it in two steps, one for black and one for ruby. The process took forever. Very quickly Gutenberg abandoned the two-color printing and instead left the accented letters blank so that a scribe could later write them in ruby ink by hand. In a similar manner, richly ornamented capital letters at the beginning of chapters, as well as pictorial embellishments called illuminations, could be added by hand. All that mattered was that the printed Bible would have the look and feel of a handwritten book. For the same reason, Gutenberg opted for parchment, the prepared animal skins perfected by the librarians of Pergamum.

At the Gutenberg Museum in Mainz, I was able to inspect one of Gutenberg's Bibles, which are magnificent objects. Their large format, with strange letters, elaborate flourishes, and ruby-colored lines for emphasis, made them look almost like handwritten books painstakingly produced by devoted monks.

But to Gutenberg's contemporaries, they looked very different. Thanks to differently sized letters and abbreviations, each line could be set so that both margins were justified, an ideal no calligrapher, not even the best, could ever hope to achieve. Each page of the Bible was now composed of two geometrical columns of dense black text. Gutenberg's Bible didn't just look as if it was written by hand. It looked much better, achieving a level of precision and symmetry undreamed of by even the most pious monk. Having started out with the hope that the printed Bible might approximate the look of a handwritten one, Gutenberg ended up exceeding his task, creating a new standard by which books would be judged. Print wasn't just a way of mass-producing books; it completely changed the way books should look. A machine had triumphed over the human hand.

The new mechanical reality had many consequences. One concerned the writing surface. Even though parchment was prestigious, it was expensive. For a parchment Bible, the skins of well over a hundred calves were needed. Fortunately, paper had found its way to northern Europe when a clever businessman in Nuremberg had set up a water-powered paper mill there, and thanks to the Arabs, all that was needed to produce paper was a pile of rags. As Gutenberg realized the possibilities of the new mechanical Bible, he decided to increase the print run to about 180, with most versions printed on paper. Clearly, the mechanical mass production of books favored paper.

As Gutenberg and his partners were laboring on the Bible project, there was one question left hanging in the air: What would the
Church say about these printed Bibles? Gutenberg had asked no
one for permission. In the rigidly regulated medieval world, where
much was controlled by guilds, Gutenberg had set up a secret society and gone into business for himself. What he was proposing was
surely shocking to the Church, for which copying scripture by
hand was a holy duty performed by devoted monks. Cheap indulgences and pamphlets were one thing, but the Book of Books,
printed on recycled rags? Had this entrepreneur and opportunist
finally crossed a line, sullying the words of God with his furnaces,
inks, and wine presses, replacing scribal monks with mindless machines?

Gutenberg took precautions. The first was the choice of translation. In his Bible, of course, God was going to create the world in
Latin. True, the Old Testament had been written in Hebrew, and
Jesus had spoken Aramaic, but the original language of Christianity
had been Greek (brought by Alexander to the Near East), and it
had been in Greek that the words of Jesus had been committed to
writing. But then Christianity had gained prominence in the
Roman Empire, which had required an authoritative translation of
both the Old and the New Testament into Latin. The task had
been accomplished by Saint Jerome, who had studied with Donatus. It was Saint Jerome's Latin Bible, commonly called the Vulgate, that had become the Bible of European Christianity. Recently,
some scholars had questioned the quality of Saint Jerome's translation, but Gutenberg used it anyway. The Vulgate was the traditional, authorized version favored by the Church, and Gutenberg
wasn't going to risk his capital outlays on a new and untested translation.

If Gutenberg was still worried about what the Church would
say, he didn't need to be. Presented with Gutenberg's mechanically
produced Bible, the Church admired it; it was more beautiful than

what even the most pious monks could produce. And despite their inhuman beauty, Gutenberg's Bibles were cheap enough for parishes and monasteries to buy. Gutenberg's high-stakes gamble to move print from the marketplace to the pulpit had paid off.

There was an additional reason why the Church readily accepted the new technology. Gutenberg's method promised to reduce the countless errors that copyists introduced into the holy text. The Church representative who worried about this issue with particular urgency was Nicholas of Cusa. Today known as one of the most important theologians of his era, Nicholas had studied in Heidelberg and Padua and then returned to Germany to teach at the University of Cologne. He was a precise thinker and valued churchman who had traveled to Constantinople before its fall to seek reconciliation with the Greek Orthodox Church. A diplomat working directly for the Pope, he was also in favor of establishing better relations with Islam, arguing that the Qur'an was compatible with Christianity.

But if Nicholas was open-minded with respect to the Greek Orthodox Church and Islam, he was exacting in how Christianity should be practiced. During his extensive travels, he had witnessed the most shocking inaccuracies and mistakes in matters of scripture and ritual. In church after church, the words of God were different, often grotesquely distorted, due to the mistakes copyists had introduced, which were then copied and multiplied by a new generation of scribes, and so on through the generations. Given this system of transmission, it was close to a miracle that the text produced by Saint Jerome in the fourth century still contained complete sentences a thousand years later. Missals and breviaries, the books that told priests and monks how to pray and conduct the mass, were similarly flawed, which meant that in no two churches was mass celebrated in the same way, with the same words.

Faced with this sea of errors, Nicholas of Cusa had called for new, authoritative, and error-free missals, breviaries, and Bibles.

But how could these new texts be kept from breeding errors when they would be copied by scribes in the future? Nicholas realized that the answer was Gutenberg's invention. True, printers might introduce errors as well, but these errors could be corrected more easily. Each page could be carefully proofread, and if a letter was out of place, or upside down, as sometimes happened, it could be fixed and the page printed anew. Once the corrected page was set, all copies would be the same. It wasn't quite foolproof. In England, a printer produced a Bible that encouraged its readers to commit adultery, having accidentally omitted the "not." But overall, the errors introduced by human scribes would stop. Print was perfect for allowing the Church to exert control over its scripture. The Church and print were made for each other.

Martin Luther:
The Outrage of a Bible Scholar
—
1517, Wittenberg

The alliance between the Church and print did not last. Without realizing it, Gutenberg and the Church had set in motion forces that would change the Church by changing the role of writing and reading. Neither Gutenberg nor the Church understood that institutions and societies based on sacred scripture were especially vulnerable to new writing technologies. Nor did they anticipate that the person who would exploit this vulnerability was a monk with little interest in writing technologies of any sort, who was happy with his printed Bible, and who otherwise expressed himself with quill and paper.

Some sixty years after Gutenberg's Bible, the monk, Martin Luther, employed his usual writing method when he composed a letter to the archbishop of Mainz. Luther had studied philosophy and law before taking his vows, deliberately withdrawing from rambunctious university life to the quiet of an Augustinian cloister. He hoped to combine the abstraction of philosophy and theology with the lived experience of devotion and the love of God. After being ordained, he had been called to the University of Wittenberg to teach arcane theological arguments.

It was from Wittenberg that Luther was now addressing his archbishop. The letter was written by hand, in Latin, and it called the archbishop's attention to an agent of the Church who was peddling printed indulgences in the most outrageous manner. Even if you had raped the Virgin Mary, prospective buyers of these indulgences were told, you could get remission from your sins as long as you paid between one and twenty-five guilders, depending on your income. The writer was sure that the archbishop did not know about these abuses and would promptly put a stop to them.

The writer also took the liberty of including some theses on indulgences for the archbishop's perusal. In these, he questioned the role of indulgences, their sale for money, but he also added some questions about the status of confession, about purgatory, and about the role of the Pope. It was nothing unusual. This was how theological debates were being conducted at Wittenberg and many similar institutions. The main point, though, was indulgences. Something needed to be done about them.

The production and sale of indulgences had come a long way since the fall of Constantinople and Gutenberg's first print run. The threat of the Turks had remained undiminished, requiring fresh funds from across Christendom to fight it. Fortunately, Gutenberg's invention had come along just in time to help multiply indulgences, a heaven-sent invention that the Church had put to immediate use. Indulgences were now printed and sold by the thousands, even tens of thousands; in one instance, 190,000 copies of a single indulgence letter were produced. Some printers came up with the brilliant idea of putting indulgence letters in books, as a kind of bonus coupon. An elaborate organization was set up to distribute indulgences, with (printed) brochures recommending the best ways of selling them in each territory. One such brochure had fallen into the hands of Luther, causing additional indignation.

The archbishop of Mainz had other worries on his mind. He had borrowed a large amount from the Fuggers, a rising banking family, to purchase the archbishopric of Mainz. The loan was secured through a clever scheme. He promised to oversee the sale of the Pope's indulgences, with half the proceeds going to the Pope and the other half to the Fuggers, paying back his loan. Everyone benefited. The archbishop could finance his Mainz seat; the Fuggers got sure collateral for the loan; and the Pope not only received money for the archbishopric, but also knew that his indulgences would be sold as aggressively as possible. It was this carefully constructed scheme that Luther was now threatening, and understandably the archbishop was not amused. He was not going to discuss any of the theses attached to the letter, and he was certainly not going to stop the sale of his indulgences.

Luther had no idea of what he had stumbled into—a perfect business deal. He simply waited for an answer. But the archbishop wasn't writing back. After a while, Luther might have decided to publish his theses against the selling of indulgences and related matters, all ninety-five of them, himself. At his university, in Wittenberg, publishing meant posting them on the door of the castle church, which was how debates were announced. But no one came to debate his theses, apparently for lack of interest. Even the few like-minded friends to whom Luther had sent his theses didn't respond. His letter and his theses were going nowhere.

The quiet was deceptive; behind the scenes things were moving. The archbishop had sent the theses to his business partner in Rome and was trying to figure out how to placate this troublemaker. Luther's friends were busy as well. Instead of responding to Luther's call for debate, they opted for a different form of publication, one that never occurred to Luther himself. They took the theses to the

printers. The theses, carefully handwritten by Luther in Latin, were not meant for public consumption, but the friends thought they should be published anyway. In Nuremberg, a councilman translated them into German, and within weeks the theses were available in several towns.

It was a surprising development. In the first sixty years of print, most printed matter had been drawn from works that were already well known, such as Gutenberg's Latin grammar or the Bible. In Italy, so-called humanists, entranced with the literature of classical Greece and Rome, printed ancient texts (print had arrived just in time to preserve the Greek scrolls that had been brought to Italy after the fall of Constantinople). But who would want to read the difficult words of a young, unknown monk? To everyone's surprise, there turned out to be a modest market for such things.

Luther himself wasn't very interested in this new form of publication—not yet. He still hoped to reform the Church through the official channels, by handwritten letters sent to those in authority. He wanted his theses debated in person, if only the archbishop would allow it. But the archbishop was not interested in debate. He wanted Luther to recant so he could keep on selling printed indulgences to pay back the Fuggers and to raise money for the Pope and his new cathedral, St. Peter's.

Faced with resistance, Luther took up the pen again. This time he wrote not in the difficult language of Latin theology, but in the popular form of a sermon. His sermon against indulgences expressed his thoughts more intuitively and directly; it was written to convince his audience and to produce outrage against widespread abuses. Remembering what had happened to his theses, Luther not only preached this sermon but also, perhaps still as an afterthought, printed it. The sermon was of course written in German, so it didn't need to be translated, and it turned out that Luther, this unworldly monk who didn't care about the newfangled world of print, had a way with language.

The sermon against indulgences was only the beginning. Slowly, Luther realized just what a weapon the printing press could be for a writer such as himself, without institutional power but with public sentiment on his side. He discovered a gift for expressing outrage. Sometimes he asked seemingly naive questions; at other times, he hurled invectives against the Pope; and always he wrote in pithy, pointed sentences in the language of the common people.

It was a style perfect for the printing press. Editions ran out, reprints had to be ordered, and reprints of reprints, leading to more than twenty editions in different cities. Print had fueled the wide availability of indulgences, and now it fueled the polemics against them. Print runs of Luther's texts exceeded by orders of magnitude anything ever printed before; his texts were available in hundreds of thousands of copies. Unwittingly, Luther had begun the age of popular polemic, an age in which a single writer could publish under his own name, an age in which success would be measured by the size of print runs and the number of reprints, an age in which writers and readers were connected more efficiently than ever before, and outside traditional institutions. The printing press was creating a new reading public and a new, powerful form of literature: polemical writing fueled by print. Polemics itself was not new, of course; some of the great teachers had excelled at it, and one wonders in retrospect what Jesus' followers could have done had they been able to combine Jesus' provocations with print.

Luther could be stubborn—that was what made him dig in when the archbishop of Mainz was dismissing his complaint—but he was not incapable of learning something new. He was doing that now, learning to handle the new world of print by perfecting the art of print polemics. The Church could be stubborn and tradition-bound, but it, too, was waking up to the fact that something new was happening with print, that the printing press was more than just a means for multiplying indulgences and Bibles. The Pope's denunciations of Luther, so-called papal bulls, were no longer posted on church doors, as was customary, but given to the printers. The presses didn't take sides, and they happily fanned the flames of a fight that was increasingly defined by their output. Luther was denounced as a heretic; he shot back that the Pope was the Antichrist. It was unclear which insult was the more damaging one, but what was clear was that the Church was not winning this fight. In the new world made by print, it didn't matter that you were the leader of the mightiest organization in the world or that you could claim to be speaking for God. What mattered was how good you were as an author; it was the only thing that gave you authority. Luther, the poor monk who was merely pointing out abuses, who was learning how to speak to and for common people, managed to acquire more authority than the Pope because he was an author; the Pope was only the Pope. A full one-third of all works published in Germany during Luther's life were by Martin Luther. He was the first superstar of the new public of print, the master of the new genre of printed polemics.

When the Church found that it couldn't beat Luther at his own game, it reverted to an older technique. Within a few years after Luther's theses were printed, the Church staged the first public burning of Luther's writings. Luther, emboldened by his success, had done the same. With the help of students at Wittenberg, he had held his own book burning, giving over to the flames volumes of canon law, on the basis of which the Church was threatening to excommunicate him. Then he himself approached the fire and ceremonially threw in the papal letter that had demanded his recantation. Bystanders overheard him say that the papal throne should have been burned as well.

It was good theater, the burning, but it wasn't very effective. Book burnings were no match for the flood of print, which Luther had become adept at channeling against the Church. Printers were able to print Luther's sermons more quickly than the Church could burn them. Book burnings only led to new editions and reprints. In the new world of print, paper was stronger than fire. As if to prove this point, Luther immediately wrote an account of the book burning and took it to the printer. Print was God's greatest act of grace, as Luther liked to put it—and Luther thought of himself as print's most faithful agent.

If the archbishop of Mainz was losing faith in the printing press, he could still enjoy the thought of Gutenberg's most glorious creation, made right here in his own city, the Latin Bible. Thanks to Gutenberg, more Bibles had been printed, and their prices had kept falling and their formats shrinking, until individual priests and monks could possess their own copies, often in the smaller octavo or duodecimo formats, pocket books almost. At the same time, Nicholas of Cusa's dream of a more uniform, standardized, and centrally controlled Vulgate, purged of many errors and corruptions, had come true. There could be no doubt that the Bible had increased its reach and potency, and with it the reach and potency of the Church.

Luther himself, upon admission to his order, had received for his study a copy of the Latin Bible, the Vulgate, and in Luther's hands that copy of the Vulgate had begun to do its work. Luther's letter to the archbishop, his arguments against indulgences, against the authority of the Pope, were all based on his close study of his copy of the Bible. It was this copy he was thinking of when he declared with utmost conviction that scripture was more important than the Pope, that the institution of the Church wasn't even mentioned in the Bible, nor were indulgences. Luther's handy printed copy of the Bible had been his most important source of inspiration and was becoming his battle cry. *Sola scriptura*, he shouted, politely, in Latin: Scripture was the only authority to which he would bow. Show me the passage in the text, and I will burn my own sermons and theses. The idea of sacred scripture, first instituted by Ezra the scribe, was asserting itself powerfully in the new world of print.

Given Luther's insistence on scripture and his success with print, it was only a matter of time until he would put the two together. The occasion arose after he publicly refused to recant and was taken into protective custody by a supporter. Hiding from the henchmen of the Pope at Wartburg Castle, Luther had time to devote himself to a project of the highest importance: a Bible that lay people could read. He was not the first to do so. More than a dozen German versions of the Bible, many fragmentary, had appeared during the past decades, finding readers and markets. None of them had enjoyed much success. He would have to do better and translate the Bible from the original into the language of the people. If he could give his followers access to the Bible, rendered into forceful, easy-to-understand German, and multiply the result with print, he would be able to attack the Church at its center of power.

With little else to do, under self-imposed house arrest, it took him just eleven weeks to translate the New Testament. Later he added the Old Testament. When the work was printed, it dwarfed in distribution everything that had been printed before, reaching half a million copies. If he had still been alive, Gutenberg would have been amazed. His Latin Bible had stood as the first achievement of bookmaking by means of print, but it hadn't yet tapped into the real source of power of the press: the mass audience. Gutenberg had merely sought to meet an existing, finite demand, namely large Bibles for churches and monasteries, more cheaply. He hadn't realized that his invention would radically expand demand and thereby change it. Sixty years after its invention, the printing press was reshaping how books were read and by whom.

Luther's Bible became the prototype for other Bible translations. Many were now faced with censorship by the Church, ultimately leading to the infamous index of forbidden works, the vehicle by which the Church sought to control print. The index, too, was printed, of course, and almost simultaneously the first printing press was set up at the Vatican.

But against print, censorship could do only so much. The best proof was England, the only country that already had a law against unauthorized Bible translations, stemming from before the advent of print. Even such laws didn't prevent an English Bible, modeled on Luther's, from going to press. The person who seized this chance was William Tyndale; he meant to translate the Bible into English and achieve for the English language what Luther had achieved for German.

There were only seven printers in London, most of them tightly controlled by the crown, so Tyndale left for Germany, spending time in Luther's Wittenberg. In Worms, Tyndale found a printer who was ready to print his English Bible and smuggle it back to London.

The printer was Peter Schöffer, the son of Gutenberg's apprentice by the same name who had helped Gutenberg produce the first Latin Bible in Mainz. While Peter Schöffer the elder had carved the beautiful types for Gutenberg's Latin Bible, his son set the page in which God created the world in the English language, the basis for the Bible that Frank Borman and his crew on Apollo 8 read in 1968. Within the lifetimes of the two Schöffers, more books had been printed than had been produced by scribes in the whole of human history before them.

The differences over print became differences over many things, ultimately leading to the splintering of Christendom. Luther, the ordained priest and monk, married a nun; he instituted a different type of mass; he gave ordinary sinners the chalice; he rejected the authority of the Pope. The entire fabric of Christianity was changing.

AT THE END OF my research, I found myself in Mainz again, contemplating the large cathedral, the river Main, and the Gutenberg Museum and considering how they were all connected. The river had led to the emergence of long-distance traders who had amassed the capital for funding an expensive project such as the one Gutenberg had undertaken. Trade had put Mainz in contact with distant lands and ideas, including the idea of print. The cathedral represented the first beneficiary of print, but also, shortly thereafter, its first victim.

There was a larger lesson here about inventions: They are often the result of independent developments that suddenly converge, and those we call inventors are people who see those convergences for the first time. The story of Gutenberg and Luther also shows that changes in how texts were produced and transmitted, in who read them and to what end, had an outsize impact on societies based on sacred scripture. This is an important lesson for us in the early twenty-first century, as we are living through another revolution in writing technologies, more fundamental than the print revolution. It will be good to remember that while print popularized the Bible, wresting it from the control of the Church, print also empowered a Christian form of textual fundamentalism, demanding of its readers that they live according to the rules set down in a text from the remote past.

Will our own writing revolution further encourage fundamentalist readings of sacred texts? Will it further undermine the institutions in control of those texts?

On October 31, 2016, Pope Francis traveled to Lund, Sweden, to commemorate the 499th anniversary of Luther's ninety-five theses, as a gesture of ecumenical reconciliation. Perhaps this is a sign that the division brought about by Gutenberg and Luther is waning in the era of the Internet.

CHAPTER 8

THE *POPOL VUH* AND MAYA CULTURE: A SECOND, INDEPENDENT LITERARY TRADITION

A TRAP AND A BOOK

1532, PERU

THE SPANISH SOLDIERS HAD BEEN LYING IN WAIT ALL DAY. AFRAID AND exhausted after their long sea journey down the coast from Panama and the never-ending hike up the mountains, they had few provisions and few prospects. On the way, many had given up hope of ever getting a foothold in this strange land, with its well-kept roads, impressive buildings, and above all gold. But just when their campaign had seemed hopeless, news had reached them that the Inca emperor, Atahualpa, was nearby. Contact had been made and the Spaniards had been invited to spend the night here in this town, to meet His Highness the next day.

The next morning, their commander, Francisco Pizarro, decided to risk everything on this one chance. He divided his 106 foot soldiers and 62 horsemen into three groups and hid them in buildings around a square. The Indians were afraid of horses, so he attached bells to them to heighten their effect. Their two cannon were in position. Only twenty soldiers remained with

Pizarro. On a signal, they would all rush toward Atahualpa and seize him.

As they lay waiting, a messenger came informing them that Atahualpa would not be coming today after all. Pizarro knew that his exhausted soldiers could not bear the tension any longer. The trap would work now or never. Desperate, he sent one of his people to the emperor, inviting him in the politest terms to visit today. Nothing happened.

Suddenly they saw movement in the camp. First a few, then a hundred, finally thousands of the emperor's attendants were swarming into formation. A litter became visible, and then the whole train began to move toward them, with pomp befitting the ruler of a vast realm. Before long the retinue entered the square and Atahualpa's bearers set down the litter. Pizarro was jubilant. They would use their superior weapons, swords made of the best Toledo steel, crossbows firing with precision and power. Their muskets and cannon, though cumbersome to load and use, were terrifying because of their novelty. The most useful domestic animal in South America was the llama, little more than a large sheep, completely useless in warfare, in comparison to the armored horses bearing Spanish riders. Even more important was the weapon Pizarro and his men had brought unwittingly: smallpox, to which the Indians were not immune. An epidemic of gigantic proportions had preceded Pizarro, triggering a bloody civil war, which had further weakened the empire. Pizarro and his men were battling a civilization already under serious assault.

The Spanish had another weapon that has attracted much less attention, perhaps because it was so small, barely the size of two outstretched hands. A number of witnesses nevertheless noticed it being deployed at the center of the trap Pizarro had set for Atahualpa. Pizarro didn't handle it himself, but he sent an expert, a Dominican friar named Valverde, to place it right in front of the emperor.

Atahualpa saw the friar approaching, and through an interpreter he understood that the Castilian was imploring him to accept the authority of the king of Spain and of the Christian God. When the Castilian was finished, he held up a square device, which turned out to be a book, and claimed that it contained the voice of his god.

Some bystanders later remembered that Atahualpa had taken the book but didn't know what to do with it. When the friar offered help, the emperor slapped away his arm rudely. After some fumbling, Atahualpa managed to open the book, but, annoyed by the many pages, he threw it into the air. Other witnesses remembered that he held the book to his ear, listening for the voice of this Spanish god, and when no voice was forthcoming, he threw the strange object to the ground. One thing was clear: Atahualpa did not know what a book was. He had never encountered paper. He could not conceive of a sacred text. The Incas, for all their impressive roads and buildings, were ignorant of writing.

As soon as the book hit the ground, the friar signaled to Pizarro that the assault should begin. Some Incas had arms hidden beneath their clothing, but in the confusion of horses and bells, of the cannon firing, and of sharp swords doing their work on an enemy trapped in a small plaza, the Incas didn't put up much resistance. They were slaughtered, and the emperor was seized.

Valverde's encounter with Atahualpa was a triumph. His book was a Bible, or more likely a breviary, a one-volume compilation of psalms and other excerpts from the Bible condensed into a travel-friendly format to help preach the mass according to the Christian calendar. This book, this object that Atahualpa could not fathom, was the culmination of thousands of years of innovation, combining the invention of writing, in Mesopotamia, and of the alphabet, in Greece, with paper from China and the book format from Rome. Recently, Johannes Gutenberg had reinvented print with movable type, similar to a Chinese technique. Print shops were springing up everywhere in Europe, turning out Bibles and breviaries, increasingly in small octavo formats, just in time for the conquest of the New World.

We have so many accounts of this memorable encounter because several of the participants wrote about it afterward, including Pizarro's brother and his first cousin but also Atahualpa's nephew, who dictated his memories to a mixed-race scribe. The one notable missing account was from Francisco Pizarro himself. He left no written record of this day. In fact, we do not have a single piece of writing from him. Even the contract he had drawn up with his co-investors to outfit his ships does not bear his signature. Pizarro did not know how to write his own name. Like his Inca adversary, he was illiterate.

THE BATTLE OF THE BOOKS

1519, YUCATÁN

The conquest of the New World consists of many similar scenes: A handful of Europeans, armed to the teeth, aided by the fact that they had inadvertently spread smallpox, making clever use of civil wars and divisions among native peoples, prevail against overwhelming numbers. If you look closely enough, there is usually a book involved.

Fourteen years earlier, in 1519, Pizarro's second cousin, Hernán Cortés, had sailed from Cuba to explore the mainland, which they proudly called Yucatán, using the native name. Later, it turned out that the word they had taken to be the name of this peninsula was garbled Maya for "The way he talks is funny," the expression Mayas who encountered Spaniards had repeated to them over and over again.

The natives also kept saying something that sounded like "Castilano." After some back-and-forth, it dawned upon Cortés that there was a Spaniard somewhere, perhaps a survivor from a ship that he knew had been stranded here nine years before Cortés arrived. He sent a messenger after this fellow Castilian but readied his ship to leave when he did not hear back. At the last moment, a canoe of natives arrived, and one of them, to everybody's great surprise, identified himself, in a perfect Castilian accent, as Jerónimo de Aguilar. Even more surprising was what Aguilar said next: "It's Wednesday, right?"

Aguilar, it turned out, was a Franciscan friar, and throughout his nine years of captivity and enslavement by the Mayas, he had managed to hold on to his breviary, similar to Valverde's, which is how he had been able to count the days.

Aguilar was not the only survivor of the shipwreck. There was another, Gonzalo Guerrero, who had not come in the canoe to greet the new Spanish arrivals. Guerrero, Cortés learned, had taken a native wife and adopted native ways, including long hair, tattoos, and a pierced nose. He didn't want to join the Spaniards, and he spent the rest of his life organizing resistance to their increasingly aggressive colonization of these lands. Guerrero, to state the obvious, did not keep a breviary with him to count the days. The episode taught a valuable lesson about the importance of writing in the midst of a foreign culture: The breviary had kept Aguilar from going native. Upon encountering Aguilar, Cortés promptly adopted him as his interpreter, and Aguilar stayed with him through the conquest of Mexico.

Cortés picked up something else on his initial foray into Yucatán: two Maya books. He included them in his first shipment to the king of Spain, that all-important bribe that would bolster his case against his rivals at home and his superiors, whose orders he had ignored in his reckless dash to the mainland. The two books weren't the most important items; what really mattered was gold, gold that could be melted down to bolster the royal coffers, or gold in the form of curious artifacts that could be displayed with pride. But the books were there, proof that in the Mayas, the Spaniards had encountered a people that knew writing.

In contrast to Pizarro, Cortés could write, quite well, in fact. His eloquent letters to the Spanish court, in which he justified his expeditions, succeeded in swaying the king in his favor. Maya writing did not overly impress Cortés, however, perhaps because he was comparing everything he saw to Europe and Asia. In Eurasia, every early civilization from China to the Near East had been in occasional contact with others. The single landmass, stretching from east to west along roughly the same climate zone, had allowed laboriously cultivated crops and domesticated animals to spread from one culture to the next in a continent-spanning web of exchange. This exchange included writing. It was possible, even probable, that writing—the idea of writing—was developed only once, in Mesopotamia, and then spread to other early writing cultures like Egypt and perhaps as far as China. Writing, and with it literature, could be thought of as a single stroke of good luck.

But unlike Cortés, we know that the Americas had been out of contact with Eurasia since long before the invention of writing. Of all the patterns in the story of literature, I find this the most intriguing: Humans came up with writing, perhaps the most fundamental of all inventions, twice.

So far, I have been following the consequences of a single invention of writing in Mesopotamia, which led to the emergence of a class of scribes, the decision by one of those scribes to write down stories, and the habit of bundling those stories into larger texts, some of which acquired the status of holy scripture, aided by improved technologies such as paper, the book, and print. Thanks to the Mayas (and other people in the Americas who invented writing systems that are less well known), we can compare the story of literature told so far with a second, completely independent tradition.

Surprisingly little attention has been paid to the two thousand years of Maya literature and writing culture, perhaps because Maya writing has been deciphered only within the last half century, through the combined efforts of Russian and American linguists. Step by step, they realized that this intricate system consisted of almost six hundred signs, some of which expressed ideas and others combinations of sounds. While not every sign has been deciphered, we are now in a position to ask whether literary history in the Americas followed a path similar to that of Europe and Asia.

The person who pioneered the study of Maya glyphs was Diego de Landa. Landa had been born in 1524 in Cifuentes, in the middle of Spain, a town that still contained a community of converted Muslims (after the defeat of Muslim rule in Spain). At age sixteen, Landa joined the Franciscan brotherhood, and when he was twenty-four, he decided to take the plunge into the unknown and joined the mission to the American mainland, following in the footsteps of his fellow Franciscan, Aguilar. His purpose was to save the souls of the Mayas; his main instrument, a (printed) breviary.

When he arrived in Yucatán, Landa soon realized that he had encountered a complex civilization. Intrigued, he began to take notes and ultimately produced an account of the region before and after the Spanish conquest that has remained the primary source of information on Maya culture. With the interest of a proud new owner, he described the cultural achievements of the Mayas, including their impressive pyramids and cities, many of which had been abandoned by the time the Spaniards arrived, as a result of unknown environmental or cultural forces. For me, Landa became an important guide, similar in some ways to Layard and the other excavators and discoverers of distant civilizations. Like them, Landa was also a destroyer in that he came to the New World as part of an occupying force. His observations about the Mayas are our primary source of information, but it is information that came at a steep price.

In order to understand this culture and its mysterious history,

Landa needed to befriend a Maya. He was lucky in his choice. Nachi Cocom came from an old dynasty and was himself the leader of Sotuta, an important Maya chiefdom in the middle of Yucatán. Cocom had access to all aspects of culture and society, including writing, and provided Landa with the best information to be had. The Mayas, Landa learned, had invented not only a writing system but also many of the other writing technologies that the Inca emperor was so puzzled by when confronted with them by Pizarro. Above all, Cocom showed him Maya books, which Landa studied in detail. They were similar to the Roman invention, with one difference: The pages were attached on both ends and folded in an accordion pattern rather than bound on one end and open at the other. Maya books were prestigious objects, held within the most powerful families, such as the Cocom clan.

In order to create books, the Mayas had invented a suitable writing surface. In Eurasia, it had taken more than a thousand years for Chinese paper to arrive in the Near East, and hundreds of years more for it to arrive in Spain, just in time for the Spaniards to take their paper books to the New World. The Maya equivalent relied on soaking bark in a lime solution, then beating it into sheets and gluing several of these sheets together. The white sheen was achieved by coating the sheets with calcium carbonate and then smoothing it with a pebble. Writing was done in several colors, with dyes that were kept in conch shells, and the books were sometimes reinforced on the outside with wood or jaguar skin embellished with ornaments. Maya writing, paper, and books had not spread to South or North America because movement along a north-south axis, across different climatic zones and difficult terrain, was much harder than the lateral movement possible in Eurasia, which was oriented along an east-west axis.

The difficulty of the Maya writing system led to the emergence of a class of scribes who were also priests and guarded their technology jealously, although some women and other outsiders knew how to write as well. A writing system had created a powerful scribal class, whose activities were bolstered by the inventions of paper and a type of accordion codex. So far, history seemed to be repeating itself. But what were these books used for? Had some of the scribes taken down stories and combined them into larger foundational texts, such as the ones the Spaniards were now bringing to the New World?

Maya books were closely connected to the Maya science of "reckoning of years, months and days," as Landa realized—the one thing everyone now associates with the Mayas: their calendar. It was an elaborate system, or rather several interlocking systems, beginning on August 11, 3114 B.C.E., and ending on December 21, 2012. Since that date, we have been living in the second 5,126-year cycle of the Maya calendars. (In 2012 some people believed that the end of the cycle meant the end of the world, but that turned out to be a wrong reading of the Maya calendars.)

The Maya calendars were a unique cultural achievement, closely connected to religion, the means "by which they regulated their festivals, their counting and contracts as business, as we do ours," Landa found. *As we do ours*: For all the strangeness of these calendars, they were used in a way Landa could recognize. Landa's impression of the religious significance of the calendars was confirmed when he observed firsthand how the highest priest "opened a book, and . . . preached to them." Ezra's invention, holding up scripture as a sacred object, seems to have occurred here as well. So far, Maya literary history had gone through similar stages of development, with a small class of scribes presiding over sacred books.

THE GREAT AUTO-DA-FÉ OF 1562

One question remained, the most important one: Were these Maya calendars based on sacred stories, foundational texts? Here I could no longer rely on Landa's observations, because his studies were interrupted by a crisis that brought out Landa the destroyer. In the spring of 1562 a young Maya boy discovered a cave near the village of Mani that contained idols and human skulls, evidence of human sacrifice. Landa was horrified. What he had taken for a great civilization was barbaric after all.

He rose in fury to suppress these secret practices, launching a regime of mass arrests and torture that lasted for three months. His favorite method was hanging by the hands, extracting confessions through torture, and then, based on the confessions, meting out severe punishment. One recurring problem was that after the torture regimen, there usually wasn't enough intact skin for beatings. Of Landa's 4,500 torture victims, 158 died, and at least 13 committed suicide. The Mayas, not exactly hesitant when it came to spilling the blood of their enemies, were shocked. Their own system of cutting out the heart was much quicker and therefore less cruel.

Landa was shocked as well, shocked by what he heard amid the tortured cries of his victims about their secret worship of the old gods. Even his old friend and informant Nachi Cocom, who had been baptized and had taken the name Don Juan Cocom, had encouraged some of these practices. The worship of the old gods had persisted in secret under a thin veneer of Christianity. All of Landa's efforts at conversion had been for naught.

There was only one conclusion Landa could draw: Maya culture needed to be torn out by the root. Based on everything the traitor Cocom had told him, Landa realized that the basis of Maya practices was their sacred writing. This was how Landa, who more than any Spaniard had taken the trouble of learning about Maya books, decided to burn every single one that he could find. He hunted for them everywhere, books that had been passed down within noble families like that of his former friend Cocom, books that had been held up as sacred scripture, books that kept track of the stars and the calendar. Landa gathered them all, those precious handcrafted objects he had admired so much, and piled them in a big heap, along with all the idols whose worship was anchored in those texts. Then he celebrated the auto-da-fé ("act of faith") of 1562, the public reading of confessions and of sentencing, illuminated by the flames that were consuming the books of the Mayas. It was a technique Landa had seen at work in his native Spain, where the Church was fighting a losing battle with Luther (if Landa had known about the burning of Confucian classics in China, he might have taken inspiration from that event as well). The history of literature is a history of book burnings—a testament to the power of written stories.

This festival of fire was so violent that Landa was called back to Spain to face an inquiry. Even the Spanish crown had found the performance excessive. The crown was all for torture, but had established a highly regulated, controlled system with extensive rules and procedures, the great Inquisition, which Landa and his zealous underlings had violated. The legal proceedings against him lasted for years, and Landa escaped more or less unscathed only because of his diplomatic skills. Eventually he managed to return to the New World in triumph, as Bishop of Yucatán.

It was during those difficult years back in Spain, with his future uncertain, that Landa wrote down all he had learned, producing his great work on Maya culture. What was he thinking as he described the beautiful books, the achievement of the calendar? Did he see them all before his mind's eye going up in flames? His account does not betray any emotion: "We found a great number of books . . . and since they contained nothing but superstitions and falsehoods of the devil we burned them all, which they took most grievously, and which gave them great pain." Landa sounds unrepentant—he was, after all, trying to justify his actions to the court—and even feigns surprise that the Mayas did not want their books burned. But he must have had an inkling of the oddity of his position. He was the person whose writings preserved most of what we know about Maya literary culture. It was thanks to him that lin-

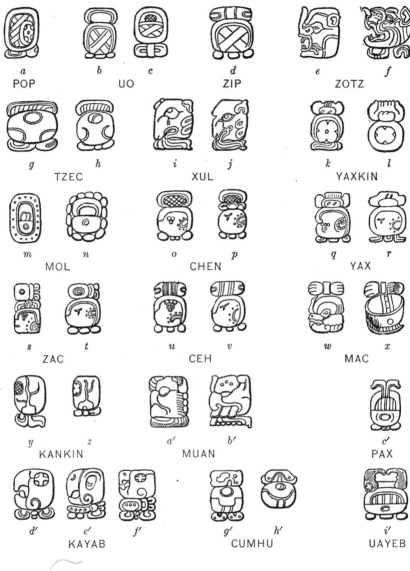

MAYA GLYPHS, ONE OF SEVERAL WRITING SYSTEMS
DEVELOPED IN MESOAMERICA, THE ONLY CONFIRMED
INVENTION OF WRITING OUTSIDE EURASIA.

guists were able to decipher Maya writing hundreds of years later.
At the same time, he was also the person who did more than anyone else to destroy it.

The bonfire of 1562 was not the end of the battle of the books.

More and more books were coming to Yucatán, and the Spanish were no longer just relying on imports. As early as 1539, the latest technology, a printing press, was brought to the New World. At first, production was slow; only thirty-five books were printed over the next few decades. But the new technology proved invincible in the long run.

THE *POPOL VUH:* THE COUNCIL BOOK
—

Maya scribes needed to save their own culture from this Spanish onslaught, but how? Fortunately, some had gone underground well before Landa's campaign. But going underground was not enough. They knew that they could not hold out against this literary flood forever. If the secret line of transmission broke, knowledge of Maya characters would die, and the culture distilled within the few remaining books would die as well.

At this moment of crisis, the Maya scribes came to a painful realization: The future would be dominated by the format of the victors. In order to preserve their own literature, they would have to give up on their own precious writing system and use the weapons of the enemy: Spanish paper and books and the Roman alphabet. They called the great work the *Popol Vuh,* the Council Book. They wrote it using the Roman alphabet, but they used that alphabet to write down their native language. The book preserved what was most precious about their culture. It also supplied an answer to the last question of the Maya test case, that is, whether the calendars, with their minute attention to the stars, were telling stories like other foundational texts. It turned out that they were: stories set in the Maya sky.

What I love most about the *Popol Vuh* is its creation myth, the creation of sky-earth, as the universe is called, out of unformed matter. The principal creator is Sovereign Plumed Serpent, a "Creator, Maker," but he is not alone. In quick succession we are introduced to a whole cast of godlike creatures, who soon embark on the difficult task of fashioning humans. Several attempts, using mud and carved wood, fail. Either the creatures fall apart or they can't talk, becoming nothing more than animals. Creation here is described as difficult, an experiment that may well go wrong, introducing a humorous note into the awe-inspiring event.

What draws me to creation myths in general is that they put on display the ability of literature to create worlds. While these myths putatively praise some powerful creator god, they also compete with the gods in imagining what creation would look like. The astronauts on board Apollo 8 might have sensed this as well. To be sure, they felt dwarfed by the expanse of nothingness that is space, but they were also reciting a creation myth at the moment of technological confidence.

In the *Popol Vuh*, after creation is accomplished, the gods embark on their own adventures, the most important of which were the famous Maya ball games. For me, the Maya ball game is the most ambivalent feature of the *Popol Vuh*, because my parents barred me from joining a soccer club on the grounds that kicking a ball with one's foot originated from the Maya practice of playing with the heads of their enemies. It had always sounded like a crazy story to me, but when you are young, you hear so many crazy stories that one more doesn't seem all that unusual. In any case, when I finally read the *Popol Vuh*, I paid particular attention to the ball game.

The game, it turned out, was first played by two brothers, semidivine heroes, Hun and Vucub Hunahpu. They play so vigorously that they disturb the gods of the underworld. Irritated, these gods summon them and challenge them to a match. The two brothers follow the summons, but they are tricked and killed before they even get to play, with one of them, Hun, being decapitated and his head put in a tree. The place where the severed head is displayed has an ominous name: Place of Ball Game Sacrifice. I had to admit that this didn't sound too good. Perhaps my parents had a point.

The head in the tree has one more role to play: It spits into the lap of a young goddess of the underworld, impregnating her. Her father is not pleased, and she must flee, moving in with the in-laws, the father and mother of Hun, where she gives birth to another pair of hero brothers, Hunahpu and Xbalanque. These two are among the most entertaining characters in the entire work, a pair of rambunctious tricksters who are always up for a bit of fun. All goes well until they come across the discarded playing equipment of their father. Nothing can prevent them now from trying the game themselves, and promptly history repeats itself: The underworld gods are disturbed once more and summon them down to play a game.

Smart tricksters that they are, the twins have come prepared and manage to evade all the traps the gods have laid for them. Even so, before the game begins, one of them is decapitated, his head snapped off by a killer bat. Will it be displayed in the Place of Ball Game Sacrifice as his father's head was? No, it actually rolls onto the court. This inspires the gods of the underworld to use the head to play their game. The head, unperturbed, encourages the players to keep playing: "Punt the head as a ball." Now the other twin hits the head and strikes it outside the court, where a rabbit, who is on the side of the brothers, takes it and runs away, with all the gods of the underworld following in hot pursuit. This buys the intact twin enough time for a canny move. He seizes upon a squash made to look like a head, and when the ball game continues, the gods are tricked into playing with the squash.

As I was trying to make sense of this complicated story, I kept wondering whether this text advocated playing with heads. True, twice someone is decapitated in connection with the game, and at one point the game is actually played with a head. At the same time, the defeat of the underworld is accomplished once the head is replaced with a squash. Let's not play with heads anymore, the

Popol Vuh seems to be saying, let's play with squashes instead. I felt vindicated: I should have been allowed to play soccer after all. (Later, I read that soccer originated when Englishmen played with the skulls of Danes, another unconfirmed story.) After they defeat the underworld, the twins end up being killed for good, but rather than disappearing altogether they ascend to the sky, where they now exist as constellations.

The story of the two-generation ball game explains how the stars, whose movements were captured with so much precision by the Maya calendar, became stars in the first place. I sometimes wonder what Mayas would have done if they had been the first to go to the moon. They might have looked back at Earth and imagined the moment of its creation as the Christian astronauts had done. But I like to think that instead they would have looked at the stars, reading from them the drama of the skies as recounted by their foundational text.

The *Popol Vuh* reports that finally, after three failed attempts, the gods tried one last time to make humans. This time they used maize, and the experiment succeeded. From this point on, the *Popol Vuh* deals with the human world. Some episodes sound strangely familiar, including the story of a great flood. Had the flood been part of Maya culture before the Spaniards arrived, a residual memory of worldwide rising sea levels at the end of the most recent Ice Age? Or did the anonymous scribes copy it from the Bible, just as the biblical scribes had copied this episode from the *Epic of Gilgamesh* or another, even older source?

The Spanish onslaught was certainly on the minds of the scribes as they wrote down the last sections of the *Popol Vuh*, which deal with the fate of Maya territory. At the time of writing, of course, this territory had been overrun by foreigners, and the book ends on a wistful note: "This is enough about the being of Quiché, given that there is no longer a place to see it. There is the original book and ancient writing owned by the lords, now lost, but even so, everything has been completed here concerning Quiché, which is now named Santa Cruz."

The sense of loss is pervasive. The original book, which the three scribes had decided to preserve by rendering it in the Latin alphabet, was lost, along with Maya writing, perhaps their greatest cultural achievement. The most important loss, however, is that of place. The land of the Maya has been renamed Santa Cruz: "there is no longer a place to see it."

The *Popol Vuh* preserved a Maya culture that was already lost when it was written down. Around 1701 a Dominican friar found the manuscript, copied it, and added a translation into Spanish. More than 150 years later, a French priest published it, allowing the *Popol Vuh* to enter the world of Gutenberg.

SUBCOMANDANTE MARCOS, EL SUB

2004, CHIAPAS

After I first read the *Popol Vuh*, I was so intrigued by this text's sense of place that I decided to travel to the mountains of southeastern Mexico. My journey began in the Lacandon jungle. A bus dropped me at the border of the Maya territory, where a beat-up truck picked me up at the side of the road. The village of several dozen huts was located in a clearing in the jungle. Everyone but me was dressed in what looked like long white nightgowns. Men and women both wore their black hair shoulder length (I thought of the shipwrecked sailor who had gone native), and most of them walked around barefoot, sometimes donning rubber boots. Nighttime in the clearing revealed an astonishing sky, the memory of the stories told in the *Popol Vuh* written overhead.

The next day, I went on an all-day jungle tour. There were rumors of jaguars, the animal whose name was given to the early ancestors in the *Popol Vuh*. Soon we came across the first piles of stones, ruins of Maya monuments. The jungle here was full of them, many still unexplored. I had visited some of the great sites such as Palenque and Yaxchilan, excited to see their well-preserved ball courts, but it was here in the Lacandon jungle, amid the many unknown and unnamed ruins, that I felt most acutely the sense of loss that is so pervasive in the *Popol Vuh*.

After leaving the low-lying jungle, I drove into the mountains. Before long, I passed a handwritten sign informing me that I was entering an "autonomous Zapatista zone." Some people were hanging out next to the sign with old rifles, but otherwise all looked

A MURAL CREATED IN THE WAKE OF THE ZAPATISTA REBELLION IN
SOUTHERN MEXICO, ADVOCATING LITERACY FOR THE POOR.

peaceful. By the early 2000s, a status quo had been reached that tolerated such autonomous areas, though the Mexican army heavily patrolled their borders.

The military buildup and the autonomous zones were the fallout of an insurrection that had been going on for more than a decade. On January 1, 1994, soldiers calling themselves the Zapatista Army of National Liberation (EZLN) had occupied San Cristóbal de las Casas and a number of other towns in Chiapas. The EZLN fighters soon drifted back to their villages, but the Mexican army was unforgiving. New barracks were built in the district, roadblocks were erected, and ultimately more than seventy thousand soldiers and armed paramilitary troops were dispatched to pacify the area. On December 22, 1997, forty-five people, including twenty-one women and fifteen children, seen as loyal to EZLN were massacred during a prayer meeting by a right-wing paramilitary group supported by local police and government.

Despite overwhelming firepower, the state was forced to the negotiating table by an anonymous writer from the Lacandon jungle, where a small group of Mayas preserved vestiges of the people's former ways while the majority of Mayas had long since been pushed to the margins of Spanish-speaking culture, their way of life under threat everywhere. The Lacandon writer, who hid his face behind a ski mask, came to be known as Subcomandante Marcos, El Sub. The Mexican army hunted him everywhere but could never catch him. He was too fast, too mobile, and could rely on the support of Maya villagers. Through a cunning use of the media and the emerging Internet, El Sub turned the insurrection, and the harsh response by the army, into an international cause.

As I was contemplating the elusive Marcos while driving across the mountains, I realized that he derived considerable power from literature. When he had first entered the jungle in the early 1980s, the main weapon in his possession had been a backpack full of books. Ten years later, when the insurrection finally began, he made good use of them, issuing communiqués, declarations of war, and open letters denouncing everything from the central government to NAFTA, the North American Free Trade Agreement, which had contributed to falling coffee prices. The writing technology at his disposal was an old Olivetti portable typewriter. Underground couriers took the typed texts into San Cristóbal, in the mountains, where they were leaked first to a local newspaper and increasingly to the international press. The return address was invariably "From the Mountains of the Mexican Southeast."

The worldwide response to these missives was beyond what anyone had expected, and El Sub took the hint and increased his literary output even more. In addition to manifestos calling for revolution, he showed a whimsical side when he responded to statements coming from the Mexican government and surprised political observers with parables drawn from folktales. He also created a character, Don Durito, known as the Don Quixote of the Lacandon jungle. The world was enthralled by this irreverent and moving voice.

Recognizing that literature had become his most important tool, Marcos decided to modernize his weapons, acquiring a used laptop and a dot matrix printer. They proved to be decisive tools in sustaining the rebellion. On August 13, 1999, Marcos wrote the following words on his laptop and sent them out into the world:

This is the story of how all was in suspense, calm and silent, how all was motionless and still, and how the expanse of the heavens was empty.

This is the first story, the first talk. Man didn't yet exist, nor the animals, birds, fish, crabs, trees, stones, caves, ravines, grasses or forests. There was only the heavens. The face of the earth had not yet appeared. There was only the calm sea and the expanse of the sky. There was nothing brought together, nor anything that could move, or quicken, or make a noise in the heavens.

There was nothing standing, only the calm water, the placid sea, alone and tranquil. Nothing existed.

There was only stillness and silence in the dark night. Only the Creator, the Maker, Tepeu, Gucumatz, the forefathers, were in the water surrounded by light. They were hidden beneath green and blue feathers, so they were called Gucumatz. They were great sages, great thinkers by nature. This was how the heavens were, and also the Heart of Heaven. That's how they told it.

And then came the word. Tepeu and Gucumatz came

together in the darkness, in the night, and talked together. They talked and considered. They agreed, uniting their words and their thoughts.

And then as they considered, it became clear to them that when dawn broke, man must appear. Then, they planned the creation and the growth of woods and thickets, the birth of life and the creation of man. That's how it was arranged in the darkness of the night by the Heart of Heaven who is called Hurakán.

Writing from the mountains of Mexico's southeast, El Sub was issuing forth the opening of the *Popol Vuh*.

Once again, a written story proved to be a weapon that could be hidden for centuries only to emerge in the distant future. Did Marcos see this old text as an ally in his attempt to lay claim to the land of the Mayas? Did he, hidden behind his ski mask, recognize a kinship with the anonymous Maya scribes who had sought to preserve a culture on the verge of extinction? The part of the *Popol Vuh* that El Sub chose reveals an additional attraction: the creation of the world through words. It was the ultimate power of literature, the same power that had drawn the astronauts of Apollo 8 to the opening of Genesis.

With this latest use of the *Popol Vuh* on my mind, I drove into San Cristóbal, the beautiful baroque city high up in the mountains and the center of the Zapatista revolt. Marcos was in hiding, but images of him were everywhere. Handmade Marcos figurines were for sale in the market, as were T-shirts bearing slogans from his manifestos. On the next day, Easter Sunday, a crowd assembled around large papier-mâché dolls representing Mexican president Vicente Fox and NAFTA. Suddenly, the dolls erupted in simultaneous explosions. I ducked, but then I realized that they had been merely stuffed with firecrackers that were shooting out in every direction—not exactly safe, but no cause for great concern.

Sadly, I could never find Marcos, not in the jungle, not in San Cristóbal, and not in the mountain villages, with their churches and syncretistic rituals that would have enraged Landa, his project of Christianization still incomplete four hundred years later. The Zapatista rebellion of 1994 did not lead to Maya independence from Mexico, but it reminded the world that the Mayas still existed, that they still rejected the rule imposed on them by others—and that the *Popol Vuh* could still serve as a weapon in the battle for their lands.

In 1995, the Mexican government announced that it had identified El Sub, the person behind the mask. He was not a Maya at all but a certain Rafael Sebastián Guillén Vicente, born in Tampico, hundreds of miles north of Chiapas. Vicente had been educated by Jesuits, the order that had taken over from the Franciscans as the dominant force of Christianizing the New World. Vicente had then become a lecturer in philosophy in Mexico City before heading to Chiapas in the early 1980s.

How could a Mexican presume to speak for the Mayas? The answer was: through literature. Vicente had spent ten years in the Lacandon jungle organizing his insurrection. His work included teaching villagers the Roman alphabet, while they taught him essential survival skills. He also struggled to learn Maya languages and dialects. Above all, he studied the *Popol Vuh*, to preserve that epic for the future. Finally, he donned a ski mask and became an anonymous Maya writer in the tradition of these scribes. His slogan was "Our Word Is Our Weapon"—the battle cry since the dawn of the written world.

The Italian
Baroque painter
Ciro Ferri (1634–
1689) imagines
Alexander the
Great reading
Homer in bed.

Painting by Albrecht
Altdorfer (c. 1480–
1538) of the battle at
Issus, with Darius
being pursued by
Alexander the Great.

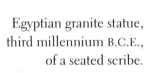

Illustrated version of the Persian *Book of Kings*, from the fourteenth century, depicting the death of Alexander the Great.

Egyptian granite statue, third millennium B.C.E., of a seated scribe.

Clay envelope and clay letter, both containing cuneiform writing, circa 1927–1836 B.C.E.

This nineteenth-century lithograph, by James Fergusson, imagines the palaces of Nimrud restored to their full beauty.

Ezra writing in his study, as imagined by medieval Christians in the *Codex Amiatinus*, one of the earliest surviving manuscripts of the Latin Bible.

Tibetan painting from the eighteenth century depicting the Buddha teaching on the Vulture Peak Mountain in India.

Japanese woodblock print by Yashima Gakutei, dating from the early nineteenth century, of ten disciples of Confucius.

French painter Jacques-Louis David (1748–1825) shows Socrates philosophizing shortly before his death, in the company of his students.

A 1481 fresco painting by Domenico Ghirlandaio, connecting Moses and the Old Testament, on the left, to Jesus and his disciples.

Roman fresco from Pompeii depicting a young woman with wax tablets and stylus, implements used for everyday writing and accounting.

This painted silk scroll from China (fifth to eighth century) shows a female court instructor admonishing her pupils.

Murasaki being divinely inspired to write the *Tale of Genji*. The artist, Suzuki Harunobu (1725–1770), used separate woodblocks for each color to accomplish multicolor printing.

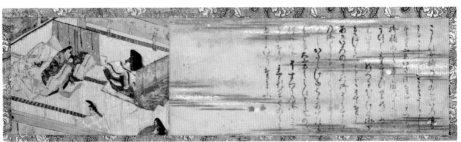

A thirteenth-century edition of Murasaki's diary. Murasaki is probably the serving woman in the bottom right corner.

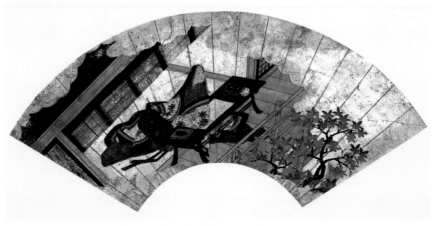

Seventeenth-century fan made of gold paper showing Murasaki writing at her desk.

Scholars and students in a Baghdad library in 1237, as depicted by artist Yahya ibn Mahmud al-Wasiti in an illuminated Arabic manuscript.

Seated Scribe, attributed to Gentile Bellini (circa 1429–1507), combining Western and Ottoman painting styles.

This Qur'an from circa 1180 was written in a distinct style of calligraphy: two letters, alif and lam, are much taller than the others.

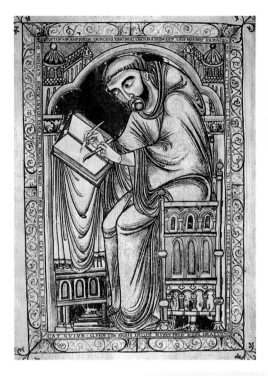

Portrait of Eadwine the Scribe, twelfth century, laboring over a folio manuscript.

The opening of Genesis from the Latin Bible printed by Johannes Gutenberg circa 1455, with letters carved by the scribe Peter Schöffer.

Title page of a 1534 Bible translated by Martin Luther, with color woodcuts.

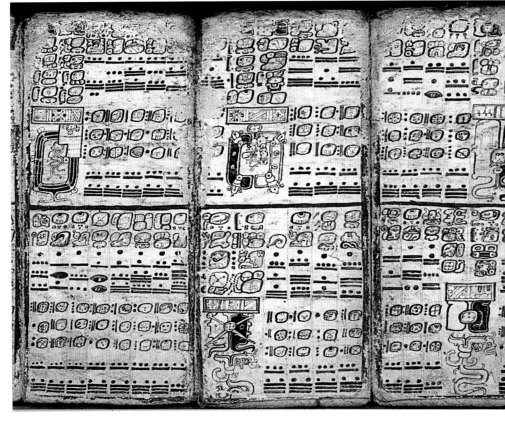

Six pages from the *Dresden Codex* (thirteenth to fourteenth century), one of the few Maya books to survive the Spanish Conquest.

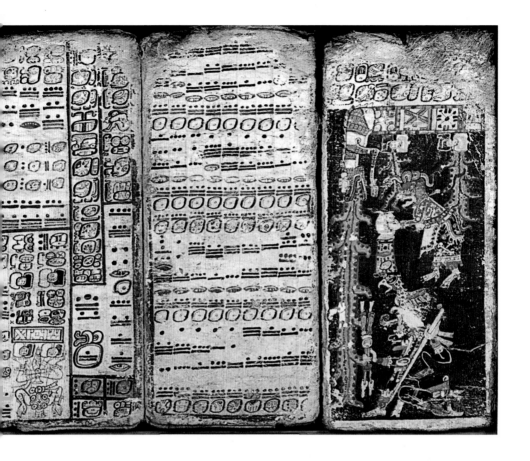

The Maya ball game had a ritual function captured in the *Popol Vuh*.

A
CONTINUATION
Of the Comical
HISTORY
Of the moſt Ingenious Knight,
DON QUIXOTE
De la Mancha.

By the Licentiate
ALONZO FERNANDEZ de Avellaneda.

Being a THIRD VOLUME;
Never before Printed in Engliſh.

Illuſtrated with ſeveral curious Copper Cuts.

Tranſlated by Captain JOHN STEVENS.

LONDON:
Printed for JEFFERY WALE, at the Angel in
St. Paul's Church-yard; and JOHN SENEX,
next the Fleece Tavern in Cornhil. 1705.

An English translation of the unauthorized sequel to *Don Quixote* by Alonzo Fernandez de Avellaneda.

A seventeenth-century peddler hawking books and pamphlets, catering to an expanding market in literature.

This painting from circa 1770 by Jean-Honoré Fragonard captures the importance of women readers.

The painter Johann Joseph Schmeller (1796–1841) depicts Goethe dictating to his scribe, who also recorded many of his conversations.

The library of Duchess Anna Amalia in Weimar, used by Goethe to satisfy his far-flung reading habits.

Photograph by Eugène Atget, in late-nineteenth-century Paris, of a rag picker collecting the raw material for making paper.

Writing ball invented in the 1870s by Rasmus Malling-Hansen in Denmark: the first commercially produced typewriter.

This Russian propaganda poster from 1920 recommends reading because "knowledge will break the chains of slavery."

Cubist painter Nathan Altman's portrait of Anna Akhmatova in 1914.

Paraphernalia used in the Soviet Union for duplicating and circulating censored literature (samizdat).

A CPT 8100 word processor desktop microcomputer from the 1970s.

Annenberg Hall, at Harvard University, considered by some students to be the model for the Great Hall at Hogwarts.

CHAPTER 9

DON QUIXOTE AND
THE PIRATES

I'T'S NOT SUCH A TERRIBLE JOB, BEING AN AUTHOR. YOU DO SOME research, come up with characters, shape a plot that unfolds central themes and ideas. Once you're done, you find a publisher, who in turn finds a printer; the book gets set in type, a nice cover is added, and the final object lands in your local bookstore. It all seems natural enough, but in fact it's a relatively recent arrangement that emerged only gradually over the last five hundred years (and is changing again now). The arrangement involves people who own machines and people who sell their stories to them, which in turn means that there have to be people who own stories, original stories that can be stolen, plagiarized, and pirated.

When I wrote the book you are reading, these questions were on my mind pretty much constantly. I was very pleased when I found a publisher, Random House. During the writing process, I tried to anticipate what Kate Medina, my editor, would say, and once she had read a first draft and supplied extremely helpful comments, I tried my best to respond to them (for example, Kate felt that I needed to have a more consistent presence in the book). In order to publish the book, Random House had to engage in negotiations with my agent, Jill Kneerim, and drew up a rather long contract, which I never read all the way through; I just initialed each page and signed the whole thing at the end.

Throughout the process of writing, I was careful to acknowledge the work of others, since my book relied on countless scholars, whose work I have credited in endnotes; a particularly generous group of experts even agreed to vet individual chapters, for which I thank them in the endnotes as well. And yet, while acknowledging all this, I nevertheless asserted that the story of literature I was telling was my own, claiming copyright over the particular way in which I expressed it. If someone were to copy that particular expression and make it available on, say, the Pirate Bay or a similar website offering pirated materials, I would be very unhappy (or, if the book sells very poorly, I'll be glad that at least someone is bothering to steal it).

I have always felt a particular affection for Don Quixote, that most hapless of modern heroes, but it took me a while to realize that my experience with modern authorship had put me in the perfect frame of mind for approaching this novel and its author, Miguel de Cervantes Saavedra. It was with Cervantes that the features of modern authorship, from the printing press and a market for literature to ownership, plagiarism, and literary piracy, came together as never before. He was the first modern author.

1575, MEDITERRANEAN SEA

For the longest time, Miguel de Cervantes knew nothing of his future as an author; he was interested only in gaining fame as a soldier. He achieved his goal at the Battle of Lepanto, in 1571, off the western coast of Greece, at the age of twenty-four. Ever since the Ottoman Turks had taken Constantinople more than a century earlier, Christendom had been seeking to stop their westward advance. To this end, sea-bordering Catholic states had formed the Holy League and dispatched a large fleet of several hundred galleys, along with 40,000 sailors and 28,000 troops, including the feared Spanish infantry. Along with his fellow soldiers, Cervantes had been promised a plenary indulgence from the Pope—complete remission of all sins—for his services in battle. The Holy League was faced with a smaller fleet of Ottoman galleys, many of them rowed by captured Christian slaves. In order to keep the slaves motivated, they were promised freedom if the Ottomans won.

During the days leading up to the battle, Miguel de Cervantes had been kept belowdecks by a severe fever, but he refused to stay away while his comrades faced the enemy. The two fleets engaged, pitching hundreds of galleys, sixty thousand humans, and hundreds of cannon against each other on the treacherous seas. Ships rammed each other, went up in flames, and sank. Caught between water, steel, and fire, soldiers fought for every inch of their ships, which were wildly swaying from sudden maneuvers and the impact of cannonballs. The battle cry of the Turks was notoriously frightening, but it was drowned out by the sheer noise of cannon firing and wild cries of desperation as more and more soldiers were killed by fire and blade or flung overboard to find their death amid the waves.

The Battle of Lepanto was won for the Holy League—the Turks were defeated—but it left Cervantes with a maimed left arm. A turning point in the centuries-long war against the Ottoman Empire, the Battle of Lepanto put a stop to the Turkish advance, allowing Don John of Austria, who had led the Holy League, to return home in triumph.

Four years after the battle, Cervantes and his brother returned home as well, and they had every reason to expect a warm welcome. Cervantes was carrying a letter from Don John commending him for his bravery in the Battle of Lepanto. He would be able to use the letter to find employment despite his wound once their ship had finally arrived in Spain.

As the galley carrying the Cervantes brothers made its way along the coast to Barcelona, a ship appeared on the horizon. At first the ship was difficult to make out, but it kept coming straight at them, and at last they realized that they were being pursued by North African pirates. The galley tried to flee, but the pirates, equipped with a faster ship and more slaves to man the oars, closed on them quickly. Some Christians were killed right away, while others were bound and taken to Algiers, on the North African coast, where pirates could operate with impunity—the Ottomans tolerated them as long as they served the purpose of disrupting Christian commerce. The Cervantes brothers, who had been within striking distance of their home, were among the prisoners taken to Algiers.

Miguel de Cervantes was lucky. The letter from Don John, victor of Lepanto, was found on him and identified him as a valuable prisoner. He would not be put to the sword, nor would he be forced to work the oars. Instead, the pirates would try to extract a hefty ransom, the main business of Algiers. But the letter was also unlucky, since it made Cervantes seem a much more important, and therefore richer, person than he actually was.

As a ransomworthy slave in Algiers, Miguel received better treatment than the others. To be sure, he had to observe curfew and, like many other slaves, had to scramble for food. Three times he and his companions tried to flee, but each time they were caught, betrayed by paid helpers and bad luck. In the most elaborate plot, Miguel's brother, who had been ransomed already, sent a ship to rescue Miguel, only to be discovered and chased away. Each failed attempt meant more severe punishment, but the promise of ransom kept Miguel alive. Finally, after several years, with the help of a loan from the Trinitarian order, enough ransom was raised to free Miguel when he was about to be sold to Constantinople. After five years as a soldier and five years as a slave, Cervantes was finally allowed to go home.

Miguel's problems were not over. Now he had to repay the money for the ransom, which his family had scraped together by borrowing and begging. There existed a possible avenue for raising funds: to write up the experience of captivity as a story. His bravery at Lepanto, his daring escape attempts from Algiers—wasn't all this great material for literature? It would bring his readers to the front lines of the battle against the Ottoman Empire through a brave Christian soldier who was wounded and abducted but fought his way back to freedom. The heroic deeds of the writer could be set in a richly textured account of Algiers, with its sailors and slaves, Muslims and Christians, all packed together in a seaport town that had become the scourge of the Mediterranean.

This was one of the consequences of print: a market for stories. To be sure, Cervantes would not be the only one writing such an escape narrative. Similar accounts had been produced in great number as piracy itself had increased. The market for these stories was very peculiar, however. Slave narratives were often self-published, in small print runs, but that didn't matter, since the writers of such narratives weren't contemplating careers as professional authors. Their ultimate goal was to curry favor with the monarch.

But Cervantes had a larger ambition than that: to become a professional writer and succeed in this new market. There was one type of popular writing that promised both quick fame and a chance of making a living. Cervantes lived during the golden age of theater in Spain, comparable to that in Shakespeare's England, an art form equally adept at entertaining kings and the illiterate masses. The theater industry was hungry for new plays, especially plays about Spanish history and folktales, and writers were rushing to supply them. If they found the right tone, they could make good money, and if they did it over and over again, they could make a fortune. The most successful ones could capitalize on their theatrical success by having their plays printed, thus capturing a reading public as well. The master of the craft was Lope de Vega, who had pioneered a modern, varied style and become a national celebrity—

his most ardent fans even put his picture in their homes. He gave them some fifteen hundred plays in return, making him the most prolific playwright in history.

Cervantes had begun writing plays before Lope de Vega's spectacular success, but the rise of theater as a popular art gave Cervantes ideas. He decided to turn his best material, the tale of his captivity, into drama. Drama was a genre that demanded immediate success. If a play failed to attract the interest of a theater manager, or if audiences disliked it, it would die, with little chance of a revival. In this high-stakes environment, Cervantes was bested by others. Most of his comedies fell flat and are lost. The drama of his captivity suffered, perhaps, from an oversupply of such stories. The result was that Cervantes's plays never enjoyed much success, although they give us a rich account of his experience in Algiers. (His earliest play, with its depiction of Algiers, was probably begun while he was still a captive.)

A failed dramatist scraping together a living with various schemes, Cervantes ended up in captivity again, this time on his home turf, where he was accused of having defrauded the state while working as a tax collector raising funds for the Spanish Armada. In prison, Cervantes had plenty of time to contemplate his life's intimate relation to history, from Lepanto to the brewing conflict with England. But he also used this time to reflect on his own career and his dwindling options. What should he do?

What's Wrong with Medieval Romances?

In addition to plays, another type of story enjoyed great popularity: tales of knights roaming medieval Christendom, slaying monsters, worshipping damsels, and obeying a strict code of honor. These stories catered to a desire for a simpler world in which good and bad were easily identified and heroic action rewarded—a world without confusing new continents in the west, the painful loss of

Constantinople in the east, or the sudden threat from the English fleet in the north.

Even though these romances were set in an idealized past, they profited from the new world of print. The cost of producing books had been dropping rapidly, and books had begun circulating more widely than ever before, not just among rich clergy and the high aristocracy, as had been the case during Gutenberg's life, but also among the merchant class; even innkeepers might possess a few volumes. The wider availability of books fueled literacy, and literacy in turn fueled the demand for more books, a cycle that was turning with increasing speed. This cycle also expanded the types of literature that were circulating, from autobiographical accounts and biographies to grammars and almanacs and works of law, medicine, and geography. Rising demand for printed matter also led to economic changes, including cash payments to authors and advances for manuscripts, features that still dominate the book publishing industry today. In this environment, chivalric romances were so successful that they were being exported, especially to France, through a brisk international trade in books. The demand for romances was so strong that Parisian booksellers didn't even wait for whole works to be translated and instead sold them part by part.

Cervantes might have tried his hand at chivalric romances and perhaps even adapted his own captivity tale for the purpose. Instead, he turned against them. It can't have been their popularity, since he had sought popularity through his plays. But there was something in these romances that irked him; perhaps it was the idealized past in which they were set, or their pat morality. Or he simply felt that they bore no relation to the world in which he lived. No matter what it was, Cervantes decided that these romances needed to be stopped.

Cervantes's invented tool in this battle against romances was an impoverished aristocrat by the name of Don Quixote, an avid consumer of romances, of which he possessed an entire library. The more Don Quixote read of these tales set in the medieval world, the more he was taken with them; he simply couldn't get these stories out of his mind, and he started to see everything through their lens. In the end, he put himself in these stories and started to act them out. He found an old suit of armor, lying neglected in a corner of his run-down residence, and repaired a helmet with the help of cardboard; his emaciated horse he henceforth considered his most noble mount, and he set out to face the world as a knight-errant. Windmills became giants that needed to be battled according to the chivalric code of honor, and illiterate country wenches became elegant damsels who had to be worshipped according to the high art of courtly love. Everything that did not fit his picture he ignored or interpreted according to the world he knew from his books.

Don Quixote's single-minded quest made him look ridiculous, even dangerous, especially once he developed the habit of charging unsuspecting opponents as if they were rival knights. Often they were surprised and didn't know what had hit them, but usually they saw pretty quickly what this strange man was up to. While no one had ever seen a real-life knight-errant, people could figure out what Don Quixote was doing and even play along. This was the ingenious part of Cervantes's strategy: Because chivalric romances were so popular, everyone knew the script. In the novel, not just impoverished aristocrats such as Don Quixote but also innkeepers and ordinary travelers owned books and knew these stories, and those who didn't read had heard of romances and their heroes. Don Quixote's own squire, Sancho Panza, wasn't entirely immune to their influence even though he was illiterate. Cervantes had realized that the proliferation of stories through print meant that more and more people saw the world through literature. In a way, everyone was a Don Quixote, their heads alive with plots and characters, even if they didn't act on them directly. The world was becoming full of literature, and in that world, it mattered very much what and how you read.

As soon as Don Quixote's friends figured out that he had been deranged by reading the wrong kind of literature, they decided to attack his madness at its source. Gaining entrance to his library, they went through its shelves, taking out book after book, and they threw most of what they found into the fire (while speaking favorably of such valuable books as Alexander's copy of the *Iliad*). Book burning was of course a tactic the Catholic Church had employed in its fight against Martin Luther and Maya books. Cervantes seemed to be making common cause with this practice; at least he seemed to agree that the cycle of literacy wasn't always virtuous. Random reading, whether of the wrong kind of religious texts or of popular romances, could do a great deal of harm.

Unlike Don Quixote's friends and the Church, Cervantes knew that book burning was ineffective in the world of print. Against the power of storytelling, only more storytelling would prevail. He needed to establish the story of Don Quixote as more believable, more realistic, and savvier than these outdated plots. In the character of Don Quixote, the everyday world of readers was readily recognizable, governed by the laws of physics and modern social codes, a world in which characters had to pay for their supper or receive a beating if they couldn't. Only Don Quixote, his mind full of romances, lived in the medieval world of knights and damsels. Nothing captured the battle between romance and reality better than Don Quixote's famous fight against windmills. He spotted them, identified them as monstrous, readied his lance, and charged. There was no way he could win, and he knew it. But such was his belief in his chivalric duty that he did not hesitate for a moment. Destined to lose, Don Quixote was knocked off his horse by giant arms. If you read too much of the wrong kind of literature, Cervantes was warning, you will get hurt.

In mobilizing reality against romance, Cervantes was entering uncharted territory. He was writing not simply a different kind of romance, but one for which a new name was needed. And since newness was precisely what distinguished it from previous forms of literature, the most convenient name was newness itself: *novela*. Because they were new, *novelas* could do pretty much anything— the only thing they couldn't do was conform to existing literature such as romances.

With his audacious ploy, Cervantes had invented the modern novel for early modern Europe, a Europe transformed by new mechanical contraptions, windmills among them. Windmills were enormous, visible from a distance, and louder than anything before produced by man. Able to move millstones and other heavy machinery with the power of giants, they were among the first harbingers of mechanical civilization, the perfect opponent for someone like Don Quixote who insisted on living in the past.

By feeling overwhelmed, puzzled, and provoked by machines, Don Quixote became more than a sad case of bad reading, he became something of a modern hero. I myself feel, in my weaker moments, when my computer freezes for no reason at all, when any of the machines that surround me and over which I have absolutely no control breaks down, or threatens me, or simply makes me feel helpless, that I would like to grab a lance and charge it. This is the genius of Don Quixote, a helpless fool who is mad as hell at the world, capturing our collective experience of modern mechanical civilization.

Mechanical civilization was powering Cervantes's novel itself. Arabs had introduced the art of papermaking to Spain, laying the foundation for the golden age of Spanish letters. Papermaking required rags and clean water, but it also required energy, because rags or wood chips needed to be broken down in order to separate the fibers. Ingeniously, Spanish and other European papermakers had come up with the idea of using mill power for this purpose, thus becoming early adopters of this mechanical contraption, along with smiths and milliners. The paper on which the first edition of *Don Quixote* was printed came from the paper mill at El Paular, which was part of a monastery situated below the Guadarrama Mountains, which supplied clear, fresh water. Despite these advantages, El Paular paper was not particularly good. It was lumpy, with many impurities and wrinkles, and quickly became brittle. Still, with demand for paper high, El Paular sold its paper in large batches to an eager market.

An ample supply of paper was particularly important for *Don Quixote* since demand for this novel quickly exceeded expectations. Ever since the Catholic Church had woken up to the power of print, each book needed to get a license. Fortunately, *Don Quixote* received approval in the fall of 1605, allowing the publisher, Francisco de Robles, and the printer, Juan de la Cuesta, to produce a first edition, which sold out with gratifying speed. It only took a few months for new editions to be printed across Castile and Aragon; in the first ten years, an estimated 13,500 copies were produced. *Don Quixote* quickly became popular abroad as well, with editions printed as far away as Brussels, Milan, and Hamburg. Almost immediately an English translation was published to great effect as well, inspiring Shakespeare to base a play (now lost) on one of the episodes. So popular was this novel that people started to dress as Don Quixote and his wily servant Sancho Panza, perhaps in deference to this pair's insistence on letting fiction spill over into the real world.

Don Quixote also became a favorite in the Americas. A shipment of 184 copies of the very first edition left Spain shortly after its publication, with 100 copies bound for Cartagena, on the coastline of Colombia, and 84 for Quito, Ecuador, and Lima, Peru, less than a hundred years after Pizarro had brought his printed Bible to this part of the world. The books took close to a year to get there, first by ship, then by donkey, then by boat again. In the New World, rich colonists were the first buyers, but soon others purchased copies as well. In the 1800s, pirates apparently read the novel, and even named a hideout in the bayous south of New Orleans "Barataria," after the island over which Sancho Panza briefly rules in the novel—an unlikely tribute to an author who had himself been imprisoned by pirates.

How to Fight Literary Pirates

By the time *Don Quixote* had become a success, Cervantes no longer had to worry about seafaring pirates; instead he had to worry about literary ones. Even though the king's license to publish a work gave ownership to the author or printer for a set period of time, the rules were fuzzy and often ignored. It took only months for pirated editions of the novel to appear in Lisbon and Valencia, and many more would follow. The world of paper and print, which had allowed a wounded soldier, failed dramatist, and convicted tax collector to publish a new story, was now making it even easier for others to copy it.

Thus began the ongoing struggle between those who create literary works and those who control the machinery that disseminates them. This struggle was the inevitable consequence of technological progress: the costlier the machines used for producing literature, the more difficult for writers to own and operate them. True, earlier scribes had to negotiate with makers of papyrus and paper, but the new industrial-scale production of paper and print took the tools of the trade completely out of the hands of writers and put them into the hands of entrepreneurs and industrialists. The result was that writers either depended on printers and publishers or else embarked on the dubious enterprise of self-publishing. (Before print, all writers self-published in that sense, although they might use scribes to copy their work.) In a preface, Cervantes had written a manifesto of modern authorship, presenting himself in the typical pose of an author, sitting with an elbow on the table in front of an empty sheet of paper, cheek in one hand, pen in the other, ready to invent a new story—but he left out all the machines he had no control over.

Literary pirates, printers, and publishers were not Cervantes's only problems. In 1614 an unknown writer brazenly published a sequel to *Don Quixote*. Even though he hid behind a pseudonym, Alonso Fernández de Avellaneda of Tordesillas, he took out a royal license, found a printer, and published the result as the story's second part. The character and story of Don Quixote, he claimed, weren't the exclusive property of Cervantes. The public demanded a sequel and a sequel it should get, no matter who would write it. Cervantes found himself embroiled in a battle about modern authorship, a battle over the very idea of whether authors could own the stories they created.

Cervantes's travails throw the preceding history of authorship into relief. In the era of foundational texts, sacred scripture, charismatic teachers, and story collections, authorship and originality were of minor importance; only gradually did authors invent new stories to challenge or replace established ones, as when Virgil wrote his *Aeneid*, a Roman version of Homer's epics. Cervantes in turn had Don Quixote boast that if he had been alive during antiquity, he would have saved Troy and Carthage from being destroyed, thus challenging both Homer and Virgil.

Coming up with a new story to challenge older ones was fraught, because these new authors had to establish their own authority. Cervantes pretended that he had merely found the manuscript of *Don Quixote*, attributing its authorship to an Arab, a representative of a culture he had spent his life fighting. Had he become enchanted with Arab storytellers in Algiers during his captivity? We will never know. What we do know is that Cervantes included an account of his Algerian captivity in *Don Quixote* as one of the novel's many interpolated tales (another reason, perhaps, why his novel enjoyed popularity among the pirates of the bayous). This tale is unusually textured, betraying Cervantes's intimate knowledge of the terrain, including details of how a slave might escape from Algiers and a minute account of the Turks, Christians, and North Africans living in this town, speaking a mixture of several languages. Clearly, the experience of Algiers remained a crucial one for Cervantes, and he felt that this, too, was an important part of life in Spain and therefore needed to find a place in his novel. (The interpolated tales also made *Don Quixote* echo story collections such as *One Thousand and One Nights*.)

With the explosion of print, the quest for originality and ownership of new plots gained importance and found its way into the law. Unfortunately, most of the provisions protecting modern authors came too late for Cervantes, and he had little legal recourse against the anonymous copycat. Indeed, the very notion of literary piracy was only beginning to emerge at the time.

To defend himself, Cervantes used the only weapon at his disposal, the weapon he had previously used against chivalric romances: his own power as a storyteller. He worked feverishly and within a year had finished his own sequel. Much better than the lackluster product of his rival, it quickly supplanted the fake version. Mischievously, he had Don Quixote avoid everything the fraudulent second part attributed to him, thereby proving the unauthorized version wrong at every turn. Cervantes even sent Don Quixote to defeat an acquaintance of the fraudulent Don Quixote, thus showing his rival author who was really in charge.

Cervantes knew that the real culprit was not the copycat author but the new world of print, which had made both his story and its imitation so widely available. He drew the only logical conclusion, namely to send his knight out to confront this print culture head-on. In the second part, when Don Quixote learns that a novel has been written about him, he decides to visit a print shop in Barcelona. The experience is eye-opening for Don Quixote, and for his readers as well:

There he saw some working off the Sheets, others correcting the Forms, some in one Place picking of Letters out of the Cases, in another some looking over a Proof; in short, all the Variety that is to be seen in great Printing-Houses. He went from one Workman to another, and was very inquisitive to know what every Body had in Hand; and they were not backward to satisfy his Curiosity. At length coming to one of the Compositors, and asking him what he was about; Sir, said the Printer, this Gentleman here (shewing a likely sort of a Man, something grave, and not young) has translated a Book out of Italian into Spanish, and I am setting some of it here for the Press. [. . .]

But tell me, pray Sir, do you print your Book at your own Charge, or have you sold the Copy to a Bookseller? Why truly, Sir, answer'd the Translator, I publish it upon my own Account, and I hope to clear at least a thousand Crowns by this first Edition; for I design to print off two thousand Books, and they will go off at six Reals apiece in a Trice. I am afraid you'll come short of your Reckoning, said Don Quixote; 'tis a sign you are still a Stranger to the Tricks of these Booksellers and Printers. [. . .]

Then passing on, and enquiring the Title of a Book of which another Workman was correcting a Sheet, they told him 'twas the Second Part of that ingenious Gentleman Don Quixote de la Mancha, written by a certain Person, a Native of Tordesillas. I have heard of that Book before, said Don Quixote, and really thought it had been burnt, and reduc'd to Ashes for a foolish impertinent Libel; but all in good Time, Execution-day will come at last. [. . .] And so saying, he flung out of the Printing-house in a Huff.

When it came to printing, Don Quixote was no fool. While he admired the complex machinery of the printing house, he immediately realized that authors and translators now depended on the owners of these wonderful machines, who might blithely print a copycat version if it made money. In this new world of machines, authors clearly got the short end of the stick.

THIS ENGRAVING BY JAN VAN DER STRAET DEPICTS A MID-SIXTEENTH-
CENTURY PRINT SHOP OF THE KIND VISITED BY DON QUIXOTE.

Authors have been applauding Don Quixote ever since. (I know I did when I first read this passage.) The division of labor between people who invent stories (authors), people who own the machines for producing printed books (printers and publishers), and people who sell those books (distributors and booksellers) has certainly benefited authors, allowing them to reach many more readers than ever before. But it has also limited their control over their own works. Through his character Don Quixote, Cervantes took the measure of the glories and the dilemmas of modern authorship.

Don Quixote's encounter with the machinery that ensured his success yet made him a helpless bystander marked the end of his exploits. But the age of novel writing was just beginning. Very soon, print shops similar to the one he visited unleashed a flood of fiction the likes of which the world had never seen. Fighting off rival authors and literary pirates, Cervantes had created a new form of literature that easily dwarfed the popularity of romances. Independent, confident, and ruthless, authors started to absorb everything that had been written before and added their own outrageous inventions to the mix. A traveler reported meeting giants, dwarfs, and rational horses. A bored French housewife indulged in an illicit affair and killed herself. A crazy white whale hunter hunted a crazy white whale. Previously, collections had captured the ocean of stories and made them available to readers, but now all these brand-new plots were eclipsing the earlier story collections. Even though the idea of individual authorship had first emerged in the classical world, its breakthrough occurred only once it intersected with print and the mass production of literature.

Cervantes, it turned out, had stumbled on a winning formula. The new novels were author-based, premised on originality, and prone to deflating other forms of writing. Part of the deflation was an insistence on prose rather than poetry, and a suspicion about older languages—few people were writing novels in dead languages or outmoded idioms. Novels were also particularly good at giving readers access to the minds of others, especially once they developed an interest in minute psychological processes and techniques for capturing the drift of emotions and thoughts as they occurred in everyday life. Less beholden to convention than epics, novels could also adapt more quickly to changing circumstances such as serial publication in newspapers, becoming the genre of choice during what one might call the mechanical age of literature, the age when the reproduction of literature became a matter of complex machines. The novel itself preceded these machines, but once it intersected with them and used them more and more effectively, it became the dominant literary form of the modern age.

Authors were as varied as the stories they invented. Because novels were less encumbered by tradition, the barriers of access were lower, especially for women. While some female novelists would adopt a male pseudonym, as George Eliot did, more often they wrote under their own names, recording everything from life in the Parisian court to the plight of governesses in England. Female authorship became a career option in an age when few such options existed for women. Access to authorship was more difficult to gain for former slaves in the United States and elsewhere, because they had been systematically kept from literacy. And yet many freed or escaped slaves, most famously Frederick Douglass, authored the story of their escape, and often described the moment when they learned to read and write in secret as the beginning of their freedom. While some of these narratives were autobiographical, others were fictionalized in ways that Cervantes, who had turned his own escape from slavery into a tale, would have appreciated.

With the novel's success, history repeated itself. Just as Cervantes had worried about popular romances, so now people worried about novels (as had already been the case in Japan, when Buddhists and Confucians attacked Lady Murasaki's early novel). Educators and priests started to warn against novels, and doctors treated readers like addicts, hoping to keep them, women in particular, away from reading fiction. But it was becoming increasingly difficult to control access to literature. Women, former slaves, every group and class was pressing into the world of literature, and there was no way to stop them.

The suspicion about novels has disappeared only recently. We are so worried about children not reading enough, about literature losing out to video games, that we consider most novels as preferable to screen time. But the sense that not all reading is equal still exists. It has shifted to the Internet, the new unruly place for the greatest variety of questionable reading and writing. Will there be a time when we will look back at the Internet with nostalgia the way many now look back longingly at the age of the novel?

CHAPTER 10

BENJAMIN FRANKLIN:
MEDIA ENTREPRENEUR IN THE
REPUBLIC OF LETTERS

1776, NORTH AMERICAN COLONIES

ON AUGUST 2, 1776, THE MEMBERS OF THE SECOND CON-tinental Congress gathered to sign the Declaration of Independence. The talented Thomas Jefferson had drafted the text on a custom-made lap desk and sent it to the Congress, where it was put on the table, which meant that it was laid on a table where each member could read it and offer amendments and changes. After Congress had agreed and voted on the revised document, it was ceremoniously read aloud by Colonel John Nixon on July 8. Several weeks later, the Congress hired Timothy Matlack, a former beer brewer who also excelled at the elegant English round hand, with its open, flowing script. Using a quill pen, Matlack wrote out the entire Declaration on a single sheet of parchment, leaving the bottom fifth free for the required signatures.

One by one, the members of the Congress stepped forward to sign. Benjamin Franklin waited for his turn and, after half the signatures had already been applied, he approached and signed the document with a graceful hand, styling himself "Benj. Franklin." Most signatories simply wrote their names, but Franklin took the liberty of adding an elaborate flourish under the length of his signature, drawing a long figure 8, then a smaller circle across it, and finishing off with another figure 8. Perhaps he felt that he had saved room for this extravagance by abbreviating his first name.

BENJAMIN FRANKLIN IS SO WELL KNOWN for his role in the founding of the United States that it's difficult to remember his contribution to the history of literature. To get a better sense of that contribution, I traveled again. Conveniently, since Franklin was the one local figure I was writing about, all I had to do was take the subway from Cambridge into Boston. My destination was the Freedom Trail, a red path painted onto the pavement that winds its way through downtown Boston, hitting all the major locations connected to the American Revolution. There is much that the Freedom Trail leaves out, but I didn't worry about that because I was not following it to learn about the American republic. I was here to find clues about Franklin's services to the Republic of Letters.

I turned a corner and there it was, on a small street in downtown Boston: a statue of Franklin. He looked benevolently down on me, his hat politely in his arm, even though he was standing outside, in a little courtyard set back from the narrow street. Below the statue were reliefs depicting scenes from his life, including the most famous one, of Franklin signing the Declaration of Independence.

Pondering this scene located on the base of the Franklin statue, I went around the corner to 1 Milk Street, where his birth house had once been located. The address is across the street from one of the main attractions on the Freedom Trail, the Old South Meeting House, a nicely preserved redbrick building from the seventeenth century. The Franklin birth house, by contrast, was a humble wooden affair that had long since burned down. In its stead, there stood a six-story house with a stucco façade in the nineteenth-century style. On the second floor, it boasted a bust of Franklin and an inscription stating that the great statesman was in fact born here.

The house had seen better days. Some windows were boarded up, and it was hard to tell whether it was actually occupied. The entryway smelled of piss. A flyer announced that an institution called the International Academy had moved to a different location. Another, from the City of Boston, promised that improvements to the sewage system would soon be made. Someone had stuck a business card selling vintage posters to the door. Amid the revitalized Boston downtown, 1 Milk Street looked like something out of the old, seedy downtown Boston I remembered from decades ago.

The ground floor was abandoned. A sign that looked as if it dated from the eighties announced Sir Speedy, a business offering "graphic design, color copying, digital services, and color printing." At first I was excited by this coincidence: Franklin would have liked the idea of a printing service setting up shop at his birth house. But the faded sign of the abandoned print shop looked sad and outdated, and Franklin was not prone to nostalgia. While he might have liked the print shop, he would have liked even better the idea of one type of print shop going out of business and being replaced with a new one. Despite his wig and his stockings, Franklin was one of the great pioneers of modern information technology.

The more I thought about Franklin's relation to technology, the more I became convinced that as his quill scratched across the parchment bearing the Declaration of Independence, he must have realized just how antiquated it was, even in 1776, to sign a document written by a scribe, as if hailing from the dawn of writing, and on parchment, a writing surface invented at Pergamum two thousand years before. To be sure, in the age of print, handwriting and parchment had become something special, reserved for important documents (in a similar fashion, the U.S. Constitution would be written by a scribe on four sheets of parchment). But

Franklin knew that the Declaration of Independence relied on newer technology, more in keeping with its revolutionary aims.

As soon as the Declaration had been voted into effect on July 4, a full month before the beautifully handwritten parchment copy was made and signed, the ratified text had been sent to a printer, John Dunlap, who had produced some two hundred broadside copies overnight. The copies were immediately dispatched on horseback to the other twelve colonies via postal roads. On July 6, a newspaper, *The Pennsylvania Evening Post*, carried the Declaration on its front page; on July 10, Mary Katherine Goddard did the same with *The Maryland Journal*; and many other newspapers followed. It was in the form of printed newspapers and broadsides that the United States first declared its independence from England.

Among the framers of the Declaration, Franklin was in the best position to appreciate the role of print that day. At the court of France, Marie Antoinette would disparage him as lacking in aristocratic refinement because he had been a printer's foreman. Though unkind, Marie Antoinette was not wrong. Franklin had learned the trade as a quasi-indentured apprentice to his brother, who introduced him to every step in the printing process, including the making of inks and the different types of paper, letters, and layout. The process hadn't changed significantly since Gutenberg. What had changed were the uses to which print was being put: cheap new formats, above all newspapers and broadsides, that fundamentally altered how ideas spread. While Franklin didn't contribute much to the technical process of printing, he realized what could be done with it, and he spent his career expanding and perfecting the infrastructure of print, from securing paper supply and maintaining the postal roads over which printed matter was distributed across the thirteen colonies to newspaper and broadside publishing networks. A media entrepreneur, Franklin did more than anyone else to cre-

THE DECLARATION OF INDEPENDENCE AS PRINTED ON
SATURDAY, JULY 6, 1776, BY *THE PENNSYLVANIA EVENING POST.*

ate the world that would bring the Declaration of Independence into being.

THE NEW ENGLAND INTO which Franklin was born took pride in literacy, but it was a literacy centered on a single book: the Bible. Puritans had brought the Geneva Bible, an English Bible translated secretly in Geneva, Switzerland, to the New World on the *Mayflower* (it was also the Bible used by William Shakespeare). Less than two decades later, in 1636, they founded a college—what would become Harvard University—to ensure higher levels of literacy among the clergy. But ministers were not the only ones focused on literacy. Schools were founded to ensure that children, both male and female, would learn to read the Bible. To satisfy the new demand for books and other printed matter, Puritans set up the first printing press in the English colonies in 1638 (a hundred years after the Spaniards had set up the first printing press in Mexico), creating the most literate society on earth at the time, with 45 percent literacy among white women and 70 percent among white men. By 1790, the latter rate had reached an astonishing 90 percent.

Franklin cared deeply about books. He would go on to found the Junto, a club of like-minded book lovers, as well as the Library Company, a membership-based lending library. Once he had made his fortune, he built a personal library containing 4,276 volumes, with custom floor-to-ceiling shelves and an elaborate inventory system. He even devised a mechanical arm to retrieve books that couldn't be reached by hand.

But Franklin didn't print more than a few dozen books in his entire life. He once brought out the New Testament without a license, but it didn't yield much in terms of profit. Even though novels had become popular in the wake of Cervantes, Franklin printed only a single one, Samuel Richardson's *Pamela*. (Fiction amounted to barely 4 percent of total print output in the colonies.) Franklin himself was fond of John Bunyan's *Pilgrim's Progress*, an allegorical tale of a Christian who resists temptation and overcomes doubt, which had become the second most commonly possessed book after the Bible (Bunyan, too, preferred the Puritan Geneva Bible to the official King James Bible). But Franklin printed neither *Pilgrim's Progress* nor *Don Quixote*, although he possessed a copy of the latter in his personal library. The problem with books was that they were prohibitively expensive to make, requiring significant capital investments in paper, type, and binding, not to mention labor. Franklin was happy to sell books, but often it was cheaper to import them from England.

A New Market for Newspapers

Despite his love for books, Franklin realized that the combination of high literacy and print technology had created the conditions for new forms of print publication, above all newspapers. The first newspaper of the colonies had been produced in Boston in 1690, mostly reflecting the views of the ruling class. But Franklin's brother challenged the status quo by starting his own newspaper, whose success set him on a collision course with the authorities. When he landed in jail, he continued to publish the paper in Benjamin Franklin's name, showing the younger brother just how powerful a newspaper could be. The experiment also demonstrated that there was an untapped market for newspapers. Towns didn't need just one newspaper, as had been thought; there was room for several. And with competing newspapers would come controversy, the testing of ideas, and polemical exchange from which the best ideas would emerge victorious.

Soon Franklin broke his contract with his brother and fled to Philadelphia, where he set his sights on newspapers. He acquired his own print shop and bought *The Pennsylvania Gazette*, and from that moment on, newspapers were at the core of his growing business empire. The newspapers of the day were typically short, just four pages, with advertisements on the last page. They were read in homes, clubs, taverns, and coffeehouses, places that allowed for social encounters in which new ideas could be debated and could thrive. The philosopher G.W.F. Hegel would compare the ritual of reading the morning paper to the morning prayer, an idea Franklin would have liked; having abandoned the Puritan faith of his fathers, he had opted for the republican faith in the newspaper.

Increasingly difficult to control, newspapers involved a growing portion of the literate population in the exchange of ideas, fostering a climate in which independence could arise. When Franklin was born, there existed only a single newspaper in the colonies; by the time the Declaration of Independence was printed, there were thirty-seven, in part thanks to Franklin's own efforts. The proliferation of newspapers didn't reach all colonies in the same way, with many fewer newspapers in the South, which also meant that there were fewer independence-minded colonists there. (The comparison with England is instructive as well. The colonies possessed fewer newspapers but more towns with printing presses than the mother country, where printing was centered in London and could be more easily controlled.)

While newspapers were the most important novelty in the world of print, broadsides were significant as well. Shorter, cheaper, and even easier to distribute than newspapers, single-page broadsides consisted of one large, folio-sized page that could be posted on a wall or door. Alternatively, a page could be printed on both sides and folded once or twice, yielding four and sixteen pages respectively. Combining three such twice-folded pages produced a sizable pamphlet of forty-eight pages that could be stitched together with needle and thread. As long as the stack of pages didn't need to be laboriously bound, as long as a needle could still pierce the pages and thread them together, which was possible up to about one hundred pages, the result could be made cheaply.

Of the four hundred pamphlets produced before 1776, the most famous was Thomas Paine's *Common Sense*, written half a year before the Declaration of Independence, powerfully articulating the rationale for independence. Franklin helped Paine publish this pamphlet and bought a hundred copies of the first print run. Paine would ultimately sell 153,000 copies in the first year alone (cunningly, he not only forwent all royalties but also renounced his copyright, giving any printer the right to publish the pamphlet). As the cheapest vehicles for spreading new ideas, broadsides and pamphlets had contributed to the climate of democratic unrest among the colonists. The print run of the Declaration of Independence in the form of a broadside was the culmination of decades of broadside publishing.

Sensing that newspapers and broadsides were the way of the future, Franklin focused his energies on these two formats and made sure that he would command every aspect of their production. It wasn't enough to have a print shop; he also needed to control the necessary raw materials, above all paper. After failing to buy out the paper supplier from his Philadelphia rivals, he helped papermakers set up their own business and shared profits. Paper was still made from rags, and Franklin himself collected them and sent them to the paper mills that were part of his sphere of influence before buying back the finished paper. Eventually his supply network expanded all the way to the South, including a paper mill at Williamsburg, Virginia, which, like the many Dutch mills that produced the paper exported to the colonies, was driven by a windmill. Franklin was essentially creating a vertically integrated industry, controlling the process from the rags that were turned into paper to the printing and distribution of his newspapers and broadsides.

Printing in the colonies was highly localized, in part because of the difficulties of transportation, but Franklin recognized that having a network of printers would be a great advantage. In addition to his vertical integration, he needed a horizontal one. Just as he himself had been apprenticed to his brother, so Franklin now placed his own children and nephews as apprentices in other print shops or bound others to him through marriage. Franklin would lend money and types and help with contacts, demanding in return one-third of the profits. He trained his nephew, who became a printer in Rhode Island, and sent a former associate all the way to Antigua.

All told, he helped set up two dozen printers, from New England to the Caribbean. The official printer of the Declaration of Independence, John Dunlap, was part of Franklin's network as well. Franklin had helped John Dunlap's uncle, William, to establish himself as a printer, and approved of William's marriage to Franklin's wife's niece, Deborah Croker. William Dunlap was so grateful to his patron that he named one of his sons Benjamin Franklin. Eventually William gave his business to John, who became the official printer of the Declaration of Independence.

Not all of Franklin's ventures succeeded. The first newspaper to carry the news that a declaration of independence had been signed was the *Pennsylvanischer Staatsbote*, on July 5. Franklin must have observed the success of the Declaration in German with a mixture of triumph and regret because he had failed in his attempt to establish a German newspaper. First he was hampered by the fact that he didn't have the gothic types preferred by German readers; he also proved tone-deaf to the pacifist-leaning community. As a general principle, Franklin did not use his newspapers to advance a particular political agenda, something for which he was often criticized. When he broke this rule with the Pennsylvania Dutch by criticizing their pacifism, his venture failed.

While Franklin was working on both vertical integration and horizontal print networks, he also realized that print was dependent on the government and governmental infrastructure. Perhaps the most lucrative government print job was not laws and declarations but money, since all he had to do was print identical blanks; the numbers were added later by hand.

Even more important than government print jobs were government roads, called postal roads because they enabled the distribution of mail in the colonies, which placed them under the control of the postmaster. The position didn't offer much by way of a salary, but it came with the privilege of sending items free of charge and deciding who else could do so, a significant savings for a printer. As soon as Franklin had established himself as a printer, he had started a lobbying campaign to become postmaster, and he succeeded nine years later, when he was named postmaster of Philadelphia. Not content with this accomplishment, he brought nearby post offices under his control as well and did not rest until he became the postmaster general for all the colonies, in 1753. In 1775 he switched his allegiance from the British crown to become the first postmaster general appointed by the Second Continental Congress. (The position of postmaster general today comes with the second-highest salary in the federal government, right after the president.)

The job of postmaster came not only with privileges but also with responsibilities, chief among them the postal roads. They were not in good shape. A British inspector sent to investigate the postal roads in 1773 was shocked by the decrepit roadbeds, drunken drivers and riders, and lack of inns. Franklin was not easily deterred by

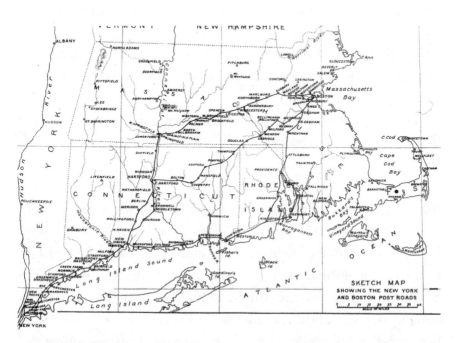

A MAP OF POSTAL ROADS IN NEW YORK AND NEW ENGLAND, WHICH WERE PART OF FRANKLIN'S PRINT AND DISTRIBUTION NETWORK.

such conditions and decided to inspect his roads personally, traveling some sixteen hundred miles from Virginia to New England.

He made significant improvements, cutting down the time it would take for mail to get from Philadelphia to New York (faster than it does today: a round-trip in twenty-four hours) and setting up a new postal road to Montreal. Of all the signatories of the Declaration of Independence, Franklin knew the most about the technologies that had made this document possible because most of those technologies were concentrated in his own hands.

The Republic of Letters

In 1747, with his career as printer and publisher firmly established, Franklin left the running of his business to associates and became a man of leisure. He immersed himself in scientific papers and books and undertook his own experiments, especially in the burgeoning science of electricity, which led him to discover and name the negative and positive charges of electric currents. He also demonstrated the practical uses of science by inventing the lightning rod, becoming the continent's first natural philosopher and recognized scientist.

These scientific activities profited from print as well because they depended on what we would now call knowledge networks. Philosophical and scientific societies created an international exchange of ideas that was independent from older centers of learning such as the Church and royal courts. The advocates of these new networks realized the political implications of their activities and began to think of themselves as citizens of a Republic of Letters. Ever the entrepreneur, Franklin contributed to this Republic of Letters by founding the American Philosophical Society and becoming an enthusiastic member of the Freemasons, the influential but secretive international association devoted to promoting Enlightenment values.

These more specialized societies were the flip side of the print revolution, the counterpart to popular newspapers and broadsides. Many natural philosophers dismissed the crude tone of newspapers and broadsides, but Franklin's experience made him appreciate these popular forms alongside those for scientific exchange. The Enlightenment, he knew, was the product not only of philosophers enjoying prestige and autonomy from established centers of power, but also of the democratic cacophony of ideas disseminated by newspapers and broadsides.

The most important intersection of print and the new knowledge networks was the *Encyclopédie*, undertaken by a number of French philosophers under the guidance of Denis Diderot and Jean Le Rond d'Alembert. The project started as an attempt to translate the English *Cyclopaedia, or an Universal Dictionary of Arts and Sciences*, a two-volume encyclopedia published in 1728, into French. But soon the French editors realized that they needed a more comprehensive and all-encompassing publication, something that would gather, organize, and distribute the rapidly changing knowledge of the time, including the new mechanical, technical, and scientific discoveries that were being produced by natural philosophers such as Franklin. Between 1751 and 1772, they published seventeen volumes, plus eleven volumes of illustrations, a comprehensive distillation of knowledge in the eighteenth century.

Just like its more modest British predecessor, the French *Encyclopédie* was premised on print. It was because of print that more literature and science, both ancient and modern, was circulating, and print made it possible to gather all this knowledge in a single venture and hope to sell enough copies to make a profit. There was too much to know; new devices for filtering and organizing knowledge were necessary. Given the importance of print as a facilitator for encyclopedias, it is not surprising that print and related matters occupied more than sixty entries in the *Encyclopédie*, from "rag

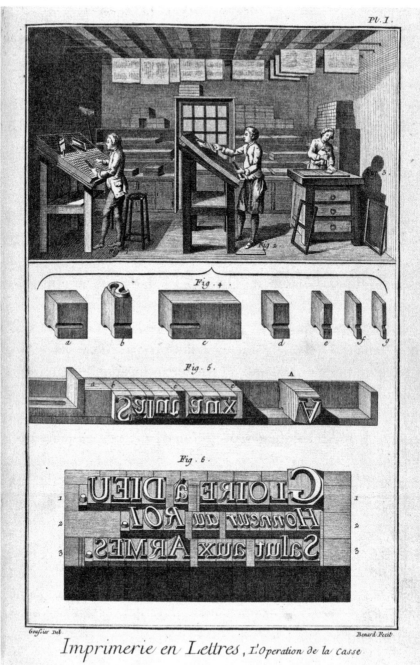

THIS PLATE FROM DIDEROT AND D'ALEMBERT'S *ENCYCLOPÉDIE,*
WHICH INCLUDED MANY ENTRIES ON LITERATURE AND WRITING,
DEPICTS THE WORK OF COMPOSITORS.

sellers" and "paper makers" to "ink balls" and "typefaces," with detours to "copyright" and "censorship."

The *Encyclopédie* also included entries on the history of literature with an emphasis on writing technologies, from Chinese writing and the invention of the alphabet to the idea of holy scripture (though only of the Christian variety) as well as the Septuagint, the Greek translation of the Hebrew Bible. The most significant entry, written by Diderot, was on "encyclopedia" itself, a passionate defense of the entire enterprise as a unique effort to gather all knowledge and preserve it for future generations. In it, Diderot made it clear that the technology behind this hope was print. Perhaps thinking of Don Quixote, the editors also included an entry on bibliomania, the mental disorder of manically collecting books. Franklin, with his large library, surely fit that definition.

These encyclopedia projects resonated with printers and publishers in the colonies, who wanted to tap into this new source of knowledge and instruction. The Pennsylvania newspaper that Franklin would take over was called *The Universal Instructor in all Arts and Sciences: and Pennsylvania Gazette*. Each issue carried one page from the British *Cyclopaedia* on which the French *Encyclopédie* was originally based, beginning with A. The plan was to proceed alphabetically to arrive, one day, at Z. The attempt to publish an encyclopedia in a newspaper and to name the newspaper after an encyclopedia was a perfect example of how exclusive knowledge networks intersected with popular ones.

The intersection didn't always work. In October 1729, the newspaper went bankrupt and was bought out by Franklin, who quickly recognized the folly of the undertaking. He got rid of the encyclopedia-sounding part of the name, *Universal Instructor in all Arts and Sciences*, and kept only the second, *Pennsylvania Gazette*, explaining to his readers that at the present pace, it would take more than ten years to get through the entire two-volume *Cyclopaedia*. Furthermore, a newspaper, bought and discarded daily, was the wrong medium for an encyclopedia, which depended on the reader's ability to flip back and forth among cross-references. The clear-eyed decision to cut the encyclopedia project from his newspaper did not mean that Franklin dismissed encyclopedias—quite the contrary. In 1749 he purchased the expensive two-volume set of the *Cyclopaedia* for himself. Two decades later he advised the Library Company, which he had helped found, to purchase the large French *Encyclopédie* at the staggering cost of £300 (roughly $100,000 today). Newspapers were good at creating a lively but chaotic atmosphere of colliding ideas. Encyclopedias were good at ordering knowledge. The two shouldn't be forced together. This was Franklin at his best: understanding the connections but also the differences between technologies and applications, formats and content.

Taxing the Republic of Letters

Together, newspapers and encyclopedias helped create the explosive Enlightenment mixture that would lead to the Declaration of Independence. All that was needed was a match. According to conventional wisdom, the match was the Boston Tea Party. The British had imposed taxes on the colonists even though the colonists had no representation in Parliament. In protest, freedom-minded Bostonians, disguised as Indians, threw newly taxed tea into Boston Harbor.

The story is true, but incomplete. The first tax imposed on the colonists that triggered widespread resentment was not on tea but on paper and printed matter, the so-called Stamp Act. Despite the attempts by Franklin and others to establish a domestic paper industry, most paper in the colonies continued to be imported, often Dutch paper that was distributed via English wholesalers. This import was the target of the Stamp Act, which aimed straight at the rapidly expanding colonial network of paper mills and printers, postal roads, and newspaper distributors. It was not the smartest way for the British to raise revenue, because the colonial publishing industry fought back with all its newfound might. Newspapers ran front page stories about the injustice of the Stamp Act; some added black funereal frames, and one paper printed a gravestone across the front page. Printers boycotted, protested, decried, and openly defied the tax by using paper that had not been stamped. When paper exports to the colonies dropped 90 percent, the British Parliament relented and repealed the Stamp Act.

In ending the hated Stamp Act, Parliament did the right thing for the wrong reason. Thinking that the problem had been the structure of the tax (an external rather than an internal tax, a distinction suggested by Franklin himself), it came up with the Townshend Acts, which still taxed paper, in addition to tea. Angry printers destroyed stamped paper publicly, in a kind of dress rehearsal for the Boston Tea Party, which could just as easily have been named the Boston Paper Party. The importing of paper almost ceased after 1775, when the First Continental Congress imposed a systematic boycott on all imports from Britain, laying the foundation for the Second Continental Congress to declare independence. The paper Jefferson used for drafting the Declaration of Independence, however, was imported from a Dutch mill, probably via a British wholesaler.

While Jefferson could take pride in having authored the Declaration of Independence, Franklin could take pride in the fact that he had created the print infrastructure that had made it possible. He also contributed the document's most important phrase. Jefferson had opened the document with the sentence "We hold these truths to be sacred"; Franklin replaced "sacred" with "self-evident," using a term favored by natural philosophers. Marie Antoinette, no doubt, would have found it strange that it was a printer who added a crucial word to the most important document of the Enlightenment. But then again, she didn't know that the technology that would lead to her death was not the guillotine but the printing press.

A CONTENT PROVIDER

The word "self-evident," of course, was not Franklin's only act of authorship. Having full control over everything from rags and paper to print and newspapers all the way to the postal service and roads, Franklin was in a most enviable position as an author: He could write what he wanted, print it, and force it down the throats of the public.

Surprisingly, young Franklin rarely wrote to earn money (nor did he seek to profit from his scientific discoveries even when they yielded practical results). This famous businessman, who seized every opportunity for making and saving money, did not initially think of the act of authoring literature as an appropriate source of income. He earned his money with his printing network, the infrastructure of literature, not with literature itself. He wrote when the network demanded it, and then mostly under assumed names. While still a teenager, he adopted the character of a middle-aged widow and mother; many other characters would follow, intervening in political debates, satirizing the follies of his countrymen, instructing and amusing his readers. More often than not, Franklin wrote to defend his newspapers and his publishing decisions or to attack those of his rivals.

Franklin's greatest financial success as an author was *Poor Richard's Almanack,* a publication based on the days of the month and lunar cycles as well as proverbs, sayings, and aphorisms. Written in a folksy tone, it shared hard-earned wisdom and provided readers with advice and encouragement. For all the success of his almanac, Franklin wasn't really its author. Not only did he strenuously hide behind the name of Richard Saunders, he did not write many of the sayings associated with Poor Richard in the first place. He found them, changed them, arranged them, and placed them in Poor Richard's mouth. Even when he collected the best sayings of Richard in a freestanding pamphlet, *The Way to Wealth*, he refused to attach his own name to it. Later critics didn't accept this stance and accused him of plagiarism, as if he were a modern author like Cervantes, hoping to sell original stories on the literary market. But Franklin was not a modern author in that sense. He was an entrepreneur of writing who cut and pasted, assimilated and transformed the literature of the past into a product that would work for his readership, acting more like ancient scribes—or the content aggregators of our own time.

The other piece of literature closely associated with Franklin's name was his autobiography, which provided a powerful account of Franklin's life, from his apprenticeship to his business success. While it left out much, including many business failures, it chronicled Franklin's struggle with his personal shortcomings, including pride. At the heart of the autobiography was a chart through which he kept track of his virtues and vices, a kind of moral account book. Franklin's autobiography was so powerful that it laid the foundation for many future autobiographies both in America and elsewhere.

But Franklin never wrote it—that is to say, he never wrote a text called *The Autobiography of Benjamin Franklin*. Much like Lady Murasaki in her autobiographical letter to her daughter, Franklin gave an initial account of his life to his wayward son William (who became the last colonial governor of New Jersey and a notorious Loyalist). To this letter he later added others as well as bits of narrative, but he, the printer, the person uniquely positioned to publish whatever he wanted, never published any part of it. After his death, the pieces were cobbled together by editors and labeled *The Autobiography of Benjamin Franklin*, in which form they became a classic. As a print entrepreneur who used whatever content he could find, Franklin would probably have approved of this unlicensed editorial practice.

The most important text associated with Franklin's name remains the Declaration of Independence, which was increasingly celebrated as the foundational document of a rising nation. During the War of 1812, the original document was deemed unsafe in Washington, D.C., and was evacuated just in time before the burning of the city in 1814. During World War II, even greater precautions were taken, and the Declaration was placed for safekeeping in Fort Knox, in Kentucky. Lying secure amid the gold reserves of the United States, this handwritten piece of parchment had acquired the status of a sacred text. By that time, the Declaration had also begun to inspire others, including the proclamation of the independence of Haiti. Along with the Constitution, the Declaration would also spawn its own form of textual fundamentalism, the insistence that henceforth the United States would have to live by the original, literal meaning of this text.

Franklin's life was so closely connected to print in all of its forms that he saw his life through print, or even as print. In his youth, he had written a mock epitaph:

> The Body of B. Franklin, Printer
> Like the Cover of an old Book
> Its Contents torn out
> And stript of its Lettering and Gilding
> Lies here Food for Worms.
> Yet the work shall not be lost
> For it will (as he believ'd) appear once more
> In a new & more beautiful Edition
> Corrected & amended
> By
> The Author.

While wittily referring to a godlike author in the afterlife (which he didn't believe in), Franklin described his life from the perspective of a printer. And indeed, his life has been corrected and amended, not by a deity but by generations of biographers who turned him into one of our most revered founding fathers. But perhaps we should respect his wish and remember him primarily as the person who brought the power of print to the struggle for independence. More than simply a republican printer, as he liked to call himself, he was the printer of the Republic of Letters.

CHAPTER 11

WORLD LITERATURE:
GOETHE IN SICILY

1827, WEIMAR

ON THE TWENTY-FOURTH OF MAY, 1823, THE ASPIRING POET
Johann Peter Eckermann gathered his courage and sent his manuscript titled "Reflections on Poetry with Particular Reference to Goethe" to the famous writer himself. Eckermann was thirty years old, and no one would have predicted that he would ever write a piece of literary criticism. He had grown up in abject poverty. The family's survival depended on a cow, which supplied them with milk for their own consumption and occasionally allowed them to sell a little surplus. Since that time, Eckermann had come up in the world. He learned how to read and write, attracted the notice of the village doctor, and finally secured a low-level secretarial position. He took Latin and Greek lessons with a private tutor and eventually was accepted at the University of Göttingen, in his late twenties, to study law. A bright future was within his reach.

But this ordinarily disciplined man couldn't stay focused on the law and kept getting distracted by literature, writing poetry, a play, and literary criticism when he should have been studying. Then a friend recommended that he read Goethe, and Eckermann was hooked. He dropped out of law school to embark on a book about his new idol and sent it off to the seventy-three-year-old Goethe, who was then at the height of his fame, presiding, in the Duchy of Weimar, in eastern Germany, over a large number of acolytes and admirers. (In 1850, only eighteen years after Goethe's death, Ralph Waldo Emerson would include him among his six "representative men," as the sole writer, along with Plato, the philosopher; Swedenborg, the mystic; Montaigne, the skeptic; Shakespeare, the poet; and Napoleon, the man of the world.)

The day after Eckermann sent off the manuscript, he hit the road. Traveling by coach was out of the question; he was much too poor for that. Instead he did what he always did: He walked. He started walking on the twenty-fifth of May, heading south in the summer heat along the river Warre, and didn't stop until he arrived at his destination over a week later.

Immediately upon arriving in Weimar, he left a note for Goethe and was invited to visit. He entered a large and sprawling house, one room giving way to another, almost labyrinthine in design. The rooms were as far-flung as Goethe's interests. There was a room for receiving guests, a drawing room, a dining room, and a room for conversation. There was Goethe's study with an adjacent library, and a music room. There was a room for Goethe's collection of statues and busts, a room for his collection of coins, and a room for his minerals. A servant took Eckermann up the stairs and through some of these rooms and left him in the presence of Goethe. Goethe graciously invited Eckermann in. He had been spending all morning with Eckermann's excellent manuscript, he said, and would help him publish it. He hoped that Eckermann would stay in Weimar for a while.

Why was Goethe so welcoming? Eckermann had sent not only the manuscript, but also a letter praising his own talents as a secretary. He was looking for an employer, and the aging Goethe was looking for a personal assistant, a role that Eckermann readily assumed. In the nine years until Goethe's death, he came to Goethe's house more than a thousand times, helping the writer with the publication of his work, making selections, and researching topics, all free of charge.

Eckermann also started to record his conversations with Goethe, initially to aid his own memory but more and more because he realized how valuable they might become. Instinctively, Eckermann did what students of teachers had done in the centuries before the Common Era, namely write down their masters' conversations and publish them under their own name. Eckermann was Goethe's Plato and his chief evangelist.

Thanks to Eckermann, we know that on the afternoon of January 31, 1827, a Wednesday, a new vision of literature was born in the small town of Weimar, a vision that has remained current to this day. On that Wednesday, Eckermann hadn't seen his master for several days, so Goethe had all kinds of thoughts and reflections pent up and was holding forth, reporting on what he had done and read since they last met. Apparently, he had been reading a Chinese novel. "Really? That must have been rather strange!" Eckermann exclaimed. But this was not the right reaction. After more than four years with Goethe, Eckermann did not yet fully understand his master. "No, much less so than one thinks!" Goethe reprimanded him, and began to lecture.

Eckermann liked it when Goethe lectured; there was always something to be learned. Goethe started talking about the influence of the British writer Samuel Richardson on his own work, but before long he came back to Chinese novels and manners, emphasizing how morally elevated this Chinese novel was. Eckermann was surprised again: "Isn't it strange that the works of this Chinese writer are so morally elevated while those of the foremost poet of France [Pierre-Jean de Béranger] aren't?" "I suppose you're right," Goethe answered, throwing the disoriented Eckermann a bone. "It just goes to show the topsy-turvy world of today." But Eckermann still couldn't believe what Goethe was telling him about China and ventured that surely this Chinese novel must be quite unusual, the exception to the rule. The master's voice was stern: "Nothing could be further from the truth. The Chinese have thousands of them, and had them when our ancestors were still living in the trees."

Eckermann was speechless, realizing that Goethe had opened a can of worms. One sympathizes: Who wants to read thousands of Chinese novels? But one also sympathizes with Goethe. Someone like Eckermann, full of prejudice, ignorance, and incredulity, is just asking to be shocked a little. Faced with Eckermann's obstinacy, Goethe reached for the term that would truly jar him out of his complacency, and intoned: "The era of world literature is at hand, and everyone must contribute to accelerating it."

World literature. Goethe realized that literature was expanding, that more literature from more periods and places was becoming available to more people than ever before. Hitherto confined to particular places and traditions, literature was becoming a single, integrated whole.

We owe this insight, the coinage of the term "world literature," to Eckermann, to his persistence, his decision to walk for two weeks to Weimar, his willingness to serve as Goethe's interlocutor and to write down the wise man's thoughts. But we also owe "world literature" to Eckermann's ignorance, his inability to imagine Chinese novels, his assumptions about the superiority of what he knew. "World literature," like many new ideas, needed a straw man.

A WORLD MARKET IN LITERATURE

Eckermann recorded the conversation that gave birth to the idea of world literature, but he didn't explain why this cosmopolitan vision should emerge from the provincial town of Weimar, located some-

where in eastern Germany. Didn't the grand idea of world literature belong in one of the great capitals of the nineteenth century,
such as Paris or London?

Goethe had grown up in privileged circumstances in cosmopolitan Frankfurt, where Gutenberg had sold his first printed Bible
three hundred years earlier. After some notable successes with plays
and poetry, Goethe had come to prominence with a bestseller, *The
Sorrows of Young Werther*, the story of a love triangle leading to a
suicide. The novel triggered "Werther Fever" by encouraging over-
wrought young men and women to express their emotions freely in
letters (the novel contains many epistolary exchanges) and to wear
the distinctive clothes of the characters (blue frock coat, yellow
vests, high boots). Napoleon claimed to have read the novel in detail and made a point of meeting Goethe in person. Apparently, he
criticized certain passages, though Goethe never revealed which
ones.

Riding this early success, Goethe could have gone anywhere,
but he followed an invitation from the duke of Weimar to join him
in his remote duchy. The inducements were considerable. Before
long, Goethe found himself showered not only with praise and recognition but also with a handsome salary, a house, a title, and an
increasingly far-flung job description. The duchy numbered only
about two hundred thousand subjects, and the town of Weimar
only seven thousand, but it was an independent entity. Goethe
soon realized that the town was in need of better management and
made himself indispensable. Acquiring the title of privy councilor,
he took charge of everything from the theater to roads, finances,
and even warfare; he was also sent on diplomatic missions. In addition to his position as the best-known German writer, he had become a man of the world.

In Weimar, Goethe found himself on the receiving end of cultural imports despite his growing fame. The cultural center at the
time was Paris (London, though larger in size, was a distant sec-

ond), and Parisians happily exported their national culture, making Europeans read French novels, recite French poetry, and watch French plays. To counter French influence, Goethe turned to England, above all to Shakespeare, along with Samuel Richardson and Laurence Sterne, but these, too, were metropolitan products. As an alternative, he might have fallen back on his own national traditions, but his duchy was part of a patchwork of small and medium-sized German states that had not yet coalesced into a nation-state. Goethe appreciated German literature and enjoyed an unrivaled status among German writers, but that was not enough for him. He was not content to promote German national culture as an alternative to England and France. While Parisians and Londoners admired the grand history of their national literatures, and younger nations were eager to boost their own national traditions, Goethe was becoming interested in literature from farther afield.

In his far-flung reading interests, Goethe was helped by an increasingly developed world market in literature, which allowed works from remote locales to find their way to this provincial town and its gorgeous Duchess Anna Amalia Library, where he worked frequently. *Hau Kiou Choaan or The Pleasing History: A Translation from the Chinese Language,* one of the first Chinese novels to be translated into a Western language, was a typical example. Its initial translator was James Wilkinson, a British subject working in Canton for the East India Company, through which England was establishing trading posts and colonies in Asia (especially after having lost the thirteen North American colonies to independence). Stuck in China, Wilkinson decided to learn Chinese and soon took it upon himself to translate the popular novel *Hau Kiou Choaan* into English. His manuscript contained many corrections that reveal how much he labored over it. When he was called back to England, he abandoned the effort, leaving the work only three-quarters complete.

Decades later, the manuscript found its way into the hands of

Bishop Thomas Percy, who corrected Wilkinson's manuscript, adjusted expressions when they didn't make sense to him, and cut repetitive passages until he was satisfied with the product and published it in 1761. The result was still far from perfect. Seventy years later, John Francis Davis, the second governor of Hong Kong (and son of the director of the East India Company) undertook a new translation, wryly observing that the original translator not only was guilty of innumerable errors and omissions, but had also managed to mistranslate the very title of the work. His new translation, now more correctly called *The Fortunate Union*, was published with the Oriental Translation Fund in 1829.

For Goethe, Davis's painstaking labor came too late. Always looking for new literature from abroad, he had gotten his hands on a German translation of the flawed English translation in 1796. Despite its faults, this translation made him a convert to Chinese literature, which he followed as best he could for the rest of his life. Library records show that he borrowed several volumes on China in 1813, including the *Travels* of Marco Polo, the first Western account of China, published around 1300. Goethe particularly appreciated the combination of finely observed description and completely invented fantasy that gave this work the quality of a fairy tale. A few years later, Goethe got in touch with one of the earliest professional experts on China to seek further information about this mysterious culture, and in 1827 he lectured about another Chinese novel, *Les Deux Cousines*, which he read in a French translation by Jean-Pierre Abel-Rémusat, the first chair in Chinese at the Collège de France. Some months earlier, Goethe had read yet another Chinese novel, *Chinese Courtship*, in an English translation. It was in the course of commenting on this last reading experience that he coined the term "world literature" in his conversation with Eckermann in 1827. So few Chinese novels were available in the West that Goethe basically read everything he could find through booksellers, libraries, and scholarly networks.

What impressed Goethe about this foreign literature? The first Chinese novel he read, the badly translated *Pleasing History*, was a fast-moving story of a young man and woman who got caught in convoluted plots and schemes, full of adventures and cunning deceptions, before they were united in marriage. This contrived plot did not bother Percy, the second translator, perhaps because it reminded him of Western novels such as *Don Quixote*. Goethe was not bothered by this plot, either, and publicly read from the novel in 1815, almost two decades after having first encountered it. *Les Deux Cousines*, the last Chinese novel he was able to find, was even more extreme in this regard, premised entirely on strange coincidences, oracular predictions, and a contrived happy ending.

But *Chinese Courtship*, the novel that prompted Goethe to coin the term "world literature," was different. Composed in verse, it presented a male protagonist who was widely admired for his literary education and his ability to dash off sophisticated poems on a whim. The novel rewarded him for his literary prowess with a lucrative government post and marriage to his beloved, using this plot as an excuse for elaborate descriptions of gardens and the recitation of poetry. At a time when the Western novel was considered a latecomer to the literary canon and mostly middlebrow, a verse novel such as *Chinese Courtship* showed Goethe the possibilities of a high-art novel.

Goethe didn't limit himself to Chinese novels. He got his hands on folktales, Serbian poetry, and classical Sanskrit drama (part of his play *Faust* was inspired by the Sanskrit play *Shakuntala*). And then there was *One Thousand and One Nights*. Even as a child Goethe had been fascinated by this collection of tales. They were read to him in the way Scheherazade had told them to the king, namely night after night with cliff-hangers. The young Goethe was more imaginative than the king because each night he would try to finish the story and tell his parents his own ending the next morning, comparing it to the original. In middle age, Goethe deepened his interest in the Arabic world and worked on a play about the prophet Muhammad. Voltaire, the Enlightenment writer with a penchant for provocation, had written a play on the prophet as well, portraying him as a fraud. Goethe, by contrast, showed Muhammad as a charismatic teacher who managed to turn scattered desert tribes into a unified force.

The most important writer Goethe encountered was the medieval Persian poet Hafez. He was so taken with this poet that he wrote a book of notes and essays as well as an entire collection of poetry called *West-Eastern Divan* as a response to his reading experience. Unable to travel to Persia, he imagined visiting the oases and great cities of the Orient with his "master" Hafez through poetry.

Goethe's reading habits puzzled most of his contemporaries and friends, not only his narrow-minded secretary. Wilhelm Grimm, an associate of Goethe, wrote to his brother Jacob in utter confusion: "He is into Persian stuff, composed a collection of poems in the manner of Hafez [. . .] and is studying Arabic," while noting that Goethe was also seen "reading from and explaining Haoh Kioh Tschwen" (A *Pleasing History*). The brothers Grimm were younger than Goethe and fascinated by German folk art. They collected fairy and folktales and had just begun the monumental work of publishing their findings, now known as *Grimm's Fairy Tales* (as well as a German dictionary). Focused on the popular products of their own culture, they did not share Goethe's cosmopolitan interest in world literature. In fact, very few of his associates did. The best his friends could do was to present him, for his birthday, with a turban. Goethe was unperturbed and pursued his fascination with world literature as a reader and writer despite the mockery of his contemporaries. His stature allowed him to ignore the opinions of others and follow his own curiosity.

In gathering these works of literature, Goethe was not only aided by Gutenberg's printing press, conceived more than three hundred years earlier, but also by European colonial empires. A handful of European nations had set up trading posts across the globe, and over time these European traders had settled permanently in their adopted countries and gained control of the hinterland. Portugal and Spain had led the effort, but soon England and France took over as dominant colonial powers. More and more swaths of the world were forced into trade or outright submission, at great human cost. Often these territories were under the control of corporations, such as the East India Company, that had been granted exclusive trading privileges by their home governments.

Begun for purely economic reasons, imperialism made it useful, even necessary, to learn something about foreign cultures. Some agents of imperial powers took the trouble to learn native languages and writing systems, and before long, fragments of translations began to arrive in Europe (including the first Chinese novel Goethe had read). Eventually specialists in these cultures emerged, a first generation of orientalists, as they were called, who made it their business to study the literature and culture of the Middle East and Far East. Much of the foreign literature that was arriving in Europe, including what Goethe read, was translated in this way.

The commerce in world literature went both ways. European agents and specialists not only translated and imported foreign literature from the colonies to the West, they also took their own literatures and print technologies to the colonies. Portuguese and Spanish traders set up the first printing press in India (India had welcomed Chinese Buddhist monks and scholars, and used paper, but had not adopted print). Often working together, native scholars and European orientalists recovered and disseminated literary texts that had hitherto been the province of small elites. Through force and suppression, but also through print technologies, colonialism was connecting literary traditions in new ways.

Most colonial powers felt the need to justify their actions by arguing that European colonists were bringing civilization to other parts of the world. This meant that orientalists who were studying colonial possessions tended to carry with them condescending ideas about the quality of these cultures. Here, Goethe's provincial position in Weimar turned out to be an advantage. His Weimar duchy was not connected to imperialism—none of the many small and medium-sized German states had colonies. This meant that he could indirectly profit from the imperialism of others while being removed from the experience of subjugating foreign cultures and the false feeling of superiority it often induced.

As someone who read a dozen languages and who tried to teach himself Arabic at an advanced age, Goethe also recognized that world literature depended on the painstaking and underpaid work of translators and that it was based on a market, the unlikely by-product of European imperialism, which had brought literature from the remote corners of the world—along with raw materials, handicrafts, and other wares—and made it available for purchase. Goethe's view of world literature as based on a global marketplace in literature, fueled by translation, is still very much valid today.

In Search of Origins

1787, Sicily

In 1786, despite the advantages of his position in Weimar, Goethe resolved to escape his provincial routine and experience the world. Without telling anyone except his duke and his butler, he got in a coach and traveled to Italy. Sensing that this travel must have shaped his vision of world literature, I decided to follow in his foot-steps, all the way to Sicily, where his travels culminated.

I have always had a particular admiration for travel writers: Driven by curiosity and daring, they venture forth and capture en-tire worlds through their writings. Even though I traveled quite a bit in the process of writing this book, I never felt like a real travel writer, in part because I was always too late: Invariably others had been there already and reported back. All that was left for me to do was retrace their steps, imagining what real travel writing would have been like. (Possibly these earlier travel writers felt the same way.)

The passage to Sicily was difficult for Goethe. The boat from Naples was driven off course by a storm and he became seasick. But once he arrived in Palermo, he knew that he had chosen the right destination; Sicily would provide the answers to many of his questions, as he noted in his travel journal. More than a journal, it was something closer to an early blog. Goethe would send periodic updates to his friends at home, long letters to be shared among them. He also included pictures. To this end, he hired a painter to come along with him and sketch whatever Goethe wanted to remember. Upon his return, Goethe compiled his letters and the sketches and published them as a travelogue, *Italian Journey*, one of his most charming works.

Equipped with Goethe's travelogue, smartly downloaded from Project Gutenberg, the online platform that makes public domain literature available free of charge, I followed Goethe around the island, beginning in Palermo, looking for anything that might have played a role in Goethe's interest in world literature.

To my surprise, I learned that one of the first things Goethe did upon his arrival was to go to the botanical gardens to feed an old obsession: finding the "original plant," the Adam-and-Eve plant from which he believed all others must have descended. Instead of accepting the classification proposed by the Swedish botanist Carl Linnaeus, with its fine distinctions among different types of plants, Goethe was determined to trace all plants to a single origin. How do we know that a plant is a plant? he asked. Because we have an idea of what a plant is, of *plantness*. This ur-plant was what Goethe went looking for in the botanical gardens of Palermo, where he spent hours comparing specimens.

As I contemplated this strange obsession I began to wonder whether Goethe's literary mission in Sicily was similar to his search for the original plant, in that it was an attempt to grasp an entire system, to think of different works of literature as part of an integrated whole.

On my way back to the hotel, looking at the map, I noticed a street called Via Goethe, and of course I went there immediately. The Via Goethe was unpretentious, in a newer part of town, running just a few blocks. It was not where Goethe stayed, and perhaps he never went there at all, but I liked it. Everything a modern inhabitant of Palermo might need could be found here, including coffee, sandwiches, a copy shop, a hardware store, and, most important, a place to get a scooter fixed. The Pizzeria Goethe looked uninviting, and it was closed anyway, but there was a charming little carpenter's shop, with old boards and tools strewn about, spilling out onto the street. There was also a Vetreria Goethe, which sold glass kitsch. When I asked, none of the owners knew anything about the writer. They had named their stores after the street, not the man.

I dropped off my dirty clothes at the Lavanderia Goethe, and while I waited, I began to wonder how Goethe did his laundry. I skimmed through his travelogue and found quite a bit about clothing. Gradually, Goethe had dropped his northern European attire, especially his leather boots, and tried to go native. At the same time, he became more German, extravagantly so when he had his portrait done in Rome, elegantly vested with a long white traveler's coat and a German hat, one leg in breeches, flirtatiously exposed, pointing toward the viewer. The picture, entitled *Goethe in the Roman Campagna*, now adorns many of his books. Goethe mentioned the costume in his travelogue, making it sound as if the whole getup was the painter's idea. When one reads between the lines, however, one can see that he was quite taken with these garments. This, too, seemed to reflect his experience with world litera-

JOHANN HEINRICH WILHELM TISCHBEIN PORTRAYED GOETHE
ON HIS ITALIAN JOURNEY IN 1787.

ture, which allowed him to inhabit other cultures while also rediscovering his own.

As I was waiting for my laundry (I couldn't find any information about who did Goethe's), I realized that Goethe was on a mission similar to mine, that he, too, hoped that his travels to Sicily would help shape his view of literature. He had purchased an edition of the *Odyssey* in German and Greek, knowing that Sicily would be the closest he would ever get to the origin of Greek antiquity, since he was too far from Greece. In Sicily, Goethe imagined himself in the land of Homer. "There is no better commentary on the *Odyssey* than being in this environment," he wrote triumphantly in his travelogue. This was when it struck me that Goethe had indeed come to Sicily to look for what he thought of as the literary equivalent of the original plant: Homer.

Goethe's idea of Sicily being part of the Homeric world wasn't so far-fetched, because Sicily had been a Greek colony. In many ways, the *Odyssey* is an early example of travel literature, which is probably why Goethe was so interested in it during his time in Sicily (and why I, following both Goethe and Odysseus, paid attention to it). But had Odysseus actually set foot in Sicily?

The question of Odysseus's travel itinerary has been hotly disputed since antiquity. Odysseus started his voyage in Troy, but even the location of that famous city was unknown in Goethe's time. Only in the late nineteenth century, decades after Goethe's death, did a German American amateur archaeologist who had made a killing in the California gold rush, Heinrich Schliemann, manage to find ancient Troy on the western coast of Turkey. During a trip to Troy, I was able to see the large trench Schliemann had dug into the mountainside. Even though he found ancient ruins and treasures, Schliemann also created a great deal of chaos that archaeologists have been sorting through ever since.

Thanks to Schliemann's trench, we now know exactly where the *Odyssey* started, but as soon as Odysseus leaves Troy, we enter a fantasyland inhabited by the sea monsters Scylla and Charybdis, the Sirens, Circe, and the island of the one-eyed giants—none of which can be found on a real map.

As the *Odyssey* grew in importance, more and more places started to lay claim to these settings, above all Sicily. The narrow Strait of Messina between Sicily and the mainland became the location of Scylla and Charybdis, one grabbing poor sailors and smashing them on the rocks, the other sucking them into a deadly whirlpool. The island of the Sirens was claimed by Capri, off the coast of Naples, but some Sicilians argued that it was really located among the Aeolian Islands, off the northern coast of Sicily. When I took a boat there, I couldn't have agreed more: The islands were composed of sharp volcanic rock, definitely a suitable home for dangerous harpies.

The most inventive theory I heard was told to me in Taormina,

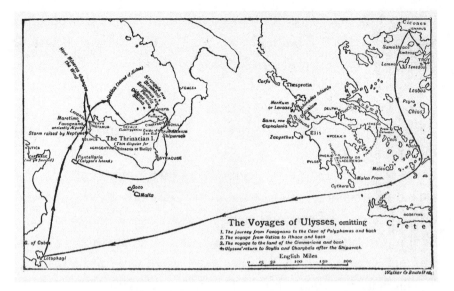

A RECONSTRUCTION OF ODYSSEUS'S WANDERINGS BASED
ON CIRCUMSTANTIAL EVIDENCE.

a small town carved high up into the mountain, overlooking the sea and overlooked, in turn, by Mount Etna, the active volcano that dominates Sicily. My friendly host, who ran a casual bed-and-breakfast, explained that in addition to Scylla and Charybdis and the Sirens, Sicily was also the island of the one-eyed giants. Do you remember, he asked as I tried to keep up with his rapid Italian, how Odysseus escaped by making the Cyclops drunk, then holding a stick in the fire until it was red and thrusting its burning point into the Cyclops's eye? *Sì*, I nodded. And once Odysseus made his escape, how he taunted the giant? *Sì, sì*. And then, what happens? I answered, like a good student, that the angry giant throws a rock after the boat and almost hits Odysseus, except I couldn't think of the Italian phrase for "missing a target," so I acted out the whole thing with my hands instead. You see, exclaimed my host, triumphantly: The Cyclops? With his one burning eyehole? That throws a rock? And he pointed out the window. I was puzzled. "It's Mount Etna!" He showed me, through one window, the volcano, smoking ominously, and through the other, rocks in the sea, near the shore.

I finally followed the drift of his thought and said, several seconds too slow: *Certo* . . . Goethe, I was sure, would have liked this story and written home about it in his travelogue.

Inspired by Sicily, Goethe wrote a play based on the Nausicaa episode of the *Odyssey*, though there is no proof that the episode was set in Sicily (some ancient sources favor the island of Corfu). In the episode, the shipwrecked Odysseus was washed ashore and found by the young princess Nausicaa, who took the traveler to the palace of her father, the king, where Odysseus was bathed and dressed, feted, and sent on his way. The episode is one of the happiest in the entire epic, but for some reason Goethe thought that it was perfect for a tragedy. Perhaps this skewed view of the material was the reason he never finished it. He kept working on it throughout his travels, complaining afterward that he had wasted his time with the play instead of enjoying Sicily.

Given Goethe's fascination with Homer, I expected that Goethe would go out of his way to admire every Greek ruin on the island, but he turned out to be surprisingly critical. Upon seeing the unbelievably beautiful temple of Segesta, situated among lovely hills and well preserved, he observed that the temple had never been completed, as if that mattered two thousand years later, when most other temples were nothing but piles of stones. He admired the temples of Agrigento, on the southern coast, and spent several days in them. His glowing reports helped turn them into a nineteenth-century tourist destination. Goethe got even more excited about the Greek theater in Taormina, where my host had explained his theory of the Cyclops, calling it a perfect combination of art and nature:

> If one takes a seat in the upper part of the auditorium, one has to admit that never has a theater audience seen such sights. On the right side, castles rise from large rocks, the town lies far below, and even though the buildings them-

selves are of a newer vintage, they are arranged just as in ancient times. Mount Etna rises from a long mountain range,
and on your left, you see the shore all the way down to Cata-
nia, even Syracuse. The awe-inspiriting fiery volcano com-
pletes the panorama, but it does not seem all that terrifying
because the mild atmosphere makes it seem farther away and
milder than it really is.

If you turn from this view to the pathways located in the
back of the theater, you see a steep wall of rock and the paths
that wind their way down to Messina between the rock and
the sea. There are also rocks and rock formations in the sea
itself, and the coast of Calabria is in the far distance, barely
distinguishable from the rising clouds.

This accomplished playwright and theater director found that the
best spectacle in the world was one in which the audience was
perched between Etna and the sea, between town and rock, between art and nature.

Goethe is a great travel writer because he never gushes for very
long. After the passage, he suggests that an architect should restore
the theater, now in ruins, to its former splendor, at least on paper,
just as he thought that ruined Greek temples should be reconstructed. Far from being overcome by reverence in the face of antiquity, Goethe was refreshingly pragmatic about it all, much less
concerned about preserving originals than we are. The same, it occurred to me, was true of his attitude toward literature, which he
enjoyed mostly in translation, the literary equivalent of a historical
reconstruction (Goethe also decorated his house with plaster copies of classical statues).

As Goethe was touring the coastal towns of Sicily, he abruptly
decided to avoid Syracuse, the most important Greek settlement,
and turned inland. He was driven by an idea, or rather, a phrase:
Sicily, "the granary of the Mediterranean." He wanted to see the

THE ANCIENT THEATER OF TAORMINA, WITH MOUNT ETNA
IN THE BACKGROUND.

fields of grain, to know how they looked, how they smelled, what kind of soil they grew in. It was part of his larger interest in the lay of the land. "He must have thought me very strange indeed," Goethe noted about one of his nonplussed guides who caught him exploring a riverbed instead of listening to stories about antiquity. What he wanted to study in the riverbeds were rock formations. The brittle white limestone was the first thing Goethe had noted as he approached the island by boat, and it became a theme throughout his travelogue. He had with him a book on minerals, and he brought back what he could for his collection.

But when it came to geology, Goethe's greatest fascination was with volcanoes, which gave him the rare opportunity to gaze into the mysterious depths of the earth. Goethe almost died when Vesuvius, the active volcano near Naples, erupted during his visit. Even after this experience he wouldn't stay away from Sicily's volcano, Mount Etna, and insisted on hiking halfway up, despite the danger. Perhaps Goethe's interest in literature wasn't so different from his interest in rocks and minerals and in plants, namely the passion of a collector who has gone out into the world and brought back as many specimens as he could find.

Sicily also laid the foundation for Goethe's future coinage of the term "world literature" by giving the poet, who had grown up land-locked, the experience of being on an island, which is to say in a miniature world. "One doesn't have a notion of 'world' unless one finds oneself surrounded on all sides by water," Goethe summed up his experience. Forty years later, he would put the two, "world" and "literature," together in a single phrase.

CHAPTER 12

MARX, ENGELS, LENIN, MAO: READERS OF *THE COMMUNIST MANIFESTO*, UNITE!

1844, PARIS–1848, LONDON

THE TWO YOUNG MEN HAD ARRANGED TO MEET AT THE CAFÉ de la Régence, conveniently located in the center of Paris, near the Louvre. Elegant chandeliers illuminated a large space with rows of tables, each occupied by men facing each other with intense concentration. From time to time, someone would go up to a long counter to speak to an attendant, who consulted a ledger and arranged a meeting with another man. Some tables attracted bystanders, who whispered to one another or even made loud comments, which was frowned upon. The atmosphere was quiet, even when it got so crowded that everyone had to keep their hats on because there was nowhere to put them.

If the two young men were unfamiliar with the café and surprised by these mysterious practices, it wouldn't have taken them long to figure out that the Café de la Régence was dedicated to the increasingly popular game of chess. For more than a century, all the great chess players had come here to play, which in turn attracted interested amateurs. Benjamin Franklin had played here, as had Voltaire, and just months earlier, the café had hosted the most famous match of the era, between the French civil servant Pierre Saint-Amant and the English actor Howard Staunton. Staunton, who had perfected the art of the opening, had emerged victorious.

The lesson about the importance of a strong opening was probably lost on the two young men who met there on August 28, 1844. They had come to strategize about a different kind of game: world revolution. Each of them brought very different skills to the table. The younger of the two, Friedrich Engels, twenty-three years old, had just arrived from Manchester, where his father, a rich cotton textile manufacturer, had sent him to study advanced manufacturing techniques. Manchester was the center of cotton—some called it Cottonopolis—the place from which cotton fabric was being shipped to the rest of the world and where new methods of industrial production changed how it was processed. Because cotton and cotton-based products were central to the new machine-based economy, the smokestacks of Manchester had become the emblem of the Industrial Revolution.

Engels studied Manchester closely and found himself deeply affected not only by the marvels of industrialization, as his father

THE SMOKESTACKS OF CROMPTON, NEAR MANCHESTER.

had hoped, but also by the masses of impoverished workers who had come to serve under the chimney. He began to investigate their living and working conditions and became convinced that here, in the most advanced industrial city of the world, became visible the dire consequences of replacing artisans with factories. The Industrial Revolution was creating an army of destitute workers utterly dependent on the owners of machines.

The other young man, Karl Marx, was two years older and knew little about the workingmen of Manchester, or of any other place, for that matter. He had come to Paris from Berlin, where he had immersed himself, against his father's wishes, in philosophy. He was lucky in his choice of city, because if Manchester was the center of the Industrial Revolution, Berlin was the center of a philosophical one. Previously, philosophy had been concerned with abstract principles, with the definition of knowledge, seeking to distill general laws and, more recently, to collect all knowledge in great encyclopedias. In Berlin, however, philosophy concerned itself with thinking in historical terms, recognizing that all its definitions, abstractions, and insights were subject to change, to historical evolution. The person who had taught this history lesson was Georg Wilhelm Friedrich Hegel. His philosophy was still interested in laws, only now they were the laws of history, the laws that governed the rise and fall of entire civilizations.

Marx didn't like the particular history Hegel was telling, which favored the Prussian state and the status quo, but he was intrigued by philosophy's new storytelling powers all the same. He was not alone. A similar interest in history brought travelers to the Middle East to investigate how Jesus had lived and to understand religion in historical terms. Novelists wrote historical novels and developed new, multiplot techniques of capturing social reality. And Charles Darwin brought historical thinking to bear on a new grand story of human evolution. In retrospect, this new mode of thinking would be called *historicism,* and at its heart was a struggle over which story would prevail.

At the Café de la Régence, the meeting between the man who had studied factories and the man who had studied philosophy went surprisingly well because despite their differences in training and interest, each realized that he had much to learn from the other. They began to collaborate, combining Engels's knowledge of factory work and Marx's knowledge of philosophical storytelling into a new and powerful vision of a revolution that would change all aspects of society. Their collaboration would result in one of the most influential texts of the modern era, *The Communist Manifesto.*

Growing up, as I did, during the Cold War, fifty miles from the Iron Curtain, it was difficult for me to remember that the Soviet Union, a world power that had amassed a large conventional force of tanks and was pointing short-range atomic missiles straight at me, had started in this way, with the meeting between Marx and Engels and the text that resulted from it. The other influential texts in the history of literature accrued their power over time, sometimes over hundreds or even thousands of years. The success of *The Communist Manifesto* was more immediate: It unfolded its greatest influence barely seventy years after its first publication. No other text in the history of literature had such an impact in so short a time. How to account for this rapid success?

A New Genre Is Born: The Manifesto

Marx and Engels came to write *The Communist Manifesto* a few years after their first meeting, when they were contacted by an organization called the League of the Just, which consisted of artisans embittered by industrialization and political repression, headquartered in London. To become a member, candidates had to swear an oath of secrecy, and the league's meetings were dedicated to hatching plots, conspiracies, and violent uprisings. In 1839 the league had participated in a failed insurrection in Paris and been forced to relocate to London to avoid arrest and execution. Its members now turned to Marx and Engels to seek their advice and leadership. Marx and Engels immediately saw that the league's invocation of universal brotherhood and its predilection for secrecy and conspiracies were all wrong. The former disregarded the specific plight of the industrial proletariat Engels had studied, and the latter, the laws of historical change Marx had distilled. In search for a new purpose, the league was happy to have Marx and Engels suggest a change in direction.

In November 1847, the two friends traveled from Brussels to London with a plan that entailed a new name, the Communist League, and a new vision. The League of the Just complied and officially commissioned them to write up a statement that would outline the new approach. Engels had taken a first stab at the document before the London meeting, a text called "Principles of Communism," which listed articles of faith similar to a catechism, the question-and-answer form familiar from religious instruction. This form, however, soon proved inadequate for the more ambitious task the two authors had in mind. "Think a little about the confession of faith. I believe that the best thing is to do away with the catechism form and give the thing the title: Communist Manifesto," Engels wrote to his collaborator. When Engels proposed the new title, the word "manifesto" didn't have the meaning we associate with it today, post–*Communist Manifesto*. It had sometimes been used for important declarations of emperors or the Catholic Church, making the wishes of these sovereigns known to their subjects. The cobbled-together Communist League didn't have any authority or subjects. Calling their text a manifesto was preposterous, signaling an ambition that had not yet been earned.

There was another meaning associated with the new title: to make one's views manifest and public. This was an important change from the league's conspiratorial past. In order to overcome this history, Marx and Engels now insisted that the league needed to publish its views for all to see, going against its most ingrained instincts for secrecy. To underscore this point, the two authors opened with the famous sentence, "A specter is haunting Europe — the specter of Communism." It was an ominous beginning, putting to mind the world of ghosts, as if the *Manifesto* were trying to spread fear, delighting in its role as a scary apparition (the first English translation warned: "A frightful hobgoblin stalks throughout Europe"). But actually, the opposite was the case. Marx and Engels were tired of being in the shadows, scaring children as if in a fairy tale. They wanted to leave behind the world of ghosts and hobgoblins, of conspiracies and assassinations, and become an open, legitimate force. This was what the *Manifesto* was supposed to achieve, turning Communism from a specter into the real thing.

There was another reason why the old catechism didn't work. Again, it was Engels who noticed the problem: "Since we basically have to tell a historical narrative, the present form does not work. I take with me from Paris what I have written; it is a simple story, but miserably composed, in an awful hurry." Engels had stumbled on a key ingredient of the *Manifesto*, something he had learned from Marx: storytelling. During their years of collaboration in Paris and Brussels, Marx had developed a powerful alternative to Hegel. In Hegel's version, imagination and ideas were the driving forces of world history. In Marx's version, it was humans transforming the world through their labor. This meant that the new key discipline was not philosophy but economics.

The economic narrative Marx wrote with the help of Engels was breathtaking, a story of the massive forces of industrialization and trade that were changing the world on an awe-inspiring scale:

By exploiting the world market, the bourgeoisie has made production and consumption a cosmopolitan affair. To the annoyance of its enemies, it has drawn from under the feet of industry the national ground on which it stood. All traditional national industries have been destroyed or are daily being destroyed. They are pushed aside by new industries, which all advanced nations need in order to thrive. These industries no longer use local materials but raw material drawn from the remotest zones, and its products are consumed not only at home, but also in every quarter of the globe. In place of the old needs, satisfied by domestic production, we find new needs, which can only be satisfied by the products of distant lands and climes. In place of the old local and national seclusion and self-sufficiency, we have commerce in every direction, universal interdependence of nations. And as in material, so also in intellectual production. The intellectual creations of individual nations become common property. National one-sidedness and narrow-mindedness become increasingly impossible, and from the numerous national and local literatures there arises a world literature.

This description of the world market sounds almost as if Marx and Engels were admiring capitalism for its unheard-of power, but they added a dramatic twist: At the very moment of triumph, capitalism would suddenly be confronted with an enemy of its own making, namely the industrial proletariat Engels had studied so closely. The more places in the world looked like Manchester, the larger the industrial proletariat would become, until it would be numerous enough to overthrow its oppressors. This was storytelling at its most powerful, transforming helpless victims into come-from-behind heroes.

There was one more wrinkle to this story about industrialization, namely that it affected not only material goods but also ideas,

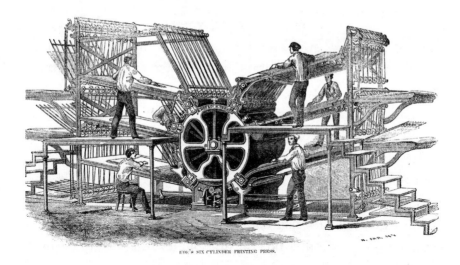

HOE'S SIX CYLINDER PRINTING PRESS.

IN 1847 THE AMERICAN INVENTOR RICHARD HOE
INTRODUCED HIS LITHOGRAPHIC ROTARY PRESS,
USED FOR CHEAP MASS-CIRCULATION NEWSPAPERS.

as they put it in the culminating sentence: "From the numerous national and local literatures there arises a world literature." *World literature*—this was a strange term to use in the context of mines, steam engines, and railways. Goethe, with his aristocratic leanings, surely would have objected to the proletarian revolution Marx and Engels were advocating. However, he might well have agreed that world literature was a consequence of world trade. By noticing an emerging world market in literature, Goethe had caught a glimpse of the powers of capitalism that Marx and Engels were now describing in much greater detail. And through advanced printing machines that resembled other industrial production processes, literature increasingly looked as if it came out of places like Manchester.

World literature was also on Marx's and Engels's minds when they contemplated the fortunes of the text they had just finished. They concluded their preamble with the bold announcement that the *Manifesto* would "be published in the English, French, German, Italian, Flemish and Danish languages." While modest in comparison to today's book launches, which can include dozens of languages, this was quite ambitious for a far-flung group of revolutionaries in 1848, requiring translators, printers, and distributors in many different countries. Just as the story told by the *Manifesto* was international, the *Manifesto* wanted to be read internationally as well; it wanted to become world literature.

Toward the end of January, Marx received a sternly worded letter from London reminding him of his deadline: February 1. The two authors would miss that deadline, but not by much. Over the course of a few months, they had managed to distill everything they had learned from each other into an unusual text that would become the prototype for all subsequent manifestos. Without intending to do so, they had contributed a new genre to world literature: the genre of the manifesto.

If the London headquarters of the Communist League realized that they had received a masterpiece, they didn't say so. They did, however, immediately proceed to place the text in a journal, although only piecemeal, for the *Manifesto* was published serially. Since the death of Benjamin Franklin, the number of newspapers had increased rapidly, printing longer pieces, even entire novels, installment by installment. It was a sign of the power of serialization that even *The Communist Manifesto*, numbering only twenty-three pages, was published in this way despite the fact that it was written to be read in one sitting. For this reason, the league decided to publish the text as a freestanding pamphlet as well. Through these two forms of print publication, the world would know, for the first time, exactly what the league intended to do.

Within weeks of publication, revolutions broke out across Europe. Demonstrations led to strikes and strikes to insurrections, resulting in new national assemblies demanding new constitutions and new rights. Marx and Engels were delighted. It didn't matter that Marx was forced to leave Brussels; he simply went back to Paris, the center of revolutionary activity. In Paris and in Germany, Marx and Engels organized and strategized and published newspapers and pamphlets, desperately trying to steer the events that were unfolding at a rapid pace.

The only disappointment in these exciting times was that these revolutions had absolutely nothing to do with the *Manifesto*. Their work had simply fallen flat. There was almost no response to *The Communist Manifesto*, which had no measurable impact on events. Increasingly, it was also getting difficult to publish new versions of this text, as the old regimes were fighting back not only with armies and police forces, but also with tightened censorship. The league was forced underground again, back into the secrecy it had tried to leave behind, and it ultimately splintered. Helplessly, Marx and Engels had to watch the revolution die away, and with it the text through which they had tried, unsuccessfully, to guide its course.

In the first decades after 1848, it was unclear whether the *Manifesto* would survive at all. Despite the grandiose plans to publish this text simultaneously in many countries, very few editions actually came to fruition. Between 1853 and 1863, only a single new edition was printed, as presses were pushed underground and few places existed where subversive literature could be published with impunity. The first Russian translation was produced in relatively liberal Geneva, not in czarist Russia; a Swedish translation was printed in the United States. Scattered groups of true believers were trying to get the *Manifesto* translated and into the hands of readers, but without much success. In this era of reaction, the *Manifesto* became outdated, a remnant of a revolutionary time that was receding into the past.

The two authors were now faced with a stark choice: Should they let the *Manifesto* become a historical document, one of the countless pamphlets accompanying the failed 1848 revolutions, or should they update it to address new political realities? Initially they chose the second path. As early as August 1852, Engels admitted, "California and Australia are two cases not considered in the *Manifesto*: creation of new markets out of nothing. They need to be added." The two authors began writing prefaces to incorporate new developments while insisting that the core ideas remained as true as ever. Things became more complicated after Marx died. In 1883, Engels wrote ruefully: "Since his death, there can be even less thought of revising or supplementing the *Manifesto*." The *Manifesto* had become part of the historical record—and the legacy of his dead friend.

Powerful literature has always been able to bide its time, and the *Manifesto* was no exception. After decades of stagnation, things began to look up in the seventies and eighties. New print technologies, which brought the full power of industrialization to literature, also helped. The printing process had finally seen significant improvements and could for the first time be automated to a much greater degree. There was even a mechanical way of selecting letters and assembling them into a page-sized frame ready to receive ink and paper. Printers became more ubiquitous and cheaper, and therefore more difficult to suppress, while commerce among nations made it easier to print a German edition in London or a Russian edition in Geneva and smuggle it back.

As more editions of the *Manifesto* came to fruition, an intriguing pattern emerged: The more copies of the *Manifesto* were published in a given place, the more likely that a revolution would occur. This correlation was true in Paris, when angry workers barricaded the streets and announced the formation of the Paris Commune in 1871, and it was even more true in 1905, when a coalition of workers and a rising bourgeoisie rebelled in Russia. Did the *Manifesto* simply profit from revolutionary fervor, or did it have a hand in inciting these sentiments? Probably both. The *Manifesto*, in any case, was finally becoming a true revolutionary text, finding readers ready to take its historical lessons and turn them into action.

THE READERS:
LENIN, MAO, HO, CASTRO

One of the eager readers of *The Communist Manifesto* was Vladimir Ulyanov, a Russian revolutionary living in Zurich during the Great War. Switzerland was one of the few countries in Europe that had stayed out of the war, but that didn't mean that it was peaceful. The city was crawling with diplomats, weapons dealers, spies, draft dodgers, and refugees, but it was the best place from which to watch the war wreak havoc on the regimes that had gotten the world into this war. And it was a good place to wait for the right moment to strike.

Vladimir had learned to be patient. Back in Russia, he had watched his older brother be arrested and executed after a hasty assassination attempt on the czar. Undeterred, he had followed in his brother's footsteps, but realized that assassinations were ineffective. Even if they succeeded, a new czar would take the place of the old one, as had happened before. It wasn't enough to replace the head; the whole system had to change. Casting about for intellectual guidance, Vladimir had immersed himself in revolutionary literature, little of which he found inspiring, until he came across *The Communist Manifesto*. It offered a powerful historical perspective that showed him that the struggle against oppressive regimes had been going on for thousands of years; it pointed him to the roots of problems; it predicted that revolutionary change was around the corner; and it inspired him to act on that prediction.

One action Vladimir took upon reading *The Communist Manifesto* was to translate it into Russian, so that more of his fellow Russians could read it. Then he tried to put it into practice. Unfortunately, avoiding assassinations such as the one plotted by his brother didn't prevent him from getting arrested, though it meant that he was only sent to Siberia, not executed.

His prison sentence over, he went to Europe, where he devoted

himself to reading and writing, combining history with calls for action in the manner of the *Manifesto*. He also realized that this text,
hailing from a different time and place, needed to be updated and
related to the specific situation in Russia. As Vladimir Ulyanov was
waiting for the right moment to put the *Manifesto* into action, he
also took a new surname: Lenin. Decades after it was written, *The
Communist Manifesto* had found an ideal reader, one ready to use
this obscure text to change the course of history.

During the Great War, Lenin lived at Spiegelgasse 14, right in
the old center of Zurich. Across the street, at Spiegelgasse 1, an
international group of artists and provocateurs had talked the owner
of a bar into letting them start a cabaret. The group organized poetry readings and presented rambunctious performances of all
kinds, often with strange, geometrical costumes, dissonant music,
and plots that didn't make sense. Above all, the group recited and
published manifestos. In those manifestos, they announced, with
great fanfare, the creation of a new revolutionary movement called
Dadaism and simultaneously denounced every art movement that
had come before it. How did this group of provocateurs come to
write a manifesto in the tradition of *The Communist Manifesto*?

Since the deaths of Marx and Engels, the *Manifesto* had found
admirers not only among professional revolutionaries like Lenin
but also among artists. The peculiar force of this text, its combination of grand history with a call to action, appealed to artists who
wanted to change the face of art. At first hesitantly then more boldly,
art manifestos started to appear across Europe, beginning with Nat-
uralism and Symbolism, and continuing with Futurism and Dadaism. In each case, small groups of artists, often under the leadership
of a single charismatic figure, denounced all traditional art in the
name of a yet unaccomplished future. Realist painting, traditional
storytelling, harmonic music—they all needed to go. It was less
clear what should take their place. Sometimes artists wrote manifestos announcing the latest movement before any artwork had

A RAMBUNCTIOUS EVENING IN 1916 AT THE CABARET VOLTAIRE IN
ZURICH, THE BIRTHPLACE OF DADAISM. THE PAINTING, BY MARCEL JANCO,
IS LOST, BUT THIS PHOTOGRAPH OF IT SURVIVES.

been created, as if writing manifestos had become more important
than actually making art. When they got around to creating art-

works, these works resembled manifestos in their shrill tone, aggressive attitude toward the audience, and programmatic ambition.

Art manifestos and their movements had begun before the Great War, but it was during these brutal years that they came into their own, since they articulated the sense that European culture was coming apart at the seams. Clearly, the arts of the nineteenth century could not do justice to the mechanized slaughter of trench warfare. Of all the new avant-garde groups, the Dadaists and their Cabaret Voltaire in Zurich best captured the sheer aimlessness and absurdity of the war. Marx had had a lively interest in culture—his writings were full of literary quotations, particularly from Shakespeare—but inspiring revolutionary art was the last thing he had intended. With his relatively conservative taste, he would have been appalled.

Lenin would probably have objected as well, but he was unaware that an offshoot of *The Communist Manifesto* had taken up residence right across the street. Instead he was too focused on following the war and its effect on Russia, where things were heating up. Beginning in February 1917, more strikes and demonstrations broke out, and policemen and soldiers joined the demonstrators rather than arresting them. The czar abdicated in favor of his brother, an honor the brother wisely declined. Russia was now without a sovereign. A provisional government was formed while workers and soldiers set up councils, called soviets, and elected representatives to form a new parliament. Lenin sensed that it was time to act. Germany was at war with Russia, but the German authorities let Lenin pass through Germany and enter revolutionary Russia via Finland.

Lenin traveled to Petrograd (St. Petersburg) with a seemingly impractical plan. Instead of working with other democratic and revolutionary groups, he would focus exclusively on the working class. The working class, or *proletariat* as *The Communist Manifesto* called it, was the only genuinely revolutionary group in Russia, and only the Communist Party could act on its behalf.

This unwise plan, which made Lenin break with many of his natural allies, was based on the story of world history as told in *The Communist Manifesto*. Marx and Engels had identified the bourgeoisie, the class in control of industrial production, as a revolutionary force, one that could wrest power from feudal monarchies. But *The Communist Manifesto* had gone on to predict that history would move from this bourgeois revolution to one driven by the proletariat, the ultimate agent of history. Impoverished by industrialization and utterly dependent on the owners of production, the proletariat would rise up against its oppressors. This was the story animating Lenin and his comrades, and it now gave them confidence to put their faith in the slogan ALL POWER TO THE PROLETARIAT. When Lenin arrived at the Finland Station in Petrograd in April 1917, he immediately undertook to turn this story into reality. He created a party capable of staging coups but also of winning the battle of ideas, for which purpose he revived a newspaper to propagate Marx and Engels's historical narrative.

In working toward a proletarian revolution, Lenin and his com-

LENIN SPEAKING TO A CROWD IN PETROGRAD ON
THE EVE OF THE RUSSIAN REVOLUTION.

rades received unexpected aid from the *Manifesto*'s artistic admirers. The manifesto fever that had taken hold of the Dadaists in Zurich had spread to Russia, where different groups of artists wrote manifestos in the name of artistic revolution. While Lenin had not paid any attention to the Dadaists in Zurich, he now took notice of their Russian counterparts, whose manifestos contributed to the revolutionary atmosphere in Petrograd and Moscow. The two strands of the manifesto movement were reacting like two wires, one polarized toward politics, the other toward art, that suddenly touched, setting off revolutionary sparks. (The same thing happened when the French Surrealist André Breton and the Russian revolutionary Leon Trotsky co-signed a manifesto called *For a Free Revolutionary Art*.) Against all odds, Lenin and his comrades managed to turn the political chaos between February and October 1917 to their advantage. When a coup attempt from the right failed, they decided to counter it with a coup from the left, and succeeded. The revolution had reached a tipping point, suddenly leaving Lenin and his party in control of the state. For the first time in history, a party representing the impoverished working class was running an entire country.

RUSSIA WAS NOT THE ONLY STATE transformed by *The Communist Manifesto*. Mao Zedong also remembered when he read this text for the first time. Originally, his father, a rice farmer, had sent him to a Confucian school to learn the Confucian classics by heart. Disappointed with rote learning, Mao decided not to study for the imperial exam, which was still based, as it had been for hundreds of years, on the same set of texts. Even before the fall of the last emperor, he cut off his pigtail, prescribed by tradition, in an act of open rebellion, and joined an armed student group. Moving to a larger town, Mao studied Chinese novels, Western philosophy, and newspapers that kept him up to date with the events of the Great War. When he finally managed to move to Beijing, he became involved with rebellious intellectuals including editors of *New Youth* magazine, an organ designed to modernize Chinese culture. Mao attended group meetings in which different political philosophies were discussed, and he became involved with a literary magazine as well as a cooperative bookstore. Looking back at this period, it all seemed to Mao merely the disoriented period prior to his conversion to Russian-style Marxism, and that conversion took place when he first read *The Communist Manifesto*.

It had taken this text a long time to arrive in China. Unlike Lenin, who knew German, Mao read only Chinese and was therefore dependent on the text's slow translation into his native language. *The Communist Manifesto* had first been mentioned in China in 1903, and the preface was published in 1908. Mao's mentor, Chen Duxiu, an editor of *New Youth* magazine, had published a shortened version some time thereafter, but a full translation wasn't available until the summer of 1920, which was when Mao first read it. By then Lenin had managed to consolidate his hold on Russia.

Almost eighty years old, the *Manifesto* did not address the specific situation in China (just as it hadn't said much about Russia), and yet a few months after reading this text, Mao would form a Communist cell and turn himself into the leader of a Communist revolution, certain that he would succeed with *The Communist Manifesto*, and history, on his side.

Similar experiences were multiplying. The young Ho Chi Minh had traveled the world while working on a steamboat, but it was in Paris that his political education took place. Having grown up in Vietnam under French colonial rule, he knew French, and it was in that language that he read *The Communist Manifesto*, which had long been available in French. The reading experience, which

took place just after the Great War, moved him to become a Marx-
ist. He joined the French Communist Party and began to adapt the
Manifesto to the struggle against European colonizers. His own
text, *The Process of French Colonization,* contained a manifesto
whose ending echoed the celebrated last sentence of *The Communist Manifesto,* "Workers of the world, unite!" (Prior to writing this
manifesto, Ho had written a declaration of independence for Vietnam, modeled on the American Declaration of Independence.)

Fidel Castro also remembered his first reading of the *Manifesto,*
which he dated to 1952, when the U.S.-backed dictator Fulgencio
Batista had orchestrated a coup to seize power in Cuba. "Then, one
day a copy of *The Communist Manifesto*—the famous *Communist
Manifesto!*—fell into my hands and I read of things I'll never forget. . . . What phrases, what truths! And we saw those truths every
day! I felt like some little animal that had been born in a forest
which he didn't understand. Then, all of a sudden, he finds a map
of that forest."

And so it kept happening, from Lenin in the 1880s to Castro in
the 1950s, *The Communist Manifesto* provided revolutionaries
from Russia and China to Vietnam and Cuba with a map through
the forest. Those equipped with this map were able to throw off the
czar of Russia, the emperor of China, the French colonists, and the
U.S. Army. *The Communist Manifesto* kept finding readers, con-
verting them and inciting them to action until it became one of the
most revered, and feared, texts in history.

THOSE THREATENED BY COMMUNISM reacted with arrests, executions,
and wars, leading to the long twentieth-century battle against Communism that came to an end only in 1989 (or, if you will, with the
death of Fidel Castro in 2016). But the reaction against Communism also took the form of literature.

The most ferocious reactionary was an Austrian by the name of Adolf Hitler, who promised to put an end to the red tide sweeping Europe. While imprisoned for a failed coup in 1923, he wrote an autobiography that was also a campaign biography for his future political career. Once he had seized power, he was able to foist this text on his subjects in a gigantic vanity publishing project. At the height of Nazi rule, *Mein Kampf* became the most widely owned book in Germany, going through 1,031 editions totaling 12.4 million copies; every sixth German possessed a copy of *Mein Kampf*, with counties required to give a copy to all newlyweds.

Books could be forced into every household, but no one could force people to read them. Hitler's long-winded rants made *Mein Kampf* the most unread book in history, a stark contrast to *The Communist Manifesto*, with which it competed so desperately. (Another government-sponsored book, Mao's *Little Red Book*, was more successful in actually getting read, perhaps because its pithy quotes and reflections were the exact opposite of Hitler's extended harangue.)

Marx and Engels had forged a captivating text that had absorbed valuable lessons from literary history. From foundational texts, it learned how to tell a story of origin; from the texts of ancient teachers, it learned how to address all people and not just those of one nation; from quasi-sacred historical texts like the Declaration of Independence, it learned how to bring a new political reality into being; and from Goethe it learned about the dynamics of world literature.

Just as *The Communist Manifesto* had been catapulted to the forefront of history by the Russian Revolution, so its prestige has suffered since the fall of the Soviet Union. Today it is once again considered outdated, as it was in the 1850s and '60s. In the past, the *Manifesto* has been able to rise again from obscurity, adjusting to new political realities. Even now, it is finding readers who feel that this text predicted our current backlash against globalization. Be this as it may, what is certain is that *The Communist Manifesto* became one of the most influential texts of the modern era within a few decades of its emergence. In the first four thousand years of literature, few texts have been able to shape history so effectively.

CHAPTER 13

AKHMATOVA AND SOLZHENITSYN: WRITING AGAINST THE SOVIET STATE

CIRCA 1935, LENINGRAD

AT FIRST, ANNA AKHMATOVA, THE RUSSIAN POET, WORKED ON HER poem in the usual way. She always composed by hand, writing out the lines on paper; then she would make corrections and perhaps read the lines aloud to see if they sounded right. Normally, she would produce a fair copy and send it to a magazine, or put it aside until a whole cycle of poems had emerged and then approach a book publisher. Before the Great War, she had published several volumes in this way, to great acclaim. She had become a celebrated poet in Russia while still in her early twenties, a dashing figure with her long shawls, black hair, and a bearing that betrayed her aristocratic heritage. In Paris, she had made the acquaintance of Amedeo Modigliani, a painter already confident of his future success, and he had fallen for her. Modigliani produced several drawings and paintings of the young Akhmatova that captured the elegant lines and distinct features of the poet whom critics would soon call the Russian Sappho.

Akhmatova held on to one of Modigliani's drawings and gave it pride of place above her bed, but the time of her Paris triumph was

ITALIAN SCULPTOR AND PAINTER AMEDEO MODIGLIANI
MADE SEVERAL SKETCHES OF ANNA AKHMATOVA WHEN THEY MET IN PARIS.

long past. No thought of publication crossed her mind now, in the middle of the 1930s, as she was composing her new poem. The state would simply not allow it. Ever since Martin Luther had demonstrated what could be done with print, authorities had been trying to control publishers and authors. Permission had long been required for many publishing projects, forcing the likes of Cervantes to apply for a royal license. But licenses could be circumvented, as Franklin knew when he published a Bible without one, and books could be printed abroad and copies smuggled back into censored territory, as Marx and Engels found. Only in the twentieth century was control over print finally within the reach of the state, at least some states. Equipped with centralized power, totalitarian states such as the Soviet Union and Nazi Germany commanded guns and manpower, but they also relied on a large bureaucratic apparatus to keep track of their citizens. Innumerable dossiers were created, processed, and stored. Bureaucracy, first developed five thousand years earlier with the invention of writing, had become an all-encompassing force. Anna Akhmatova never engaged in any political activity, and yet her police file grew to some nine hundred pages.

Knowing that the state would not allow her poem to appear in print did not deter Akhmatova from writing it, even in these dangerous times. After a leading functionary was assassinated in 1934, arrests and executions had become a daily occurrence. No one was safe from Genrikh Yagoda, the head of Stalin's secret police, who arrested potential rivals of Stalin, old comrades, anyone who might harbor thoughts of opposition or who simply happened to be in the wrong place at the wrong time. Yagoda also dragged prisoners who had been tortured to confess their sins in show trials that spread fear across the entire population. When Yagoda himself was arrested, people became even more frightened: If even the head of the secret police was not safe, then truly no one was. Yagoda was swiftly replaced with someone even worse, Nikolai Yezhov, who oversaw the deadliest period of the Great Purge, until he, too, followed the fate of his predecessor.

Throughout this period, Akhmatova knew that she was at great risk of arrest. Ever since her former husband had been executed on fabricated charges, she had been on the radar screen of the security forces. Their son had also been arrested, released, arrested again, and tortured. At any moment, the secret police might come and search her apartment, and a single line of poetry, the wrong line of poetry, would be reason enough to land her in front of a firing squad. This was why she memorized each section of the poem as soon as she had finished it, and then burned the paper on which it had been written.

Akhmatova was particularly exposed because the Soviet Union was a totalitarian state with a keen interest in poetry. Akhmatova's early fame came from the time before the Russian Revolution, which meant that she was now suspect as a writer from another era, even though she had never been a traditionalist. Together with her first husband and a group of like-minded young artists, she had founded a movement, Acmeism, that sought to do away with the heavy symbolist poetry of the turn of the century and replace it with more simplicity and clarity (the word "Acmeism" might have been inspired by Akhmatova's name). In the heady days after the revolution, this relatively modest movement with its relatively modest manifesto was quickly overtaken by more radical movements such as Futurism, which wanted to do away with the past entirely and quickly flooded the market with increasingly shrill pronouncements. (One of the differences between the older Acmeists and the new Futurists happened to be one of paper: The Acmeists used expensive paper, while the Futurists liked their paper cheap and disposable.)

The leaders of the Russian Revolution knew only too well that their own revolution had been prepared by underground texts such as *The Communist Manifesto* and that this text had filtered into the world of art, inspiring revolutionary literary and art movements. Leon Trotsky, the intellectual leader of the Russian Revolution, had found the time to write *Literature and Revolution,* a book about the new literary movements, in which he attacked Akhmatova, barely thirty years old, as already outdated. Anatoly Lunacharsky, the powerful commissar of education, denounced Akhmatova in similar terms. After Lenin's death in 1924, Stalin managed to consolidate his power by forcing Trotsky into exile, but he retained Trotsky's interest in poetic affairs and kept track of Anna Akhmatova's doings (Akhmatova was not the only poet he read; one of his favorite writers was Walt Whitman). Being the object of Stalin's attention could cut both ways. When Akhmatova's son was arrested in 1935, Akhmatova was able to write to Stalin directly and plead for her son's life. To her own surprise, her son was released. But for the most part, Stalin's interest severely restricted her ability to write and publish. Worse than a state indifferent to poetry, it turned out, was one obsessed with it.

For a poet like Akhmatova, poetry was dangerous, but also necessary; it enabled her to channel the sadness, fear, and desperation of an entire people. She called her new poem *Requiem*. It didn't tell a straightforward story. The Stalin years were too overwhelming, too confusing, too disjointed. Instead, Akhmatova offered snapshots, a few lines of dialogue here, a remembered incident there, reduced to a sentence or an image that would turn history into a matter of minutely crafted moments. The most telling passage spoke of women, mothers and wives, who gathered every day outside a prison, waiting to learn whether their loved ones had been executed or exiled. "I'd like to remember them all by name," Akhmatova wrote about these women, "But the list has been confiscated and is nowhere to / be found."

The evolving poem was safe as long as Akhmatova memorized each section and immediately burned it, but it would survive only as long as she herself survived. In order for the poem to live, it needed to be shared, carried in the minds of others. Cautiously Akhmatova summoned her closest friends, no more than a dozen women, and read the poem to them over and over until they knew it by heart. Perhaps this was how Sappho had taught her poems to groups of female friends more than two thousand years ago. But Sappho had not lived in fear of writing down her lines. Scraps of her poems, recorded on brittle papyrus, have come down through the ages, bearing witness to her extraordinary imagination and the durability of writing. Such writing, even on papyrus, was not something the Russian Sappho could risk.

Forced to learn her poetry by heart, Akhmatova and her female friends had to make do without the skills of singers from oral cultures. Those professionals had trained their memories to hold long narratives as well as set pieces, but they also knew that they could adapt this memorized material to new circumstances. Akhmatova, by contrast, didn't want her friends to change a single word. She had composed her poem on paper, worrying over each phrase, and now insisted on the precision typical of a literary writer. Her friends were expected to remember *Requiem* exactly as she had written it.

Their job was made even more difficult when Akhmatova did something else that was typical of a literary poet as opposed to an oral one: She kept making revisions. Because the poem was now distributed among the minds of her close friends, she needed to make sure that they would all remember the updated version. Her friends weren't oral poets and singers with a license to improvise; they were the paper on which Akhmatova wrote, and revised, her most important work.

To better cope with Akhmatova's demands, one of her friends visualized the poem as if it were written down, divided into sections, and numbered with roman numerals. It was an old memory technique that depended on separating a long piece into short segments and visualizing the sequence with distinct markers or numbers. When, many years later, Akhmatova finally dared to prepare the poem for publication, she used her friend's numbering, remarking: "See, as you said, roman numerals."

The irony of her position as a poet living in a highly literate society who was forced to resort to memorization didn't escape Akhmatova. She called her situation "pre-Gutenberg" and declared, sarcastically, "We live according to the slogan 'Down with Gutenberg.'" Akhmatova was highly attuned to the history of writing technologies. She had learned to read and write on her family's estate with the use of a schoolbook written by the greatest Russian writer, Leo Tolstoy, whose literary works she later came to dislike. The Russian alphabet, she knew, was modeled on the Greek alphabet, allegedly brought to Russia by two Greek monks, Saint Methodius and Saint Cyril, in the ninth century C.E.

Akhmatova's deepest insight into the history of writing came from her second husband, a scholar of Sumerian cuneiform. Oc-

cupying two rooms of a former palace strewn with books and manuscripts, the couple worked together, with Akhmatova typing up her
husband's translations as part of a project to bring world literature
to the masses. Between 1918 and 1924, no fewer than forty-nine
volumes of world classics, including the Indian story collection
Panchatantra, were published, Goethe's dream of world literature
updated for the revolutionary workers' republic. Akhmatova was so
struck by cuneiform, including the *Epic of Gilgamesh*, that she
wrote a play based on Sumerian material. During a period of intense persecution, in the 1940s, she burned the draft, along with
many other manuscripts, but throughout her life she toyed with the
idea of someday rewriting the play from memory.

Contemplating her unusual position with respect to literacy,
Akhmatova realized that literary history didn't move steadily forward, from oral recitation to cuneiform and then to print; it could
move sideways, stall, and even move backward, depending on
who controlled the means of literary production. If those means
were in the hands of a hostile, totalitarian state, a writer might be
forced to live in a pre-Gutenberg era or even in a world before
writing, as if the two monks had never arrived with the Greek alphabet at all.

For Akhmatova, state oppression and censorship eased somewhat in the forties, but only because the greater horror of World
War II took their place. In 1941, Adolf Hitler broke the military
pact he had made with Stalin and declared war on the Soviet
Union. Stalin was temporarily distracted from Akhmatova as he
prepared for war. His bloody purges had left the army without an
officer corps, which now needed to be rebuilt overnight. Many of
Akhmatova's friends had gone into exile, but she refused to leave
the country and instead participated in the war effort by reading
patriotic poetry to soldiers. She even took to the latest technology,
the radio, encouraging her fellow residents of Petrograd—now re-

named Leningrad—to defend this city of Russian writers and poets (before she was evacuated). Of her poem *Requiem* she did not speak, but she and her friends kept it safe throughout the war.

AKHMATOVA MEETS BERLIN

In the months after the war, Akhmatova found herself reciting *Requiem* again. This time it was not to her close circle of friends but to a visitor from abroad, the first one she had received in a long time. During the purges, it would have been suicidal to meet a foreigner, more dangerous even than committing poems to paper. But the war had softened some of the worst repressions, and the visitor was from the United Kingdom, an ally in the struggle against Hitler. His name was Isaiah Berlin. Born in Russia, he was raised in England, where his parents had fled after the revolution, and he would go on to become one of the great intellectuals of the middle of the twentieth century.

Berlin was not yet famous as a critic of totalitarianism when he came to see Anna Akhmatova in November 1945; he was simply someone bringing news from the West. It was Berlin's first time back in his former homeland, whose language he still spoke fluently. He was there in an official capacity as a member of the British Foreign Office with a brief to report on the situation in the country that had survived the brutal purges of its paranoid leader, helped to defeat Nazi Germany at enormous human cost, and was now facing an uncertain future. He also had ties to the British secret service. Probably he was not on a secret mission, but he later falsified his account of the meeting, suggesting that it was a chance encounter when in fact it had been set up by a contact. In a dispatch to the Foreign Office, Berlin informed the British government that Russia took poetry more seriously than any other country. The British Foreign Office, at least in the person of its officer Isaiah Berlin, seemed to share this disposition.

By 1945, Akhmatova had long since divorced her cuneiform-deciphering husband. She lived in a communal apartment, in which Akhmatova didn't enjoy much privacy because they shared it with her former companion, Nikolay Punin, his daughter, his former wife, and a changing number of visitors. The lodgings were part of a research facility with special security measures. When Berlin entered, he had to show his papers to a guard. He then crossed a courtyard and ascended the stairs. The door was opened by a woman in tattered clothes. Upon being asked to enter the apartment, he realized Akhmatova lived in extreme poverty. In a city still ravaged by war, all she had to offer was a boiled potato. But Berlin was smitten. Called away, he returned later that night, eager to talk to Russia's most acclaimed poet. The meeting left a deep impression on Akhmatova as well, who kept her visitor until morning. They spoke of literature, the West, and the Soviet Union, and after some hours they spoke of more intimate matters as well. Berlin came back the following night, and for one more night after that.

Most memorable was the moment when Akhmatova recited to Berlin her poem *Requiem*. Berlin was so struck by it that he twice begged her to allow him to write it down. She demurred. After the easing of repressions, she was planning to publish a new volume of poetry; soon Berlin would be able to read *Requiem* in print. After ten years of existing in her mind and the minds of her friends, *Requiem* would finally enter the world.

But things didn't turn out that way. The problem was, once again, Stalin. Amid the effort to rebuild the war-torn Soviet Union, he found time to worry about the fate of Soviet poetry as represented by Akhmatova. When he heard of the meeting (one of Akhmatova's friends turned out to be an informer), he was enraged and exclaimed: "So the nun [an old slur directed at Akhmatova] has been meeting with foreign spies?" He proceeded to unleash the full force of his totalitarian state against her. He could have arrested her and tortured a false confession out of her, or simply let her disappear into his prison system. Instead he chose to fight Akhmatova with literary means, mobilizing against her the state's monopoly on print.

The campaign began with a speech given by the cultural commissar appointed by Stalin denouncing two literary magazines for the errors in judgment they had committed in publishing the work of Anna Akhmatova. The speech was printed in a high-circulation newspaper and then reissued as a pamphlet with a print run of one million copies. This was a clear signal for others to produce similar denunciations, which they quickly did. Akhmatova became the target of the country's literary wrath, remarking sarcastically to a friend: "Just think, what fame! Even the Central Committee of the Communist Party writes about me."

Publishing *Requiem* was now out of the question. The campaign against her had other consequences as well. A declared enemy of the state, Akhmatova found herself under police surveillance and excluded from the writers' union. In a country in which everything depended on such membership, this meant that she was no longer a practicing poet. It also meant that she no longer received food coupons, a significant loss in the rationed postwar Russian economy. Before long, her son would be arrested yet again, and this time she could not plead with Stalin to have him released. Her son was sentenced to ten years in a labor camp, a pawn to keep Akhmatova from seeing foreign spies ever again.

The three meetings with Berlin came at a steep price, but Akhmatova never regretted them, although she probably regretted not letting Berlin commit *Requiem* to paper. In the several poems Akhmatova later wrote about the meeting, she called Berlin her almost-husband and a visitor from the future. She even claimed that the encounter, and Stalin's reaction, had triggered the Cold War. Akhmatova may have been overestimating her own importance, but as a well-known poet, she knew that she was a thorn in the side of Russia's most powerful leader. Her meetings with Berlin may well have been an additional trigger for the Cold War. Be that as it may, the result was that *Requiem* continued to exist exclusively in the minds of its creator and her friends.

LITERATURE OF BEARING WITNESS: AKHMATOVA MEETS SOLZHENITSYN

Seventeen years later, in 1962, Akhmatova found herself reciting *Requiem* to yet another visitor. This time, he was not a foreigner; she had learned the bitter lesson of 1945. Instead, he was a younger Russian writer who was about to test the limits imposed on published literature in the Soviet Union. Stalin had been dead for several years, and the worst of the purges were over. After an internal power struggle, Khrushchev had won the upper hand and had begun to distance himself from Stalin's most extreme crimes. The period was called the Thaw, and it allowed an influential literary editor to write to Khrushchev on Akhmatova's behalf, suggesting that she be rehabilitated after so many years of enforced silence and exclusion. Once again, the head of state had to decide what to do with Russia's Sappho. Khrushchev agreed that Akhmatova was no longer a threat and might even be given a minor place in the Soviet literary universe. For the first time in decades, Akhmatova could write with the hope of publication.

Even under these new circumstances, however, *Requiem* was too risqué to be published, which was why Akhmatova was reciting it to the younger Russian writer from memory. The writer, Aleksandr Solzhenitsyn, didn't know *Requiem*, but he did know some of her other poems from a publication system called *samizdat*, the Russian word for "self-publishing." While the safest method for composing secret poems under Stalin was to commit them to memory, after Stalin's death an underground method of self-publishing had emerged as an alternative. The tools were not printing presses, which were difficult to acquire in a totalitarian state—samizdat was still pre-Gutenberg, as Akhmatova had called the era—but it used another mechanical instrument, barely a hundred years old, relatively cheap, and more difficult to control: a typewriter. With the aid of carbon paper, a single typewriting session could produce around ten copies, which would then be passed on to other readers, who might in turn duplicate the text secretly and give it to more readers still.

Samizdat started after Stalin's death with the poetry of Akhmatova and a few others. Poems were short, the most compressed way of capturing the helplessness and terror that had seeped into every corner of Soviet life. In the beginning, these unauthorized, handmade poems circulated among groups of friends, each group barely larger than the one to whom Akhmatova had whispered her poems in the thirties. But during the Thaw following Stalin's death, samizdat became bolder. Copies circulated more widely and more people dared to read them. People might be allowed to keep a text for only one day, reading it greedily on their own or to friends all night before passing it on to the next group. The process was primitive, labor-intensive, and limited in reach, but it was a beginning. Soon, samizdat expanded from poetry to essays, political writings, and even novels, especially from abroad, all typed on cheap paper, without covers, unbound, strewn with errors, and often divided into loose chapters so that several people could read a work simultaneously. As samizdat increased, the method of duplication improved, with professional samizdat typists aiding the literary underground while also supplementing their income.

The Soviet state was not oblivious to the growing samizdat movement, but short of turning back the clock to the terror of the Stalin period, samizdat was difficult to control. Apartments were searched, and the mere possession of samizdat would be met with swift punishment, usually based on article 190-1, "Slander of the Soviet State and Social System," or article 162, "Engaging in Prohibited Manufacturing." But no matter how many readers and distributors were arrested, samizdat could not be stopped, because it produced the only literature worth reading. A joke circulated in which a grandmother tried and failed to interest her granddaughter in Tolstoy's *War and Peace*. Desperate, she retyped the sprawling novel by hand to make it look like a samizdat publication.

By the time Akhmatova read *Requiem* to Solzhenitsyn, some three hundred authors were circulating in this way. Solzhenitsyn was one of them, which is how Akhmatova had read a samizdat version of Solzhenitsyn's novel *One Day in the Life of Ivan Denisovich*. While Akhmatova's *Requiem* had described what it was like to wait without hope outside a prison, Solzhenitsyn took the reader into the heart of the gulag, the prison camp system known by its acronym. The novel was chillingly matter-of-fact. Solzhenitsyn recounted a single day in the life of a typical inmate, beginning with the wake-up call and the scramble for extra food and describing the day's work on a building crew at below-zero temperatures with inadequate clothing. Solzhenitsyn realized that life in the gulag was so inhuman that no amount of outrage could do it justice. The best weapon was bone-dry description, giving readers the chance to generate outrage themselves. Unbeknownst to him, a similar approach had been used by writers such as Primo Levi in trying to capture the even more inhuman experience of the Nazi labor and death camps.

When I contemplate the fortunes and function of literature in the twentieth century, authors bearing witness to the horrors of fascism and totalitarianism rank high. To be sure, earlier writers had not been shy about depicting violence. In the *Iliad*, Homer and his scribe capture in stark detail how a spear might enter a human body or crash through a head. But describing the systematic mass incarceration of ordinary people was a new challenge. Literature was prepared to meet this challenge because it had learned to care about the lives of common people, not just the fates of kings and heroes. In the twentieth century, these two developments, mass internments and literature, converged in the extraordinary literature of bearing witness.

Solzhenitsyn knew what he was writing about. While serving in World War II, he had made a derogatory remark about Stalin in a letter to a friend, which led to his being arrested and sentenced to eight years in the gulag. Upon his release, made possible by Stalin's death, he was forced into exile in Kazakhstan, where he took up residence in a primitive clay hut. The first thing he did was to buy a Moskva 4 typewriter to put his experience of the gulag into words. It was a laborious process because Solzhenitsyn was not a fast typist. When he remarried his former wife, who had divorced him while he served his sentence, the pace of production increased because she knew how to touch-type, like the better samizdat duplicators. Writing about the gulag was taboo, so Solzhenitsyn burned all drafts and kept only one version, which he carefully secured in a complicated system of hiding places.

But by the time he was meeting Akhmatova in 1962, things were

A MOSKVA 4 TYPE-
WRITER, THE MODEL
USED BY SOLZHE-
NITSYN UPON HIS
RELEASE FROM THE
GULAG TO COMPOSE
HIS FIRST BOOK, *ONE
DAY IN THE LIFE OF
IVAN DENISOVICH.*

changing. The main reason for Solzhenitsyn's visit to Leningrad was not to pay homage to Akhmatova, but the astonishing fact that *One*

Day in the Life of Ivan Denisovich was to be printed in *Novy Mir*. The magazine occupied a crucial place in Russian literature, situated at the border between the secret world of samizdat and the official world of state-sanctioned print. The plan to publish Solzhenitsyn in an official journal almost failed. Editors at the magazine had to be placated, and Khrushchev himself, acting on his reformist impulses, persuaded the party presidium to authorize publication. The efforts were worth it: Around one million copies of the magazine version would be produced, as well as a separate book publication with a print run of more than one hundred thousand. During their meeting, Akhmatova and Solzhenitsyn didn't know these numbers, but they knew that the publication would create a sensation. A text channeling the pent-up power of samizdat was about to burst into the public eye with the state-controlled might of Gutenberg.

Akhmatova profited from these new possibilities as well. *Novy Mir,* the magazine that would publish *One Day*, had brought out some of her poems, though not *Requiem*, which continued to circulate in samizdat only. By the early sixties, there existed another possibility: publication abroad. Presses had sprung up in different countries, especially in Germany, ready to publish Russian works. The process was difficult and dangerous. Manuscripts had to be smuggled out of Russia, often on microfilm, and the printed books smuggled back. There were also risks to the authors, which was why foreign publications, called *tamizdat* (publishing abroad), usually carried a note saying "published without the consent of the author." After having lived in the minds of Akhmatova and her close friends and then been circulated through the secret samizdat network, *Requiem* was printed for the first time in the form of *tamizdat* in 1963.

THE NOBEL PRIZE IN LITERATURE

There was another important undercurrent to the meeting between Akhmatova and Solzhenitsyn in 1962: the Nobel Prize in Litera-

ture. Both writers knew that the publication of *One Day* in an official Soviet journal was going to put Solzhenitsyn on the radar of the
Swedish Academy. Akhmatova had been nominated several times
in the past, but had been passed over in favor of her countryman
Boris Pasternak, who had been forced to decline the prize in 1958.
With the Thaw in full force, the Swedish Academy might well try
to bolster Soviet writers again by supporting Solzhenitsyn and his
backers. The prize had become undeniably political, a testament to
the importance of literature during the Cold War.

The beginnings of the Nobel Prize had been much more modest. It had been endowed by a Swedish weapons manufacturer and
inventor of dynamite who was hoping to leave a legacy in the sciences and the arts. The Swedish Academy, the body responsible for
the prize, at first chose many writers who did not stand the test of
time. But thanks to a generous endowment and increasing experience, the academy developed ways of avoiding the more blatant
types of favoritism as well as other pitfalls and managed to establish
its prize as the single most important one in the world. Sweden's
small size and peripheral position helped as well, just as a similar
position had helped Goethe conceive of world literature without
being drawn directly into world politics. Even in its early decades,
the Swedish Academy had gotten something else right: Literature
was much broader than fiction and poetry. It had awarded the prize
to many nonfiction writers, including philosophers (Henri Bergson
and Bertrand Russell) and historians as well as writers of autobiography (Winston Churchill) and essays, in order to signal just how
varied the power of literature could be. (The last fifty years have
seen a narrower focus on novels, poetry, and drama, although the
2015 prize went to a writer of nonfiction journalism from Ukraine
and Belarus and the 2016 prize to an American singer and song-
writer, Bob Dylan.)

The event anticipated during the meeting between Akhmatova
and Solzhenitsyn finally occurred in 1970 when the Nobel Prize in

Literature went to the author of *One Day*. By 1970, the Soviet Union no longer forced its writers to renounce the prize, but it did not permit Solzhenitsyn to attend the award ceremony. It would be another four years before the prize was handed to Solzhenitsyn in a small ceremony arranged just for this purpose. By that time, he had been expelled from the Soviet Union and taken up residence in the West, and he would spend the following decades in the United States.

Akhmatova did not live to see the award go to Solzhenitsyn. She died four years earlier, in 1966, her most important poem, *Requiem*, still unpublished in her native country. At least she had been allowed to travel to receive a literary prize in Sicily (in Taormina, which Goethe so admired) as well as an honorary degree at Oxford, masterminded by Isaiah Berlin. On her way back home she stopped in Paris, full of memories of her affair with Modigliani. In the meantime, she had recited *Requiem* to some new friends. Some of those who had served as guardians of the poem in the thirties experienced pangs; having been the carrier of the poem had been a burden but also a privilege that was now slipping away.

Akhmatova's official rehabilitation took another twenty-two years and involved yet another general secretary of the Communist Party of the Soviet Union. In a ceremony in 1988, Mikhail Gorbachev revoked the official note of censorship from 1946, which Akhmatova believed to have been occasioned by Isaiah Berlin's visit. By then, the Soviet Union was in the process of dissolution, brought to its knees by the desperate arms race of the Cold War but also by the secret publication system called samizdat, with which Anna Akhmatova was so closely identified. This persistent poet, who had perhaps exaggerated her role in triggering the Cold War, had done her part in bringing about its demise.

CHAPTER 14

THE *EPIC OF SUNJATA* AND THE WORDSMITHS OF WEST AFRICA

THE *EPIC OF SUNJATA* IS SET IN WESTERN AFRICA, IN WHAT today is Mali and Guinea, and it tells the story of how the Mande Empire came to be founded sometime during the late Middle Ages.

Like many foundational stories, the *Epic of Sunjata* begins with the drama surrounding the hero's birth. A regional chief has been trying to locate the woman prophesied to become his wife and to bear his son, the son who was to become Sunjata, who would unify the Mande people. The chief takes many wives, but none of them bears the right boy. The chief's difficulties increase when a buffalo begins terrorizing the region. The birth of Sunjata seems all but impossible. Desperate, the chief offers the most desirable woman to anyone who would vanquish the buffalo.

As with many stories, help arrives from unexpected quarters. Two foreign hunters from the north, attracted by this reward, come to the area. On the side of the road, they encounter a sorceress, who turns out to be the shape-shifting buffalo. Unexpectedly, this sorceress is ready to reveal to the hunters the secret of how she, in the form of the buffalo, could be killed in exchange for a promise: From among the village girls offered as the chief's prize, they would have to select the least attractive woman.

The young hunters kill the buffalo with weapons provided by the sorceress, and they keep their promise, selecting a deformed woman as their reward. Observing everything, the chief now realizes that this woman must be the future mother of Sunjata. He compensates the two hunters from the north and takes the woman as his own wife. Before long, young Sunjata is born.

The drama of the hero's birth is over, but Sunjata's difficulties have only begun. Like his mother, Sunjata is deformed, unable to stand or walk. As with many other heroes, Sunjata now must prove his worth. For seven long years, he endures this condition, biding his time, but eventually he manages to rise by the sheer power of his will, breaking the witchcraft that had kept him down.

His growing power attracts envy, particularly from his father's many wives. When one of Sunjata's half brothers tries to kill him, Sunjata's mother knows that the only way to save her son is to take him into exile. Sunjata must now endure the hardship of exile, which will last for twenty-seven long years, while his half brother lets the country be dominated by a hostile sorcerer. Desperate, his kinsmen track down the exiled Sunjata and persuade him to return home. Sunjata assembles a force, frees his homeland, and unifies it into a regional empire.

As with many other foundational stories, there is no independent historical proof that Sunjata ever existed (just as there is no proof, outside foundational texts, that Gilgamesh or Moses did). The *Epic of Sunjata* bears many resemblances to other foundational texts, which often portray a hero, seemingly overpowered by strong adversaries, rising up to meet a challenge. Like Odysseus, Sunjata experiences a period of exile and wandering before he can claim his homeland, a story that also resonates with the exile of the Jewish people. And like the Maya *Popol Vuh*, the epic lists the names of important ancestors all the way back to the dawn of life.

What is unusual about the *Epic of Sunjata* is that it has survived as oral literature until our own time. There isn't a single version, fixed through writing, but instead many local variations performed by trained storytellers to live audiences. These storytellers sometimes use musical instruments, such as the kora, a harplike device, to accompany their performance, and include the lineages of prominent families in attendance. Each performance is different, as each storyteller selects from the store of remembered episodes those that are most relevant for a particular time and audience. These storytellers enjoy an exalted status in Mande society. Since their profession requires long training and complex skills, they are considered artisans. Alongside the men who work with wood, leather, or metal, they work with words and are called wordsmiths.

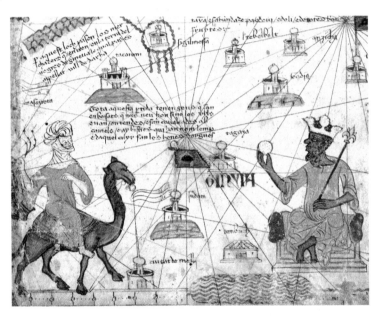

THIS DETAIL FROM A 1375 MAP OF WESTERN AFRICA
SHOWS MANSA MUSA, A SUCCESSOR TO SUNJATA,
SITTING ON HIS THRONE.

Still alive as oral literature, the *Epic of Sunjata* was written down only in our own time. This gives us the unique chance to observe a process that has happened over and over ever since Gilgamesh and Homer: the process by which oral stories are transformed into written literature.

An Epic Is Being Performed
—

My favorite version of *Sunjata* was performed by a storyteller, and written down by a scribe, in 1994. The performance took place in the village of Fadama, near the Niandan River in Guinea, West Africa. The village contained only about one hundred inhabitants, most of whom lived in small round mud-brick huts with cone-shaped thatched roofs. Depending on a family's size, a compound might contain a half dozen or so dwelling huts, a roofed, open-sided cooking area, and a granary or two.

The storyteller was Djanka Tassey Condé. Condé had been trained in the traditional manner by his father and brother. His father, the famous Babu Condé, had long presided over their family compound and become the *jeli nagara*, or chief of the bards, in the region, and Tassey had inherited the position.

Tassey Condé performed in his own hut, which was crowded with a dozen or more people seated, backs against the curved wall, on mats and goatskins. During the long performance, male family members and neighbors would drift in and out as space opened up, with younger people always making way for their elders, and women peeking in from outside the door. Wearing a brightly patterned traditional gown over baggy trousers, Condé acknowledged the arrival of visitors before launching into the story.

Given limited time, he would have to pick and choose, deciding which story lines to pursue, which to elaborate, and which to leave for other occasions. Over the course of four performance days, spread out over several weeks, he would craft a version of *Sunjata* that was true to tradition but that was also his own.

Audience participation was encouraged. Two or three bards from other lineages in the village alternated as formal responders, uttering encouraging exclamations at the end of every sentence. Virtually every phrase was hailed by a *naamu* ("We hear that!") or *tinyé* ("True!"), expressing the audience's appreciation of the story and the performer's expertise.

There was one unusual audience member: the scribe who would write down this story. The scribe was the American scholar David Conrad.

It had not been easy for Conrad to reach this remote village. He had traveled by jeep, making his way through grazing cattle, then crossed a stream in a dugout canoe, and finally walked the last part to the village. Conrad knew what he wanted, namely to turn *Sunjata* into literature. This was the ultimate purpose of Condé's performance—not the live recounting of the story for a local audience, but a performance that would end up in David Conrad's book.

In order to record Condé's version, Conrad did not use a pen, at least not right away. He used a Sony TCS-430, a hand-sized tape recorder, as well as a Marantz PMD-430, a somewhat larger portable recording machine. Tape recorders had been familiar sights around storytellers since the 1970s. They allowed them to record stories in oral form without translating those stories into literary genres like plays or novels (or children's stories). Often coming from Nigeria, tape recorders had started to appear in larger numbers in West Africa and were now used to record oral storytelling without imposing literary expectations. Cassettes, usually pirated, were sold in market stalls across the region, often without casing and proper labels, giving those who could not read access to the story as well.

Like other new technologies, cassettes changed oral performance culture. They allowed storytellers to reach audiences across distances, radically expanding the range of their influence (similar to the effects of writing in this regard). Whereas previously bards had been reciting to audiences congregating in a particular place, they now competed with one another across the region. One result was that bards tried to impose their own personality more strongly onto the material, producing their own distinct interpretations to differentiate themselves from rivals, which is what Condé was doing as well.

Cassettes, along with radio and television, also changed the social position of storytellers. Traditionally, they had been tied to powerful patrons, but this system of patronage had been disrupted by the arrival of the French colonists. The economic and social fabric surrounding storytellers changed again when Mali and adjacent countries gained independence after World War II, leaving bards scrambling to find new patrons among the new political and economic elite. In this situation, the cassette tape, along with radio and television, offered a new source of income to supplement what bards could earn by reciting at naming ceremonies and weddings.

The financial incentive for Condé's 1994 performance was not radio or cassette sales, but the world market in literature. Conrad had paid Condé between twenty-five thousand and fifty thousand Guinean francs per session (about twenty-five to fifty U.S. dollars), a significant sum at the time. After the recording, the tapes were painstakingly transcribed into the Mande language spoken by Condé, using the French alphabet, and then translated into English. Conrad then edited the result, reducing it to about a third of the length, to produce a version that worked as a piece of literature while capturing the cadences of oral storytelling, including interjections from the audience (Conrad later published an excellent prose version as well). He then wrote the text in lines of poetry, like a Homeric epic. An oral story had been transformed into a literary text.

THE FIRST WAVE OF LITERACY

LATE MIDDLE AGES, MANDE TERRITORIES

David Conrad's tape recorder and transcription were not *Sunjata*'s first encounter with writing. The epic had coexisted with different

writing cultures for centuries, and these cultures had influenced
the oral story. Bards like Condé had not simply rejected writing,
but incorporated written stories—and writing itself—into their narrative. This is the second process *Sunjata* lets us observe in detail:
how oral storytelling can exist side by side with literary cultures.

Condé began his story with the origin of all mankind in Adam
and Eve, whom he called by the Arabic names Adama and Hawa.
He then moved on to Abraham and his descendants down to Jesus
and Muhammad. These figures had come to the Mande territories
via Islam and its sacred text, the Qur'an.

Bards like Condé not only accepted stories from sacred scripture
into their oral narrative, but also related Sunjata's genealogy to that
of Islam. For this purpose, they turned to Muhammad's companion, Bilal ibn Rabah. Because of his beautiful voice, Ibn Rabah had
called the people to prayer and came to be known in Islam as the
first *muezzin*, the caller to prayer. Interested in this vocal performer,
Mande bards now described Ibn Rabah as an ancestor of Sunjata,
thus intertwining their own storytelling tradition with Islamic belief.

But that was not all. Aware that Islam relied on sacred scripture,
Condé's version also honored writing as an important cultural force
in the person of Manjan Bereté. A prophet and counselor to Sunjata's father, Bereté had correctly predicted that foreigners would
identify the woman destined to give birth to Sunjata. Significantly,
all of Bereté's wisdom was derived from written books. Condé told
his audience how Bereté had brought a sacred book to Sunjata's
father and persuaded him to convert to Islam. The *Epic of Sunjata*
had maintained its oral nature by including many aspects of Arab
writing in its narrative.

Tassey Condé was responding to a long tradition of West African
literacy. In the centuries after the death of Muhammad in 632,
Arabic-speaking tribes had spread the words of the prophet across

the Middle East through a series of military conquests. Then Arab and Berber armies conquered the northern coast of Africa and crossed into Europe, extending their empire to the Spanish peninsula, until Christian armies managed to take possession of these territories again through the so-called reconquest of Spain in 1492. Ultimately Islam would reach all the way to India, where rulers in Delhi converted to the religion, giving rise to the Mughal Empire.

Only the path southward continued to be barred by the Sahara, one of the most formidable natural barriers in the world. Ultimately, Arabs, who were adept at desert technology, figured out how to cross the Sahara by importing the one-humped camel, or dromedary. With the help of caravans of such camels, Arab traders brought the products of their vast network, including spices and crafts, to Mali.

They also brought a literate culture based on a sacred text, the Qur'an, and a rich tradition of commentary and scholarship on this text. Recognizing the advantages of becoming part of this large cultural sphere, the Mande rulers converted to Islam sometime during the Middle Ages.

Ibn Battuta Visits Mali

1352, Tangiers

The best witness for the early contact between the Mande and the Arabic world is Abu Abdullah Muhammad ibn Battuta, one of the great travelers and travel writers in world literature. He was one of the first Arabs to write about the Mande Empire, whose founding was commemorated in the *Epic of Sunjata*.

Ibn Battuta's enchantment with travel had begun when the young native of Tangiers, in Morocco, decided to make the pilgrimage to Mecca required by Islam. His pilgrimage complete, he didn't feel like returning home to Tangiers right away. He would spend the next twenty-three years on the road, traveling thousands of miles toward the east, across the vast territory dominated by Islam, stretching all the way to India.

Ibn Battuta made his way into the land of the Mande in 1352, his final journey, which led to one of the earliest written accounts of the successors of the mythic Sunjata. While the oral—and now written—story of Sunjata is the only account of this mythical founder, Ibn Battuta's travelogue shows that the story may have had some historical basis.

Taking two camels, one for riding and one for provisions, Ibn Battuta set off, noting various strange sights along the way, including a salt mine, camels carrying slabs of salt, one on each side, and a village whose buildings were made entirely of rock salt.

Mostly, Ibn Battuta focused on staying alive. The only way to survive the ordeal of crossing the desert was to be part of a caravan, and even that was dangerous. The hardest part was a ten-day stretch without any source of water. One member of their caravan had stayed behind after a quarrel, lost his way, and died. Ibn Battuta encountered another caravan that reported missing members. He and his companions soon found them dead along the way, a gruesome reminder of the dangers they all faced. None of their group ever strayed from the caravan after that.

The only thing they didn't have to worry about was other people—the Sahara was free of robbers. Ibn Battuta was pleasantly surprised that the roads continued to feel safe even after they had traversed the desert, and he decided to continue on his own. The roads were controlled by Mande rulers, but actual trade was in the hands of Muslims, including Berbers and Arabs who had settled there, bringing their culture, their know-how, and their writing. Ibn Battuta took it all in, admiring the zeal with which some local youths were studying the Qur'an, and he particularly noted a boy who was shackled until he learned it by heart. And he noted with satisfaction a ceremonial reading of the Qur'an.

A THIRTEENTH-CENTURY BOOK ILLUSTRATION BY AL-WASITI SHOWING A
GROUP OF PILGRIMS ON THEIR WAY TO MECCA.

There was one event that attracted his particular attention, a
festival involving a group of singers in costumes made of feathers.
They stood before the king reciting their poetry, which told of the
deeds of previous kings. Then the chief singer approached the king
and placed his head on the king's lap, then on each of his shoul-
ders, all the while reciting an ancestral story. What struck Ibn Battuta about this display of oral storytelling was how ancient it was;
apparently, this type of recitation "was already old before Islam."
Even though writing had long been introduced to some segments
of Mande society, these older oral traditions had continued undiminished, even while adapting to the new book-based religion.
Thanks to Ibn Battuta, we know that the dynamic relation between

Islamic writing and Mande orality that was playing out in 1994 in Tassey Condé's version of *Sunjata* had been going on at the very least since the fourteenth century.

Ibn Battuta finally made it into the presence of the Mande king, Mansa Sulayman, a successor of the mythical Sunjata. The encounter didn't go well. During his almost thirty years on the road, Ibn Battuta had become a demanding traveler. He expected to be showered with gifts, as he had been in India, where he had also been asked to go on a diplomatic mission to China. This king didn't pay much attention to him, giving him nothing but three pieces of bread, a piece of fried beef, and a calabash of sour milk as welcome presents. Ibn Battuta laughed out loud in anger and surprise.

Unfortunately, the king had offended not just any traveler, but someone who would shape the Arabic world's view of sub-Saharan Africa for decades, even centuries. Throughout his travels, Ibn Battuta had kept copious notes, impressions of his encounters and exploits. He turned them into one of the most influential travel stories of all time.

Ibn Battuta didn't write up the story of his travels with his own hand but dictated it to a professional scribe, while also working with another collaborator. The result was the greatest eyewitness account we have of the Islamic world during the late Middle Ages, much to the detriment of the Mande king with his paltry gifts. Never shy about expressing his opinion, Ibn Battuta denounced the king in no uncertain terms, calling him the most miserly king he had met and reporting widespread dissatisfaction among his subjects.

Despite his invectives against the king, Ibn Battuta did the Mande a service by giving us an early account of their storytellers. In the centuries following Ibn Battuta's visit, these bards continued to practice their art by incorporating Islamic material but without feeling the need to learn how to read and write. Arabic writing remained mostly confined to the relatively small number of Arabic speakers, Qur'anic scholars like Bereté from the story of Sunjata. A significant literary culture developed in such places as Timbuktu, which became a center of Arabic learning, but it did not fundamentally affect oral storytelling.

Mande singers, for their part, didn't see the need to translate the stories of Sunjata into Arabic for the purpose of writing them down. Perhaps they even worried, as bards of other oral cultures had done, that once their most important story was written down, they would lose control of it. Instead these storytellers continued to transmit the story orally, mostly within families such as Tassey Condé's clan. They performed it on special occasions, such as the one Ibn Battuta had witnessed during his journey.

In this way, Arabic writing and Mande storytelling continued to exist simultaneously in parallel worlds—as they still do today. Tassey Condé himself could have gone to one of the many Qur'anic schools, learned Arabic letters, and turned his oral version of *Sunjata* into a written story in that language. But he didn't. And why should he? He was trained to remember and recite the story of Sunjata in live performance, as its official guardian, and that is what he did until his death in 1997.

THE SECOND WAVE OF LITERACY

Even if oral and written cultures can exist side by side for centuries, as was the case in the Mande territories, eventually they will intersect. They did intersect in the late nineteenth and early twentieth centuries. However, the writing culture with which they intersected was not Arabic, but European.

Europeans had first made contact with western Africa in the fifteenth century and subsequently established trading posts along the coast, leaving the interior relatively untouched. This changed with the Berlin Conference of 1884–85, when European powers, emboldened by superior war technology and steamships, carved up Africa among themselves. The Mande heartland fell to France. Politics, trade, and worldly power now spoke—and wrote—in French.

While importing French writing and culture to Africa, some French colonists and military officers became interested in the culture of their latest acquisition, including the stories of Sunjata, and started to write them down. (Perhaps they were drawing on Arabic writers from the late nineteenth century who had finally taken an interest in Mande culture.) These first French accounts presented the Sunjata tale as a local legend, or even as a children's story, with little awareness that its central figure was revered as the founder of a large and ancient empire. This was not a glorious beginning for the literary career of *Sunjata*, but a beginning it was.

The next stage in *Sunjata*'s literary life was initiated by students at the École Normale William Ponty. Schools had been the prime vehicle for making Africa more French, although only a small number of Africans were educated in this way, just enough to meet the demand for people to fill lower-level administrative offices. In some of these schools, French colonists experimented with giving more scope to African culture and tradition, which was how students at Ponty were exposed to stories of Sunjata. On the occasion of a school festival in 1937, they decided to present *Sunjata* as a play. Drama combined the advantages of writing with those of live performance, allowing the students to perform the story of Sunjata in front of an audience with musical accompaniment in the manner reminiscent of traditional storytellers.

The first widely read version of *Sunjata* was published several decades later, in 1960, by Djibril Tamsir Niane, who had also gone through the French school system in western Africa before earning a degree from the University of Bordeaux. Writing in French and working with a storyteller, Mamoudou Kouyaté, the two collaborators produced what they called an *Epic of Old Mali*. Niane took the material provided by the bard and turned it into a novel. This form confronted them with some difficulties in that the characters and plot of *Sunjata* lacked the realist style and psychological insight readers had come to expect from novels. Niane tried to rectify this situation by adding realistic touches and character motivation typical of novels (he also related Sunjata to other historical figures such as Alexander the Great). The result was an easily readable version of *Sunjata*, which enjoyed, for the first time, a wider readership. *Sunjata* had undeniably become literature.

Both the play and the novel were in French because literacy remained confined to those who attended French schools (in addition to Arabic for those who attended Qur'anic schools), which meant that Mande languages had remained mostly spoken.

A New Writing

One of the most prominent critics of importing European writing was Souleymane Kanté, a strong-minded reformer and linguistic entrepreneur living in Guinea, West Africa. Kanté was convinced that the only way to spread literacy more widely was to turn Mande, the family of closely related Mande languages and dialects spoken at home and in the street into writing.

Kanté knew that first attempts had been made in the late nineteenth century to adapt the Roman alphabet, brought by the French, to local languages. The French alphabet came with significant drawbacks. It wasn't designed to capture tonal languages such as Mandingo (Arabic writing wasn't suited to this task either). Even more problematic was its cultural and political baggage as the alphabet of the colonizers. African students remembered with resentment the lessons taught by their French teachers about the superiority of the French language. A backlash was inevitable. For Kanté and many others, political independence from France meant rejecting French as the language of education, administration, and commerce, and with it the French alphabet.

For Kanté, the only solution was a brand-new alphabet, one specifically designed to capture the languages spoken by the people and without a colonial history. In 1949, he presented such an alphabet, custom-tailored to the language it was meant to represent. It steered clear of French and looked much more like Arabic, with connected letters written from right to left. Kanté called this alphabet N'ko, Mande for "I speak," a phrase prominently used in the stories of Sunjata.

Even though this was an alphabet designed for independence from France, when independence finally arrived eleven years later, in 1960, the new state opted for the French alphabet, despite its colonial baggage, mostly for pragmatic reasons. For sixty years, the country's literacy, however limited, had been based on the French alphabet, and that alphabet now offered itself as the path of least resistance. Undeterred by the lack of state support, Kanté decided to start his own underground movement, recruiting volunteers to set up schools based on the new alphabet.

In order to take hold, the new alphabet needed a body of literature. Once again Kanté decided to take matters into his own hands, and he embarked on the heroic undertaking of producing a literature to be written with the new N'ko system, including a grammar, the Qur'an, and *Matrimonial Laws of Islam* as well as self-help pamphlets. One volume offered advice on "Breast feeding and the best way to avoid pregnancy (Contraceptive)." Finally, the N'ko movement shifted to the oldest stories of this culture, those from before the arrival of Islam.

In 1997 a history of the region during the Sunjata era appeared, written in N'ko. In this way, *Sunjata* entered literature through an alphabet specifically designed to capture the tones and cadences of the language in which it was performed.

———

THE *EPIC OF SUNJATA* now exists in several excellent written versions, which have entered the literary canon, college syllabi, and anthologies. The version Condé and Conrad produced is in English, the new lingua franca of world literature. At the same time, the epic continues to be performed live by trained storytellers in Mande languages.

The story of how *Sunjata* became literature is one that speaks to the ways in which oral cultures survive by adapting to the realities of writing. It also reminds us that the dynamic process between oral storytelling and writing technologies continues to this day. The sea of unwritten stories is still infinite and waiting to be transformed into literature.

CHAPTER 15

POSTCOLONIAL LITERATURE: DEREK WALCOTT, POET OF THE CARIBBEAN

2011, ST. LUCIA

NEW NATIONS NEED STORIES TO TELL THEM WHO THEY ARE, AND never was this clearer than in the middle of the twentieth century, when European nations lost control over their colonies and dozens of new nations were born virtually overnight. The number of nation-states in the world quadrupled from around fifty to more than two hundred. Independence, it turned out, was a boom time for literature. The new nations faced considerable challenges because European colonists had drawn territorial boundaries at their own convenience, often forcing rival groups, language communities, and tribes into a single administrative entity. These challenges made it all the more important to create cultural cohesion and identity through foundational texts. Sometimes, older oral stories were revived and turned into written epics, as had happened with *Sunjata* in West Africa. But not all new nations were fortunate enough to have a native epic tradition, which meant that new texts had to be written by individual authors, as Virgil had done for Rome. Hence the explosion of what we now call postcolonial literature in the second half of the twentieth century.

———

I HAD ALWAYS BEEN fascinated by the most extreme case in point: the small Caribbean island of St. Lucia and its resident writer Derek Walcott, author of *Omeros*, an epic poem in the tradition of Homer, and winner of the Nobel Prize in Literature in 1992.

Unlike many other former colonies with ancient literary traditions, St. Lucia had little literature before Walcott's works. With the native population wiped out within two centuries after the arrival of European colonists, and the forced importation of slaves from Africa to work the sugar plantations, the island's purpose had been agricultural, not cultural. Walcott was, for all intents and purposes, the island's first writer of note. When he was awarded the Nobel Prize, he could enjoy the thought of being a laureate from a nation with only 160,000 inhabitants. Even more remarkable was the fact that he had effectively taken the island from zero to Nobel Prize in a single generation. Iceland, with a population around 300,000, boasts a Nobel Prize winner as well, won in 1955 by Halldór Laxness, but Iceland has a literary tradition that goes back to the sagas of the Middle Ages. Walcott had managed single-handedly to write his postcolonial nation into world literature. I decided to pay him a visit.

From the air, the island looked striking, an eruption of green mountains piled sky-high, topped by a bouquet of clouds. There didn't seem to be a place to land, but after some circling we suddenly descended onto an airstrip on the southern tip, Hewanorra Airport, one of the few Amerindian names on the map. Most others were French. The airport was in Vieux Fort. The route from the airport went by small villages and towns—Laborie, Choiseul—and landmarks, including Soufrière, where volcanic activity creates bubbling hot springs and releases foul-smelling sulfur into the air. THE CARIBBEAN'S ONLY DRIVE-IN VOLCANO—COME FEEL THE HEARTBEAT OF THIS TROPICAL ISLE, a sign promised. Except for the sign, Walcott has incorporated all of this into his work. Choiseul was where his grandfather lived—we even get the street address in one poem—and the mouth of the volcano doubled in his work as entrance to the underworld. No matter where I went on St. Lucia, I saw it through Walcott's work, above all his greatest work, *Omeros*, Walcott's attempt at writing a foundational text for his new nation.

I was here with Amanda, my partner, and a friend, Maya, and we stayed at Fond Doux, a working plantation that grew cocoa, cinnamon, and many other tropical flowers and fruits. Some plants were native, others had been brought here from elsewhere, Africa or the Pacific, along with slaves.

The plantation consisted of five or six main buildings and various cottages scattered about the estate, located in the foothills of St. Lucia's green mountains. We soon met the plantation manager, Lyton, a tall man in his forties. As soon as he heard of my interest in Derek Walcott, he started giving us free drinks. Walcott clearly was a highly valued currency.

Walcott had been to the plantation many times, Lyton said; once with another Nobel laureate—he couldn't remember the name (Walcott told me later that it was the Irish poet Seamus Heaney). With a conspiratorial smile, Lyton reported that during one visit Walcott complained that there were no pictures of him anywhere on the plantation. Once I had a look around, I saw Walcott's point. The estate was plastered with photographs of Prince Charles. Prince Charles with Lyton (several); Prince Charles with the staff; Prince Charles on the terrace; Prince Charles looking at the movable racks on which cocoa is dried; Prince Charles next to the iron vessel in which the cocoa beans are pounded. There wasn't a single building or wall that didn't have a smug-looking Prince Charles, joined by Camilla, looking down at you. Surely, in the midst of this attachment to the former colonial power, there would have been room for the island's national poet? Lyton had promised Walcott that he would correct the situation, but hadn't gotten around to doing it.

While Walcott had failed in Fond Doux, he had succeeded at the symbolic center of St. Lucia, the central square of the capital, Castries. Under British rule, the square had been named Columbus Square (even though Christopher Columbus never set foot on the island), but most St. Lucians refused to recognize this name and simply called it "the square." It now contained a statue of Derek Walcott and was named after him. Walcott, the island's native son, had managed to displace the Italian explorer. Through literature.

A BUST OF DEREK WALCOTT IN COLUMBUS SQUARE IN CASTRIES, ST. LUCIA. IN 1993, THE SQUARE WAS RENAMED DEREK WALCOTT SQUARE.

To further my research, Lyton had kindly arranged a meeting with the island's unofficial historian, Dr. Gregor Williams, once a student of Walcott's. "Tell your driver to meet me at the gas station on the Morne," Dr. Williams had said on the phone, and so, lacking a driver, I had chauffeured us to what looked like the appointed gas station on the top of a steep hill. Before long a small car pulled in, from which emerged what I thought looked like a picture-book rendering of a Caribbean intellectual: an older man with large, heavy-framed glasses that looked as if they were made in Moscow circa 1962, a flowing mane of white hair, and a white beard. He switched into my car and directed me up the hill to the St. Lucia campus of the University of the West Indies, which was housed in the former colonial barracks of the British army.

As soon as we got out, he launched into a dramatic description of St. Lucia's colonial history, beginning with the American Revolution. We were standing on the spot from which the island could be ruled, Williams explained, Morne Fortuné, "Lucky Hill." Its fortunate holder commands two important bays; one is now dominated by oil tankers, the other by the island's capital, Castries, home to half of its population and the best natural harbor in the Caribbean. Striding across the area with expansive gestures, Williams explained the drama of the British and French navies making their way down to St. Lucia unbeknownst to each other during the Revolutionary War. When the two fleets finally noticed each other, they engaged in a fierce battle, right here. Subsequently, the island went back and forth between the French and the British, and each switch involved laying siege to the spot where we were standing. For this reason, St. Lucia was sometimes called "the Helen of the West Indies," a gorgeous prize fought over by rival colonial powers.

A CARIBBEAN HOMER

Throughout the history lesson, I experienced a sense of déjà vu: I had heard all this before, and from Walcott himself. The work that earned him the Nobel Prize was *Omeros*, which sought to recount the island's history in its entirety.

Writers living in cultures with long literary histories could rely on earlier works to tell the collective story of a people, works like the Greek *Iliad* or the Indian *Ramayana*—or the Icelandic *Eddas*. Writers in new nations, especially in the New World, often have had little foundational literature to draw on and have been obliged to create one for themselves (the Mayas and their *Popol Vuh* were an exception). It was a project that could go terribly wrong, leading to works that seem pompous, or simply fake. For every Virgil, who managed to manufacture a successful foundational text for Rome, there was a Joel Barlow, whose *Columbiad* of 1807 did not become the foundational work for the United States.

Walcott succeeded where Barlow failed. In *Omeros* we learn about the European conquest of the New World, beginning with the earliest Spanish conquistadors such as Pizarro and Cortés. Then came the slaves, who brought West African traditions. Walcott even mentions Mande culture and its bards, whose legacy lives on in the Caribbean because many slaves brought to the New World came from western Africa. Sir George Rodney, commander of the British fleet, makes an appearance, as do the battle for Morne Fortuné, the Revolutionary War, and the abolition of slavery.

But even as Walcott was telling a New World history, he was drawing on Old World models, specifically Homer. While there were thousands of miles and thousands of years between Bronze Age Greece and twentieth-century St. Lucia, Walcott recognized underlying commonalities, notably island life exposed to the vagaries of the sea.

The result was not a resetting of the *Iliad* or the *Odyssey* in St. Lucia (though Walcott did later write a dramatic adaptation of the *Odyssey*). Instead he created contemporary St. Lucian characters with Homeric names. They include the fisherman Achille and the delivery truck driver Hector, who vie for the hip-swinging, insouciant Helen. Wittily, Walcott lets their heroic names clash with the mundane reality on the island. And yet, in the process, he elevates the mundane to the mythic (as James Joyce had with the ordinary Irishman whom he made the protagonist in his novel *Ulysses*).

The result is an epic poem that tries to make sense of St. Lucia's volatile history by using all available literary resources. Homer's *Iliad* and *Odyssey* are there not so much to supply particular stories as to signal an ambition, namely to write a foundational text for the Caribbean. If St. Lucia was called the Helen of the Caribbean because of rival colonial powers fighting for its possession, Derek Walcott declared himself the island's Homer.

Among the many attempts at foundational texts in the twentieth century, Walcott's *Omeros* is the most audacious. It is also the most accomplished and rightly recognized with the most important literary prize, and has stood as a model for postcolonial literature.

GROS ISLET

Gros Islet, the northern tip of the island, where some of the action is set, is also where Walcott lives, and I headed there to meet him. It had not been easy to set up the meeting. When I first called, Walcott, eighty-three years old, had answered the phone himself. His voice sounded frail, and he was unsure how to handle me. "Call back when Sigrid is here," he said, and hung up. I did call back, and Sigrid, his longtime companion, was ready to arrange the visit, with Walcott on the other line listening in; I could hear his breathing, but he didn't say a word. Sigrid could not give me a date, only a window of several days.

As soon as I landed in St. Lucia, I called again. Walcott appeared to have forgotten all about the visit. After some back-and-forth, he dimly remembered. "Call back when Sigrid is here." When I did, Sigrid was all business and happy to arrange the visit. "You don't know how to get here," she announced. "It's too complicated. Meet me at the Shell station two miles north of Castries." (Gas stations seemed to be the place to meet in St. Lucia.) After I found a gas station that seemed right, I waited, and before long a white woman appeared: Sigrid. "So are you German or is it only your name? Derek and I were debating it," were the first words out of her mouth. I mumbled something in the affirmative. She seemed mollified by the answer and waved: "Follow me."

Derek Walcott and Sigrid Nama were living right on the water in three nicely proportioned buildings, one of them his painting studio. The interior was simple, modernist, with well-designed bookcases. The terrace commanded a view of the water that I admired so much that I almost missed Walcott sitting at a table in the corner. He was old, hunched over, small. He did not get up, and motioned me to sit near him. Sigrid was going off to buy some chairs. "Bis später," she called, and added: "Translate!" I suggested, "See you later?" And then she was gone.

"What are you interested in?" Walcott asked, and I tried to explain something about Goethe's journey to Sicily and how it had inspired me to travel and look for literary traces whenever I could. I was not doing a very good job. "I'm interested in literature and places," I finally blurted out. "You mean geographically?" Yes, I nodded vigorously. He took a moment to think about what St. Lucia meant to him, geographically, and the first thing that came to his mind was language. He explained that the language used by most people here was French Creole, a spoken language without connection to written literature. An aspiring writer from St. Lucia needed to turn this purely spoken language into a literary one. Walcott had to create not only a foundational text, but also the language in which it would be written.

Walcott himself didn't speak French Creole at home—that is, he didn't speak it to his mother; he spoke it only to a widow who was helping his mother around the house (Walcott's father died when Derek was only a year old). His own relation to French Creole was somewhat distant. "I don't think in Creole," he admitted, but added, "When I am writing, my instinct is French Creole." The difference between the two was left hanging in the air.

Finding the right language was connected to finding the right literary form. Walcott's upbringing was in English literature, and it was tempting to combine French Creole with Western literary traditions. Walcott experimented with ballads, closer to the folk songs of

French Creole, but also with more formal meters and schemes, such as quatrains, to forge a new English. Some reviewers had been critical of Walcott's marriage of Western literary conventions with the vernacular of St. Lucia, though others had come to his defense, including his friend Joseph Brodsky (the Russian poet and protégé of Anna Akhmatova who had been forced to leave the Soviet Union in 1972). Such controversies had made Walcott wary of academic debates. "I distrust intellectuals," Walcott told me, "because they don't have a sense of humor," and he went on to describe jolly evenings of crude humor with Joseph Brodsky and Seamus Heaney. The latter was due to visit again in a few weeks. I thought it made an appealing scene, three Nobel laureates hanging out on Walcott's terrace cracking jokes. Walcott had also painted a portrait of Heaney, executed in strong, striking colors, to which he directed me in his studio.

We had veered from geography, I observed. "Okay, I can talk about place," he said, but he continued with language as well. "Now that you mention it, I remember a tremendous excitement to name a place on paper, or even to name things. There was a time early on, if somebody would say the word 'breadfruit,' for instance, it would create laughter in the theater, from the recognition and almost from embarrassment." Breadfruit was familiar to the audience—but unfamiliar in art because most art was imported and didn't bear traces of their island and its life. Yes, he had made an effort to represent St. Lucia, Walcott went on; it was all part of the project of writing St. Lucia into literary history, adding new place names, new characters, new fruit to the literary lexicon. This is what a foundational text has to do: translate a place, a culture, and a language into literature for the first time.

On the Nerve-Wracked Atlantic Coast

My favorite text by Derek Walcott, after *Omeros*, has always been *The Sea at Dauphin*, a one-act play from 1954. Much more modest than *Omeros*, it is set in the same world as the epic poem, but without the interest in its deep history—and without Homer. And yet, for me, it shows Walcott's literary imagination in its most distilled form. The opening stage direction describes "A Windward island in the West Indies, on its nerve-wracked Atlantic coast." I didn't know what a windward island was when I first read this line, but the image stuck with me, perhaps because it was so diffuse, demanding to be brought into focus.

Before coming to St. Lucia, I had spotted Dauphin, the small fishing village where the play was set, on a map way out there on the Atlantic coast. Judging from the map, a tiny road wound its way across the mountains and then stopped well before the village, which just sat there, a forlorn dot exposed to the wind and the sea.

Toward the end of my conversation with Derek Walcott, I brought up *The Sea at Dauphin*. Drama presented a particular challenge in the Caribbean, Walcott said, because it was not just a question of creating a language appropriate to the place, but also of having a theater in which to perform as well as an audience willing to attend. Walcott had tried to create such a culture with his twin brother, first in St. Lucia and then in Trinidad, by founding the acclaimed Trinidad Theatre Workshop in Port of Spain. Port of Spain was then the largest city in the eastern Caribbean, and in his Nobel Prize acceptance speech, Walcott paid homage to it. A proper city was precisely what was necessary for theater to thrive; an island by itself was not enough. Now that Walcott had moved permanently back to St. Lucia, after having spent time in Port of Spain and Boston, where he had taught playwriting, he felt the lack of an adequate theater as acutely as ever. Even the Trinidad Theatre Workshop, once the poster child of Caribbean theater, had fallen on hard times.

Walcott explained to me that for all its difficulties, drama also had an advantage over epic poetry or other forms of literature. While St. Lucia may not have had a theater culture, it had something else: a carnival. The carnival was the product not of a single author but of a collective; it was the primary art form of St. Lucia itself—and the reason why Walcott got interested in theater.

Walcott's voice lit up when he spoke about it. The central character in the carnival, Walcott explained, was a creature called Papa Jab (a shortened form of the French *Diable*), an old man with a beard, like Father Christmas, even like God, but he was really the Devil, with horns.

In the course of the action, Papa Jab gets killed, but three days later, he is resurrected. "Do you know any other example of the Devil being resurrected?" he asked, delighted with this twist. Another favorite moment is when Papa Jab complains that it's too hot for him in hell, asking for water. "The children sing along," Walcott said, and broke into French Creole: "Voyé glo ba mwê / Mwê ka bwilé" (Send water for me / I am burning). He found the idea of the Devil burning in his own hell, asking for water, hilarious. Papa Jab also has a trident, and when the children become too annoying he chases them around. Everyone plays along.

"I have been thinking about going out to Dauphin," I finally ventured, cautiously, explaining how much I liked this play and how intrigued I was to see the place, with its out-of-the-way location. Walcott found the idea of going to Dauphin absurd. "No, don't go, it's way out on the coast there; you probably just see a lot of cliffs. There is no village or settlement."

I was surprised. "No village?" "I don't think so," he said, but he no longer sounded quite as certain. I was puzzled and disappointed.

Before I could get my bearings, Sigrid was back. "I have brought you coconut water. It's very healthy. It's the only drink that has the same electrolytes as human blood. Here." We all drank it, contemplating its health effects. It tasted good. But Walcott was getting tired, despite the electrolytes. "Is it enough?" he asked me, touchingly. I had been pushing him to talk about his relation to St. Lucia, its language and geography, for almost an hour and a half, and he had been playing along valiantly. As I left, I heard Walcott speaking French Creole. Surprised, I looked around: Was this how he talked with Sigrid? No, he was talking to the maid. Walcott may not have thought in French Creole, but Creole was still the language in which he spoke to many people, just as an English version of it was the language of the fishermen in his play *The Sea at Dauphin*. I closed the door, got into the car, and drove back to Fond Doux.

Walcott's dismissal of Dauphin was nagging at me. "What's wrong?" Amanda asked when I returned. "Nothing." Sullenly I opened Google Earth and zoomed in on Dauphin. Just as Walcott had predicted, I saw nothing. A small bay, overgrown. No sign of a settlement or village. Should I go there anyway? I asked a young man working on the plantation whether my small rental car could navigate the road to Dauphin. "Yes, sure you can drive there." He was surprised that anyone would want to go there, but confident that I could. Had he been there himself? No, actually, he hadn't been there himself.

Later that night, after dinner, we hung out at the harbor in Soufrière, a small town on the coast. People were milling about, drinks in hand. There was a gas station (of course) and a hole-in-the-wall bar, packed with people. We hesitated, but the bartender had spotted us. "Come have a drink with the locals," he said good-humoredly. We did, and ordered Piton, the St. Lucian beer. Everyone else was drinking Heineken: We were trying to be local, while they were trying to be cosmopolitan.

I asked him about Dauphin. "You want to go to Dauphin?" he said incredulously. "Talk to this guy over there, he has been all over the island." I did. Was the road navigable? Yes, sure it was, but the village had been abandoned since the sixties. Or the fifties. But, yes, I could drive there. No problem. Had he been there himself? No, he hadn't actually been there himself. Very strange—on an island of less than 240 square miles, no one had been to Dauphin.

That night, I decided to go anyway. After having missed so many

destinations on my travels (I longed to go to Mali, but couldn't because of the civil war; ditto for Mosul), I was not going to let anyone
stop me from going to Dauphin. I got up early in the morning, and
the day started well. I got in the car and made my way back to the
north, on mountain roads. There were few cars in the south, only
the minibuses most people took and an occasional limousine from
one of the exclusive resorts. It was Sunday, and people were walking along the road in their best clothes, on their way to church.
There were many potholes, but stretches of the road were in excellent condition; inevitably, a sign informed me that the road was
being paid for by the European Union. When I left the coastal
road, I found that there was quite a bit of settlement in the interior,
at least up here, not the wild forest I was expecting. Asking for directions several times, I made my way across the mountains. Houses
became less frequent, and the road less good. Then the houses
stopped, and before long the paving as well, but I cheerfully drove
on, avoiding the increasingly large potholes. In the distance, I could
see the sea: the sea at Dauphin, as described so vividly in Walcott's
play.

And then the car tilted to the side, there was a nasty scraping
sound across the bottom, and I was stuck.

I tried to be calm. I found a jack in the trunk and tried to dig out
the front tires, to no avail. It was beastly hot. I hadn't seen a soul for
quite a while. I remembered that I had declined any form of car
insurance, and now I had probably ruined the car.

I hiked back. When I arrived at the first house, three teenagers
offered to help. When we got to the car, they shook their heads at
my predicament but then started to discuss strategy among themselves. They motioned me to get in the car and started giving me
instructions, pushing and lifting the car every which way. Forward;
stop; turn wheels this way; back up a bit. None of it made any sense
to me, but I followed their instructions, not always swiftly enough,
earning exasperated looks. They knew what they were doing and

got the car free, directing me, driving in reverse around the massive potholes, as we carefully wound our way to where the road was a little better. Only now did I register that the car was actually fine. We drove back to their house and even managed to turn the car on the small road. I was elated. In my post-scare high, I decided to make one more attempt. I told my new friends that I was going to walk down to Dauphin. They offered no commentary on my plan, I thanked them, and they were gone.

The dirt road had clearly been neglected for decades and had been given over to hurricanes. I was beginning to understand why no one I'd met had ever gone down to Dauphin. But I was in a good mood, hopping from stone to stone. After about ten minutes, a new problem arose: My feet began to hurt because I was wearing thin canvas shoes. Not ideal for hiking, as I was finding out. I tried to tread more carefully, wondering whether the teenagers could still see me, picking my way down the empty dirt road as if on eggshells, feeling like an idiot.

But soon I found myself thinking about the play. *The Sea at Dauphin* is set among a handful of fishermen braving the hostile sea. There are rough words spoken between Afa, the toughest fisherman in the village, and Augustin, his companion; there is an old man, Hounakin, an East Indian, who asks to be taken along for the ride, but he is too old, and too drunk, and too afraid. Left behind, he falls from the cliffs; probably suicide. Shaken by these events, Afa agrees to take a young boy on board as an apprentice.

The real drama, the protagonist of the play, is the sea, an alien force that shapes everything, bending plants, houses, and humans to its will. Gacia, the most reasonable character, sums it up in his rhythmical English Creole: "This sea not make for men." It sure isn't, but these fishermen have to deal with it anyhow. In the process, they become hardened and beaten down. "The sea is very funny, papa," Afa says to the old man, "but it not making me laugh." Echoing the opening of Yeats's poem "Sailing to Byzantium"—

"That is no country for old men"—Afa warns: "This sea no cemetery for old men." Augustin finally observes, "The sea is the sea,"
expressing resignation that we must accept the sea as it is, in all its
alien cruelty.

Thinking of these characters and their struggle against the sea as
I approached Dauphin, I found myself engaged in a daydream,
imagining the place as a kind of romantic ruin: a simple, wind-
beaten fishing village, abandoned but picturesque. There might be
a single old fisherman refusing to leave, holding down the fort. He
would be standing there by the sea, fishing, and telling me how
everyone up and left to seek their fortunes in Castries ("Ask him
why he not going to Castries to learn mechanic," Afa says in the
play about the boy). As I imagined the aftermath of Walcott's play,
they would all have left except this old man. His father and grandfather had lived and died here, and he, too, would die in Dauphin,
just as Dauphin would die with him.

My musings were interrupted when suddenly I found myself at
the foot of the road; there was a small brook, and I knew that I was
near the ocean. It had been only an hour since the car broke down.
There was a small clearing, with bananas; a goat, tied to a pole, was
grazing lazily. A little farther on, a fire was smoldering by the road.
Finally, I saw a shack, a wooden contraption with a corrugated iron
roof. I called out; no one answered. After another bend in the road,
I had arrived at Dauphin.

And I couldn't believe my eyes: There he was, the solitary figure
I had imagined in my daydream, standing at the beach, fishing.
Giddy with excitement, I walked toward him. As I approached, I
noticed that he was wearing the jersey of the Brazilian soccer team.
This wasn't quite the worn, hand-sewn garb in which I had draped
my imaginary lonely fisherman (in Walcott, the characters wear
old, moth-eaten sweaters). I called out so as not to startle him, and
he turned around, fishing rod in hand. He looked only mildly surprised to see me; he must have spotted me approaching. He was

about fifty years old, strongly built. As I stepped up to him and extended my arm to shake his hand, my eyes caught his belt: a holster
and a gun. With my other hand, I started groping for my cellphone.
Aware what was going through my mind, he grinned. "Hi, I'm
George. I sometimes come here for fishing. I'm a policeman."

Relieved, I told George that I had come to look around Dauphin, which I now did for the first time. The small bay was not a
pretty sight. It was swampy and littered with trash—plastic bottles,
plastic bags, everything imaginable. The same wind system that
had brought Columbus to the West Indies now delivered the trash
of the oceans to its shores. This was what a nerve-wracked coast on
the Windward Islands looked like these days: full of Atlantic debris.

George told me that this was the site of the earliest settlements
on St. Lucia: Shipwrecked sailors came here and stayed. I assumed
he was referring to Spanish explorers. "There are some ruins over
there, if you walk along the swamp," he added. I went, gingerly
walking along the perimeter of the trashy swamp, which was as
disgusting as it could be. The terrain was not navigable unless you
walked along a little creek, which had combined forces with the sea
to flood everything. I waded along, under trees and bushes, trying
not to notice how filthy I was getting. After ten minutes, I spotted
the remnants of two stone structures. Three walls, no roof, nothing
else. Could this be the remnant of the church that Walcott mentions in the play? Encouraged by my find, and hoping to escape the
swamp, I climbed up a steep hill, overgrown with all kinds of bushes
and roots and small trees. I almost fell several times. But I couldn't
find any more ruins. There were boulders lying about; were they
from houses? It was difficult to imagine buildings on this slope.

All this crawling around made me remember the other side of
The Sea at Dauphin: the land. The play contrasts the dangerous
sea, and the hardened fishermen braving it, with those who remain
on the land, seeking to eke out a living through agriculture. The
rough fishermen look down on farming, though it isn't much easier

than what they do: The land at Dauphin is rocky, as I was finding out right now, and not particularly fertile. Goats could survive on dry grass, but come to think of it, the goat that I had encountered on my way had looked pretty thin.

I climbed farther up to look around and down toward the water, but all I could see was bushes and rough undergrowth. Carefully I slid down again, frequently on all fours, back to the swamp, the trash, and George. Except that suddenly there was a second pickup truck with two more men. It was getting positively crowded here at Dauphin on this sunny Sunday afternoon. "Talk to him, he knows Dauphin," George called out when he saw me. I approached the beat-up truck. The owner, in blue overalls, introduced himself as Rogence. He and his companion were shoveling sand into their truck: They had just slaughtered pigs, he explained. When they were done, his companion stripped naked and waded into the re-pellent brown water.

I couldn't decide how to broach the topic of Dauphin and what had brought me here. Would Rogence, slaughterer of pigs, even know who Derek Walcott was? I asked him about the settlement. Dauphin had been abandoned since the fifties, Rogence con-firmed. A few people kept fishing boats here until the seventies, but since then the place had been pretty much abandoned. He himself came here only because he had a plantation nearby.

I felt that I had to explain what brought me to this remote place after all, so I finally mentioned Derek Walcott and *The Sea at Dau-phin*. "Of course, *The Sea at Dauphin*. My grandfather is the boy in the play." "Excuse me?" "Yes, my grandfather lived here. He was a foreman on the plantation. He is in the play." "What was your grandfather's name?" "Duncan." My head was spinning, and I couldn't even remember the characters' names anymore, but I was pretty sure none of them were called Duncan. "But there is no character named Duncan," I said hesitantly. "He is the boy," Rogence repeated. The matter was settled. I was speaking with the grandson of a dramatic character.

His silent companion had come back, apparently refreshed, and was slowly putting on his clothes; his muscular body had a heroic look to it. He had not uttered a single word. Rogence paid him no heed and offered me a ride. I got in the cab with him; his companion jumped in the back, with the sand. I was somewhat gratified that even this large pickup truck was having trouble navigating the potholes, and we almost got stuck a couple of times. Along the way Rogence told me about his farm. Originally it had been owned by a Frenchman, then by an Englishman, and after his grandfather had bought it, it had stayed in the family. His main livelihood was not pigs, it turned out, but cassava. He had a good hand for growing cassava, and he would make it into bread. He showed me some cassava trees on the way, and some moldy leftover loaves in his car. The loaves he sold directly to people in the area, but he also ground up the cassava and sold the product in the market at Castries.

Suddenly, while driving around the potholes, he fumbled for his cellphone and called his daughter. "Someone will come to pick up a packet" was all he said, and then turned to me: "Ask people where Rogence lives. It's a green house. My daughter will give you cassava." He dropped me off and turned right toward his farm, somewhere up in the mountains. When I got out, the farmworker spoke for the first time and demanded that I take his picture. He raised his shovel high over his head, triumphantly, posing for the shot. I didn't even know his name. I wanted to ask, but they were already on their way. The image of him, with his raised shovel, stayed in my mind. Of the three people I met at Dauphin, this silent man alone had the bearing of a Homeric character.

I hiked back to my car, got in, and started to drive back, still a bit worried. But all went well. The road got better, more houses appeared, and I stopped to ask two women for Rogence. "You drove this car to Dauphin?" They giggled. Then I recognized them: I had asked them for directions earlier. "No, I got stuck," I admitted, which they found uproariously funny. I smiled and didn't point out that they could have warned me. In return for my restraint, they told me how to get to Rogence's house. A teenage girl opened the door and looked at me with suspicion. "Rogence told me to pick up a package?" I said. Without a word, she disappeared. After a minute, she was back with a hand-sized package of finely ground cassava and gave it to me, smiling shyly. I was delighted with my trophy, thanked her, and drove home. The packet was labeled DAUPHIN HARVEST. In the battle between sea and land, the land had won.

THE WHOLE REST OF MY TIME in St. Lucia, I kept thinking about Dauphin. If Rogence was right, then Dauphin had been abandoned by the time Walcott was writing the play. Did he know that he was commemorating a fishing village on the brink of collapse or already abandoned? The play did not paint life at Dauphin in a rosy light. The fishermen risk their lives every day, going out even when the sea is rough. But as hard as this life is, there is no mention in the play of the village being abandoned or doomed. Come to think of it, it is not even clear when the play is set. Its ingredients are timeless: poor fishermen, in an isolated village, eking out a living from the sea and the land.

I went through the play, carefully noting anything that might fix its action in time. Tin cans seem to be around (as they are today, floating in the bay), but tin cans have existed for two hundred years. There was another hint: The fishermen smoke American cigarettes. This, again, was too general to date the play.

Back home, I discovered two additional pieces of information about Dauphin. The first was a recent newspaper article mentioning that the water at Dauphin seemed to contain clumps of oil. Even Rogence is quoted, saying that the water has always been dark, rather oily. Apparently, there are negotiations going on about oil exploration. History may erupt again in Dauphin, and now that Walcott has passed away, in March 2017, someone else will have to write a sequel to his play: *The Oil at Dauphin*.

The second was a report on an archaeological find from the pre-Columbian period. Dauphin, it turns out, does indeed contain one of the earliest signs of human settlement on the island. This is what George must have been referring to. Walcott had captured something archaic about Dauphin in the play—the struggle against the sea, the simple canoes. In doing so, he had put Dauphin on the map by making it literature.

CHAPTER 16

FROM HOGWARTS
TO INDIA

As MY RESEARCH AND TRAVEL, MY EXPLORING OF LITERATURE, CAME to a close and I found myself back in Boston, I was asked by an undergraduate student to join him for dinner in Annenberg Hall, the freshman dining hall of Harvard University. It is an imposing hall, with high Gothic ceilings. When the student met me outside, he mentioned, proudly, that Annenberg was the model for the Great Hall at Hogwarts. I nodded politely, hiding my skepticism. Clearly, my student was living in Harry Potter's world and I was, too. While I had traveled far and wide in search of literature, literature had caught up with me right here at home. It was time for me to face up to Potterworld.

Like a young novice wizard, I started with *The Tales of Beedle the Bard*, the book of wizarding tales, published in 2007. Originally, the volume was published in a limited edition of seven copies, bound in Moroccan leather and studded with precious stones and silver pieces. What made it most valuable, however, was the fact that J. K. Rowling had written each copy by hand, to be auctioned off at Sotheby's. Was this a capitalist version of samizdat? I contented myself with a printed version, which I purchased for a mere $7.92 plus tax on Amazon.

I enjoyed it much more than I expected. Rowling used the structure and the moral tone of the fairy tale very neatly. What I liked best was the commentary—I am a teacher, so it's a professional deformity, no doubt: There was Dumbledore's commentary and then Rowling's commentary on Dumbledore's commentary, all of which captured how simple texts accrue significance through later interpretations.

Before I proceeded to read the actual Harry Potter books, I went on Pottermore.com, the official Potter website, to be sorted into one of the houses—aspiring students are assigned to one of four houses based on their personalities. In the novels, this is accomplished by a magical hat; on the website, it was done by means of a questionnaire. I am embarrassed to report that I was sent to Slytherin (Harvard has abandoned sorting and assigns students by lottery). I didn't fully understand what this meant about me at the time, having lived more or less exclusively among Muggles, in ignorance of the wizarding world and its rituals. But even I could tell from the way the website tried to make me feel better about it that Slytherin didn't have the best reputation. It was morally suspicious. I suffered my next blow when I found out about my Patronus, the animal-shaped magic that can defeat dark creatures. My Patronus, based on the questionnaire I had to fill out, was the hyena. I was somewhat consoled when the website decided to assign me a 14.5-inch laurelwood wand with a unicorn-hair core. Unlike the hyena, the unicorn was an elegant magical creature I was happy to be associated with.

The grueling initiation over, I decided I was ready for the full Hogwarts experience and embarked on an intensive program of binge-reading and binge-watching my way through the Harry Potter stories. It took me about a month, and I arrived at the other end a bit bleary-eyed and with my ears ringing from the way Severus Snape, the master of my own house, would say "Harry P'otter," a contemptuous *P* exploding into a vicious *o*.

After I finished the last volume, my immediate response was immense relief. As a Slytherin, I had been traumatized by the thought that the master of my house had gone over to the side of You-Know-Who, as we wizards call the dark lord, whose very name is taboo among us. Imagine, therefore, my delight when I learned, on the last pages of the last volume, that Snape had been a double agent run by Dumbledore to spy on You-Know-Who.

On the whole, though, I don't recommend binge-reading or binge-watching Harry Potter, as it becomes repetitive—again and again, there's a new teacher for the defense against the dark arts; another hidden chamber; another task Harry must accomplish, seemingly abandoned by adults. It made me realize how much better it must be to grow up with Harry Potter, to begin reading the books when you are his age or perhaps a year or two younger, and then mature with him as he and his world get more complex. I suppose the generation that really grew up in this way were those who had turned nine or ten in 1997, when the first volume came out, and who had to wait for each of the following volumes to appear as they grew older.

Otherwise, Harry Potter reminded me of a hodgepodge that borrows from medieval romances in ways that would have driven Cervantes crazy (when I ask novelists about Potter, they usually react allergically, as if still fighting Cervantes's fight against medieval romances). To this medieval mash-up, Rowling adds the boarding school novel, having Harry and his friends worry about popularity, school bullies, and eccentric teachers who induct them into the strange world of adulthood. The world of fantasy is grounded in the lived reality of teenagers.

Even though Potter's story is officially complete, Rowling has not been able to stay away from her creation entirely. She keeps adding new pieces of information (such as revealing that Dumbledore is gay) and has recently written a sequel in the form of a play. But the main form in which the Potter universe keeps expanding is merchandise. As I am writing these lines, on Halloween 2016, I was just trick-or-treated by a neighbor disguised as Hermione Granger (whom I will always admire as the translator of *The Tales of Beedle the Bard*, my first induction into the Potter world). Sadly, I haven't been able to go to The Wizarding World of Harry Potter™ in Orlando, where I could buy a real wand at Ollivanders, or rather at Ollivanders™, for a mere $49. The theme park has re-created not only Hogwarts itself, but also Hogsmeade™ village and Diagon Alley™. After a moment of reflection, I realized why: At Hogwarts there's nothing to buy, while Hogsmeade and Diagon Alley are the two dedicated shopping destinations in Harry Potter's universe.

Like the content of the Potter books, the form of publication is an odd mixture of old and new. One of the seven handwritten copies of *The Tales of Beedle the Bard* was purchased by Amazon for four million dollars, perhaps to acknowledge how much Rowling and Amazon have profited from each other.

But the question of who will be the ultimate beneficiary of Amazon's services, and the other new technologies on offer today, is very much an open one. Will it be bestselling authors like Rowling? Internet platforms? Publishers? And which types of stories will thrive in this new environment?

A NEW REVOLUTION IN WRITING TECHNOLOGIES

—

Our current revolution in writing technologies has its roots in two interlocking inventions—and both happen to be related to Apollo 8. Landing a man on the moon and bringing him back alive, as John F. Kennedy had demanded, required complicated calculations on board the spaceship. Computers necessary for this feat were available, but they were much too large. Making computers smaller, faster, and lighter for the space mission ultimately allowed them to enter people's homes, where they were soon used for everything from bookkeeping to writing stories.

Even more transformative was a second invention, made less than a year after Apollo 8, when researchers at UCLA managed to communicate with a computer at Stanford through an ordinary phone line, made possible by a new technology that allowed switching between voice and data packages. The message, LOGIN, did not go through, because the network crashed when they got to the letter G, but the idea of a computer network, called the Arpanet, had been established. Personal computers and computer networks have changed everything from how literature is written to how it is distributed and read. It is as if paper, the book, and print had emerged all at the same time.

Some publishers have been looking back at the era of print as a golden age in which they had a near-monopoly on literature. True, any writer could pay a printer to produce copies, but the problem was getting the book into the hands of readers. This is what publishers did, connecting printers with customers. Along the way, they shouldered some of the risk and pocketed much of the profit. But now, thanks to computers and the Internet, inexpensive apps allow authors without coding experience to produce handsome ebooks and market them directly via Amazon and similar sites. Online publishers and bookstores, of course, also take a hefty cut, often over 30 percent, but this is small compared to the percentages siphoned off by the traditional mode of publication.

While these changes worry publishers, they seem to be good news for authors. Computers—once called word processors—make their daily work more efficient, allowing them to erase and add words, move whole sections, and revise entire documents with ease.

The Internet also enables authors to access information and literature as never before. In writing this book, I was able to read and run searches on a large body of literature put online by the Internet

Archive, which makes public domain literature available at no charge. It is explicitly modeled on the library of Alexandria. (A backup copy of the Internet Archive is housed in the Bibliotheca Alexandrina, the rebuilt library of Alexandria, the first such storage facility outside the United States.) I also used another not-for-profit site, which was begun in 1971 when a student, Michael S. Hart, typed the Declaration of Independence into a computer connected to the Arpanet. Six users downloaded it, and Hart decided to call his enterprise Project Gutenberg (even though Gutenberg was much closer to our profit-driven Internet entrepreneurs).

The most influential new vehicle for organizing knowledge is the online encyclopedia. I remember the early days of Wikipedia, when its crowdsourced approach was ridiculed by academics. The ridicule has stopped because those same academics now routinely use Wikipedia as their first source of information, yours truly included. I like to think that Benjamin Franklin and the French encyclopedists would have embraced the Internet Archive, Project Gutenberg, and Wikipedia.

But even though authors seem to be the winners of our writing revolution, they are at least as worried as publishers. While Gutenberg had taken writing tools from authors and given them to publishers, the printing press had also been a boon to authors, giving those who managed to become professional writers access to a large readership at a low cost. But now, suddenly, everyone can become a writer and find readers through social media. Other authors worry that in the future they will become mere content providers, whose products will be regarded not as original contributions of independent minds but as a form of customer service, designed to meet a particular demand. At the high end, some of these service providers might well become celebrities, working with a whole workshop of assistants, but they, too, would not be authors in the traditional sense of individuals originating new stories. It is true that computers can facilitate the creation of original content, but they lend themselves much more easily to remixing what already exists. To what extent is the age of Cervantes, which is to say the age of modern print authorship, waning, giving way to the curator, the celebrity, and the customer service provider hoping to stay afloat in a sea of user-generated content?

As my thoughts returned to Rowling, I realized that perhaps it was too easy to poke fun at the out-of-control merchandising of Harry Potter, at his appearance in all possible types of entertainment, from film and theater to the Internet and theme parks. Potter, after all, was not born in some corporate boardroom or dreamed up by a marketing department, but invented by an unknown author who, working very much on her own, created an entire universe.

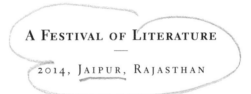

A FESTIVAL OF LITERATURE

2014, JAIPUR, RAJASTHAN

In order to take the measure of literature today—and for a change from Potterworld—I decided to travel one last time, to a medium-sized town in Rajasthan called Jaipur, some 170 miles from Delhi. Ten years earlier, the British writer William Dalrymple and the Indian writer and publisher Namita Gokhale had started a series of literary events that, within a few years, had grown into a festival that made Jaipur a place where world literature happens.

The drive from Delhi was pretty much what I expected, with cars going the wrong way, trucks adorned with beads and colorful paint jobs encouraging other travelers to honk at them, and any number of animals wandering about, including cows, camels, goats, donkeys, elephants, sheep, hogs, and dogs. It was hard to imagine literature taking place here. But suddenly, there it was, the festival, and nothing like what I had anticipated. Instead of depressing gatherings in convention hotels or large trade facilities, this was more like a rock festival, with food stands everywhere and people camped out on the ground or gathered in tents and buildings. It was large, drawing close to a hundred thousand visitors.

Among the visitors, I met a car mechanic from the outskirts who had borrowed a motorcycle to come here, an engineering student who took a day off to attend, and a rickshaw driver who held forth about this year's celebrities as he honked his way through the traffic. "Oprah very nice lady—dark skin like me," he shouted, referring to the previous year's star, Oprah Winfrey. Not everyone was here for literature. Some had come to spot Bollywood stars and talk show hosts, while others were hunting for invitations to exclusive after-parties and private dinners, and some had come just for the fun of it. But the main draw was literature in all of its forms. Poets, dramatists, novelists, and nonfiction writers were here for readings, lectures, discussions, dialogues, interviews, and informal conversations. Goethe, with his advocacy of far-flung world literature, would have been pleased.

Not all parts of the world were equally represented. Perhaps because of the background of the two founders, the festival revolved around a British-Indian axis, though there was a smattering of writers from other parts of the world, including the United States. English dominated, and there was a good deal of hand-wringing, mostly in English, about the dominance of global English. But there were also sessions held in Indian languages ranging from Tamil in the south to Himalayan languages in the north. Most striking, perhaps, was the near-absence of writers from China, India's Asian rival.

While the festival has grown, it has faced a number of crises. The most significant one had occurred two years prior to my visit and had involved Salman Rushdie, whose novel *The Satanic Verses* was (and still is) banned in India, in deference to its Muslim minority population. The Rushdie controversy was a typical world literature clash. Rushdie had made his name with a novel, *Midnight's Children*, set at the moment of India's independence, a classical gesture of writing a foundational text in a postcolonial situation.

This success turned sour when Rushdie's subsequent novel, *The Satanic Verses*, was seen by the Ayatollah Khomeini of Iran as being offensive about a sacred text, the Qur'an. In response, he famously issued a religious edict and death sentence against the writer, who was forced to go into hiding.

Even though the edict had been revoked by the time I went to Jaipur, the controversy hadn't ended. In 2012, the festival had invited Rushdie, who promptly received death threats. Even the compromise solution, that Rushdie would deliver his address via Skype, had not mollified protesters. In the interest of safety, the organizers decided to cancel his address entirely. Outraged by this form of censorship, some participants had started to recite from the novel at the festival, an illegal reading that had forced them to leave Jaipur, and India, immediately afterward.

When I visited, the crisis was still on people's minds. During one of the sessions revolving around censorship, several participants made veiled references to the incident, at which point someone got up and said: "You mean Rushdie; I'm not afraid to say his name." The Rushdie affair was resonant with the story of literature, as a story of old foundational and newer texts struggling for prominence.

The affair, while sobering, wasn't able to squash the festive atmosphere at Jaipur. There were too many authors, both well known and obscure, too many people eager to celebrate literature. I began to think of this literary festival as another (and yes, better) version of Potterworld, a place where people came to demonstrate their enthusiasm for literature. For anyone worried about the future of reading and writing, I recommend very highly this true combination of literature and festival.

THE NEW AND THE OLD

The festive atmosphere at Jaipur made me take one last look back at the history of literature. It began in the fertile river valleys of

Mesopotamia where literature originated and followed its triumphal march across the globe. Along the way, literature evolved from being the exclusive possession of scribes and kings to reaching increasingly larger numbers of readers and writers. This democratization of literature was aided by technologies from the alphabet and papyrus to paper and print, all of which lowered the barriers of entry, opening the literary world to more people, who then innovated new forms—novels, newspapers, manifestos—while also affirming the importance of older foundational texts. Jaipur, with its readers from every walk of life and the clashing of old and new texts, seemed like a good bookend to this story.

I also remembered that this story of expansion harbored within it many twists and turns, and many surprises, at least for me: The story of literature wasn't a straight line, but one with sideways and even backward movements. Writing was invented both on the Eurasian continent and in the Americas. Individual stories moved back and forth on the network of story collections stretching from Asia to Europe. The rise of writing brought forth opposition by charismatic teachers in different parts of the world. New technologies led to format wars such as the one between the papyrus scroll and the parchment book, while sacred texts often became early adopters of new methods of reproduction. But despite the dramatic explosion of literature, oral storytelling continued to exist, as the example of the Mande bards, with the story of Sunjata, shows.

The greatest difficulty in writing a history of literature wasn't these surprises and complex story lines. It was the recognition that we are still in the middle of this, an ongoing story. Even the idea of a single world literature whose story can be told is barely two hundred years old. When Goethe coined the term "world literature," he didn't know about the Maya *Popol Vuh*, which was languishing in some library, or the *Epic of Gilgamesh*, which was buried underground in Mesopotamia, nor did he know of *The Tale of Genji*, which was unknown outside Japan and East Asia, or *Sunjata*, of western Africa, which hadn't been written down yet. And of course Goethe could never have predicted that his idea of world literature would inspire the authors of *The Communist Manifesto*. With each new addition and each discovery from the past, the story of literature keeps changing.

The same is true of technologies. Perhaps you are reading these words in a book printed on paper or on a screen, unless you are wearing glasses that somehow project words into your field of vision. But no matter what device you're using, you'll either be flipping through pages or scrolling through a continuous piece of text. Notice the combination of old and new. Most people had stopped scrolling ever since the papyrus scroll gave way to the parchment book, but now, after two millennia, this act of scrolling has suddenly come back because the unending string of words stored by computers is closer to a continuous scroll than to discrete pages. Similarly, people hadn't been writing on tablets for hundreds of years, but now we see them everywhere. When I squint, today's tablet users look strangely like ancient scribes sitting cross-legged with their writing implements in their laps.

The more I look back, the more I see the past in the present. The 140 characters of Twitter are perhaps crude versions of the short poems with which the Heian court communicated at the time of *Genji* and Lady Murasaki, and romances have made a comeback as bestsellers on electronic self-publishing platforms, which displeases any number of modern authors writing in the tradition of Cervantes. The Internet has made possible both new forms of surveillance and new ways to evade censorship, like a modern samizdat system. Oral storytelling has returned as well, as you well know if you are listening to these words on an audio device. The Mande bards, who prefer cassette tapes to writing, would be pleased.

On my travels, I looked for moments when I could observe literature shaping history. I found such moments when encountering the traces of extraordinary readers like Ashurbanipal and Alexander, who turned their reading experiences into action, as well as those of illiterates like Pizarro, proudly bringing books to the New World. History has also been shaped by believers in sacred scripture, who turned their worship of writing into a powerful historical force, sometimes leading to clashes between sacred texts as well as between different interpretations of a single text. And I found myself traveling on the infrastructure laid for the dissemination of literature, such as Franklin's postal roads, right in my own backyard.

The most striking feature of literature has always been its ability to project speech deep into space and time. The Internet has supercharged the first, enabling us to send writing to any place on earth within seconds. But what about time? As I started using the last four thousand years of literature as a guide to the changes taking place around me, I began to imagine literary archaeologists of the future. Will they be able to unearth forgotten masterpieces such as the *Epic of Gilgamesh*?

The answer is far from certain. The endurance of electronic media over time has already emerged as a problem because of the rapid obsolescence of computer programs and formats. If we are lucky, future historians will be able to transcode outdated data sets or reconstruct old computers to access otherwise illegible files (much as the cuneiform code had to be reconstructed in the nineteenth century). Librarians warn that the best way to preserve writing from the vagaries of future format wars is to print out everything on paper. Perhaps we should carve our canons into stone, as Chinese emperors did. But the most important lesson from the history of literature is that the only guarantee for survival is continual use: A text needs to remain relevant enough to be translated, transcribed, transcoded, and read by each generation in order to persist over time. It is education, not technology, that will ensure the future of literature.

No matter what future historians will find, they will understand better than we do just how transformative our current writing revolution will have been. What we can say for sure is that the world population has grown even as literacy rates have risen sharply, which means that infinitely more writing is being done by more people, and published and read more widely, than ever before. We stand on the verge of a second great explosion—the written world is poised to change yet again.

ACKNOWLEDGMENTS

—

As I was writing this book, which draws on the work of writers and scholars since the dawn of literature, I naturally felt more like a scribe assembling a text from existing sources than a modern author inventing a new story. I give credit to the hundreds of people who contributed to my story of literature in footnotes, but the enormous help I received from some should be given particular mention here.

A special round of thanks goes to my agent, Jill Kneerim, who helped me shape this book at its inception, and my editor at Random House, Kate Medina, who contributed so much to giving this book its final form, together with Erica Gonzalez and my editor at Granta, Bella Lacey. My particular gratitude goes to those friends and colleagues who read individual chapters, namely Peter Burgard, David Conrad, David Damrosch, Wiebke Denecke, Barbara Fuchs, Stephen Greenblatt, Paulo Horta, Maya Jasanoff, Luke Menand, Parimal Patil, Elaine Scarry, David Stern, and Bill Todd. The book was also inspired by teaching, with my friend and colleague David Damrosch, a course on world literature to students at Harvard and in 155 other countries, thanks to the new technology of online education. I could not have written this book without the experience of putting together a large anthology of world literature with a wonderful team of colleagues that included Suzanne Akbari, David Conrad, Wiebke Denecke, Vinay Dharwadker, Barbara Fuchs, Caroline Levine, Pericles Lewis, Pete Simon, and Emily Wilson.

Many friends lent an ear and offered wise counsel, including Tim Baldenius, Leonard Barkan, Michael Eskin, Ariane Lourie Harrison, Seth Harrison, Ursula Heise, Noah Herringman, Sam Haselby, Maya Jasanoff, Caroline Levine, Sharon Marcus, Luke Menand, Bernadette Meyler, Klaus Mladek, Franco Moretti, Bruce Robbins, Freddie Rokem, Alison Simmons, Matthew Smith, Kathrin Stengel, Henry Turner, and Rebecca Walkowitz, as well as my brothers, Stephan and Elias, and my mother, Anne-Lore.

Amanda Claybaugh has done more than anyone else to give shape to this story of literature—and to bring pleasure and meaning and love to the story of my life. This book is dedicated to her.

NOTES

—

INTRODUCTION: EARTHRISE

xii **"Alright, Apollo 8. You are go"** *Apollo 8 Technical Air-to-Ground Voice Transcription* (Manned Spacecraft Center, Houston, Tex.: National Aeronautics and Space Administration, December 1968), tape 3, page 3.

xii **At any moment, they would speed** Lunar injection occurred at 35,505.41 ft/sec. See "Apollo 8, The Second Mission: Testing the CSM in Lunar Orbit," December 21–27, 1968, history.nasa.gov/SP -4029/Apollo_08a_Summary.htm, accessed January 10, 2017.

xii **Borman interrupted procedures** *Apollo 8 Onboard Voice Transcription As Recorded on the Spacecraft Onboard Recorder (Data Storage Equipment)* (Manned Spacecraft Center, Houston, Tex.: National Aeronautics and Space Administration, January 1969), 41.

xii **"We would like you, if possible"** *Apollo 8 Technical Air-to-Ground Voice Transcription*, tape 37, page 3.

xiii **"These in particular bring out"** *Apollo 8 Technical Air-to-Ground Voice Transcription*, tape 57, page 6.

xiv **"The vast loneliness up here"** *Apollo 8 Technical Air-to-Ground Voice Transcription*, tape 57, page 6.

xiv **"It makes you realize"** *Apollo 8 Technical Air-to-Ground Voice Transcription*, tape 57, page 6.

xiv **"a space scientist is an engineer"** Pat Harrison, "American Might: Where 'the Good and the Bad Are All Mixed Up,'" *Radcliffe Maga-*

zine, 2012, radcliffe.harvard.edu/news/radcliffe-magazine/american
-might-where-good-and-bad-are-all-mixed, accessed August 5, 2016.

xiv **"It's a vast, lonely"** *Apollo 8 Technical Air-to-Ground Voice Transcription*, tape 57, page 5.

xv **"Good to hear your voice"** *Apollo 8 Technical Air-to-Ground Voice Transcription*, tape 46, page 5.

xv **"May I see that blurb"** *Apollo 8 Onboard Voice Transcription*, 177.

xv **"For all the people"** *Apollo 8 Onboard Voice Transcription*, 195.

xvi **"And God called the light Day"** *Apollo 8 Onboard Voice Transcription*, 196.

xviii **"reading of the sectarian Christian"** Jack Roberts, District Judge, United States District Court, W.D. Texas, Austin Division, Memorandum Opinion, December 1, 1969. O'Hair v. Paine Civ. A. No. A-69-CA-109.

xix **"I looked and looked"** The line is disputed and may have come from a speech by Nikita Khrushchev.

CHAPTER 1. ALEXANDER'S PILLOW BOOK

3 **The first was a dagger** Plutarch, *Lives*, volume VII, translated by Bernadotte Perrin, Loeb Classical Library 99 (Cambridge, Mass.: Harvard University Press, 1919), chapter VIII, section 2.

3 **And inside the box** Plutarch, *Lives*, VIII, 2–3.

4 **Alexander learned the lesson** This account of Philip of Macedon's wedding and murder is based on Diodorus Siculus, *The Library of History*, translated by C. H. Oldfather, Loeb Classical Library 422 (Cambridge, Mass.: Harvard University Press, 1933), book XVI, sections 91–94. The main classical sources on Alexander the Great are Arrian and Plutarch, as well as Siculus. These accounts are based on older, lost sources.

4 **He had become a famous horseman** Plutarch, *Lives*, VI, 1–6.

5 **Throughout his life** Plutarch, *Lives*, LI, 4.

5 **But now it seemed that Philip** Plutarch, *Lives*, X, 1–2.

5 **If the marriage produced a son** Plutarch, *Lives*, IX, 4ff.

5 **If Darius was behind the murder** Various theories have circulated about who was behind the attack. Plutarch believes that it was a maltreated guard, Pausanias. Plutarch, *Lives*, X, 4. See also Diodorus Siculus, *Library*, XVI, 93ff.

5 **Alexander used the murder** Plutarch, *Lives*, XI. I also consulted

Arrian, *Anabasis of Alexander*, translated by P. A. Brunt, Loeb Classical Library 236 (Cambridge, Mass.: Harvard University Press, 1976), book I, chapter 1ff.

7 *"With these words, resplendent Hector"* Homer's *Iliad*, VI, 491–500. Homer, *Iliad*, translated by Stanley Lombardo, *Norton Anthology of World Literature*, edited by Martin Puchner (New York: Norton, 2012), 254.

8 **He had learned to read** Plutarch, *Lives*, VII, 2ff.

8 **The copy of the *Iliad*** Plutarch, *Lives*, VIII, 2–3.

8 **The first thing Alexander did** Arrian, *Anabasis*, book I, chapter 11, section 5. Diodorus Siculus, *Library*, XVII, 17, 11.

8 **Once they had made** Arrian, *Anabasis*, I, chapter 12, section 1.

9 **They and their companions** Plutarch, *Lives*, XV, 4.

9 **When Alexander was given** Aelian, *Historical Miscellany*, edited and translated by N. G. Wilson, Loeb Classical Library 486 (Cambridge, Mass.: Harvard University Press, 1997), book 9, 38; Plutarch, *Lives*, XVI, 5.

9 **and he took armor** Arrian, *Anabasis*, book I, chapter 11.

9 **The first clash between Alexander** Arrian, *Anabasis*, book I, chapter 13ff.

9 **By tightening the discipline** Joseph Roisman and Ian Worthington, *A Companion to Ancient Macedonia* (New York: Wiley, 2010), 449.

10 **When his men** Plutarch, *Lives*, LXIII, 2ff.

10 **Darius panicked and fled** Arrian, *Anabasis*, book II, chapter 5ff; Plutarch, *Lives*, XX–XXI.

11 **Alexander wasn't done** On Alexander's identification with Achilles, see also Andrew Stewart, *Faces of Power: Alexander's Image and Hellenistic Politics*, volume 11 (Berkeley: University of California Press, 1993), 80ff.

11 **When he conquered Gaza** Quintus Curtius Rufus, *History of Alexander*, translated by J. C. Rolfe, Loeb Classical Library 368 (Cambridge, Mass., Harvard University Press), IV, 29.

11 **The armies met** Arrian, *Anabasis*, book III, chapter 9ff.

12 **The Persian Empire was his** Arrian, *Anabasis*, book III, chapters 14–16.

12 **He didn't behave** Plutarch, *Lives*, XXI, 2–3.

12 **Darius was killed** Arrian, *Anabasis*, book III, chapter 21.

12 **Alexander grieved** Arrian, *Anabasis*, book III, chapter 23, section 1ff; chapter 25, section 8.

12   **The story was set**   There is one reference to writing in the *Iliad*, when Proteus sends Bellerophon, whom he wishes dead, to the king of Lycia with a written message "in a folded tablet" instructing the king to kill the bearer of the tablet. Homer, *Iliad*, VI, 155–203.

12   **True, the Minoan civilization**   For a gripping account of the deciphering of Minoan Linear B, see Margalit Fox, *The Riddle of the Labyrinth: The Quest to Crack an Ancient Code* (New York: HarperCollins, 2013).

12   **Those stories were sung**   The idea that Homeric material had been composed and preserved orally was advanced by Milman Parry and Albert Lord in the 1920s. I also consulted Walter J. Ong, *Orality and Literacy: The Technologizing of the Word* (New York: Methuen, 1982).

13   **Giving up on objects**   The mental breakthrough that led to a purely alphabetic system has been captured by Robert K. Logan, even if the consequences ascribed to this breakthrough are exaggerated, in *The Alphabet Effect: A Media Ecology Understanding of the Making of Western Civilization* (Cresskill, N.J.: Hampton Press, 2004).

14   **Writing would be attached**   Henri-Jean Martin, *The History and Power of Writing*, translated by Lydia G. Cochrane (Chicago: University of Chicago Press, 1994), 31.

14   **The new phonetic alphabet**   This argument is based on the fact that there are no early uses of the Greek alphabet specific to economic transactions, with the exception of Linear B texts.

14   **It's even possible**   This argument is made by Barry B. Powell in *Homer and the Origin of the Greek Alphabet* (Cambridge, U.K.: Cambridge University Press, 1991).

15   **The power of the new alphabet**   Martin, *History and Power*, 37.

15   **As Alexander's realm**   Plutarch, *Lives*, XXVIII; Arrian, *Anabasis*, book VII, chapter 29.

15   **He demanded that**   Arrian, *Anabasis*, book VII, chapter 23.

16   **"Since Alexander wishes"**   Aelian, *Historical Miscellany*, II, 19.

16   **To retain possession**   Plutarch, *Lives*, XLV, 1.

16   **He admitted**   Plutarch, *Lives*, XLVII.

16   **And he let his Eastern**   Arrian, *Anabasis*, book IV, chapters 5–6.

16   **Alexander's Greek**   Plutarch, *Lives*, L, 5–6.

16   **"I shall be poorer"**   Arrian, *Anabasis*, book IV, chapter 12; Plutarch, *Lives*, LIV, 4.

17   **In possession of Babylon**   Arrian, *Anabasis*, book IV, chapter 14, section 7.

17   **Soon a whole network**   William V. Harris, *Ancient Literacy* (Cambridge, Mass.: Harvard University Press, 1991), 118ff.

17   **The empire comprised**   Harris, *Ancient Literacy*, 138.

17   **The *Iliad* was the text**   Harris, *Ancient Literacy*, 61.

17   **This was the language**   George Derwent Thomson, *The Greek Language* (Cambridge, U.K.: W. Heffer and Sons, 1972), 34; Leonard R. Palmer, *The Greek Language* (London: Faber and Faber, 1980), 176.

17   **Local rulers**   Thomson, *Greek Language*, 35; F. E. Peters, *The Harvest of Hellenism: A History of the Near East from Alexander the Great to the Triumph of Christianity* (New York: Simon and Schuster, 1970), 61.

18   **He also circulated**   *Hellenism in the East: The Interaction of Greek and Non-Greek Civilizations from Syria to Central Asia After Alexander*, edited by Amélie Kuhrt and Susan Sherwin-White (Berkeley: University of California Press, 1988), 81; Peter Green, *Alexander the Great and the Hellenistic Age: A Short History* (London: Weidenfeld and Nicolson, 2007), 63. I also consulted M. Rostovtzeff, *The Social and Economic History of the Hellenistic World*, volume 1 (Oxford: Clarendon Press, 1941), 446ff.

19   **Lydian ultimately died out**   Peters, *Harvest of Hellenism*, 61, 345. I also consulted Jonathan J. Price and Shlomo Naeh, "On the Margins of Culture: The Practice of Transcription in the Ancient World," in *From Hellenism to Islam: Cultural and Linguistic Change in the Roman Near East*, edited by Hannah M. Cotton, Robert G. Hoyland, Jonathan J. Price, and David J. Wasserstein (Cambridge: Cambridge University Press, 2009), 267ff, and *The World's Writing Systems*, edited by Peter T. Daniels and William Bright (Oxford: Oxford University Press, 1996), 281, 515, 372.

19   **The effects of this unprecedented**   Harry Falk, *Schrift im alten Indien: Ein Forschungsbericht mit Anmerkungen* (Tübingen: Gunter Narr Verlag, 1993), 127.

19   **When a new Indian king**   Falk, *Schrift im alten Indien*, 81–83.

19   **His own army**   Plutarch, *Lives*, LXII, 1ff.

20   **Anticipating that his own deeds**   Arrian, *Anabasis*, book I, chapter 12, section 2; Plutarch, *Lives*, XV, 5.

20   **Callisthenes refused**   Arrian, *Anabasis*, book IV, chapter 12, section 5.

20   **implicated in a revolt**   Arrian, *Anabasis*, book IV, chapters 12–14.

20   **Several contemporaries**   The most explicit Homeric ambition is that of Arrian, who notes that Alexander did not have a poet worthy of

a Homer to sing his praises and offers to fill the gap with his own account. Arrian, *Anabasis*, book I, chapter 12, sections 4–5.

21   **It is not associated**   Peters, *Harvest of Hellenism*, 550.

21   **The Greek version**   *The Greek Alexander Romance*, translated with an introduction and notes by Richard Stoneman (London: Penguin, 1991), 35. I also consulted Joseph Roisman and Ian Worthington, *A Companion to Ancient Macedonia* (New York: Wiley, 2010), 122.

21   **In the Persian *Book of Kings***   Abolquasem Ferdowsi, *Shahnameh: The Persian Book of Kings*, translated by Dick Davis, with a foreword by Azar Nafisi (New York: Penguin, 1997), 454–55.

21   **Alexander was so devoted**   Plutarch, *Lives*, XXIX, 2.

22   **Alexander was planning to found**   Plutarch, *Lives*, XXVI, 3.

22   **Alexandria boasted**   *The Library of Alexandria: Centre of Learning in the Ancient World*, edited by Roy MacLeod (London: Tauris, 2000).

22   **The library employed**   Galeni, *In Hippocratis Epidemiarum librum III commentaria III*, Corpus Medicorum Graecorum, V 10, 2.1, edited by Ernst Wenkebach, (Berlin: Teubner, 1936), Comment. II 4 [III 1 L.], 606.5–17, 79. I also consulted Roy MacLeod, *The Library of Alexandria*, 65.

23   **But even though hieroglyphics**   Harris, *Ancient Literacy*, 122.

23   **The ease of the Greek**   Daniels and Bright, *The World's Writing Systems*, 287.

23   **It was rediscovered**   Price and Naeh, "On the Margins of Culture," 263. I also consulted Rostovtzeff, *Social and Economic History*, 423, and Kuhrt and Sherwin-White, *Hellenism in the East*, 23ff.

CHAPTER 2. KING OF THE UNIVERSE:
OF GILGAMESH AND ASHURBANIPAL

24   **My father once told me**   I thank my friend and colleague David Damrosch for his generous help with this chapter (as well as with several others). Developing with David the HarvardX course "Masterworks of World Literature" was crucial to my writing this book.

26   **Apparently, the rulers**   Sir Austen Henry Layard, *Discoveries Among the Ruins of Nineveh and Babylon*, abridged from the larger work (New York: Harper, 1853), 292.

26   **"Their meaning was written"**   Sir Austen Henry Layard, *Nineveh and Its Remains, in Two Volumes*, volume 1 (London: John Murray, 1849), 70.

27   "restoring the language and history"   Austen Henry Layard, *Discoveries among the Ruins of Nineveh and Babylon: Being the Result of a Second Expedition* (London: John Murray, 1853), 347.

27   **Layard used moistened brown**   Layard, *Nineveh and Its Remains*, volume 1: 327.

28   **Beginning with names**   For an account of the discovery and the decipherment of cuneiform script, read the excellent book by David Damrosch, *The Buried Book: The Loss and Rediscovery of the Great Epic of Gilgamesh* (New York: Henry Holt, 2006).

29   **When presented with**   Herman Vanstiphout, "Enmerkar and the Lord of Aratta," in *Epics of Sumerian Kings: The Matter of Aratta* (Atlanta: Society of Biblical Literature, 2003), 49–96.

30   **The *Epic of Gilgamesh* received**   *The Epic of Gilgamesh*, translated by Benjamin R. Foster (New York: Norton, 2001), reprinted in Puchner, *Norton Anthology of World Literature*, 99–150. I also consulted Stephen Mitchell, *Gilgamesh: A New English Version* (New York: Simon and Schuster, 2006).

30   **The story boasted of**   Foster, *Gilgamesh*, tablet I, line 20.

32   **Victorian England**   Jeffrey H. Tigay, *The Evolution of the Gilgamesh Epic* (Philadelphia: University of Pennsylvania Press, 1982).

33   **"like a clay pot"**   Foster, *Gilgamesh*, tablet XI, line 110.

33   **"*Gilgamesh, who saw the wellspring*"**   Foster, *Gilgamesh*, tablet 1, line 10. There is some ambiguity in this passage, in how directly the activity of writing is attributed to Gilgamesh, but the hero and the written tablet are closely associated in all readings.

34   **Ashurbanipal had grown up**   Biographical information based mostly on Daniel Arnaud, *Assurbanipal, Roi d'Assyrie* (Paris: Fayard, 2007). Primary sources can be found in Benjamin R. Foster, *Before the Muses: An Anthology of Akkadian Literature* (Bethesda, Md.: CDL Press, 1993).

34   **Wandering through the streets**   Jane A. Hill, Philip Jones, and Antonio J. Morales, *Experiencing Power, Generating Authority* (Philadelphia: University of Pennsylvania Press, 2013), 337.

34   **Exposed to writing everywhere**   "To Ishtar of Nineveh and Arbela," in Foster, *Before the Muses*, volume 2: 702, and "Assurbanipal and Nabu," in Foster, *Before the Muses*, volume 2: 712–13.

34   **Taking possession of Nineveh**   Pierre Villard, "L'éducation d'Assurbanipal," *Ktèma*, volume 22 (1997): 135–49, 141.

35   **"My teacher said"**   Samuel Noah Kramer, "Schooldays: A Sume-

rian Composition Relating to the Education of a Scribe," *Journal of the American Oriental Society*, volume 69, number 4 (Oct.–Dec. 1949): 199–215, 205.

35   **"Like you, I was once"**   "A Supervisor's Advice to a Young Scribe," in *The Literature of Ancient Sumer*, translated and with an introduction by Jeremy Black, Graham Cunningham, Eleanor Robson, and Gábor Zólyomi (Oxford: Oxford University Press, 2004), 278.

36   **"Do you not remember"**   This comes from an Egyptian text, "Reminder of the Scribe's Superior Status," in *The Literature of Ancient Egypt*, edited by William Kelly Simpson (New Haven: Yale University Press, 2003), 438–39, 439.

36   **Next to them**   Martin, *History and Power*, 44.

36   **They were the original**   Samuel Noah Kramer, *History Begins at Sumer: Thirty-nine Firsts in Recorded History* (Philadelphia: University of Pennsylvania Press, 1956), 3ff.

37   **Ashurbanipal's sister**   Alasdair Livingstone, "Ashurbanipal: Literate or Not?," *Zeitschrift für Assyriologie*, volume 97: 98–118, 104. DOI 1515/ZA.2007.005.

37   **Still a teenager**   Villard, "L'éducation d'Assurbanipal," 139.

37   **The best scribal teacher**   Eckart Frahm, "Royal Hermeneutics: Observations on the Commentaries from Ashurbanipal's Libraries at Nineveh," *Iraq*, volume 66; *Nineveh. Papers of the 49th Rencontre Assyriologique Internationale*, part 1 (2004): 45–50. Livingstone, "Ashurbanipal: Literate or Not?" 99.

37   **They could tell**   Eleanor Robson, "Reading the Libraries of Assyria and Babylonia," in *Ancient Libraries*, edited by Jason König, Katerina Oikonomopoulou, and Greg Woolf (Cambridge: Cambridge University Press, 2013), 38–56.

38   **Writing was so powerful**   Frahm, "Royal Hermeneutics," 49.

38   **For Ashurbanipal, rising**   Arnaud, *Assurbanipal*, 68.

38   **His long title**   "Pious Scholar," in Foster, *Before the Muses*, volume 2, 714.

38   **Unlike his father**   Arnaud, *Assurbanipal*, 75.

40   **Layard transported**   Sami Said Ahmed, *Southern Mesopotamia in the Time of Ashurbanipal* (The Hague: Mouton, 1968), 74.

40   **He maintained informers**   Ahmed, *Southern Mesopotamia*, 87. I also consulted Jeanette C. Fincke, "The Babylonian Texts of Nineveh," in *Archiv für Orientforschung*, volume 50 (2003–2004): 111–48, 122.

40   **he succeeded only after**   Arnaud, *Assurbanipal*, 270.

40   **He raided his brother's**   Grant Frame and A. R. George, "The Royal Libraries of Nineveh: New Evidence for King Ashurbanipal's Tablet Collecting," *Iraq* 67, number 1: 265–84.

40   **He also took scribes**   Robson, "Reading the Libraries," 42, note 32.

41   **To make room**   Arnaud, *Assurbanipal*, 259ff.

41   **Each tablet was carefully classified**   Fincke, "Babylonian Texts of Nineveh," 129ff.

42   **They ended up**   Daniel C. Snell, *Life in the Ancient Near East, 3100–332 B.C.E.* (New Haven: Yale University Press, 1997), 30ff. I also consulted Martin, *History and Power*, 11.

42   **Sumerian scribes**   This was part of a larger pattern of nomadic conquerors adopting writing. See, for example, Robert Tignor et al., *Worlds Together, Worlds Apart: A History of the World*, second edition (New York: Norton, 2008), 99, 105, 252.

42   **"I was brave"**   Daniel David Luckenbill, *Ancient Records of Assyria and Babylonia*, volume 2 (Chicago: University of Chicago Press, 1927), 379. Translation adapted by me.

42   **Inadvertently, writing had kept**   On the medieval university and its focus on dead languages, see Martin, *History and Power*, 150.

42   **Thanks to Ashurbanipal**   David M. Carr, *Writing on the Tablet of the Heart: Origins of Scripture and Literature* (Oxford: Oxford University Press, 2005), 47–56.

43   **Mighty King, Without Rivals**   Arnaud, *Assurbanipal*, 278.

43   **"I, Ashurbanipal"**   Foster, *Before the Muses*, volume 2: 714.

44   **Some tablets bubbled**   See Damrosch, *Buried Book*, 194.

CHAPTER 3. EZRA AND THE CREATION
OF HOLY SCRIPTURE

46   **Foundational texts such as the**   I thank my colleague David Stern for commenting on this chapter. For the relation between Mesopotamian literature and the Hebrew Bible, see David Damrosch, *The Narrative Covenant: Transformations of Genre in the Growth of Biblical Literature* (San Francisco: Harper and Row, 1987), 88ff.

46   **After a period of hardship**   Joseph Blenkinsopp, *Judaism, the First Phase: The Place of Ezra and Nehemiah in the Origins of Judaism* (Grand Rapids, Mich.: William B. Eerdmans Publishing, 2009), 117. Settlement started as early as 597, centered in Nippur.

47   **Had he learned**   Haim Gevaryahu, "Ezra the Scribe," in *Dor le Dor: The World Jewish Bible Society*, volume 6, number 2 (Winter 1977–78): 87–93, 90. Ezra is described as an *unmanu*, the kind of scribe who had advised Ashurbanipal.

47   **They had brought with them**   On exilic redaction, see Martin, *History and Power*, 105ff.

47   **Inspired by Babylonian literacy**   Frank H. Polak, "Book, Scribe, and Bard: Oral Discourse and Written Text in Recent Biblical Scholarship," *Prooftexts*, volume 31, numbers 1–2 (Winter–Spring 2011): 118–140, 121. I also consulted William M. Schniedewind, *How the Bible Became a Book: The Textualization of Ancient Israel* (Cambridge, U.K.: Cambridge University Press, 2004), and David M. Carr, *Writing on the Tablet*.

47   **This they followed with a story of their first ancestors**   Juha Pakkala, *Ezra the Scribe: The Development of Ezra 7-10 and Nehemia 8* (Berlin: Walter de Gruyter, 2004), 256.

47   **By the time Ezra was born**   There is a debate about what text exactly is meant by the Torah that Ezra brings back. Is it only Deuteronomy? It is difficult to know. I am sympathetic to those, like Lisbeth S. Fried, in *Ezra and the Law in History and Tradition* (Columbia, S.C.: University of South Carolina Press, 2014), who argue that he brought the entire Pentateuch or at least a sense of the narrative thrust of it.

47   **They also kept alive**   Carr, *Writing on the Tablet*, 169.

48   **In weaving together**   Some even argue that Ezra and fellow scribes essentially produced the Hebrew Bible in Babylonian exile, using the relatively small hitherto existing written tradition as basis. See Gevaryahu, "Ezra the Scribe."

48   **Moses was important**   Martha Himmelfarb, *Between Temple and Torah: Essays on Priests, Scribes, and Visionaries in the Second Temple Period and Beyond* (Tübingen: Mohr Siebeck, 2013). Himmelfarb describes how Moses becomes retrospectively the first scribe, 105.

48   **God first summons Moses**   Exodus 19–20.

48   **Moses writes everything down**   Exodus 24:4.

48   **Instead of dictating to Moses**   Exodus 24:12, 31:18.

49   **He is overcome**   Exodus 32:19.

49   **God summons Moses again**   Exodus 34:1.

49   **This time, Moses has to**   In most readings of the passage, it is Moses who does the writing at this point, but there is some lingering ambiguity.

49   **He stays with God**   Exodus 34:27–28.

50   **In the year 458 B.C.E., he issued a call**   Account based on the biblical books of Ezra and Nehemiah, King James Bible. The dates are
disputed based on the assumption that the Artaxerxes mentioned is
Artaxerxes I.

50   **Descendants from**   Ezra 8:15–20.

50   **Ezra had boasted**   Ezra 8:22.

50   **It stated that the traveling Judeans**   Ezra 7:11–28. About the spread
of Aramaic, I also consulted Falk, *Schrift im alten Indien*, 77ff.

50   **In fact, Ezra was**   Fried, *Ezra and the Law*, 13, 27. Ezra is described
as one of hundreds of *gaushkaiya*, "king's ears."

51   **He was sending Ezra**   Pakkala, *Ezra the Scribe*, 13. Ezra is described
as securing the Levant after the Egyptian revolts of 464–54 B.C.E.

51   **But as they made**   Donna J. Laird, *Negotiating Power: The Social
Contours of Ezra-Nehemiah* (Ann Arbor: UMI, 2013), UMI number
3574064, 338.

51   **Those remaining few**   Laird, *Negotiating Power*, 21ff; Pakkala, *Ezra
the Scribe*, 253.

51   **The exiles had developed**   Ralf Rothenbusch, ". . . *abgesondert zur
Tora Gottes hin*": *Ethnisch-religiöse Identitäten im Esra/Nehemiabuch*
(Freiburg: Herder, 2012), 268.

51   **The city had been famous**   I follow the biblical sequence according
to which Ezra precedes Nehemiah, the rebuilder of the city walls.
This view is supported by, among others, Pakkala, *Ezra the Scribe* and
Blenkinsopp, *Judaism, the First Phase*. Others, including Fried, argue
that Nehemiah came first and rebuilt the city wall, at which point
Ezra entered the scene. Fried, *Ezra and the Law*. From a dramatic
angle, I would argue that the redactors wanted to bring the two signal
events, the rebuilding of the wall and the reading of the Torah, together. They achieved this by placing Ezra's climactic reading in Nehemiah, before the wall is completed.

52   **There was one consolation**   I am following the sequence suggested
in the Bible, which has Ezra and Nehemiah, who rebuilds the city
walls, as contemporaries. Nehemiah 2:13.

52   **Some decades earlier**   Ezra 1:1–6.

52   **All kinds of people**   Pakkala describes tensions between returning
exiles from Babylon, the *golah* group, and the so-called "people of the
land," who had stayed behind. Pakkala, *Ezra the Scribe*, 265. I also
consulted Blenkinsopp, *Judaism, the First Phase*, 48ff.

53   **Finally, he uttered a prayer**   Ezra 9.

53   **They who had brought**   Ezra 10.

53   **Everyone had been told**   Nehemiah 8.

54   **They immediately bowed**   Nehemiah 8:5–6.

54   **For the first time**   Fried, *Ezra and the Law*, 37–38, 43. Pakkala, *Ezra the Scribe*, 279. See also Jeffrey H. Tigay, "The Torah Scroll and God's Presence" in *Built by Wisdom, Established by Understanding: Essays on Biblical and Near Eastern Literature in Honor of Adele Berlin*, edited by Maxine L. Grossman (Bethesda: University Press of Maryland, 2013), 323–40, 328ff. Tigay discusses how the scroll came to embody God's presence. Karel van der Toorn compares the worship of the scroll in Judaism to the cult of the image in Babylonian religions, in "The Iconic Book: Analogies Between the Babylonian Cult of Images and the Veneration of the Torah," in *The Image and the Book: Iconic Cults, Aniconism, and the Rise of Book Religion in Israel and the Ancient Near East*, edited by Karel van der Toorn (Leuven: Peeters, 1997), 229–48.

54   **Noticing the difficulties**   John J. Collins, "The Transformation of the Torah in Second Temple Judaism," *Journal for the Study of Judaism*, volume 43 (2012): 455–74, 461. I also consulted Nehemiah 8:8.

55   **Ezra's reading**   Mark F. Whitters, "Baruch as Ezra in *2 Baruch*," *Journal of Biblical Literature*, volume 132, number 3 (2013): 569–84, 582.

55   **in order to be a scribe**   Martha Himmelfarb, *A Kingdom of Priests: Ancestry and Merit in Ancient Judaism* (Philadelphia: University of Pennsylvania Press, 2006), 12.

55   **The stronger Jerusalem became**   Nehemiah 13.

56   **With the temple gone**   Himmelfarb, *Kingdom of Priests*, 171.

57   **So crucial did Ezra's reading**   Martin Whittingham, "Ezra as the Corrupter of the Torah? Re-Assessing Ibn Hazm's Role in the Long History of an Idea," *Intellectual History of the Islamicate World*, volume 1 (2013): 253–71, 253.

57   **It was Ezra**   Ezra 4:10.

57   **They credited him**   Whittingham, "Ezra as the Corrupter," 260. I also consulted Gevaryahu, "Ezra the Scribe," 92.

57   **Some Jewish writers**   Whittingham, "Ezra as the Corrupter," 261.

57   **Somehow, Ezra must have**   Whittingham, "Ezra as the Corrupter," 264.

59   **As I was contemplating Ezra**   I thank Freddie Rokem for being my guide through the Old City of Jerusalem.

61 **The second acknowledges** Wolfgang Iser, *The Act of Reading: A Theory of Aesthetic Response* (Baltimore: Johns Hopkins University Press, 1980).

CHAPTER 4. LEARNING FROM THE BUDDHA, CONFUCIUS, SOCRATES, AND JESUS

62 **I was never a teacher's pet** I thank Parimal G. Patil and Wiebke Denecke for their help with this chapter. Wiebke Denecke taught me much about East Asian literature, including the Chinese tradition of master teachers, which she laid out in her excellent book *The Dynamics of Masters Literature: Early Chinese Thought from Confucius to Han Feizi*, Harvard-Yenching Institute Monograph Series, number 74 (Cambridge, Mass.: Harvard University Press, 2011).

63 **Many of today's philosophical** This pattern is related to Karl Jaspers's notion of the axial age, although Jaspers does not pay attention to the dynamics of literature and the influence of writing technologies. Karl Jaspers, *The Origin and Goal of History*, Routledge Revivals (Basingstoke: Routledge, 2011).

63 **I found one answer** One of the few scholars to relate Jaspers's notion of the axial age to writing is Jan Assmann, "Cultural Memory and the Myth of the Axial Age," in *The Axial Age and Its Consequences*, edited by Robert N. Bellah and Hans Joas (Cambridge, Mass.: Harvard University Press, 2012), 337–65, 397ff.

64 **His dates are disputed** Most Western scholars assume that the Buddha died in the year 400 B.C.E., at the age of eighty. K. R. Norman, *A Philological Approach to Buddhism* (Lancaster, U.K.: Pali Text Society, 2006), 51. Buddhist tradition places him about eighty years earlier.

64 **His awakening began** Account based on a variety of sources, primarily *Buddha-Karita: Or Life of the Buddha, by Asvaghosha, Sanskrit text, edited from a Devanagari and Two Nepalese Manuscripts, with variant readings, and English translation by Edward B. Cowell* (New Delhi: Cosmo Publications, 1977). See also the new translation of this text, *Life of the Buddha,* by Ashvaghosha, translated by Patrick Olivelle, Clay Sanskrit Library (New York: New York University Press, 2008). I also used Peter Harvey, *An Introduction to Buddhism: Teachings, History and Practices,* second edition (Cambridge, U.K.: Cambridge University Press, 2013).

64   **He wanted to go and see**   *Buddha-Karita*, 3:1.

64   **By the time the prince**   *Buddha-Karita*, 3:3ff.

65   **Yes, it could**   *Buddha-Karita*, 3:23.

65   **People were surprised**   *Buddha-Karita*, 10:34.

65   **Alexander encountered**   Plutarch, *Lives*, LXIV, 1.

65   **The prince followed**   *Buddha-Karita*, 12:89ff.

65   **He gave up**   *Buddha-Karita*, 12:111.

65   **It had not calmed**   *Buddha-Karita*, 12:101.

66   **He had become**   *Buddhism*, edited by Peter Harvey (London: Continuum, 2001).

66   **More and more came**   *The Collection of the Middle Length Sayings* (Majjhima-Nikaya), volume 1, *The First Fifty Discourses*, translated from the Pali by I. B. Horner (London: Pali Text Society, 1954).

66   **The Buddha continued**   Such acts are described in many sutras, including *The Diamond of Perfect Wisdom*, translated by the Chung Tai Translation Committee, January 2009, buddhajewel.org/teachings /sutras/diamond-of-perfect-wisdom-sutra/, accessed November 13, 2016.

67   **They could engage**   Richard F. Gombrich, *How Buddhism Began: The Conditioned Genesis of the Early Teachings*, second edition (London: Routledge, 1996), 15.

67   **This was very different**   Gombrich, *How Buddhism Began*, 16. See also Richard Gombrich, "Did the Buddha Know Sanskrit? Richard Gombrich's Response to a Point in the *BSR* Review of His *What the Buddha Thought*," *Buddhist Studies Review*, volume 30, number 2 (2013): 287–88. I also consulted Norman, *Philological Approach*, 34.

67   **Together they would remember**   Shi Zhiru, "Scriptural Authority: A Buddhist Perspective," *Buddhist-Christian Studies*, volume 30 (2010): 85–105, 88.

68   **Some form of writing**   This question is hotly debated. Richard Gombrich, "How the Mahayana Began," in *The Buddhist Forum*, volume 1 (1990): 21–30, 27, claims that no writing existed. I also consulted Falk, *Schrift im alten Indien*, 337. Peter Skilling, "Redaction, Recitation, and Writing: Transmission of the Buddha's Teachings in India in the Early Period" in *Buddhist Manuscript Cultures: Knowledge, Ritual, and Art*, edited by Stephen C. Berkwitz, Juliane Schober, and Claudia Brown (Basingstoke: Routledge, 2009), 53–75, 63, assumes that some writing existed but that it was used only for administrative purposes. There is also the puzzle of the so-called Indus Valley Script, considerably older, which may or may not be a linguistic script

and which has not yet been deciphered. Daniels and Bright, *World's Writing Systems*, 165ff.

68   **While no single person**   Berkwitz et al., *Buddhist Manuscript Cultures*, volume 3. An argument in favor of a fixed oral transmission was put forward by Alexander Wynne, "The Oral Transmission of the Early Buddhist Literature," *Journal of the International Association of Buddhist Studies*, volume 27, number 1 (2004): 97–127. I also consulted Norman, *Philological Approach*, 57.

68   **But even after**   Falk, *Schrift im alten Indien*, 243.

69   **The followers of Buddha**   On the differences between the two forms of oral transmission, especially the great variation in Buddhist transmission, see Wynne, "The Oral Transmission," 123. On the influence of Brahmin techniques of recitation, see Gombrich, "How the Mahayana Began," *Journal of Pali and Buddhist Studies* (1988): 29–46, 31ff.

69   **Only centuries later**   Falk, *Schrift im alten Indien*, 287ff.

70   **Writing would help**   See Gombrich, *How Buddhism Began*.

70   **All the accounts of the Buddha**   Zhiru, "Scriptural Authority," 98.

70   **Even though the state**   *The Original Analects: Sayings of Confucius and His Successors*, a new translation and commentary by E. Bruce Brooks and A. Taeko Brooks (New York: Columbia University Press, 1998), 3ff.

70   **He had advised younger**   Brooks and Brooks, *Original Analects*, 11.

71   **His students were usually**   Brooks and Brooks, *Original Analects*. I also consulted the Chinese Text Project, ctext.org/analects, accessed July 17, 2015.

71   **"Yu, shall I teach you"**   Confucius, *Analects*, translated with an introduction by D. C. Lau (London: Penguin, 1979), 2:17.

71   **He loved some of his**   *Analects*, 2:9, 5:9, 6:3, 11:7, 11:11.

71   **Many dukes came**   *Analects*, 3:19, 3:23.

71   **Once a border warden**   *Analects*, 3:24.

71   **And then there was**   *Analects*, 14:44.

71   **He loved order**   Chapter 10 of the *Analects* is exclusively devoted to Master Kung's actions and habits; not a single word is reported.

72   **He made his students read**   *Analects*, 16:13. Other positive mentions of *Odes* in *Analects* can be found at 1:15, 3:8, 7:18, 8:8, and 17:9.

72   **But when some of them**   *Analects*, 13:5.

72   **The point remained, though**   *Analects*, 13:3.

72   **"I am not one"**   *Analects*, 7:20.

72   "When names are not correct"   *Analects*, 13:3.

72   The earliest Chinese writing   Daniels and Bright, *World's Writing Systems*, 191ff.

74   One volume of the sayings   *Analects*, book 10.

74   The sayings of the various   See Denecke, *Dynamics of Masters Literature*.

74   without having written down   Michael Nylan, *The Five "Confucian" Classics* (New Haven: Yale University Press, 2001), 1ff, 36.

75   Socrates' most intense teaching   Account based on Plato, *Phaedo*, in *Euthyphro, Apology, Crito, Phaedo, Phaedrus*, translated by Harold North Fowler, Loeb Classical Library 36 (Cambridge, Mass.: Harvard University Press, 1914), 64a.

75   He had made his name   Plato, *Apology*, in *Euthyphro, Apology, Crito*, 18bff.

75   When the time came   Plato, *Apology*, in *Euthyphro, Apology, Crito*, 31d.

75   He, the provocateur   Plato, *Crito*, in *Euthyphro, Apology, Crito*, 45bff.

76   Before long, he was   Plato, *Phaedo*, in *Euthyphro, Apology, Crito*, 61bff.

76   And since he had taught   Plato, *Republic: Books 6–10*, edited and translated by Chris Emlyn-Jones and William Preddy, Loeb Classical Library 276 (Cambridge, Mass.: Harvard University Press, 2013), VII, 514a.

76   swans sing most beautifully   Plato, *Phaedo*, in *Euthyphro, Apology, Crito*, 85a.

76   The students may well   Plato, *Phaedo*, in *Euthyphro, Apology, Crito*, 116c.

76   "You have the childish fear"   Plato, *Phaedo*, in *Euthyphro, Apology, Crito*, 77d–e.

77   First his legs   Plato, *Phaedo*, in *Euthyphro, Apology, Crito*, 117e.

77   But not in the Athens   For literacy debates, see Harris, *Ancient Literacy*, 8, 13ff, 100.

78   Only the expense of papyrus   Harris, *Ancient Literacy*, 95.

78   More recently, there had   Harris, *Ancient Literacy*, 86.

78   He rarely went   Plato, *Symposium*, in *Lysis, Symposium, Gorgias*, translated by W.R.M. Lamb, Loeb Classical Library 166 (Cambridge, Mass.: Harvard University Press, 1925), 174a.

78   What did Homer know   Plato, *Ion*, in *Statesman, Philebus, Ion*,

translated by Harold North Fowler and W.R.M. Lamb, Loeb Classical Library 164 (Cambridge, Mass.: Harvard University Press, 1925), 537b.

78 **Socrates himself had fought** Plato, *Symposium*, in *Lysis, Symposium*, 219e.

79 **Phaedrus had brought** Plato, *Phaedrus*, in *Euthyphro. Apology. Crito*, 227a.

79 **Writing was all the rage** Plato, *Phaedrus*, 257e.

79 **It was therefore not surprising** Plato, *Phaedrus*, 274aff.

79 **People would no longer bother** Plato, *Phaedrus*, 275b–c.

79 **You couldn't ask** Plato, *Phaedrus*, 175d–e.

80 **All he tells us** Plato, *Phaedo*, 59b.

80 **Plato was creating** Martin Puchner, *The Drama of Ideas: Platonic Provocations in Theater and Philosophy* (New York: Oxford University Press, 2010).

81 **command that these stones** Matthew 4:1ff.

81 **a very good thing** Matthew 4:1–11.

82 **He told them to prepare** Matthew 5–7.

83 **But while he waited** John 8:6.

83 **"Do not think"** Matthew 5:17.

83 **"For this is he that was spoken"** Matthew 3:3.

83 **"This that is written"** Luke 22:37.

83 **"The Word was made"** John 1:14.

84 **Tongues of fire appeared** Acts of the Apostles 2:1ff.

84 **A Jew and Roman citizen** Acts of the Apostles 9:4–18.

85 **These letters** On the importance of letters for early Christians, see Harris, *Ancient Literacy*, 221.

85 **The library of Pergamum** The library of Pergamum may even have been the model for that of Alexandria. Thomas Hendrickson, "The Invention of the Greek Library," in *Transactions of the American Philological Association*, volume 144, number 2 (Autumn 2014): 371–413, 387ff.

86 **According to a classical source** Strabo, *Geography*, volume I, translated by Horace Leonard Jones, Loeb Classical Library 49 (Cambridge, Mass.: Harvard University Press, 1917), VIII, 1, 54–55.

87 **This way, the teachers' literature** Carr, *Writing on the Tablet*, 283.

87 **This translation took place** Daniels and Bright, *World's Writing Systems*, 487.

88   **Perhaps to soften this blow**   Abraham Wasserstein and David J. Wasserstein, *The Legend of the Septuagint: From Classical Antiquity to Today* (Cambridge, U.K.: Cambridge University Press, 2006).

89   **The librarians became so**   Rudolf Pfeiffer, *History of Classical Scholarship: From 1300 to 1850* (New York: Oxford University Press, 1976), 236.

89   **The Romans called it**   Jonathan M. Bloom, *Paper Before Print: The History and Impact of Paper in the Islamic World* (New Haven: Yale University Press, 2001), 25.

89   **Initially, the parchment codex**   Bloom, *Paper Before Print*, 27.

89   **In this it was perfect**   Carr, *Writing on the Tablet*, 279; Bloom, *Paper Before Print*, 25. See also Harris, *Ancient Literacy*, 296.

89   **Soon a format war**   Martin, *History and Power*, 59ff.

89   **Paul was an early adopter**   Colin H. Roberts and T. C. Skeat, *The Birth of the Codex* (London: Oxford University Press, 1983), 22.

90   **Even though he was not**   For an excellent account of the discovery of the *Diamond Sutra*, see Frances Wood and Mark Barnard, *The Diamond Sutra: The Story of the World's Earliest Dated Printed Book* (London: British Library, 2010).

90   **While working in one**   Wood and Barnard, *Diamond Sutra*, 32.

90   **They were miraculously preserved**   Joyce Morgan and Conrad Walters, *Journeys on the Silk Road: A Desert Explorer, Buddha's Secret Library, and the Unearthing of the World's Oldest Printed Book* (Guilford, Conn.: Lyons Press, 2012), 134.

91   **When the Buddha**   *The Diamond of Perfect Wisdom Sutra*, translated by the Chung Tai Translation Committee, January 2009, from the Chinese translation by Tripitaka Master Kumarajiva, 11, buddhajewel.org/teachings/sutras/diamond-of-perfect-wisdom-sutra/, accessed November 13, 2016.

91   **"Wherever this sutra is present"**   *Diamond of Perfect Wisdom*, 12.

92   **Previously, texts in China**   Sarah Allan, *Buried Ideas: Legends of Abdication and Ideal Government in Early Chinese Bamboo-Slip Manuscripts* (Albany: State University of New York Press, 2015).

92   **Its smooth surface**   Tsien Tsuen-Hsuin, *Paper and Printing*, in *Science and Civilisation in China*, edited by Joseph Needham, volume 5, *Chemistry and Chemical Technology* (Cambridge, U.K.: Cambridge University Press, 1985). I also consulted Dard Hunter, *Papermaking: The History and Technique of an Ancient Craft* (New York: Dover, 1978).

92   **It was also easy to transport**   Morgan and Walters, *Journeys on the Silk Road*, 135.

92   **"Reverently made"**   *Sacred Texts*, British Library Online Gallery, bl.uk/onlinegallery/sacredtexts/diamondsutra.html, accessed November 13, 2016.

94   **Later, woodblock printing**   Martin, *History and Power*, 393.

95   **An early beneficiary**   The International Dunhuang Project, idp.bl .uk/, accessed November 8, 2016.

95   **The emperor retained copies**   The main source for the incident is the great Chinese historian Sima Qian, who wrote a hundred years later. Nylan, *Five Confucian Classics*, 29.

96   **Less than a hundred years**   Nylan, *Five Confucian Classics*, 33.

96   **An Imperial Academy**   Nylan, *Five Confucian Classics*, 32–41.

97   **Beginning in the tenth century**   Simon Eliot and Jonathan Rose, *A Companion to the History of the Book* (Malden, Mass.: Wiley-Blackwell, 2007), 104.

97   **In the second century C.E.**   Liang Cai, "Excavating the Genealogy of Classical Studies in the Western Han Dynasty (206 B.C.E.– 8 C.E.)," *Journal of the American Oriental Society* volume 131, number 3 (July–September 2011): 371–94, 383.

97   **Buddhist sutras**   Katherine R. Tsiang, "Monumentalization of Buddhist Texts in the Northern Qi Dynasty: The Engraving of Sutras in Stone at the Xiangtangshan Caves and Other Sites in the Sixth Century," *Artibus Asiae*, volume 56, number 3/4 (1996): 233–61.

97   **More likely, these libraries**   Nylan, *Five Confucian Classics*, 53. I also consulted Tsien Tsuen-Hsuin, *Paper and Printing*, 156ff.

97   **I visited one such stone library**   Others include a library engraved during the Wei Dynasty (220–65). P. J. Ivanhoe, "The Shifting Contours of the Confucian Tradition," *Philosophy East and West*, volume 54, number 1 (January 2004): 83–94, 89.

CHAPTER 5. MURASAKI AND *THE TALE OF GENJI*: THE FIRST GREAT NOVEL IN WORLD HISTORY

98   **I still remember my surprise**   I thank my former colleague Haruo Shirane for helping me with this chapter.

99   **"Just my luck"**   Murasaki Shikibu, *Her Diary and Poetic Memoirs*, a translation and study by Richard Bowring (Princeton, N.J.: Princeton University Press, 1982), 139.

100 **The emperor himself** Murasaki, *Diary*, 137.

100 **To protect herself** Murasaki, *Diary*, 139.

100 **Paradoxically, the discrimination** Richard Bowring, *Murasaki Shikibu: The Tale of Genji* (Cambridge, U.K.: Cambridge University Press, 1988), 12.

101 **a history of the Fujiwara clan** *Okagami, the Great Mirror: Fujiwara Michinaga (966–1027) and His Times*, a study and translation by Helen Craig McCullough (Princeton: Princeton University Press, 1980).

101 **The court was located** Ivan Morris, *The World of the Shining Prince: Court Life in Ancient Japan* (New York: Knopf, 1964), 22.

101 **Light six-panel folding screens** Kazuko Koizumi, *Traditional Japanese Furniture: A Definitive Guide* (Tokyo: Kodansha International, 1986), 158–60. I also consulted Joseph T. Sorensen, *Optical Allusions: Screens, Paintings, and Poetry in Classical Japan (ca. 800–1200)* (Leiden: E. J. Brill, 2012).

102 **Everyone in court society** Bowring, *Murasaki Shikibu*, 68.

102 **During a normal day** Morris, *World of the Shining Prince*, 178.

103 **In Genji's present situation** Murasaki Shikibu, *The Tale of Genji*, translated by Dennis Washburn (New York: Norton, 2015), 109.

104 **The girl was sleeping** Murasaki, *Tale of Genji*, 122–23.

105 **Genji wanted to make sure** Murasaki, *Tale of Genji*, 125.

105 **"I've yet to see"** Murasaki, *Tale of Genji*, 125–26.

106 **Rome had similarly** Wiebke Denecke, *Classical World Literatures: Sino-Japanese and Greco-Roman Comparisons* (New York: Oxford University Press, 2014).

107 **The poems exchanged** Morris, *World of the Shining Prince*, 97.

107 **This exam system** Morris, *World of the Shining Prince*, 67.

107 **He would have preferred** Murasaki, *Tale of Genji*, 426–27.

108 **would sponsor mass** Murasaki, *Tale of Genji*, 675.

108 **In keeping with the Buddhist** Morris, *World of the Shining Prince*, 101, 110.

110 **"Though my body must wander"** Murasaki, *Tale of Genji*, 260–61.

111 **When the new emperor learned** Murasaki, *Tale of Genji*, 677.

111 **Instead, the emperor communicated** Murasaki, *Tale of Genji*, 678.

112 **From *The Tale of Genji*, they** Murasaki, *Tale of Genji*, 121.

112 **It is possible that** Haruo Shirane, *The Bridge of Dreams: A Poetics of "The Tale of Genji"* (Stanford: Stanford University Press, 1978), 58.

113 **In this way, Murasaki Shikibu** Morris, *World of the Shining Prince*, 280.

114 **"the fifty-odd volumes"** Bowring, Murasaki Shikibu, 78.

114 **Because the novel had** For the reception history of *The Tale of Genji*, see Haruo Shirane's excellent *Envisioning The Tale of Genji: Media, Gender, and Cultural Production* (New York: Columbia University Press, 2008).

115 **Before long, Confucians warned** Bowring, Murasaki Shikibu, 86.

118 **Like Murasaki Shikibu, most** Morris, *World of the Shining Prince*, 79.

119 **"Recently I tore up"** Murasaki, *Diary*, 141.

CHAPTER 6. ONE THOUSAND AND ONE NIGHTS WITH SCHEHERAZADE

121 **When did you first** I thank my friend Paulo Horta for helping me with this chapter.

121 **One side of the fragment** Nabia Abbott, "A Ninth-Century Fragment of the 'Thousand Nights': New Light on the Early History of the Arabian Nights," *Journal of Near Eastern Studies*, volume 8, number 3 (July 1949): 129–64.

122 **Probably the Arabic collection** Robert Irwin, *The Arabian Nights: A Companion* (London: Palgrave Macmillan, 2004), 51.

122 **Once the collection was available in Arabic** Irwin, *Arabian Nights*, 120ff. I also consulted *The "Thousand and One Nights" in Arabic Literature and Society*, edited by Richard G. Hovannisian and Georges Sabagh, with an introduction by Fedwa Malti-Douglas (Cambridge, U.K.: Cambridge University Press, 1997); Eva Sallis, *Sheherazade Through the Looking Glass: The Metamorphosis of the "Thousand and One Nights"* (Richmond, Surrey: Curzon, 1999); Paul McMichael Nurse, *Eastern Dreams: How the "Arabian Nights" Came to the World* (Toronto: Viking, 2010); John Barth, *Chimera* (New York: Random House, 1972); and Marina Warner, *Stranger Magic: Charmed States and the Arabian Nights* (Cambridge, Mass.: Harvard University Press, 2013).

123 **"Once upon a time there was a Porter"** Richard F. Burton, *The Book of the Thousand Nights and a Night: A Plain and Literal Translation of the Arabian Nights Entertainments*, volume 1 (USA: Printed by the Burton Club for Private Subscribers Only, 1885–88), 82–84.

125 **Alexander the Great, Al-Nadim reported**   *The Fihrist of al-Nadim: A Tenth-Century Survey of Muslim Culture*, edited and translated by Bayard Dodge, volume 2 (New York: Columbia University Press, 1970), book 8, 714.

125 **he also collected them**   Dodge, *Fihrist*, 714.

126 **It was a wild theory**   In his essay "The Thousand and One Nights," Jorge Luis Borges also mentions the connection between Alexander and *One Thousand and One Nights*. Jorge Luis Borges, *Seven Nights*, translated by Eliot Weinberger (New York: New Directions, 1984), 43ff.

126 **After all, Alexander's own life**   Yuriko Yamanaka, "Alexander in the *Thousand and One Nights* and the Ghazali Connection," in *The Arabian Nights and Orientalism: Perspectives from East and West*, edited by Tetsuo Nishio and Yuriko Yamanaka (London: Tauris, 2006), 93–115.

126 **"Everyone is your enemy"**   *The Book of the Thousand Nights*, Burton, volume 5: 252–54.

126 **The story comes from the *Jataka***   Irwin, *Arabian Nights*, 63.

126 **Another story**   Irwin, *Arabian Nights*, 64.

129 **The impulse to tell stories**   Jerome Bruner, *Making Stories: Law, Literature, Life* (Cambridge, Mass.: Harvard University Press, 2003), 3ff. I also consulted Steven Pinker, *The Language Instinct: How the Mind Creates Language* (New York: Harper, 1995), 6.

129 **We are driven to make connections**   Donald E. Polkinghorne speaks of humans having been engaged in a "virtually uninterrupted monologue" in *Narrative Knowing and the Human Sciences* (Albany: State University of New York Press, 1988), 160.

129 **No matter what forces**   Joseph Campbell, *The Hero with a Thousand Faces* (Princeton: Princeton University Press, 1949).

130 **While they sometimes**   Aboubakr Chraïbi, editor, *Arabic Manuscripts of the "Thousand and One Nights": Presentation and Critical Editions of Four Noteworthy Texts; Observations on Some Osmanli Translations* (Paris: espaces&signes, 2016). Chraïbi classifies this type of literature as "middle literature" (63).

131 **They created suspense**   On frames as storytelling devices, see Mia Irene Gerhardt, *The Art of Story-Telling: A Literary Study of the "Thousand and One Nights"* (Leiden: E. J. Brill, 1963), 389ff.

131 **A good number of stories**   On Harun as protagonist, see Gerhardt, *Art of Story-Telling*, 466.

132 **If the Buddha seemed**   This tale is from the *Suka Saptati*, which

was translated from Sanskrit into Persian as *Tutinama*. Irwin, *Arabian Nights*, 67ff. This text in turn was translated into Turkish and formed the basis for a German translation under the title *Papagaienbuch*, the first version to be translated into any Western language, in 1858. *Tuti-Nameh: Das Papagaienbuch, Eine Sammlung orientalischer Erzählungen, nach der türkischen Bearbeitung zum ersten Mal übersetzt von Georg Rosen* (Leipzig: Brockhaus, 1858).

132 **Like Scheherazade, the parrot** This time-gaining frame was of Indian origin and transmitted via Persia in the fourteenth century, according to Gerhardt, *Art of Story-Telling*, 397.

133 **The most frightening** Richard F. Burton, *Vikram and the Vampire: Classic Hindu Tales of Adventure, Magic, and Romance* (Rochester, Vt.: Park Street Press, 1993).

136 **For hundreds of years** Tsien Tsuen-Hsuin, *Paper and Printing*.

137 **The city of Talas** The story itself is probably false, but it reveals the strategic importance of Samarkand and of paper while it also seeks to explain the delayed diffusion of this technology. Bloom, *Paper Before Print*, 42ff. I also consulted Elizabeth ten Grotenhuis, "Stories of Silk and Paper," *World Literature Today*, volume 80, number 4 (July–August 2006): 10–12.

137 **Following the recommendation** Bloom, *Paper Before Print*, 48–51.

138 **Paper powered an explosion** Nicholas A. Basbanes, *On Paper: The Everything of Its Two-Thousand-Year History* (New York: Vintage, 2013), 48–49.

138 **The Houses of Wisdom** Bloom, *Paper Before Print*, 117.

138 **Like other charismatic teachers** Even though it is often asserted that Muhammad was illiterate, this is not certain. Claude Gilliot, "Creation of a Fixed Text," in *The Cambridge Companion to the Qur'an*, edited by Jane Dammen McAuliffe (Cambridge, U.K.: Cambridge University Press, 2009), 42.

138 **But some of his followers** Fred M. Donner, "The Historical Context," in McAuliffe, *Cambridge Companion to the Qur'an*, 31ff. I also consulted Fernand Braudel, who compares Muhammad to Homer in *A History of Civilizations*, translated by Richard Mayne (London: Penguin, 1993), 48.

138 **Originally, this writing** Gilliot, "Creation of a Fixed Text," 44.

138 **When a more complete text** Fred Leemhuis, "From Palm Leaves to the Internet," in McAuliffe, *Cambridge Companion to the Qur'an*, 146. I also consulted Bloom, *Paper Before Print*, 27.

138 **At first they continued**   Bloom, *Paper Before Print*, 68. I also con-
    sulted Oliver Leaman, "The Manuscript and the Qur'an," in *The
    Qur'an: An Encyclopedia*, edited by Oliver Leaman (London: Rout-
    ledge, 2006), 385.

140 **We still count paper**   Bloom, *Paper Before Print*, 9.

140 **Some of the most famous**   Paulo Lemos Horta, *Marvellous Thieves:
    Secret Authors of the Arabian Nights* (Cambridge, Mass.: Harvard
    University Press, 2016).

141 **The first printed version**   Leemhuis, "From Palm Leaves to the In-
    ternet," 151.

142 **While at first many Turks**   Peer Teuwsen, "Der meistgehasste
    Türke," *Tages-Anzeiger*, February 5, 2005, archived at web.archive
    .org/web/20090116123035/http://sc.tagesanzeiger.ch/dyn/news/kultur
    /560264.html, accessed August 10, 2016.

142 **After all, Pamuk was writing**   Orhan Pamuk, *The Naïve and the
    Sentimental Novelist: The Charles Eliot Norton Lectures*, translated
    by Nazim Dikbaş (Cambridge, Mass.: Harvard University Press,
    2010).

CHAPTER 7. GUTENBERG, LUTHER, AND THE NEW PUBLIC OF PRINT

145 **Every seven years**   *The Holy Relics of Aix-la-Chapelle with Copies of
    Them: To Which Is Added a Short Description of the Town, Its Curi-
    osities and Its Environs* (Aix-la-Chapelle: Printer and Editor M.
    Urlichs Son, 19–?).

145 **Then each relic**   *Gutenberg: Aventur und Kunst: Vom Geheimun-
    ternehmen zur ersten Medienrevolution*, herausgegeben von der Stadt
    Mainz anlässlich des 600. Geburtstages von Johannes Gutenberg
    (Mainz: Hermann Schmidt, 2000), 97.

146 **Pilgrims could buy**   *Gutenberg: Aventur und Kunst*, 126.

147 **The mirrors worked across distance**   *Gutenberg: Aventur und Kunst*,
    309.

147 **In anticipation of the upcoming fair**   Albert Kapr, *Johannes Guten-
    berg: Persönlichkeit und Leistung* (Munich: Beck, 1987), 80.

147 **Gensfleisch came from**   Kapr, *Johannes Gutenberg*, 35ff.

147 **But he was not a member**   *Gutenberg: Aventur und Kunst*, 119. I
    also consulted Michael Giesecke, *Der Buchdruck in der frühen
    Neuzeit: Eine historische Fallstudie über die Durchsetzung neuer Infor-*

mations- und Kommunikationstechnologien (Frankfurt am Main: Suhrkamp, 1991).

147 **In the case of Gensfleisch** Kapr, *Johannes Gutenberg*, 28.

147 **He had invented** Kapr, *Johannes Gutenberg*, 80; *Gutenberg: Aventur und Kunst*, 126.

148 **First, there was the breach-of-promise suit** Andreas Venzke, *Johannes Gutenberg* (Zürich: Benziger, 1993), 78.

148 **Gutenberg didn't want to ponder** Venzke, *Johannes Gutenberg*, 71.

148 **The only solution** Venzke, *Johannes Gutenberg*, 93.

149 **The fair of 1440** *The Holy Relics of Aix-la-Chapelle*, 6.

149 **Whatever it was, Strasburg** Venzke, *Johannes Gutenberg*, 135.

150 **This woodblock technique** Kapr, *Johannes Gutenberg*, 113.

150 **Such letters were sometimes made** Kapr, *Johannes Gutenberg*, 107.

151 **The first and perhaps most** Venzke, *Johannes Gutenberg*, 113.

151 **He would need almost** Stephan Füssel, *Johannes Gutenberg* (Reinbeck bei Hamburg: Rowohlt, 1999), 35.

152 **Here, Gutenberg's experience** *Gutenberg: Aventur und Kunst*, 163.

152 **Normal inks** Venzke, *Johannes Gutenberg*, 113.

152 **The thickened ink** *Gutenberg: Aventur und Kunst*, 172ff.

152 **A separate frame** *Gutenberg: Aventur und Kunst*, 178.

153 **The most common Latin** Füssel, *Johannes Gutenberg*, 20.

153 **Donatus was so popular** Füssel, *Johannes Gutenberg*, 61.

153 **The book he produced** Stephan Füssel, *Gutenberg und seine Wirkung* (Frankfurt am Main: Insel Verlag, 1999), 26.

154 **The result was a great** *Gutenberg: Aventur und Kunst*, 444.

154 **Those who could not** John Edwards, "'España es diferente'? Indulgences and the Spiritual Economy in Late Medieval Spain," in *Promissory Notes on the Treasury of Merits: Indulgences in Late Medieval Europe*, edited by R. N. Swanson (Leiden: E. J. Brill, 2006), 147–68, 147.

154 **All that was necessary** Füssel, *Johannes Gutenberg*, 54.

155 **Marco Polo had marveled** Guy Bechtel, *Gutenberg et l'invention de l'imprimerie: une enquête* (Paris: Fayard, 1992), 87. Marco Polo does not say whether the paper money he saw was printed, but it was certainly stamped. *The Travels of Marco Polo*, translated and with an introduction by Ronald Latham (London: Penguin, 1958), 147.

156 **He printed an anti-Turkish** Eckehard Simon, *The Türkenkalender (1454), Attributed to Gutenberg and the Strasbourg Lunation Tracts* (Cambridge, Mass.: Medieval Academy of America, 1988).

160   **In church after church**   Venzke, *Johannes Gutenberg*, 55.

161   **In England, a printer**   There may even have existed a personal relationship between Gutenberg and Nicholas of Cusa. Albert Kapr,
"Gab es Beziehungen zwischen Johannes Gutenberg and Nikolaus
von Kues?" in *Gutenberg-Jahrbuch* (1972): 32–40.

162   **The writer also took**   Martin Brecht, *Martin Luther: Sein Weg zur
Reformation, 1483–1521* (Stuttgart: Calwer Verlag, 1981), 177. I also
consulted Heiko A. Oberman, *Luther: Mensch zwischen Gott und
Teufel* (Berlin: Severin und Siedler, 1981).

162   **Indulgences were now printed**   Füssel, *Johannes Gutenberg*, 54.

162   **Some printers came up**   Swanson, *Promissory Notes*, 225.

163   **One such brochure**   Brecht, *Martin Luther*, 121.

163   **He had borrowed**   Brecht, *Martin Luther*, 176.

163   **and the Pope**   Brecht, *Martin Luther*, 177ff.

164   **In Nuremberg, a councilman**   Brecht, *Martin Luther*, 199ff.

165   **Editions ran out**   Brecht, *Martin Luther*, 213.

165   **Print runs of Luther's texts**   Rudolf Hirsch, *Printing, Selling and
Reading, 1450–1550* (Wiesbaden: Harrassowitz, 1974), 67–78.

167   **Print was God's greatest act**   Elizabeth L. Eisenstein, *The Printing
Press as an Agent of Change: Communications and Cultural Transfor-
mations in Early Modern Europe*, volumes 1 and 2 (Cambridge, U.K.:
Cambridge University Press, 1979), 304.

167   **Thanks to Gutenberg**   Eisenstein, *Printing Press as an Agent*, 46.

169   **There were only seven printers**   Brian Moynahan, *God's Bestseller:
William Tyndale, Thomas More, and the Writing of the English Bible—
A Story of Martyrdom and Betrayal* (New York: St. Martin's Press,
2002), 55.

170   **On October 31, 2016, Pope Francis**   Christina Anderson, "Pope
Francis, in Sweden, Urges Catholic-Lutheran Reconciliation," *New
York Times*, October 31, 2016, nytimes.com/2016/11/01/world/europe
/pope-francis-in-sweden-urges-catholic-lutheran-reconciliation.html,
accessed November 13, 2016.

CHAPTER 8. THE *POPOL VUH* AND MAYA CULTURE:
A SECOND, INDEPENDENT LITERARY TRADITION

172   **The Spanish had**   The following account is based on multiple
sources, among which only one is by an Inca, Titu Cusi Yupanqui,
dictated to a mestizo scribe. Titu Cusi Yupanqui, *History of How the*

Spaniards Arrived in Peru, translated and with an introduction by Catherine Julien (Indianapolis: Hackett, 2006). I also consulted Edmundo Guillén et al., *Versión Inca de la Conquista* (Lima: Carlos Milla Batres, 1974). Other accounts include Francisco de Xeres, *Narrative of the Conquest of Peru*, translated and edited, with notes and an introduction, by Clements R. Markham (New York: Burt Franklin, 1872); Pedro Pizarro, *Relation of the Discovery and Conquest of the Kingdoms of Peru*, volume 1, translated into English and annotated by Philip Ainsworth Means (New York: Cortés Society, 1921); and Augustín de Zárate, *Histoire de la Découverte et de la Conquête du Pérou*, translated from the Spanish by S. de Broë (Paris: Compagnie des Libraires, 1714). Other sources are to be found in *Die Eroberung von Peru: Pizarro und andere Conquistadoren, 1526–1712*, edited by Robert and Evamaria Grün (Tübingen: Horst Erdmann Verlag, 1973); Felipe Guaman Poma de Ayala, *The First New Chronicle and Good Government: On the History of the World and the Incas up to 1615*, translated and edited by Roland Hamilton (Austin: University of Texas Press, 2009); and Pedro de Cieza de León, *The Discovery and Conquest of Peru: Chronicles of the New World Encounter*, edited and translated by Alexandra Parma Cook and Noble David Cook (Durham, N.C.: Duke University Press, 1998). I also used Francisco Cervantes de Salazar, *Crónica de la Nueva España*, Biblioteca de Autores Españoles (Madrid: Atlas, 1971).

173 **His book was** Of the various eyewitnesses, Xeres, *Narrative of the Conquest of Peru*, calls the book a "Bible" (95) and "holy scripture." Pedro de Cieza de León, *Discovery and Conquest of Peru*, calls it a "breviary." Zárate, *Histoire de la Découverte*, speaks of a "breviary" (volume 2, 173) but also of a "book" that contains "the word of God" (177). Titu Cusi Yupanqui, *History of How the Spaniards*, speaks of a "book." Pizarro, *Relation of the Discovery*, speaks of a "breviary" (182). Guaman Poma de Ayala, *First New Chronicle*, speaks of a "breviary" (387).

174 **Like his Inca adversary** Of Pizarro's companions, only fifty-one could read and write. Rafael Varón Gabai, *Francisco Pizarro and His Brothers: The Illusion of Power in Sixteenth-Century Peru*, translated by Javier Flores Espinoza (Norman: University of Oklahoma Press, 1997), 4. I also consulted Michael Wood, *Conquistadors* (Berkeley: University of California Press, 2000), and Stuart Stirling, *Pizarro: Conqueror of the Inca* (Phoenix Mill, Gloucestershire, U.K.: Sutton, 2005).

174 **Later, it turned out** Dennis Tedlock, *2000 Years of Mayan Litera-*

ture, with new translations and interpretations by the author (Berkeley: University of California Press, 2010), 239.

175 **"It's Wednesday"** Friar Diego de Landa, *Yucatan Before and After the Conquest*, translated with notes by William Gates (New York: Dover Publications, 1978), 7. I also used Bernal Díaz del Castillo, *Historia verdadera de la conquista de la Nueva España*, with introduction and notes by Joaquín Ramírez Cabañas, 2 volumes (Mexico: Editorial Porrúa, 1966), 26, 29, and Francisco Cervantes de Salazar, *Crónica de la Nueva España II* (Madrid: Atlas Ediciones, 1971), 186. See also Inga Clendinnen, *Ambivalent Conquests: Maya and Spaniard in Yucatan, 1517–1570*, second edition (Cambridge, U.K.: Cambridge University Press, 2003), 17.

175 **He didn't want to join** Bernal Díaz del Castillo, *The History of the Conquest of New Spain*, edited and with an introduction by Davíd Carrasco (Albuquerque: University of New Mexico Press, 2008), 31, 36.

175 **The two books** Hernán Cortés, *Letters from Mexico*, translated, edited, and with a new introduction by Anthony R. Pagden (New Haven: Yale University Press, 2001), 45.

176 **The single landmass** J. R. McNeill and William H. McNeill, *The Human Web: A Bird's-Eye View of World History* (New York: Norton, 2003), 41ff.

176 **Thanks to the Mayas** There may have been as many as fifteen distinct scripts. Martha J. Macri, "Maya and Other Mesoamerican Scripts," in Daniels and Bright, *World's Writing Systems*, 172.

176 **Surprisingly little attention** The great exception, of course, is Dennis Tedlock with his fantastic book *2000 Years of Mayan Literature*.

177 **While not every sign** Macri, "Maya and Other Mesoamerican Scripts," 175.

177 **Landa had been born** Clendinnen, *Ambivalent Conquests*, 66ff. Diego de Landa's early biographer, writing a century later, was Diego López de Cogolludo, *Los tres siglos de la dominación española en Yucatán, o sea Historia de esta provincia, desde la Conquista hasta la Independencia* (1654), 2 volumes (Mérida: Manuel Aldana Rivas, 1867–68).

178 **Above all, Cocom** De Landa, *Yucatan Before and After the Conquest*, 12ff.

178 **Maya books were prestigious** De Landa, *Yucatan Before and After the Conquest*, 12, 19.

178 **Writing was done**   Tedlock, *2000 Years of Mayan Literature*, 146ff.

178 **The difficulty of the Maya**   Tedlock, *2000 Years of Mayan Literature*, 154.

179 **Maya books were closely**   De Landa, *Yucatan Before and After the Conquest*, 13.

179 **Since that date**   Tedlock, *2000 Years of Mayan Literature*, 130–36.

179 **"by which they regulated"**   De Landa, *Yucatan Before and After the Conquest*, 68.

179 **"opened a book"**   De Landa, *Yucatan Before and After the Conquest*, 71.

180 **Of Landa's 4,500 torture**   Clendinnen, *Ambivalent Conquests*, 76.

180 **Even his old friend**   Inga Clendinnen, "Reading the Inquisitorial Record in Yucatán: Fact or Fantasy?" *The Americas*, volume 38, number 3 (January 1982): 327–45.

181 **"We found a great number"**   De Landa, *Yucatan Before and After the Conquest*, 82.

183 **At first, production was slow**   The first printer was Juan Pablos, and the first book of which fragments survive was printed by Pablos in 1540. Agustín Millares Carlo and Julián Calvo, *Juan Pablos: Primer impresor que a esta tierra vino* (Mexico: Librería de M. Porrúa, 1953); Antonio Rodríguez-Buckingham, "Monastic Libraries and Early Printing in Sixteenth-Century Spanish America," in *Libraries and Culture*, volume 24, number 1, Libraries at Times of Cultural Change (Winter 1998): 33–56, 34; and José Ignacio Conde and Díaz Rubín, *Artes de México*, number 131, Libros Mexicanos (1970): 7–18, 7. See also *Colonial Printing in Mexico: Catalog of an Exhibition Held at the Library of Congress in 1939 Commemorating the Four Hundredth Anniversary of Printing in the New World* (Washington, D.C.: U.S. Government Printing Office, 1993), 3ff.

183 **In order to preserve**   Tedlock, *2000 Years of Mayan Literature*, 299.

183 **The principal creator**   I used *Popol Vuh: The Definitive Edition of the Mayan Book of the Dawn of Life and the Glories of Gods and Kings*, revised and expanded editing, translated by Dennis Tedlock (New York: Simon and Schuster, 1969), 63 (translation is slightly modified by me). I also consulted *Popol Vuh: The Sacred Book of the Ancient Quiché Maya*, translated into English by Delia Goetz and Sylvanus Griswold Morley, from the translation by Adrián Recinos (Los Angeles: Plantin Press, 1954).

185 **"Punt the head"**   Tedlock, *Popol Vuh*, 128.

186 **Later, I read that soccer**   Frank G. Menke, *The Encyclopedia of Sports* (New York: A. S. Barnes, 1939), 147.

186 **The story of the two-generation**   Tedlock, *Popol Vuh*, 142.

186 **"This is enough about the being of Quiché"**   Tedlock, *Popol Vuh*, 198.

187 **More than 150 years later**   Tedlock, *2000 Years of Mayan Literature*, 300.

189 **On December 22, 1997**   Nick Henck, *Subcommander Marcos: The Man and the Mask* (Durham, N.C.: Duke University Press, 2007), 319. I also consulted Marc Lacey, "10 Years Later, Chiapas Massacre Still Haunts Mexico," *New York Times*, December 23, 2007, nytimes.com/2007/12/23/world/americas/23acteal.html, accessed November 12, 2016. See also *Subcomandante Marcos: Ein Maskierter Mythos*, edited by Anne Huffschmid (Berlin: Elefanten Press, 1995).

189 **Despite overwhelming firepower**   Nicholas P. Higgins, *Understanding the Chiapas Rebellion: Modernist Visions and the Invisible Indian* (Austin: University of Texas Press, 2004), 84ff.

189 **When he had first entered**   Henck, *Subcommander Marcos*, 71.

189 **The writing technology**   *Shadows of Tender Fury: The Letters and Communiqués of Subcomandante Marcos and the Zapatista Army of National Liberation*, translated by Frank Bardacke, Leslie López, and the Watsonville, California, Human Rights Committee (New York: Monthly Review, 1995), 13.

189 **Underground couriers**   *Shadows of Tender Fury*, 13.

190 **He also created a character**   Subcomandante Marcos, *Zapatista Stories* (London: Katabasis, 2001), 23.

190 **Recognizing that literature had become**   Deborah Esch, "Of Typewriters and Masking Tape: A Media History of the Zapatistas," *Al Jazeera* (April 19, 2013), aljazeera.com/indepth/opinion/2013/04/2013415112152991530.html, accessed June 16, 2015.

190 **"This is the story of how"**   Subcomandante Insurgente Marcos, *Our Word Is Our Weapon: Selected Writings*, edited by Juana Ponce de León, foreword by José Saramago (New York: Seven Stories, 2002), 407.

192 **The Zapatista rebellion of 1994**   Jeff Conant, *A Poetics of Resistance: The Revolutionary Public Relations of the Zapatista Insurgency* (Oakland, Calif.: AK Press, 2010).

192 **His work included teaching**   Henck, *Subcommander Marcos*, 77ff; Higgins, *Understanding the Chiapas Rebellion*, 158.

192 **He also struggled**   Henck, *Subcommander Marcos*, 94.

CHAPTER 9. DON QUIXOTE AND THE PIRATES

193 **It's not such a terrible job** I thank Barbara Fuchs for generously helping me with this chapter.

194 **For the longest time** William Byron, *Cervantes: A Biography* (New York: Doubleday, 1978), 115.

195 **During the days leading up** Account based on Byron, *Cervantes: A Biography*, 124ff.

196 **To be sure, he had** Melveena McKendrick, *Cervantes* (Boston: Little, Brown, 1980), 63ff.

196 **Finally, after several years** Byron, *Cervantes: A Biography*, 246; McKendrick, *Cervantes*, 85.

196 **After five years as** María Antonia Garcés, *Cervantes in Algiers: A Captive's Tale* (Nashville: Vanderbilt University Press, 2002).

197 **Their ultimate goal was** Nabil Matar, "English Accounts of Captivity in North Africa and the Middle East: 1577–1625," *Renaissance Quarterly*, volume 54, number 2 (Summer 2001): 553–72, 556.

197 **Cervantes lived during** Melveena McKendrick, *Theatre in Spain 1490–1700* (Cambridge, U.K.: Cambridge University Press, 1989), 196ff.

198 **His earliest play** Jean Canavaggio, "A propos de deux « comedias » de Cervantès: Quelques remarques sur un manuscrit récemment retrouvé," *Bulletin Hispanique*, volume 68, number 1 (1966): 5–29. I also consulted Barbara Fuchs's excellent *Passing for Spain: Cervantes and the Fictions of Identity* (Urbana-Champaign: University of Illinois Press, 2002), 10–11.

199 **The demand for romances** Roger Chartier, *The Author's Hand and the Printer's Mind: Transformations of the Written Word in Early Modern Europe* (Malden, Mass.: Polity Press, 2013), 101.

201 **while speaking favorably** Miguel de Cervantes, *Don Quixote*, translated by P. A. Motteux, with an introduction by A. J. Close, Everyman's Library (New York: Knopf, 1991), part I, 48ff.

202 **Papermaking required rags** Oriol Valls i Subirà, *The History of Paper in Spain: XVII–XIX Centuries*, translated by Sarah Nicholson (Madrid: Empresa Nacional de Celulosas, 1982), 14–15.

202 **Ingeniously, Spanish and other European** Robert I. Burns, "Paper Comes to the West, 800–1400" in *Europäische Technik im Mittelalter, 800 bis 1400: Tradition und Innovation*, fourth edition, edited by Uta Lindgren (Berlin: Gebr. Mann Verlag, 1996), 413–22, 417.

202 **The paper on which** Chartier, *Author's Hand*, 131.

203 **Still, with demand for** Subirà, *History of Paper in Spain*, 15, 82.

203 **It only took a few months** Chartier, *Author's Hand*, 99.

203 *Don Quixote* **quickly became popular** Chartier, *Author's Hand*, 99; Subirà, *History of Paper in Spain*, 82.

203 **Almost immediately an English** For an excellent discussion of the influence of Spanish literature on England, see Barbara Fuchs, *The Poetics of Piracy: Emulating Spain in English Literature* (Philadelphia: University of Pennsylvania Press, 2013).

203 **A shipment of 184 copies** Irving A. Leonard, "Don Quixote and the Book Trade in Lima, 1606," *Hispanic Review*, volume 8, number 4 (October 1940): 285–304.

204 **In the 1800s, pirates** Ronald Hilton, "Four Centuries of Cervantes: The Historical Anatomy of a Best-Selling Masterpiece," *Hispania*, volume 30, number 3 (1947): 310–20, 312.

204 **True, earlier scribes** Chartier, *Author's Hand*, 17.

205 **Cervantes in turn had Don Quixote** See also Frederick A. de Armas, "Cervantes and the Italian Renaissance," in *The Cambridge Companion to Cervantes*, edited by Anthony J. Cascardi (Cambridge, U.K.: Cambridge University Press, 2002), 32–57, 44.

205 **Had he become enchanted** Robert S. Stone, "Moorish Quixote: Reframing the Novel," in *Cervantes: Bulletin of the Cervantes Society of America*, volume 33, number 1 (2013): 81–110.

206 **Clearly, the experience of Algiers** For an excellent discussion of the relation between Cervantes's Spain and the Arabic world, see Fuchs, *Poetics of Piracy*.

206 **Unfortunately, most of the provisions** Adrian Johns, *Piracy: The Intellectual Property Wars from Gutenberg to Gates* (Chicago: University of Chicago Press, 2009), 23.

206 **In the second part** Tom Lathrop, "The Significance of Don Quixote's Discovery of a New Edition of Avellaneda," in *Cervantes: Bulletin of the Cervantes Society of America*, volume 29, number 2 (Fall 2009): 131–37.

207 **"There he saw some working off the Sheets"** *The History of the Renowned Don Quixote de la Mancha, in Four Volumes, Written in Spanish by Miguel de Cervantes Saavedra, Translated by Several Hands: And Publish'd by Peter Motteux*, volume 4 (R. Knaplock et al.: Black Bull in Cirnhill, 1719), 268–70.

209 **Even though the idea**   Armas, "Cervantes and the Italian Renaissance," 58.

CHAPTER 10. BENJAMIN FRANKLIN: MEDIA
ENTREPRENEUR IN THE REPUBLIC OF LETTERS

211 **After Congress had agreed**   Chris Coelho, *Timothy Matlack: Scribe of the Declaration of Independence* (Jefferson, N.C.: McFarland, 2013), 55.

211 **Several weeks later**   Coelho, *Timothy Matlack*, 60.

214 **At the court of France**   Walter Isaacson, *Benjamin Franklin: An American Life* (New York: Simon and Schuster, 2004), 348.

216 **Schools were founded**   David D. Hall, "Readers and Writers in Early New England," in *A History of the Book in America*, volume 1, *The Colonial Book in the Atlantic World*, edited by Hugh Amory and David D. Hall (Cambridge, U.K.: Cambridge University Press, 2000), 117–51, 120.

216 **To satisfy the new demand**   Carol Sue Humphrey, *The American Revolution and the Press: The Promise of Independence*, foreword by David A. Copeland (Evanston, Ill.: Northwestern University Press, 2013), 23.

216 **By 1790, the latter rate**   Amory and Hall, *History of the Book in America*, 380.

216 **Once he had made his fortune**   Isaacson, *Benjamin Franklin*, 440.

216 **He once brought out**   James N. Green and Peter Stallybrass, *Benjamin Franklin: Writer and Printer* (Philadelphia: Library Company of Philadelphia, 2006), 70.

216 **Fiction amounted to barely**   *The Press and the American Revolution*, edited by Bernard Bailyn and John B. Hench (Worcester, Mass: American Antiquarian Society, 1980), 328.

216 **(Bunyan, too, preferred)**   Isaacson, *Benjamin Franklin*, 25; Isabel Hofmeyr, *The Portable Bunyan: A Transnational History of "The Pilgrim's Progress"* (Princeton: Princeton University Press, 2004).

216 **But Franklin printed neither**   George Simpson Eddy, "Dr. Benjamin Franklin's Library," *American Antiquarian Society* (October 1924): 206–26, 224.

217 **The first newspaper**   Humphrey, *American Revolution and the Press*, 23.

217 **They were read in homes** Jürgen Habermas, *Strukturwandel der Öffentlichkeit* (Frankfurt am Main: Suhrkamp, 1962).

217 **The philosopher G.W.F. Hegel** *Miscellaneous Writings of G.W.F. Hegel*, translated by Jon Bartley Stewart (Evanston, Ill.: Northwestern University Press, 2002), 247.

218 **When Franklin was born** Robert G. Parkinson, "Print, the Press, and the American Revolution," in *American History: Oxford Research Encyclopedias,* online publication date August 2015, 5, doi: 10.1093/acrefore/9780199329175.013.9, page 2, accessed November 2, 2015.

218 **The proliferation of newspapers** Bailyn and Hench, *Press and the American Revolution,* 334.

218 **The colonies possessed fewer newspapers** Parkinson, "Print, the Press, and the American Revolution," 2, accessed November 2, 2015; Richard Buel, Jr., "Freedom of the Press in Revolutionary America: The Evolution of Libertarianism, 1760–1820," in Bailyn and Hench, *Press and the American Revolution,* 59–97, 69.

218 **Of the four hundred pamphlets** Parkinson, "Print, the Press, and the American Revolution," 2.

218 **Paine would ultimately sell** Robert A. Ferguson, "The Commonalities of *Common Sense*," *William and Mary Quarterly,* volume 57, number 3 (July 2000): 465–504, 466; Craig Nelson, "Thomas Paine and the Making of *Common Sense*," *New England Review,* volume 27, number 3 (2006): 228–50, 243.

219 **The print run** Bernard Bailyn, *The Ideological Origins of the American Revolution,* enlarged edition (Cambridge, Mass.: Harvard University Press, 1992).

219 **Eventually his supply network** Rutherfoord Goodwin, "The Williamsburg Paper Mill of William Parks the Printer," in *The Papers of the Bibliographical Society of America,* volume 31, number 1 (1937): 21–44, 26.

219 **He trained his nephew** Ralph Frasca, *Benjamin Franklin's Printing Network: Disseminating Virtue in Early America* (Columbia: University of Missouri Press, 2006), 76ff.

220 **All told, he helped set up** Frasca, *Benjamin Franklin's Printing Network,* 19.

220 **The first newspaper to carry** Karl J. R. Arndt, "The First Translation and Printing in German of the American Declaration of Independence," *Monatshefte,* volume 77, number 2 (Summer 1985): 138–42, 140.

220 **As a general principle**   Joyce E. Chaplin, *The First Scientific American: Benjamin Franklin and the Pursuit of Genius* (New York: Basic Books, 2006), 46.

220 **Perhaps the most lucrative**   Frasca, *Benjamin Franklin's Printing Network*, 52.

221 **The position of postmaster general today**   en.wikipedia.org/wiki /United_States_Postmaster_General, accessed October 16, 2016.

221 **A British inspector**   Trish Loughran, *The Republic in Print: Print Culture in the Age of U.S. Nation Building, 1770–1870* (New York: Columbia University Press, 2007), 6–15.

221 **He made significant improvements**   Isaacson, *Benjamin Franklin*, 207.

222 **He also demonstrated**   For a discussion of Franklin as scientist, see Chaplin, *First Scientific American*.

222 **These scientific activities**   Benjamin Franklin, letter to William Strahan, August 19, 1784, in *A Benjamin Franklin Reader*, edited and annotated by Walter Isaacson (New York: Simon and Schuster, 2003), 340.

223 **There was too much to know**   See Ann M. Blair, *Too Much to Know: Managing Scholarly Information Before the Modern Age* (New Haven: Yale University Press, 2010), which compares information management before and after print.

225 **In it, Diderot**   Denis Diderot et al., *Encyclopédie, ou Dictionnaire raisonné des sciences, des arts et des métiers, par une société des gens de lettres*, volume 5 (Paris: Le Breton, 1755), 635–48A.

226 **Two decades later**   Chaplin, *First Scientific American*, 55.

226 **Despite the attempts**   C. William Miller, *Benjamin Franklin's Philadelphia Printing, 1728–1766: A Descriptive Bibliography* (Philadelphia: American Philosophical Society, 1974), xxxviii.

227 **Printers boycotted, protested**   Humphrey, *American Revolution and the Press*, 49.

227 **Angry printers destroyed**   Frasca, *Benjamin Franklin's Printing Network*, 152.

227 **The paper Jefferson used**   Julian P. Boyd, *The Declaration of Independence: The Evolution of the Text*, revised edition, edited by Gerard W. Gawalt (Washington, D.C.: Library of Congress, 1999), 65.

228 **Surprisingly, young Franklin rarely wrote**   Green and Stallybrass, *Benjamin Franklin: Writer and Printer*, 23.

229 **Even when he collected**   Green and Stallybrass, *Benjamin Franklin: Writer and Printer*, 117ff.

230 **By that time**   David Armitage, *The Declaration of Independence: A Global History* (Cambridge, Mass.: Harvard University Press, 2007).

230 **"The Body of B. Franklin, Printer"**   *Beinecke Rare Book and Manuscript Library, Beinecke Digital Collections,* brbl-dl.library.yale.edu/vufind/Record/3437127, accessed January 10, 2017.

CHAPTER 11. WORLD LITERATURE: GOETHE IN SICILY

232 **On the twenty-fourth of May**   I thank Peter J. Burgard for his help with this chapter. The following biographical account is based on Eckermann's autobiography, in Johann Peter Eckermann, *Gespräche mit Goethe in den letzten Jahren seines Lebens,* volumes 1 and 2 (Leipzig: Brockhaus, 1837), 1–34.

233 **In 1850, only eighteen**   Ralph Waldo Emerson, *Representative Men: Seven Lectures,* with an introduction by Andrew Delbanco (Cambridge, Mass.: Harvard University Press, 1996).

234 **Instinctively, Eckermann did**   In his *What Is World Literature?* (Princeton: Princeton University Press, 2003), David Damrosch describes how Eckermann's *Conversations with Goethe,* the original name of the publication, became increasingly *Conversations with Eckermann,* placing Goethe in the position of author (33).

234 **"Really? That must"**   Eckermann, *Gespräche mit Goethe,* 322.

234 **"Isn't it strange"**   Eckermann, *Gespräche mit Goethe,* 324.

235 **"The era of world literature"**   "Die Epoche der Welt-Literatur ist an der Zeit und jeder muß jetzt dazu wirken, diese Epoche zu beschleunigen." Eckermann, *Gespräche mit Goethe,* 325.

236 **The novel triggered**   Karl Otto Conrady, *Goethe: Leben und Werk,* volume 1 (Königstein: Athenaeum, 1985), 224–25.

236 **Apparently, he criticized**   Conrady, *Goethe: Leben und Werk,* volume 2, 333–35.

237 **Decades later, the manuscript**   Bishop Thomas Percy, *Hau Kiou Choaan or The Pleasing History: A Translation from the Chinese Language* (London: Dodsley in Pall-Mall, 1761). Manuscript information is based on Percy's preface to that edition.

238 **His new translation**   *The Fortunate Union: A Romance, Translated from the Chinese Original, with Notes and Illustrations by John Francis Davis* (London: Parbury, Allen and Co., 1829).

238 **Goethe particularly appreciated**   For many details on Goethe's re-

lation to China, see *Goethe und China — China und Goethe*, edited by Günther Debon and Adrian Hsia (Frankfurt am Main: Peter Lang, 1985).

238 **Some months earlier**   Peter Perring Thoms, *Chinese Courtship. In Verse. To Which Is Added, an Appendix, Treating of the Revenue of China* (London: Parbury, Allen, and Kingsbury; Macao: East India Company Press, 1824).

239 **Goethe was not bothered by this plot**   Wilhelm Grimm writes to his brother on October 14, 1815: "He [Goethe] is into Persian stuff, composed a collection of poems in the style of Hafiz, reads and explains Haoh Kioh Tschwen and is learning Persian with Paulus" (translation is mine). "Letter of Wilhelm Grimm to Jacob Grimm," in *Goethe-Jahrbuch*, edited by Dr. Ludwig Geiger, volume 1 (Frankfurt am Main: Rütten and Loening, 1880), 339. For more information on that reading, see Günther Debon, "Goethe erklärt in Heidelberg einen chinesischen Roman," in Debon and Hsia, *Goethe und China — China und Goethe*, 51–62.

239 **At a time when**   See Franco Moretti, "The Novel: History and Theory," *New Left Review* 52 (July–August 2008): 111–24.

240 **Unable to travel to Persia**   Johann Wolfgang von Goethe, *West-Östlicher Divan*, in *Gesamtausgabe*, volume 2 (Munich: DTV, 2000), 7–125, 25.

240 **"He is into Persian stuff"**   "Letter of Jacob Grimm to Wilhelm Grimm," Paris, November 10, 1815, in Geiger, *Goethe-Jahrbuch*, 339.

240 **The best his friends could do**   Rüdiger Safranski, *Goethe: Kunstwerk des Lebens* (Munich: Carl Hanser Verlag, 2013), 551.

241 **Portuguese and Spanish traders**   Anant Kakba Priolkar, *The Printing Press in India: Its Beginnings and Early Development* (Bombay: Marathi Samshodhana Mandala, 1958), 6ff. The first book printed in a South Asian language was printed in Tamil in 1578. I also consulted Dr. J. Mangamma, *Book Printing in India* (Nellore: Bangorey Books, 1975), 17ff.

242 **This meant that orientalists**   Edward W. Said, *Orientalism* (New York: Pantheon Books, 1978).

242 **As someone who read**   Johann Wolfgang von Goethe, "Preface to German Romance" (Edinburgh, 1827), in Johann Wolfgang Goethe, *Sämtliche Werke*, Münchner Ausgabe, edited by Karl Richter, volume 18.2 (Munich: Carl Hanser Verlag, 1985–98), 85–87.

243 **But once he arrived** Johann Wolfgang von Goethe, *Italienische Reise*, in *Autobiographische Schriften III, Hamburger Ausgabe in 14 Bänden*, volume 11 (Munich: Verlag H. C. Beck, 1994), 252.

245 **"There is no better commentary"** Goethe, *Reise*, 299.

246 **Only in the late nineteenth century** David A. Traill, *Schliemann of Troy: Treasure and Deceit* (New York: St. Martin's Press, 1996). For a summary of the Schliemann controversy, see Wolfgang Schindler, "An Archaeologist on the Schliemann Controversy," *Illinois Classical Studies*, volume 17, number 1 (Spring 1992): 135–51, and D. F. Easton, "Heinrich Schliemann: Hero or Fraud?" *Classical World*, volume 91, number 5, *The World of Troy* (May–June, 1998): 335–43.

248 **Inspired by Sicily** Goethe, *Reise*, 266, 298.

248 **The episode is one** Goethe, *Reise*, 299–300.

248 **Upon seeing the unbelievably beautiful** Goethe, *Reise*, 270.

248 **"If one takes a seat"** Goethe, *Reise*, 296–97. The translation is mine.

249 **After the passage** Goethe, *Reise*, 297.

250 **"He must have thought me"** Goethe, *Reise*, 233.

250 **The brittle white limestone** For a discussion of rocks and volcanism in literature, see Noah Heringman, *Romantic Rocks, Aesthetic Geology* (Ithaca, N.Y.: Cornell University Press, 2004).

251 **"One doesn't have a notion"** Goethe, *Reise*, 230.

CHAPTER 12. MARX, ENGELS, LENIN, MAO: READERS OF THE COMMUNIST MANIFESTO, UNITE!

252 **The two young men** In addition to the sources cited, this chapter is based on my own research for my book *Poetry of the Revolution: Marx, Manifestos, and the Avant-Gardes* (Princeton: Princeton University Press, 2006). A great intellectual biography of Karl Marx and Marxism is by Isaiah Berlin, *Karl Marx: His Life and Environment*, fourth edition (Oxford: Oxford University Press, 1969).

253 **Staunton, who had perfected** Philip Walsingham Sergeant, *A Century of British Chess* (London: Hutchinson and Co., 1934), 51.

253 **They had come to strategize** On the history of chess, see David Shenk, *The Immortal Game: A History of Chess, or How 32 Carved Pieces on a Board Illuminated Our Understanding of War, Art, Science, and the Human Brain* (New York: Doubleday, 2006).

253 **Because cotton** Sven Beckert, *Empire of Cotton: A Global History* (New York: Knopf, 2014).

254 **serve under the chimney** W. G. Sebald, *Die Ausgewanderten* (Frankfurt am Main: Fischer, 1992), 283.

256 **Engels had taken** Friedrich Engels, "Grundsätze des Kommunismus," in *Karl Marx und Friedrich Engels*, Gesamtausgabe (Berlin: Dietz Verlag, 1977), 361–80.

256 **"Think a little"** *Birth of the "Communist Manifesto": With Text of the Manifesto, All Prefaces by Marx and Engels, Early Drafts by Engels, and Other Supplementary Material*, edited and annotated with an introduction by Dirk J. Struik (New York: International Publishers, 1971), 60.

256 **Calling their text a manifesto** Puchner, *Poetry of the Revolution*, 69ff.

257 **"Since we basically"** Letter from Friedrich Engels in Paris to Karl Marx in Brussels, November 23–24, 1847, in *Der Bund der Kommunisten: Dokumente und Materialien*, volume 1, *1826–49* (Berlin: Dietz Verlag, 1970), 612. Translation is mine.

257 **In Marx's version** Berlin, *Karl Marx*, 124.

258 **"By exploiting the world market"** Karl Marx and Friedrich Engels, *The Communist Manifesto and Other Writings*, with an introduction and notes by Martin Puchner (New York: Barnes and Noble, 2005), 10–11. Translation is based on Samuel Moore but updated by me.

259 **"be published in the English, French, German"** Marx and Engels, *Communist Manifesto*, 5.

260 **They did, however, immediately proceed** Puchner, *Poetry of the Revolution*, 59.

260 **Since the death of Benjamin Franklin** On nineteenth-century serial publication, see Amanda Claybaugh, *The Novel of Purpose: Literature and Social Reform in the Anglo-American World* (Ithaca, N.Y.: Cornell University Press, 2007).

261 **Scattered groups of true believers** For publication information on *The Communist Manifesto*, see *Le Manifeste communiste de Marx et Engels: Histoire et Bibliographie, 1848–1918*, edited by Bert Andréas (Milan: Feltrinelli, 1963).

262 **"California and Australia"** Karl Marx and Friedrich Engels, *Gesamtausgabe*, III, volume 5, Briefe (Berlin: Dietz Verlag, 1977), 186.

262 **"Since his death"** Struik, *Birth of the "Communist Manifesto,"* 132.

263 **Vladimir had learned to be patient** For an intellectual biography of Lenin, see Georg Lukács, *Lenin: A Study on the Unity of His Thought*, translated by Nicholas Jacobs (London: Verso, 1998). For a

fuller biography, see Robert Service, *Lenin: A Biography* (Cambridge, Mass.: Harvard University Press, 2000).

265 **When they got around** Puchner, *Poetry of the Revolution*, 89ff.

266 **Russia was now without** Sheila Fitzpatrick, *The Russian Revolution*, second edition (New York: Oxford University Press, 1994), 45.

268 **While Lenin had not paid** Fitzpatrick, *Russian Revolution*, 85.

268 **When a coup attempt** Marc Ferro, *October 1917: A Social History of the Russian Revolution*, translated by Norman Stone (London: Routledge, 1980), 174ff.

268 **Originally, his father** Edgar Snow, *Red Star over China*, first revised and enlarged edition (New York: Grove, 1938).

269 **Mao attended group meetings** Alexander V. Pantsov with Steven I. Levine, *Mao: The Real Story* (New York: Simon and Schuster, 2007), 90ff.

269 **Mao's mentor** Snow, *Red Star*, 155.

269 **The young Ho Chi Minh** Jean Lacouture, *Ho Chi Minh: A Political Biography*, translated from the French by Peter Wiles, translation edited by Jane Clark Seitz (New York: Random House, 1968), 18.

270 **His own text** Nguyen Ai Quoc, *Le Procès de la colonisation française et autres textes de jeunesse*, choisis et présentés par Alain Ruscio (Paris: Les Temps des Cerises, 1925), 116.

270 **"Then, one day"** Fidel Castro, "How I Became a Communist: From a Question-and-Answer Period with Students at the University of Concepción, Chile," November 18, 1971, historyofcuba.com/history /castro.htm, accessed January 13, 2017.

271 **At the height of Nazi rule** The best scholarly information on this text and its editions can be found in the new critical edition *Hitler, Mein Kampf: Eine kritische Edition*, edited by Christian Hartmann et al. (Munich: Im Auftrag des Instituts für Zeitgeschichte, 2016).

CHAPTER 13. AKHMATOVA AND SOLZHENITSYN:
WRITING AGAINST THE SOVIET STATE

273 **At first, Anna Akhmatova** I thank my colleague William Mills Todd III for his help with this chapter.

273 **In Paris, she had** Roberta Reeder, *Anna Akhmatova: Poet and Prophet* (New York: Picador, 1994), 35–36. I also consulted György Dalos, *Der Gast aus der Zukunft: Anna Achmatowa und Sir Isaiah*

Berlin, Eine Liebesgeschichte, deutsche Bearbeitung von Elsbeth Zylla (Hamburg: Europäische Verlagsanstalt, 1969), 28.

273 **Russian Sappho** Amanda Haight, *Anna Akhmatova: A Poetic Pilgrimage* (Oxford: Oxford University Press, 1976), 80.

273 **Akhmatova held on to** Tomas Venclova and Ellen Hinsey, "Meetings with Anna Akhmatova," *New England Review*, volume 34, number 3/4 (2014): 171.

275 **Anna Akhmatova never engaged** Dalos, *Gast aus der Zukunft*, 9.

275 **After a leading functionary** Reeder, *Anna Akhmatova: Poet and Prophet*, 199–200.

275 **Yagoda also dragged** On the ideological complicity of some prisoners, see Jochen Hellbeck, *Revolution on My Mind: Writing a Diary Under Stalin* (New Haven: Yale University Press, 2006).

276 **the word "Acmeism"** Haight, *Anna Akhmatova: A Poetic Pilgrimage*, 19. See also Clarence Brown, "Mandelshtam's Acmeist Manifesto," *Russian Review*, volume 24, number 1 (January 1965): 46–51.

276 **One of the differences** Haight, *Anna Akhmatova: A Poetic Pilgrimage*, 71.

276 **Leon Trotsky, the intellectual** Leon Trotsky, *Literature and Revolution*, edited by William Keach, translated by Rose Strunsky (Chicago: Haymarket Books, 1925), 50.

276 **Anatoly Lunacharsky, the powerful** Haight, *Anna Akhmatova: A Poetic Pilgrimage*, 71.

276 **Akhmatova was not** Dalos, *Gast aus der Zukunft*, 71.

276 **To her own surprise** Reeder, *Anna Akhmatova: Poet and Prophet*, 202–203.

277 **"I'd like to remember"** Anna Akhmatova, "Requiem," in *The Complete Poems of Anna Akhmatova*, updated and expanded edition, translated by Judith Hemschemeyer, edited and introduced by Roberta Reeder (Boston: Zephyr Press, 1997), 393.

277 **Cautiously Akhmatova summoned** Haight, *Anna Akhmatova: A Poetic Pilgrimage*, 98.

278 **"See, as you said"** Haight, *Anna Akhmatova: A Poetic Pilgrimage*, 98.

278 **"We live according to"** Ann Komaromi, "The Material Existence of Soviet Samizdat," *Slavic Review*, volume 63, number 3 (Autumn 2004): 597–618, 598.

278 **She had learned to read** Anna Akhmatova, *My Half Century: Selected Prose*, translated and edited by Ronald Meyer (Ann Arbor, Mich.: Ardis, 1992), 25.

278 **Occupying two rooms**   Reeder, *Anna Akhmatova: Poet and Prophet*, 122, 119.

279 **Between 1918 and 1924**   Reeder, *Anna Akhmatova: Poet and Prophet*, 125.

279 **During a period of intense persecution**   Venclova and Hinsey, "Meetings with Anna Akhmatova," 178.

280 **Probably he was not**   Information based on Olga Voronina, *A Window with an Iron Curtain: Cold War Metaphors in Transition, 1945–1968* (Ann Arbor: UMI, 2010). Additional information based on *"I eto bylo tak": Anna Akhmatova i Isaiia Berlin* by L. Kopylov, T. Pozdniakova, and N. Popova (St. Petersburg: Anna Akhmatova Museum at the Fountain House, 2009). On his way to Moscow, Berlin had met a friend associated with the British secret service by the name of Noel Annan. Anne Deighton, "Berlin in Moscow. Isaiah Berlin: Academia, Diplomacy and Britain's Cultural Cold War," Oxford Sciences Po Research Group, Oxpo Working Paper, 5, berlin.wolf.ox.ac.uk/lists/onib/deighton.pdf, accessed December 27, 2015. Noel Annan was the man who later edited Berlin's essay about his meeting with Akhmatova.

280 **In a dispatch**   Akhmatova, *My Half Century*, 53.

281 **"So the nun"**   Isaiah Berlin, *Personal Impressions*, edited by Henry Hardy, with an introduction by Noel Annan (London: Hogarth Press, 1980), 201–202.

282 **"Just think, what fame!"**   Sophie Kazimirovna Ostrovskaya, *Memoirs of Anna Akhmatova's Years, 1944–1950*, translated by Jessie Daves (Liverpool: Lincoln Davies, 1988), 52.

283 **Seventeen years later**   Michael Scammell, *Solzhenitsyn: A Biography* (New York: Norton, 1984), 447.

283 **Khrushchev agreed that**   Dalos, *Gast aus der Zukunft*, 158–60.

283 **The writer, Aleksandr Solzhenitsyn**   Scammell, *Solzhenitsyn: A Biography*, 440.

284 **Samizdat started after Stalin's death**   Ludmilla Alexeyeva, *Soviet Dissent: Contemporary Movements for National, Religious, and Human Rights* (Middletown, Conn.: Wesleyan University Press, 1985), 13.

284 **Soon, samizdat expanded**   Alexeyeva, *Soviet Dissent*, 15.

284 **Apartments were searched**   Alexeyeva, *Soviet Dissent*, 379.

285 **A joke circulated**   Komaromi, "Material Existence of Soviet Samizdat," 609.

285 **By the time Akhmatova read**   Alexeyeva, *Soviet Dissent*, 13–15.

285 **Solzhenitsyn was one of them**   Scammell, *Solzhenitsyn: A Biography*, 440.

285 **Solzhenitsyn recounted**   Alexander Solzhenitsyn, *One Day in the Life of Ivan Denisovich*, translated from the Russian by H. T. Willetts, with an introduction by John Bayley (New York: Everyman, 1995).

286 **While serving in World War II**   Scammell, *Solzhenitsyn: A Biography*, 142.

286 **The first thing he did**   Scammell, *Solzhenitsyn: A Biography*, 319.

286 **When he remarried his former wife**   Scammell, *Solzhenitsyn: A Biography*, 370.

286 **Writing about the gulag**   Scammell, *Solzhenitsyn: A Biography*, 376.

287 **Editors at the magazine**   Scammell, *Solzhenitsyn: A Biography*, 433, 436.

287 **The efforts were worth it**   Z. K. Vodopianova and T. M. Goriaeva, eds., *Istoriia sovetskoi politicheskoi tsenzury: Dokumenty i kommentarii* (Moscow: Rosspen, 1997), 587.

287 **After having lived**   Haight, *Anna Akhmatova: A Poetic Pilgrimage*, 181.

288 **But thanks to a generous endowment**   James F. English, *The Economy of Prestige: Prizes, Awards, and the Circulation of Cultural Value* (Cambridge, Mass.: Harvard University Press, 2008).

289 **Some of those**   Reeder, *Anna Akhmatova: Poet and Prophet*, 500, 371.

289 **In a ceremony in 1988**   Dalos, *Gast aus der Zukunft*, 217.

CHAPTER 14. THE *EPIC OF SUNJATA* AND THE
WORDSMITHS OF WEST AFRICA

290 **The *Epic of Sunjata***   I thank David C. Conrad for his invaluable help with this chapter.

293 **wordsmiths**   Barbara G. Hoffman, *Griots at War: Conflict, Conciliation, and Caste in Mande* (Bloomington: Indiana University Press, 2000), 10.

293 **My favorite version of *Sunjata***   The account that follows is based on notes generously provided to me by David C. Conrad as well as telephone conversations with him. See also Conrad's introduction to

Sunjata: A New Prose Version, edited and translated with an introduction by David C. Conrad (Indianapolis and Cambridge, Mass.: Hackett, 2016). All discussions of *Sunjata* are based on this version, unless otherwise noted.

294 **Often coming from Nigeria**   Robert C. Newton, *The Epic Cassette: Technology, Tradition, and Imagination in Contemporary Bamana Segu,* dissertation, University of Wisconsin–Madison (Ann Arbor: UMI, 1997), 15.

294 **Cassettes, usually pirated**   David C. Conrad, ed., *Epic Ancestors of the Sunjata Era: Oral Tradition from the Maninka of Guinea* (Madison: University of Wisconsin–Madison, African Studies Program, 1999), 3.

294 **One result was that**   Conrad, *Epic Ancestors,* 8.

295 **The economic and social fabric**   Robert C. Newton, "Out of Print: The Epic Cassette as Intervention, Reinvention, and Commodity," in *In Search of Sunjata: The Mande Oral Epic as History, Literature, and Performance,* edited by Ralph A. Austen (Bloomington: Indiana University Press, 1999), 313–28, 325. See also Conrad, *Epic Ancestors,* 2.

296 **Interested in this vocal performer**   For an account of how the stories of Sunjata incorporated Islamic material, see David C. Conrad, "Islam in the Oral Traditions of Mali: Bilali and Surakata," *Journal of African History,* volume 26, number 1 (1985): 33–49.

296 **Significantly, all of Bereté's wisdom**   Conrad, *Sunjata: A New Prose Version,* 11.

298 **Taking two camels**   *Corpus of Early Arabic Sources for West African History,* translated by J.F.P. Hopkins, edited and annotated by N. Levtzion and J.F.P. Hopkins (Cambridge, U.K.: Cambridge University Press, 1981), 282.

298 **Ibn Battuta took it all in**   Levtzion and Hopkins, *Corpus of Early Arabic Sources,* 286, 296.

299 **"was already old before Islam"**   Levtzion and Hopkins, *Corpus of Early Arabic Sources,* 293.

300 **Ibn Battuta laughed out loud**   Levtzion and Hopkins, *Corpus of Early Arabic Sources,* 289.

300 **Despite his invectives**   Conrad, "Islam in the Oral Traditions," 37.

300 **In the centuries following Battuta's**   See Stephen P. D. Bulman, "*Sunjata* as Written Literature: The Role of the Literary Mediator in the Dissemination of the *Sunjata* Epic," in Austen, *In Search of Sunjata,* 231–51, 232. I also consulted Jan Jansen, "An Ethnography of the Epic of *Sunjata* in Kela," in Austen, *In Search of Sunjata,* 297–311, 308.

301 **A significant literary culture**   Joshua Hammer, *The Bad-Ass Librarians of Timbuktu and Their Race to Save the World's Most Precious Manuscripts* (New York: Simon and Schuster, 2016), 17.

301 **Perhaps they even worried**   Massa Makan Diabaté mentions the secret art of the griots in Diabaté, *L'aigle et l'épervier, ou La geste de Sunjata* (Paris: Pierre Jean Oswald, 1975), 17.

302 **While importing French writing**   David C. Conrad, "Oral Sources on Links Between Great States: Sumanguru, Servile Lineage, the Jariso, and Kaniaga," *History in Africa*, volume 11 (1984): 35–55, 37.

302 **Perhaps they were drawing**   Bulman, "Sunjata as Written Literature," 235.

302 **These first French accounts**   Stephen Bulman, "A School for Epic? The 'École William Ponty' and the Evolution of the Sunjata Epic, 1913–c. 1960," in *Epic Adventures: Heroic Narrative in the Oral Performance Traditions of Four Continents*, edited by Jan Jansen and Henk M. J. Maier (Münster: LIT Verlag, 2004), 35–45, 41ff.

302 **Schools had been**   Peggy R. Sabatier, "'Elite' Education in French West Africa: The Era of Limits, 1903–1945," *International Journal of African Historical Studies*, volume 11, number 2 (1978): 247–66, 265.

302 **In some of these schools**   Sabatier, "'Elite' Education in French West Africa," 247.

303 **he also related**   D. T. Niane, *Sundiata: An Epic of Old Mali*, translated by G. D. Pickett (Harlow, U.K.: Longman, 1965), 23. The French original uses the Mandingo name Djoulou Kara Naini and explains in a footnote that this is a corruption of Dhu'l Quarnein, the name given to Alexander. Djibril Tamsir Niane, *Soundjata ou L'Épopée Mandingue* (Paris: Présence Africaine, 1960), 50. David C. Conrad reported to me a conversation he had with Niane in which Niane asserted that Mande bards had no knowledge of Alexander the Great. They might have used the Arabic name without recognizing the relation to Alexander the Great.

303 **Kanté knew that first attempts had been made**   The only previous attempt to write down a Mandingo language, the Vai syllabary, had been made in the early nineteenth century to keep records of shipping cargo, mostly of slaves. Maurice Delafosse, *Les Vaï: Leur language et leur système d'écriture* (Paris: Masson et Cie, 1899).

303 **A backlash was inevitable**   Sabatier, "'Elite' Education in French West Africa," 265.

304 **For sixty years**   Dianne White Oyler, *The History of the N'ko Alpha-*

bet and Its Role in Mande Transnational Identity: Words as Weapons (Cherry Hill, N.J.: Africana Homestead Legacy Publishers, 2005).

CHAPTER 15. POSTCOLONIAL LITERATURE: DEREK WALCOTT, POET OF THE CARIBBEAN

306 **New nations need stories** I thank Maya Jasanoff for commenting on this chapter.

307 **Walcott was, for all intents** The other writer of note, Garth St. Omer, was born one year after Walcott. Patricia Ismond, "The St. Lucian Background in Garth St. Omer and Derek Walcott," *Caribbean Quarterly*, volume 28, number 1/2 (March–June 1982): 32–43.

311 **Then came the slaves** Derek Walcott, *Omeros* (New York: Farrar, Straus and Giroux, 1990), 150.

311 **While there were thousands** Walcott, *Omeros*, 14.

313 **He explained that the language** For more on this topic, see Douglas Midgett, "Bilingualism and Linguistic Change in St. Lucia," *Anthropological Linguistics*, volume 12, number 5 (May 1970): 158–70.

315 **"A Windward island"** Derek Walcott, *The Sea at Dauphin*, in *Dream on Monkey Mountain and Other Plays* (New York: Farrar, Straus and Giroux, 1971), 45.

315 **Walcott had tried to create** Errol Hill, "The Emergence of a National Drama in the West Indies," *Caribbean Quarterly*, volume 18, number 4 (December 1972): 9–40.

316 **Walcott's voice lit up** For more on the carnival, see Daniel J. Crowley, "Festivals of the Calendar in St. Lucia," *Caribbean Quarterly*, volume 4, number 2 (December 1955): 99–121.

316 **The central character in the carnival** See also Daniel J. Crowley, "Song and Dance in St. Lucia," *Ethnomusicology*, volume 1, number 9 (January 1957): 4–14.

319 **"This sea not make"** Walcott, *Sea at Dauphin*, 59.

319 **"The sea is very funny"** Walcott, *Sea at Dauphin*, 57.

320 **"This sea no cemetery"** Walcott, *Sea at Dauphin*, 64.

320 **Augustin finally observes** See also Sandra Sprayberry, "Sea Changes: Post-Colonialism in Synge and Walcott," *South Carolina Review*, volume 33, number 2 (Spring 2001): 115–20.

325 **The second was a report** C. Jesse, "Rock-Cut Basins on Saint Lucia," *American Antiquity*, volume 18, number 2 (October 1952): 166–68.

CHAPTER 16. FROM HOGWARTS TO INDIA

326 **Originally, the volume** "Amazon.com Buys J. K. Rowling Tales for $4 Million," Reuters, December 14, 2007, reuters.com/article/us-amazon -rowling-idUSN1427375920071214, accessed August 10, 2016.

326 **I contented myself** J. K. Rowling, *The Tales of Beedle the Bard, Translated from the Ancient Runes by Hermione Granger, Commentary by Albus Dumbledore, Introduction, Notes, and Illustrations by J. K. Rowling* (New York: Scholastic, 2007).

327 **Before I proceeded** Pottermore.com, visited November 2, 2016.

328 **Imagine, therefore, my delight** J. K. Rowling, *Harry Potter and the Deathly Hallows* (London: Bloomsbury, 2007), 748, 811.

329 **I haven't been able** universalorlando.com/Shopping/Islands-of -Adventure/Ollivanders.aspx, accessed November 3, 2016.

330 **The message, LOGIN** Cade Metz, "Leonard Kleinrock, the TX-2 and the Seeds of the Internet," *Wired*, October 1, 2012, internethall offame.org/blog/2012/10/01/leonard-kleinrock-tx-2-and-seeds-internet, accessed August 10, 2016. See also Walter Isaacson, *The Innovators: How a Group of Hackers, Geniuses, and Geeks Created the Digital Revolution* (New York: Simon and Schuster, 2014), 242ff.

330 **In writing this book** archive.org/about/, accessed November 13, 2016.

331 **A backup copy** archive.org/about/bibalex_p_r.php, accessed November 13, 2016. See also bibalex.org/en/project/details?documentid =283&keywords=internet%20archive, accessed November 13,2016.

331 **Six users downloaded it** Jeffrey Thomas, "Project Gutenberg Digital Library Seeks to Spur Literacy," Bureau of International Information Programs, U.S. Department of State, July 20, 2007. I downloaded this file from the Internet Archive at web.archive.org/web/20080314164013/ http://www.america.gov/st/washfile-english/2007/July/2007072015113 11CJsamohT0.6146356.html, accessed November 13, 2016.

331 **It is true that computers can facilitate** Lev Manovich, *Software Takes Command* (London: Bloomsbury, 2013), 46.

332 **In order to take the measure** I thank Homi Bhabha, Namita Gokhale, and William Dalrymple for inviting me to the Jaipur Literature Festival.

332 **Ten years earlier** Sheela Reddy, "Pen on the Rostrum," *Outlook India*, April 17, 2006, outlookindia.com/magazine/story/pen-on-the -rostrum/230952, accessed November 15, 2016.

334 **In the interest of safety**   William Dalrymple, "Why Salman Rush-
    die's Voice Was Silenced in Jaipur," *The Guardian*, January 26, 2012,
    theguardian.com/books/2012/jan/26/salman-rushdie-jaipur-literary
    -festival, accessed August 10, 2016.

334 **Outraged by this form**   Hari Kunzru, "Why I Quoted from *The Sa-
    tanic Verses*," *The Guardian*, January 22, 2012, theguardian.com
    /commentisfree/2012/jan/22/i-quoted-satanic-verses-suport-rushdie,
    accessed August 10, 2016.

ILLUSTRATION CREDITS

———

125   Cairo market street, woodcut by William Harvey. Copyright: Edward William Lane, *Arabian Nights' Entertainments*, 1853, p. 371.

128   Nineteenth-century lithograph by 'Ali-Khân included in *Hezâr dâstân* by Mirzâ Abu l-Fath Khân Dehqân Sâmâni, page 6. Private collection of Prof. Dr. Ulrich Marzolph. Image credit: Ulrich Marzolph.

153   Woodcut of print shop, c. 1520.

155   Indulgence for the Expedition Against the Turks and the Defense of Cyprus. Printed by Johannes Gutenberg, 1455. Musée Condé.

182   Maya glyphs, in Sylvanus Griswold Morley, *An Introduction to the Study of the Maya Hieroglyphs*, 1915, p. 49.

188   Zapatista school mural in Chiapas, Mexico.

208   Engraving by Jan van der Straet of 16th-century print shop.

215   Declaration of Independence as published in *The Pennsylvania Evening Post* on July 6, 1776. Library of Congress.

221   Map of old postal road. S. Jenkins, *The Old Boston Post Road*, 1913, p. 434.

224   Denis Diderot and Jean Le Rond d'Alembert, "Compositors," *Encyclopédie* (1751–1772). Houghton Library, Harvard University.

245   Johann Heinrich Wilhelm Tischbein, *Goethe in the Roman Campagna*, 1787. Städelsches Kunstinstitut.

247   Reconstruction of the wanderings of Odysseus by Walter and Boutall. Image credit: Samuel Butler, *The Authoress of the Odyssey* (New York: Dutton, 1922), p. 150.

250   Ferdinand Georg Walmüller, *The Ancient Theater of Taormina*, 1944.

253   Nineteenth-century photograph of Crompton, near Manchester.

259   Richard March Hoe's printing press, 1864.

265   Marcel Janco, *Cabaret Voltaire, 1916*. Image rights: 2017 Artists Rights Society (ARS), New York / ADAGP, Paris..

267   Lenin speaking to a crowd in Petrograd on the eve of the Russian Revolution in 1917.

274   Amedeo Modigliani, sketch of Anna Akhmatova, 1911. Heritage Image Partnership Ltd/Alamy Stock Photo.

286   Moskva Model 4 typewriter.

292   Catalan Atlas from 1375, showing Western Africa. Bibliothéque nationale de France.

299   Caravan to Mecca, by thirteenth-century illustrator al-Wasiti for the Maquamat of al-Hariri.

309   Bust of Derek Walcott in Castries, St. Lucia. Image credit: Art Directors & TRIP/Alamy Stock Photo.

COLOR INSERT

1.   Ciro Ferri (1634–1689), *Alexander the Great Reading Homer*. Image credit: Scala / Art Resource, NY.

2.   Albrecht Altdorfer (c. 1480–1538), *Battle at Issus*. Alte Pinakothek, Munich.

3.   Depiction of the death of Iskander (Alexander the Great) from *Great Mongol Shahnameh, The Book of Kings*. Freer Art Gallery.

4.   Statue of Egyptian scribe. Third millennium B.C.E. Neues Museum Berlin.

5. Cuneiform Tablet and Envelope, c. 1927–1836 B.C.E. Photo credit: Harvard Art Museum/Arthur M. Sackler Museum, Gift of Leslie Cheek, Jr. and Purchase through the generosity of the Sol Rabin and the Marian H. Phinney Fund, 1000.197.A-C. Photo: Imaging Department, President and Fellows of Harvard College.

6. James Fergusson, Palaces of Nimrud, restored. Image credit: H. A. Layard, *The Monuments of Nineveh*, 1853.

7. Ezra writing the Bible, *Codex Amiatinus*, eighth century. Biblioteca Medicea Laurenziana. Image credit: Scala/Art Resource, NY.

8. Eighteenth-century painting of Shakyamuni Buddha. Tibet. Rubin Museum of Art.

9. Print by Yashima Gakutei (1768?–1868) of the ten disciples of Confucius.

10. Jacques-Louis David (1748–1825), *Death of Socrates*. Metropolitan Museum of Art. Catharine Lorillard Wolfe Collection, Wolfe Fund, 1931.

11. Domenico Ghirlandaio, *Jesus and His Disciples*, 1481. Sistine Chapel. Image credit: web gallery of art.

12. Woman with wax tablets and stylus, Pompeii. Naples National Archaeological Museum.

13. Tang dynasty (618–907) copy of Gu Kaizhi, *Admonitions of the Instructress to the Palace Ladies*. British Museum.

14. Suzuki Harunobu, *Murasaki Shikibu at Ishiyama-dera*, 1767.

15. Portion of Lady Murasaki's diary, thirteenth century. Tokyo National Museum.

16. Lady Murasaki fan, seventeenth century. Honolulu Academy of Arts. Image credit: Honolulu Academy of Arts, gift of John Gregg Allerton, 1984 (5264.1).

17. Depiction of scholars by Yahya ibn Mahmud al-Wasiti found in the 1237 *Maquama* of Al-Hariri. Bibliotheque Nationale de France. Image credit: Zereshk.

18. *Seated Scribe*, attributed to Gentile Bellini (c. 1429–1507). Image credit: Isabella Stewart Gardner Museum, Boston, Mass., USA/Bridgeman Images.

19. Qur'an from Eastern Iran or Afghanistan, c. 1180. Metropolitan Museum of Art.

20. Portrait of Eadwine the Scribe, from Eadwine Psalter, c. 1155, Canterbury, England.

21. Forty-two-line Latin Bible printed by Johannes Gutenberg, c. 1455. Staatsbibliothek Berlin.

22. German Bible by Martin Luther, published in 1534 by Hans Lufft. Klassik Stiftung Weimar.

23. Dresden Codex, c. 1200. Sächsische Universitätsbibliothek.

24. Rollout photograph of Maya ballgame as depicted on a vessel. Photo credit: Justin Kerr File no. 1209.

25. Unauthorized second part of Don Quixote, in English translation. Image credit: Cushing Memorial Library and Archives, Texas A&M University.

26. Seventeenth-century painting of peddler. Musée des Traditions Populaires, Paris. Photo: Gérard Blot. Photo credit: RMN-Grand Palais/Art Resource, NY.

27. Jean-Honoré Fragonard, *The Reader*. National Gallery of Art. Image credit: National Gallery of Art online database.

28. Johann Joseph Schmeller, *Goethe Dictating to His Scribe*, 1834. Duchess Anna Amalia Library. Image credit: haiotthu.

29. Rococo Hall of Duchess Anna Amalia Library, Weimar.

30. Eugène Atget, Chiffonier (Ragpicker), c. 1900. Getty Center.

31. Rasmus Malling-Hansen, writing ball. Tekniska museet, Stockholm. Photo credit: Daderot.
32. Alexei Radakov, *Knowledge Will Break the Chains of Slavery*, 1920.
33. Nathan Altman, *Anna Akhmatova*, 1914. The State Russian Museum.
34. Samizdat paraphernalia, Sakharov Museum, Moscow. Photo credit: Jelena Prtoric.
35. A CPT 8100 Word Processor Desktop Microcomputer. Photo credit: LehmanUM.
36. Annenberg Hall, Harvard University. Photo credit: Katherine Taylor/Harvard Staff Photographer; President and Fellows of Harvard College.

INDEX

—

—

RANDOM HOUSE: Why is it so important for us to understand the role literature has played in great historical events?

MARTIN PUCHNER: Contemplating four thousand years of literature showed me how profoundly our lives have been shaped by stories. Storytelling is how we make sense of the world and our role within it. Sometimes these stories are personal ones, stories we tell ourselves about our own lives, but the most powerful stories are shared across entire cultures.

The reason I didn't always recognize the full impact of literature was that I tended to think of literature only in terms of what was on the fiction shelves. But once I broadened the definition of literature to include all significant written stories, I began to see its influence in many places. Most of today's dominant cultures are based on sacred texts such as the Bible, the Qur'an, the sayings of Confucius and Buddha, and modern texts like the Declaration of Independence or *The Communist Manifesto*. These texts acquired their power through the types of stories they tell: stories of the origin of the world, of how to lead your life, and of how to organize society.

Our world is full of stories, or rather, our minds are. The most important stories, and story types, get retold innumerable times—much of what we see on film, television, and the new media draws on previously written literature.

Take our last two presidents. Both launched long-shot campaigns against entrenched political dynasties, and they couldn't have done it without their bestselling books, *The Art of the Deal* and *Dreams from My Father*. It was through these books that they introduced themselves to a larger public, shaping who they were and how they wanted to be perceived. In doing so, they drew on a specifically American tradition of autobiography that goes back to Benjamin Franklin. Literature isn't just something that was important in the past. It very much shapes our lives today as well.

RH: Of the many writers and storytellers you describe in *The Written World*, which ones are especially dear to you?

MP: Lady Murasaki is the first author who comes to mind. Every time I read her work and think about her life, I find myself deeply touched by her perseverance. A lady-in-waiting at the Japanese court during the Middle Ages, Murasaki lived an extremely restricted life, mostly confined to interior chambers—we don't even know her real name. She had to acquire proficiency in Chinese literature in secret. Yet out of those constraints she wrote the first major novel in history, which gives us unparalleled access to the inner lives of her characters.

Another is the *Popol Vuh*, the Maya epic that tells the story of the creation of the earth and features fantastic trickster twins. There had been no contact between Eurasia and the New World since the invention of writing, so we know for sure that Maya literature developed completely independently, and that humans invented writing, perhaps the most important invention in our entire history, at least twice. The *Popol Vuh* was almost lost when Spaniards arrived in the New World and begun to burn Maya books. A single copy survived, because Maya scribes went underground.

Finally, there's Anna Akhmatova, the Russian Sappho as she was sometimes called, who lived under Stalin and couldn't publish her work. Instead of giving up, she composed poetry in secret and recited her poems to her friends until they knew them by heart. She called her situation "pre-Gutenberg"—censorship forced her to live as if the printing press had never been invented. In those trying circumstances, she produced some of the most important poetry of the twentieth century.

RH: Literature's "canon" is always a controversial topic. As a literature scholar whose work makes sense of how literature has evolved, how do you decide what to include in your textbooks and syllabi?

MP: This is a question that first came up when I edited *The Norton Anthology of World Literature*. Even though we had six thousand pages across six volumes, it was incredibly hard to decide what to include and what to exclude, balancing well-known works with masterpieces from ancient and modern times that were less known, and featuring new authors and texts that were just beginning to gain traction or that we felt had been overlooked. Canons change all the time: it's a very dynamic process.

I also made a point of talking to students and teachers to hear from them which authors should be included. Many colleges and universities that have large world literature programs are in the south, in places such as northern Alabama or southern Georgia, so this was an opportunity for me to travel to places I had not been before. To prepare me for one such visit, the organizer simply sent me a copy of *Garden & Gun*. Another time, I found myself paddling around alligators in Okefenokee, in Florida.

You wouldn't know this by reading the usual accounts about rural America, but world literature is thriving in the heartland. Visiting these campuses changed how my team and I shaped the anthology. I also found it rewarding to teach world literature to students who might not have had a chance to travel much, who might not own a passport. At the same time, given the large number of international students from China, Korea, and the Arabic world attending U.S. universities, we made a point of increasing our selection from those regions. World literature can be accessed from everywhere. It provides its own special opportunity for encountering other cultures and for thinking about your own.

The whole experience of shaping the canon of world literature fed into the process of writing *The Written World*, because it encouraged me to think about four thousand years of literature as a single, grand story. I realized that this story had never been told, so I decided I would take a stab at it as best I could.

RH: Were there any books that you wanted to include in this story of literature but that just missed the cut?

MP: *The Norton Anthology* includes hundreds of texts; it's an incredibly rich collection of authors and genres and periods and languages. *The Written World* is similarly broad, but it has a different goal. More than being simply a collection of important texts—or even of my favorite texts—it tells a story: the story of literature. All stories have a particular engine, some animating principle that drives them forward, and the story I wanted to tell focuses on writing technologies, how new technologies produce new stories. Each of the sixteen chapters focuses on the interaction between an important text and a new technology, such as the alphabet, paper, the scroll, the book, or print. That focus shaped my selection.

I also think of *The Written World* as an invitation to explore literature, which is why I combined some well-known texts such as the Bible or the Iliad with lesser-known ones such as the West African *Epic of Sunjata*.

All these constraints meant that there were lots of authors and texts I loved but that didn't find a place in the book. For example, I really wanted to include a chapter on James Joyce's *Ulysses*, because reading that novel converted me from being a philosophy major to studying literature (influenced, no doubt, by the setting in which I first read it, on Mount Athos, an otherworldly pilgrimage site in northern Greece closed to tourists). I also would have liked to include what is probably the best novel ever written, George Eliot's *Middlemarch*, which weaves together characters, plots, and ideas with masterful precision and imagination.

RH: *The Written World* not just chronicles the impact of some of the most important stories in world literature, but is a bit of a travelogue as well. Tell us more about the role travel and visiting new places played in your research.

MP: I felt in order to write about the impact of literature on the world I couldn't just sit in my armchair. I needed to get up and visit the places I was writing about. The fact that I had grown up in Europe and had lived in several countries helped as well. On my travels, I came across many ruins from ancient civilizations that were connected to literature. I was especially struck by this in Asia Minor, when I was traveling in the wake of Alexander the Great. These Hellenistic cities had mostly been leveled, but what was left standing—the largest ruins—were invariably theaters and libraries. Theaters were designed to host performances of stories from the Homeric world, and libraries were built around the Homeric epics, so both of these large structures were devoted to literature. The same trip also took me to Troy. From reading Homer I had imagined that this city, which had withstood the mighty Greek army for ten years, would be enormous; I was surprised how small it was, which made me realize the extent to which literature shapes how we imagine the world.

Something similar happened when I met with living writers. When I went to St. Lucia, I found that Derek Walcott's poetry and plays were constantly on my mind. And it wasn't just me. Many inhabitants I met had incorporated his work into how they saw their island. A fisherman I met claimed to be the grandson of a character from one of Walcott's plays. St. Lucia became a microcosm for the enormous impact literature has had on our view of the world.

Another trip took me to Beijing, where I visited a library containing the Confucian classics carved in stone. Given my emphasis on writing technologies, wandering amid these texts made me think about permanence, about the many texts that have been lost, but also those, such as the *Epic of Gilgamesh*, that survived only by chance and because they were written on permanent material such as stone or burnt clay. Today we put a lot of trust in electronic backup systems, but if we want to ensure that our most cherished texts survive future catastrophes, perhaps we should do what Chinese emperors did and carve those texts into stone.

RH: How do you think literature is changing in modern times? Can you predict how it will it continue to change?

MP: In studying four thousand years of literature, I noticed a pattern that emerged whenever new technologies lowered the cost of literature. On the one hand, canonical texts often became early adopters of a new technology, because these texts were in the best position to use it effectively. The earliest surviving printed text in the world is the *Diamond Sutra* (868 C.E.), and when Gutenberg reinvented the printing press for northern Europe, he printed the Latin Bible. At the same time, a second effect kicks in: an explosion of popular writing, such as the stories collected in *One Thousand and One Nights*. I think we are seeing the same pattern repeated today. Canonical texts are as easily and cheaply available as never before, but there are also new forms of writing, from fan fiction and specialized romances published online to literature written in the form of blogs and on Twitter. We are living through the second great explosion of literature (the first was ushered in by the printing press). Looking back, future historians will locate the origin of these new developments in our own era.

Thinking about our own moment from the perspective of four thousand years of history has actually made me more optimistic about the technological revolution we're living through. I understand when parents worry that their children are spending too much time online, or when teachers worry that students aren't reading anymore. I worry about these things myself. But at some point, I realized that people were writing more than ever before, so much so that "text," for the first time in the history of the English language, was becoming a verb. Surely that has to be a sign that something important is happening to writing? At the very least, it's going to be interesting.

MARTIN PUCHNER is the Byron and Anita Wien Professor of English and Comparative Literature at Harvard University. His prizewinning books range from philosophy to the arts, and his bestselling six-volume *Norton Anthology of World Literature* and his HarvardX MOOC (massive open online course) have brought four thousand years of literature to students across the globe. He lives in Cambridge, Massachusetts.

ABOUT THE TYPE

This book was set in Electra, a typeface designed for Linotype by renowned type designer W. A. Dwiggins (1880–1956). Electra is a fluid typeface, avoiding the contrasts of thick and thin strokes that are prevalent in most modern typefaces.